Ultimate Visions
Reflections on the Religions We Choose

ULTIMATE

VISIONS

REFLECTIONS ON THE RELIGIONS WE CHOOSE

EDITED BY:

MARTIN FORWARD

ONEWORLD
OXFORD

ULTIMATE VISIONS

Oneworld Publications
(Sales and Editorial)
185 Banbury Road
Oxford OX2 7AR
England

Oneworld Publications
(US Marketing Office)
PO Box 830, 21 Broadway
Rockport, MA 01966
USA

© This edition Martin Forward 1995

ISBN 1–85168–100–0

Printed and bound by
WSOY, Finland

Contents

Foreword

Interfaith Relationship

The Most Revd Desmond M. Tutu

Desmond Tutu is Anglican Archbishop of Cape Town.

MANY EARNEST CHRISTIANS reject any positive relationships between Christianity and other faiths. They make exclusive claims for the superiority of Christianity and the finality of Christ based on such New Testament texts as 'there is no other name given under heaven', and the alleged dominical words of Jesus in the Fourth Gospel that no one can come to the Father except through him. Let me state at the outset that I believe that Jesus Christ is indeed the full, perfect and final revelation of God. I will yield to no one on that point. But that does not then give me the right to ride roughshod with muddy boots on what a person of another faith considers to be her holy ground nor to denigrate and belittle what she believes is a revelation from a transcendent divine reality by whatever name it is called and however it may be conceived and described. To dismiss other faiths is not only unforgivable arrogance but is a position that flies in the face of reality. It is unreasonable and indeed unbiblical. When we assert that it is only through Christ that humans have access to God and thereby mean the incarnate Logos, we land in an untenable position. Is there any Christian who would doubt that, for example, Abraham had an encounter with God so crucial that he should be regarded as the founding father of three of the major monotheistic faiths? And what about Moses? We could extend the list. Clearly Christians do not in fact jettison all the religious experience of those who encountered God in the pre-Christian dispensation.

Some of the most sublime Christian teaching is based on what we call the Old Testament, which we read as an indispensable part of our Bible. The New Testament would in large measure be incomprehensible if we did not assume much of what is taught in the Old Testament. If it comes only through Christ and if it is true, as we clearly have to acknowledge, then we must postulate a preincarnate Logos/Word as the means of the access to God, the source of all goodness, love, life and truth.

The Fourth Gospel in which the apparently exclusivist verse occurs of people coming to the Father only through the Son asserts right at its beginning that the Word enlightens everyone who comes into the world. St Paul claims in Romans that Gentiles can be adjudged blameworthy because they have a law written in their hearts and so like the Jew to whom has been vouchsafed a direct revelation from God, they too can be accused of having fallen short of the glory of God.

God is alone the source of all goodness, truth, life and love. Whoever possesses these attributes has received them from God, otherwise we have to postulate several sources of these things and thereby administer a fatal blow to monotheism. Obviously Christians do not have a monopoly on these qualities. Often in fact they are shown up conspicuously by people of other faiths or of none. We cannot, if we want to be taken seriously, assert that Mahatma Gandhi was not a very good man, nor that the Dalai Lama is not transparently holy and serene. Is God any less glorified that these people are not Christian? Albert Einstein was a brilliant scientist. Is what he propounded any less true because he was a Jew and not a Christian? It surely would be preposterous to claim that it was.

Some of the most enthusiastic slave owners were Christians. The Holocaust was perpetuated not by pagans but by Christians. The rabid racists who are members of the Ku Klux Klan actually use a flaming cross as their emblem asserting that they are Christian.

In our struggle against apartheid in South Africa some of our staunchest allies were Muslims, Jews and people of other faiths; and we were opposing fellow Christians who spawned apartheid and sought to find biblical justification for this vicious system.

I do not know of any major religion which at its best teaches that it is morally right to oppress or to exploit fellow human beings, or that injustice and war are to be preferred to their glorious counterparts, or that it is a worthy goal to pursue development of a harsh, cruel and uncaring society that should degrade the environment and be wantonly wasteful of scarce and irreplaceable natural resources.

There is so much that conspires to separate and alienate us from one another. There is the growing intolerant fundamentalism and a resurgence of xenophobia and ethnic chauvinism. We are face to face with daunting problems that threaten us with catastrophe – Aids, poverty, disease, the population explosion, human rights violations and ignorance. We need to build coalitions with those who share our values.

The religions of the world, whilst certainly different, do in fact share some important values. Let us celebrate our diversity in culture, faith, ethnicity, etc., so that we can show that we are indeed the rainbow people of God.

INTRODUCTION

Revd Dr Martin Forward

Revd Dr Martin Forward is Senior Tutor at Wesley House, Cambridge, and lecturer in Islamic Studies in the Department of Theology and Religious Studies at the University of Bristol.

I KNEW MUSLIMS before I was a Methodist or had even heard of Methodism. I heard of the agonizing history of the Jews in the twentieth century before I read any Christian history. I attended a Confucian wedding ceremony before I remember going to church or Sunday school.

My father was a member of the Royal Air Force in the twilight years of the British Empire. I started school in Singapore, where I went to the Confucian wedding. Incidentally, I also learned to associate fireworks with the Chinese New Year festival rather than (as most British schoolchildren do) Guy Fawkes's attempt to blow up the Houses of Parliament. Between the ages of nine and eleven I spent two years at school in Aden, that barren yet entrancing heap of sand at the heel of the Arabian peninsula. My father had been to Aden twice before, so we met some of his Muslim friends there. I learned to like camels (my young daughter calls them my favourite animal, disapprovingly, since she has seen the bad-tempered one at our local zoo which kicks and spits). A Muslim friend there told me the secret of the camel's superior smile: human beings know the ninety-nine names of God, but the camel knows the hundredth! In Aden, I began my lifelong fascination with Islam.

Whilst there, I also learned of Judaism. A Jewish schoolfriend in my class told me that her grandparents and most of their friends had perished in Hitler's gas ovens. Her own parents had escaped from Austria as young children.

I was eleven years old; I lost my religious innocence then, and ever since have lacked patience with spiritual ostriches of all faiths who describe their own religion only at its best and who do not see, or else will not admit, the demonic in all religions, including their own.

When I was five years old, I read Enid Blyton's *Children's Life of Christ*. I knew then, as I know now, that he was the man for me; actually, he was the human being for me. Moreover, he is the human being for others. The feminist perspective in Christianity (and in Islam) is, in my judgement, the greatest liberation movement of our times, for men as well as women.

Like many people of faith, I refuse simply to privatize religion. The way to live faithfully in a world of many religions is not to play down the central concerns of each faith. It is how to live faithfully, penitently, obediently, humorously in a world where others are often equally so in relation to their own religious icon, guru or prophet. This is, to quote Yul Brynner in *The King and I*, 'A Puzzlement' (not a film commended by many interfaith and racial justice people). Yet from my own experience I know it to be true (even if beyond the power of words to express exactly) that one can be deeply committed to one's own faith and hold it to be universally true, at the same time as admiring, revering and learning from the faith of others.

I was a strange ten-year-old. Jesus was my friend and hero; I talked to him and thus to God. But I learned to cherish others' ways of faith. I recognized difference, and had no desire to play it down or explain it away. I have never believed that we have to agree in order to accept each other and each others' beliefs. I cannot understand the purpose of a believer who is willing to trade away bits and pieces of his or her faith in the vain hope that some common ground can be found thereby. (This is not the same as needing to contextualize and refocus or reverbalize our faith in every age, so as not to be irrelevant. This should be a holistic enterprise, not a trade-in of central beliefs.)

I also regard as bewildering, profoundly unfaithful and wholly unacceptable the 'fundamentalism' that condemns as outside the scope of transcendent grace what it cannot conform to its own point of view. This is not obedience but paranoia. How ironic that many Christian fundamentalists undermine the very notion of a loving God that lies at the heart of Christian faith, as such Muslim fundamentalists also do of the One who is the compassionate, the merciful; and so on – all religions have their zealots, who are more interested in causes (usually imperfectly understood) than people. Yet I would maintain that religions should be about people in relation to each other, and about people in awe before transcendent and universal goodness and graciousness that breaks through this imperfect world and lights it up.

My own religious pilgrimage is simply a rather extreme illustration of the possibilities that the twentieth century has opened up to many of the world's spiritual voyagers. We cannot be unmindful of the widespread poverty, warfare and death that afflict many members of the human family; indeed, television and radio bring these monstrosities into all our lives. Yet we now have an ease of transport, rapidly expanding communications and technological networks, and other factors that point us towards a global culture.

What role must faith and the faiths play in our brave new world? Some would say none, since religions have been and remain so destructive to many. Yet even in the secular west, religions flourish, if not always in traditional forms. The question to be asked is therefore not, 'Should we have religion?', but rather, 'What sort of religion should we have?'

Some would interpret this latter question in terms of a specific religion. For example, as a Christian I might simply assert, 'Everyone should be Christian.' Yet, if Christianity has many Christians, it is equally true that Christians have many Christianities. Which denomination do I see others joining?

At least as a beginning, I might settle instead for: what sort of Christians do I want to see? What moral qualities and spiritual strengths do my co-religionists need at the end of the twentieth century and how does Christian faith furnish it for them? Are there analogies or parallels to be made here with questions asked by people of other faiths?

Over the last decade, I have had the opportunity to meet with friends of many faiths, in different parts of the world. In this volume, some of them (and some of their friends whom they have recommended to me) have written about their ultimate vision for humankind. They have reflected upon their own beliefs and many of them have described aspects of their spiritual journeys. All of them have had to wrestle with the implications of living in a world of many religions. Even though some of them do not specifically mention other faiths, their own faith has been forged and lived in a context of religious diversity.

I have not attempted to get an equal number of contributors from certain specified religions. Yet you will find represented here many of the world's religious traditions, and many interpretations of them. Lots are involved in interfaith activities – no dry-as-dust and desiccated scholars, these. I am fascinated by the diversity of beliefs and hopes expressed in this book, often among people of the same religion or who have been shaped by the same religion. There are some frank and forthright statements about why some people feel themselves able to be one faith and not another. These can be placed alongside the tributes others have paid to religions that have profoundly influenced them, without persuading them to change their faith.

I am proud and glad that the British Methodist Church has encouraged and paid for me to be a wandering interfaith person during the last decade. Without its support I would have no home, and no chance to ponder the things of God in ways appropriate to my life's journey. This small Christian denomination has a large number of people involved in interfaith work, out of all proportion to its size. Maybe it is because Methodist theology has always held universal sin and universal grace in tension.

I am extremely grateful to Archbishop Desmond Tutu for writing the foreword to *Ultimate Visions*. He has done so much for interfaith work in his own country, where people of many religions have worked together to help usher in the new multiracial South Africa. His consistent grace, humour and faith under pressure have entranced and influenced people from many lands and of diverse faiths.

As I write, I remember my father with much affection. His career shaped mine. He once told me that he nearly became a Muslim, because of the experiences he had shared in the desert north of Aden in and just after World War II. My fascination with Islam began before I knew this, yet was made possible because of the man he was. He died in 1986 yet is alive to God and unforgettable by me.

The great English composer Sir Edward Elgar dedicated his *Variations on an Original Theme* to his 'friends pictured within'. I do the same, thanking the contributors warmly, and reminding them and the readers that Elgar's work is known as the 'Enigma Variations' because, in the composer's words, 'through and over the whole set another and larger theme "goes", but is not played'. Perhaps there is an analogy here. In this book, the theme and variations are played out of people's beliefs and commitments in a religiously diverse world. In and through their accounts goes the larger and somewhat enigmatic theme of what, within our differences, enables religious people to live and work together for the common good in our complex and wounded world. I hope the readers will join us in reflecting upon that theme, so that religions will give life and not deal death.

The aim of this book is to provide a forum for a diversity of approaches to God, and in view of the current variety of practice and individual preference in relation to capitalization of personal pronouns and religious terminology, I have endeavoured to accommodate authors' individual styles throughout. I could not have edited this book without the encouragement of Novin Doostdar and Juliet Mabey of Oneworld Publications. The former suggested this project, and the latter's eagle eye has brought it safely to pass. None of the three of us, however, are responsible for the views expressed herein. The major point of the exercise is a personal one, to read how people of faith express their ultimate vision.

A MUSLIM READING

Raficq Abdulla

Raficq Abdulla, *a Muslim barrister, was born in South Africa and educated in England. He is the legal adviser to several organizations and is also a poet and broadcaster.*

READING, LIKE IDENTITY, is not as simple as it looks. In fact it is quite tricky; the closer you read the more complex and ambiguous the practice becomes. Even the title of this paper can be read in at least two ways, like one of those line and shade drawings which, when looked at in one way, appears to be beautiful, and if looked at in another way, becomes ugly. It all depends upon emphasis: with the picture the eye chooses, and with the text, the ear and voice play an essential part in the creation of meaning.

Of course millions of Muslims read, or more precisely, recite, the Qur'an – the ultimate text – every day all over the world. After all, Islam is quintessentially a religion of the Book, of the holy text, which is potentially subjected to innumerable Muslim readings; more importantly it is open to an infinite number of readings as the Word of God, God who is also called the Infinite and the Ineffable. In earlier centuries, before the breach of colonialism, Muslims constructed readings of the miraculous text and of the symbols that made up the world about them, in a comparatively homogeneous way, compatible with the limits placed by the tenets of the faith.

As a divine script, the Qur'an grants the Muslim reader access to primordial truth, not only by way of its content but by its very existence. The Qur'anic words do not only translate the truth, they are considered by Muslims to be the marks of truth; their access to the Divine through the enabling sonorities of its sound. Hence great importance is placed on its recitation, which was how the unlettered Prophet Muhammad brought God's message to humankind. The Arabic language of the Qur'an, therefore, takes on a privileged status and becomes divine through God's breath. Consequently, some traditionalists, like the Wahabi *'ulama*, or religious jurists of Saudi Arabia, will not allow translations of the Qur'an into a demotic language. One can argue when we consider the status of the Qur'an that form precedes meaning, the miraculous occurrence of revelation precedes communication. So millions of children learn to read the Qur'an by rote without understanding its contents. They read or recite blindly, obtaining blessing, *barakah*, or by – so to speak – touching the hem of God's words.

The Qur'an is a text of absolute power for Muslims, which reduces all other texts to a secondary and dependent status from which they can rebel only by joining Satan's party. It is the law, and the Muslim reads it with a proper sense of humility. Like the benighted hero in Kafka's story 'Before the Law', a Muslim reads the holy text with a sense of awe, always *ante portam*, just beyond the frame of complete understanding, where the text works upon the reader subliminally. A

Muslim can never read the Qur'an deconstructively, beyond the Author's commands, or archaeologically, in the sense of digging out the underlying unconscious structures of meaning, which set limits to what is thinkable in any given epoch, from the sedimented layers of meaning that stick to words and sentences. And yet I believe that being a Muslim implies neither being subjugated to obscurantist readings of God's words, which are passed off as the real thing, nor totally and unquestioningly accepting Islamic traditional knowledge and values as the only authentic vision. One can be a Muslim and be restive, especially with those aspects of the tradition that seem to entail a submissive acceptance of a rigid consensus and a nostalgic conformity to the constructed perfection of mythic origins – allegedly the life of the Prophet and the rightly guided caliphs who followed him.

One can demonize the West and modernity, and reach for the womb as do many Islamists (by Islamist, I denote Muslim extremist), even those who enjoy the relative freedom of Western secular societies. Islam, for these people, is a form of respite care where they seek permanent relief from the travails and responsibilities of engaging with modernity.

But today, in a world dominated by a global economy and increasingly influenced by an all-pervasive media, Muslims have to encounter readings other than those steeped in traditional Islamic protocols. Even in the Islamic world Muslim readings are no longer exclusive readings, no matter how fervently the Islamists wish otherwise. In the West, the holy Scriptures were subjected to sceptical readings even as early as the seventeenth century, by the philosopher Spinoza. With due circumspection, Spinoza denied that the Scriptures could contain any kind of sacred or authoritative truth, since they were couched in language subjected to what could be described as a process of 'historico-semantic drift'. This inherent volatility of word and meaning always creates the possibility of expunging the original meaning beyond hope of recovery. Pure and sacred words, according to Spinoza, can, in other times and other places, become impure and profane. Their status does not inhere to them, nor does it entirely derive from the person who utters them. They are also received and read subsequently, they have a history that must be taken account of. This essentially secular way of regarding texts does not automatically deny all possibility of revelation or the shamanistic power of words and texts which form the basis of liturgical prayer and forms of meditative experience; but it does inject a certain element of scepticism and critical reserve towards all claims of sacred provenance and divine fiat.

We know that Muslims, who are exhorted to seek knowledge, place great importance on the virtue of intelligence and thus of independent judgement. However, the notion of 'knowledge' today has lost most of its sacred resonance and has thus become problematic. As Professor Gutting puts it:

> Our age is, no doubt, one of criticism, but not, as for Kant, criticism [critique] that can start from the fact of knowledge. Rather, our critique can

start only from the 'fact that language exists', with no assumptions about its truth or validity. We cannot expect to find large truths about our nature and destiny in the wisdom of what has been said or to evaluate this wisdom on the basis of our own uncovering of such truths . . . There is no hope of breaking through this web of language to a world of fundamental truths.

As Paracelsus claimed that snakes are repelled by certain Greek words, we, in turn, are charmed by *all* words. Different epochs and different cultures have different notions about the epistemological status of knowledge, which is grounded on how things are seen to be connected to one another and on how we read the signs about us and within us.

One extremely important weapon in one's armoury of critical independence and access to an authentic sense of self – as opposed to the more bedevilled concept of authentic truth – is to become more aware of the charm of language, notwithstanding the quixotic post-modernist notion that we are entirely structured through, and by, language. This is an uncomfortable idea, for it throws doubt on our very identity and on all thinking based on identity; but, I believe, if we really wish to face our lives and the world about us honestly, we must entertain the possibility of unending doubt. This is an attitude that values the journey more than the destination, because all destinations for the finite and contingent creatures we are, are inevitably false destinations. Destiny is a tricky idea, and manifest destiny, as history has shown us time and again, is a bloody one. For most people with a dogmatic turn of mind, however, the accumulation of knowledge is likely to be a more banal affair. The writer Genet's words come to mind: 'If you know the point of arrival as well as the point of departure, then what you are writing is not an adventure, but a bus journey.' That goes for reading as well.

My own identity is a hybrid, nebulous entity. In an earlier article, I have called it 'a work-in-progress', which is never to be completed in this life. As a Muslim I should believe in a soul which, with all other created beings, returns to God. As a product of a secular culture, I find it difficult to accept that I have a central unchanging self-present identity. Towards the end of his life, the German philosopher Fichte was obsessed, even in his dreams, with the idea of a look that sees itself. This obsession demonstrated the pathos of locating a central core of identity by which we capture and fix ourselves. Each of us has a body, is pervaded by sense impressions. Each of us has a voice, language, but where is the 'I' that contains all these attributes? Or is it a linguistic device that is absorbed by them? The question should teach us humility, and perhaps create a space in this evanescent inner world we call 'consciousness' for the graceful appearance of what the ancient Greeks called 'the unknown guest', for the possibility of being open to the Divine through silent contemplation and through the invocation of the divine names as practised by those who follow the mystical path.

My identity certainly admits of a Muslim dimension, an area that is inextricably entwined with parents, family and the Muslim community of my childhood – profound, instinctive and never entirely articulated, and thus weakened into language. These were the circumstances of my origins – if one can talk of origins without dissolving into a self-recurring solipsism – but even these origins were not 'pure', thank God. Other ideas, other values and other expectations more or less associated with the Enlightenment – a notion under siege by both Islamists and post-modernists for entirely different reasons – were in the air and entered the porous being of my yet untutored soul. Hence I am wedded to the 'self-evident values' of a democratic society: dissenting opinions, critique, freedom of conscience and speech, and the relative autonomy of art as a form of free speech. You'll notice I use the word 'relative', a weasel word that, but I use it cautiously, recognizing that there are no absolutes – not even absolute freedom! Everything may be relative, as the post-modernists tell us, but we all need values of some sort to live by. As the critic John Fekete so rightly says, 'Not to put too fine a point on it, we live, breathe and excrete values.' The problem is that they are not always the same values.

I agree with the great Russian critic Mikhail Bakhtin, who quarrelled with 'monological discourse' and resisted all forms of absolute conformity, dogmatism and the repression of dissenting voices. As the Latin American novelist Carlos Fuentes puts it, 'Ours is an age of competitive language.' But unhappily, competition can degenerate into conflict, into the obscenity of the sort of war we have been witnessing in Bosnia, where one party cannot even tolerate the existence of another – a situation cast in despair. Of course, the clinging to a desiccated notion of one's unique truth is also found in the Muslim world. As Fuentes points out, the possibility of different discourses meeting in tension and dialogue is alien to religious bigots. 'For Ayatollahs,' he writes, 'reality is dogmatically defined once and for all in a sacred text.' Not only are such people guilty of overweening and abrasive readings of such texts, but the notion of a sacred text is itself brought into question by Fuentes when he observes, 'A sacred text is, by definition, a completed and exclusive text. You can add nothing to it. It does not converse with anyone . . . It offers a perfect refuge for the insecure who then, having the protection of a dogmatic text over their heads, proceed to excommunicate those whose security lies in the search for truth.' He adds, 'Impose a unitary language: you kill the novel, but you also kill society.' It seems to me that Fuentes' diatribe against revealed texts as forms of violence inflicted on believers is extreme because he seems to legitimize only a dogmatic reading of a sacred text. But his opinion is timely in our present circumstances.

It is very difficult, and not life-enhancing, to espouse a secular hermeneutics in Islamic societies today, where it is *de rigueur* to prove one's Islamic identity by adhering slavishly to the doctrine that Islam does not differentiate between the sacred and the profane; between the state and the private realm of the spirit. This view implies an abstracted, hypostasized notion of monolithic Islam, rather than a notion of a religion and civilization in time and history and, therefore, subject to change, to the fruitful and responsive impact of *Ijtihad* (intellectual endeavour).[1] Islamists fear this historicizing of Islam, as they fear the semantic drift of language, which Spinoza alluded to, because they rightly suspect that such views detract from the unreflecting audacity of their claims to absolute, unchanging ambitions, and, I believe, their interpretation of the kernel of religious *authenticity* (yet another tricky word that needs to be read cautiously) at the heart of Islamic experience is unjustified. Spinoza warns us with premonitory insight:

> Wholly repugnant to the general freedom are such devices as enthralling men's minds with prejudices, forcing their judgements, or employing any of the weapons of quasi-religious sedition; indeed, such seditions only spring up when law enters the domain of speculative thought, and opinions are put on trial and condemned on the same footing as crimes, whilst those who defend or follow them are sacrificed, not to public safety, but to their opponents' hatred and cruelty. If deeds only could be made the grounds of criminal charges and words were always allowed to pass free, such sedition would be divested of every semblance of justification, and would be separated from mere controversies by a hard and fast line.

I think Spinoza makes a good case for the abolition of the crime of blasphemy and, with specific reference to the Islamic world, to the crime of apostasy. These offences may have made sense in the time of the mediaeval jurist Ibn Taymiya, who championed and developed such concepts as modes of treason when the Islamic world was being threatened by the Mongol invasions. But today, they have become an excuse for oppression, and a goad for mindless obedience. They have a Stalinist sting in their tails as they encourage a society of informers – a frightened, hypocritical society.

Thus, in Pakistan today, the legacy of General Zia's flirtation with the Islamists has led to a disturbing development with regard to the blasphemy laws. The law has been amended whereby 'blasphemy', now a crime, has been so loosely defined so as to encourage an atmosphere of vendetta and revenge. Formerly punishable by life imprisonment, it is now a capital offence. Fanatics are encouraged to kill members of religious minorities in the belief that they are carrying out the work of good Muslims. The rule of law is reduced to the misrule of bigots and corrupt vengeful individuals and groups who use these laws to destroy people who do not think as they do, or who refuse to enter into the diabolical compact of corruption that besets all levels of Pakistani society.

I hope I am practising a Muslim reading of texts specifically designed for reading and of situations that are not so readily read. But I am assaying a reading that is precarious, liminal and transgressive. For those of us who are familiar with

English cultural icons, the title of this essay will also echo with dramatic and tragic resonances of the imprisonment of Oscar Wilde at Reading Gaol. Wilde committed transgressions which society deemed at the time to be criminal. A transgression which today is no longer an offence, a crime which, with the passage of time (and a change in values) has ceased to be a crime, in part.

Thus we are reminded of the fact that we are in a sense imprisoned by language and by our ways of reading and the risky possibilities, but possibilities nonetheless, of transgressive readings that lay the foundations for new readings and metamorphosis, both personal and social. Like Oscar Wilde, one can be a member of society, even as an outstandingly talented socialite, and yet be marginal.

So here we have it: reading transgressively, an object or situation open to reading in several ways; readings subject to context, historical change, which are inherently contingent; readings that tease out the inherent contradictions of language beyond the intentions of the writer, which struggle for coherence and understanding at the margins; readings open to subaltern voices weighed down with irony and mute pain; voices of the oppressed, voices of artists, the peerless insights of saints, the fleeting dreams and half-realized, incubating occultations of our darker selves – shadowy intuitions we would prefer to leave alone. We can be poor readers, we can be good readers, but we will always be partial readers. Perfection does not become us. We cannot even adequately read or encounter the perfect text, which for Muslims is the Holy Qur'an. I use the word 'encounter' because as we read we more or less live our readings. We bring to it our life experiences; and as we live, we more or less reflect on, or read, our life situation. The fact is that we all read from strategic positions, culturally and geographically (which is culture materialized). We have implicit, antecedent attitudes that we bring to our reading. So in a sense, every reading has an element of self-delusion, since we always read partially a text that *represents* (some would say misrepresents) the subject of its discourse. We never get to grips with all the polyvalent complexities and obstinate contradictions of the world out there.

Each culture automatically believes that the values that underpin its existence are the right ones. Muslims discover their warrant in divine revelation with which there can be no argument. Western, secular societies may be more constrained in their rhetoric, for the belief in absolute justification and knowledge of essences, and of things in themselves, no longer holds. But they are no less entrenched in their attitudes and actions. However, the fact is that modern technologically inspired culture is agnostic, it is indifferent to the possibilities of the Divine and hostile towards the all-encompassing ambitions of divine edict.

We cannot aspire to totalizing texts as authoritative readings in a post-modern world deafened with competing explanations or as the stories we tell ourselves to make sense of our existence in an ever-expanding universe. We may still have an appetite for the Absolute but find it difficult to swallow amongst the desecrated ironies of a multicultural world. We are finite creatures who can only know finitely without the faintest hope of attaining an Olympian detachment or universality. Some would argue that our very consciousness is structured by language and that thus we are all condemned to be readers – good, bad or indifferent – of the signs bestowed on us by the culture or cultures we inherit. All we can hope to do within the limits of our linguistic natures, which are the limits of knowledge, is to know and know about our particular circumstances. There are still philosophers in the West, such as Gadamer and perhaps Habermas, who staunchly hope to attain a position of objectivity. Certainly, Gadamer's hermeneutic methodology aims to produce a coherent interpretation of a text which can produce a universally accepted mode of knowing. I am not convinced, and I would argue that for most of the philosophical endeavours in the West, absolute knowledge is not of particular interest.

Freedom of conscience and freedom of expression are rights we treasure, and I have to say, notwithstanding the fact that in Islam blasphemy and apostasy are criminal offences, I believe that religious persecution of any sort and in any cause is an unmitigated evil. Our beliefs are not entirely created by acts of choice, they arise from several causes, some of which are inevitably motivated by subconscious impulses and thus elude our conscious grasp.

If we are to read well and live wisely, we must come to terms with uncertainty . . . I would go so far as to say that we need to learn to embrace uncertainty and treat any vision that describes the world in terms of dichotomies of good and evil, us and them, and so on, with great suspicion. Post-modernist readings are opposed to such fixed oppositions that imply an insidious and destructive attitude. Notions such as unity (which has a privileged, if not *the* privileged place in Islamic discourse), fixity and consensus are demonized by post-modern writers and their readers. Yet, true to the dynamics of deconstructive readings, their position is flawed with its own contradictions or aporias, for they also have preferred values (ones I personally find convincing), expressed by terms such as marginal, ambivalence, transitional and transgressive, which are set in opposition to modernist or pre-modernist positions.

I like Bertrand Russell's comments about the philosophical vision when he writes:

> The man who has no tincture of philosophy goes through life imprisoned in the prejudices derived from commonsense, the world tends to become definite, finite, obvious, common objects rouse no questions, and unfamiliar possibilities are contemptuously rejected.

Russell goes on to commend the possibilities of self-enlargement by adopting a questioning, sceptical frame of mind; we may transcend the tyrannical bounds of custom and conventional thought and free ourselves from what he called 'the bondage of passive emotions', which exist in the quagmire of our unexamined values and prejudices. As our life, so our reading. If we capitulate to the demands to think correctly, we forgo critique and the possibility of autonomous judgement. We cease to read actively, we become passive consumers of the word, the text, the constructed values – good or bad – about us. We place the sacred in the polished and screwed-down box of dogmatic, doctrinal assertion. We are then advised to respect religious values even if we don't share them, which means granting those values total exemption from critique, never mind parody. Thus in some places they can get away with murder.

Of course, it is argued – with some plausibility – that liberalism itself is made up of an ethnocentric set of values derived from the days of nineteenth-century British imperialism, with all the arrogance and racist superiority of that period of history. Liberalism, indeed, has its own set of values and beliefs, which are not in themselves universally valid. It has its own political agenda; it is not a neutral adjudicative discourse superior to the apparently benighted values of other non-liberal or illiberal societies. God is not a liberal. But I would venture that the liberal position allows for an element of self-criticism, ironical self-awareness, of good manners – what Muslim mystics would call 'courtesy' – not to be encountered in the religious dogmas grabbing the high ground today. There is a danger of becoming complacent here, of indulging in an ever-so-fine hypocrisy that pretends to listen to or read other discourses with an 'open mind' whilst already condemning them as inferior to one's own. I have no doubt that the liberal attitude is also pitted with blind spots of prejudices and ringfenced by entrenched self-interest and selective interpretations. But I still maintain that it allows for continuous self-correction and does not reside in closure. Its central terms – freedom, justice, equality, autonomy – are subject to constant revision in the light of changing social ideas, they are not tied down to dogmatic warrant and to potent immobilizing myths.

We may be sceptics, but as Colin Wilson wrote in that wonderful early book of his, *Religion and the Rebel*:

> A sceptic must also be sceptical about his scepticism; his own judgement is
> the first thing he should doubt. And scepticism must not be limited to
> logical proportions; it must be a continual sifting of all experience.

I suppose the sceptic's scepticism about his or her scepticism enables him or her to countenance the possibility of other, more trusting visions of life, that in the heart of our being we may find God. It is a form of ironical intelligence that does not hold the world in contempt, but neither is it enslaved by it. I will draw to a close with two questions: To whom am I speaking? And why should you listen? And I end with an apostrophic comment:

> Each of us comes with his own story.
> Even where most of it is borrowed or imposed.

We are intoxicated by stories.
Poisoned and uplifted by a pharmacy of senses;
Intoxication makes life a little more bearable.
Only in the void of silent contemplation
The place where we meet what we call 'God',
Do we escape the stories, and so ourselves.
I am telling you a story at this moment
For all forms of telling
Are simply stories spilling
From our hearts to our tongues.

Notes

1. *Ijtihad* is a term referring to the disciplined but generative interpretation of Islamic law (*shari'a*) whereby the application of *shari'a* is endowed with contemporary relevance.

A CONFUCIAN-CHRISTIAN?

Dr John Berthrong

Dr John Berthrong served as the Interfaith Dialogue Secretary for the United Church of Canada. He is currently the Associate Dean for Academic and Administrative Affairs and the Director of the Institute for Dialogue Among Religious Traditions at the Boston University School of Theology.

The Context of Multiple Religious Participation

THEOLOGIANS HAVE FINALLY noticed that they live in a religiously plural world. Obviously such an assertion taken as a statement of fact or even an observation about the general sentiments of one group of religious persons is overblown. As countless biblical scholars will remind us, the Christian New Testament is the product of a relentlessly pluralistic world; the Graeco-Roman world of the Eastern Mediterranean was full of different peoples, cults and religious movements. It would not have been news to Jesus of Nazareth or to St Paul that there were many religious movements in the world. Furthermore, the recognition of religious pluralism fuelled the great waves of Roman Catholic and Protestant mission of the eighteenth, nineteenth and twentieth centuries. Generations of missionaries from the North Atlantic world went forth because of the news of whole continents beyond the reach of the Christian gospel. Nonetheless, today there is a distinctively urgent tone to the renewed recognition of pluralism that is different from the recent past of Christendom, one that is characterized by its self-reflective and nervous nature. There is also a current of apprehensiveness, apologetics and debate about what pluralism ought to mean for Christian theology and personal identity.

On the one hand there are those who maintain that all this talk of the benefits of religious pluralism is yet another sign of the decadence of the age, of the loss of evangelistic nerve. In reality, all the calls for ecumenical and interreligious harmony are attempts to make the best of a bad situation, one characterized by making a virtue of sociological necessity. Just because it may now be true that Toronto, Ontario, is the most ethnically and religiously plural city in the world does not absolve Christians of the obligation to follow the missionary imperative found at the end of the Gospel of Matthew. On the other hand, there are those who declare that modern religious pluralism, driven by the changing demography of the second truly great shifting of peoples, opens our eyes to the true nature of God's diverse manifestations among all the peoples of the world. The pluralistically inclined theologians argue that it is time to awaken to the truth of cosmological and religious diversity and that we lean to glory in primal traditions and sophisticated world-views not our own. Rather than a loss of nerve, religious pluralism gives us a chance to become truly loving neighbours to a wider world. Theologians can be found at both extremes of these debates. Regardless of their position on the issue, theologians have an obligation to discern whether religious pluralism is merely sociological and historical or truly theological in nature.

In the first instance, civil religious tolerance, driven by the changing demography of the world, has relentlessly led to a growth in dialogue between religious communities. The motives for dialogue on the part of the partners is as varied as the partners themselves. It can range from a burning concern for social and economic justice and human rights to a fascination with esoteric meditation techniques. It can be as geo-political as a learned discussion of the conflict-ridden relationships of the Christian and Muslim world to the renewed appreciation of the place of primal and tribal religions in the world's spiritual ecology. All of these considerations are having an impact on the Christian theological world.[1]

The challenge of pluralism, however, is often more than the friction of intellectual systems bumping up against each other in the buzzing complexity of any modern city. My thesis is that Christians in the North Atlantic world are now experiencing the phenomenon of 'multiple religious participation' (hereafter referred to by the acronym MRP) as a real possibility in their spiritual lives for the first time in a long, long time. Other religions, such as Islam, Hinduism or Buddhism, are no longer just objects of revulsion as the spiritual Other; they are now often considered fascinating alternatives to received tradition. The religious turf of the Western world is being contested by mosques, dharma centres and temples of all kinds. Nonetheless, MRP is nothing new in the religious history of humankind. In fact, if the noted Canadian historian of religion W. C. Smith is correct, the process of MRP is precisely what has been going on since time immemorial, even if people did not acknowledge it because they could not give a name to something that they did not conceptually recognize as religious activity, or because of fear of being denounced as unfaithful to their own tradition, and so on.[2]

There is nothing mysterious or perverse about MRP in a pluralistic world. It is as simple an action as taking part in a neighbour's religious wedding ceremony, saying a prayer before a sporting event, or arguing about the role of prayer in public education – everyone can think of their own example. What does become much more an object of concern is when contact with other religious communities begins to have an impact on an individual's personal religious thought, cultus and practice.

The Question of Religious Choice and Identity

Recently I have been presented with a theological puzzle. On a number of occasions I have been asked to make presentations about Confucianism because I am a sinologist with a specialization in Sung-dynasty Neo-Confucian studies and an additional interest in the modern Confucian movement called New Confucianism.

Less well known than traditional classical Confucianism or the later Neo-Confucianism, the New Confucian movement represents a group of Chinese scholars in Taiwan, Hong Kong, Singapore, the People's Republic of China and the wider Chinese diaspora who are seeking to understand, describe, reform and commend the Confucian tradition as a viable world-view for the modern world.[3] The puzzle is, can I participate in more than one religious community at a time without giving up my membership and my profession of Christian religious intent? Because of these invitations to take part in the New Confucian movement this has become an existential question for me.

As is well known, this is less of a problem for East Asian religious sensibilities than it is for Western religious traditions such as Judaism, Christianity and Islam. These three great monotheistic faiths have consistently argued that once a person has embraced their vision of reality all other traditions must be forsaken. This is not necessarily a contemptuous view of the other traditions; at a minimum, however, it has been a consistent teaching that a person can only set her or his heart on one master. To participate in another religious cultus would be idolatrous. The East Asian religious tradition has had a different experience of MRP. It is not uncommon for East Asians to claim that they participate faithfully in more than one tradition even if this seems impossible from a Western perspective.

The question I must pose to myself (and by extension to others faced with similar conditions) is, what has Confucianism come to mean to me? Do I have divided loyalties? Does it make any sense, from the Western Christian religious sensibility, to talk about being a Confucian-Christian? My preliminary assessment is that such a mixture does make sense. Just as St Aquinas made use of the newly rediscovered Aristotle to expound the Christian faith, I hold it possible to make use of the Confucian and Neo-Confucian tradition to do the same thing. Moreover, just as Aquinas remained a Christian, I cannot conceive of my ultimate commitment as being anything but Christian. But this is just what needs to be explored and defended.[4]

I have been delighted to be asked to participate in the discussions of the New Confucian movement, because it has helped me to understand that tradition even more clearly than my sinological studies of the Confucian way ever did. In Confucian terms, my acceptance of the invitation mandated a seriousness of response not possible without the obligation to try to think in Confucian terms about the world. As is often the case when a person learns about another religion, the new way of seeing the world has challenged, enriched and ultimately transformed my understanding of being Christian. However, just as Aquinas made use of Aristotle and Islamic materials to construct his systematic reflections on the Christian faith, I first need to outline what Boston Confucianism looks like, and whether there is anything in it that contravenes the essence of the Christian tradition.

Root Metaphors and Fundamental Perspectives

In order to deal with Confucian–Christian interaction, the primary question is, what is Boston Confucianism and how can we recognize it as part of the Confucian way? Furthermore, what would such a use of Confucianism mean to a Bostonian who is also a Christian? The complex question of image, lineage and the transmission of the Way have always been crucial parts of the Confucian tradition. From the time of Confucius and his concerns for the decay and renewal of Chou culture, to the Northern and Southern Sung attempt to repristinate the Way in light of the Buddhist and Taoist philosophic, artistic, social and spiritual challenges, to the Ch'ing attempt to get back to the original Confucian vision uncontaminated by T'ang and Sung sedimentations, Confucians have sought to hand down a cultural form that they understood as unique.

To begin, is it possible to define the 'essence' of the Confucian Way? Does it make sense to suggest that there is one Confucian Way, when Confucianism is obviously such a complex, international movement? Could a Christian scholar make a claim for a Christian essence for the entire history of the movement that began with Jesus? Or should we recognize that there are many diverse yet related Confucian ways spread across history, and then carefully delineate the special or unique philosophical way under discussion as a vehicle for Confucian–Christian dialogue?[5]

In order to deal with the question of a beginning from a fiduciary Confucian perspective, I will select and arrange one general philosophic root metaphor and five specific criteria combining elements from the greatest of the mediaeval Neo-Confucians, Chu Hsi (1130–1200) and the modern New Confucian Mou Tsung-san. I will begin with Mou Tsung-san's favourite root metaphor and short list of four essential features of Confucian discourse and add Chu Hsi's doctrine of 'residing in reverence in order to exhaust principle' to enumerate the five traits that constitute the modern Western elaboration of any Confucian tradition.

I have added Chu's notion of critical reason as the search for the principles of things in order to make the list as inclusive of the great insights of the Sung–Ming Neo-Confucian renaissance as possible. Furthermore, the inclusion of critical reason is fundamental in any dialogue with a religious tradition, such as Christianity, that stresses the prophetic and theological element in religious discourse.[6] While most prophets are not academic theologians, they certainly are disturbers of the normal use of reason – prophets as religious intellectuals are critics of the way things are in order to provoke us to think about how things ought to be.

Five Enduring Confucian Themes

The initial construction of Boston Confucianism is capped by Mou's proposal of the root metaphor of concern-consciousness for the classical, Neo-Confucian and New

Confucian movements as expressions of the foundational and enduring Confucian sensibility.[7] Of course, my presentation and modification of Mou's complex thematization of the Confucian tradition is a Western interpretation, albeit a faithful one, I hope. Mou and the earlier Neo-Confucians give direction to my Western Confucianism even if they do not determine all of its specific characteristics. On the other side, the dominant Western philosophic resources for my reconstruction are the processes of thought of A. N. Whitehead and American naturalism and pragmatism.

Mou argues that his four traits must be a part of any fiduciary interpretation of the Confucian Way in terms of its essential historical and philosophic articulation. These four traits define what Mou holds to be the Confucian concern-consciousness for the world. In short, Mou believes that without recourse to these four traits the philosophy in question would not be a part of the Confucian Way. What makes for philosophic debate is the fact that the elements are vague in terms of further specification within the larger Confucian tradition.

The use of Chu Hsi's doctrine of 'residing in reverence in order to exhaust principle' is my attempt to specify the rational and analytic side of the tradition more closely than Mou's four traits do by themselves. The specific element that Chu's trait adds to the ensemble is the notion of critical reason or the active intellect in terms of concern-consciousness. This is demonstrably one of the most important aspects of Chu's thought, because he was recognized as having a keen concern for the rational or analytic side of the Confucian tradition. Chu has always been considered one of the most rationalistic, analytic and systematic of the Neo-Confucians.

According to Chu Hsi, we need to employ reason in order to make full use of our human mind-heart; to do less would be less than human for Chu. While Chu's notion of critical reason did not lead to the typical post-Enlightenment Western sense of alienation from nature as something less than rational, it still guarded against any facile sense of mystic or overly romantic participation with the vitality of the cosmos that Chu sensed as problematic. It was Chu's way of preserving the dialectic of analytic reason alongside his robust organic or holistic vision of the Tao as the symbol for all that truly is. What is so important for New Confucianism as a modern global philosophic movement is that Chu Hsi always wanted to ask the reason why for anything whatsoever, rather than merely to assent to a vague sense of mutuality with the world. The world was real and concrete for Chu and he wanted to know, if at all possible, the reasons for these concrete object-events and their complicated patterns that contributed to human flourishing.

In summary these five traits are:

1. *T'ien-ming* as creativity itself; this is the ceaseless productivity of the Tao.
2. *Jen* as creativity mediated by a primordial concern for others; this is the Tao as manifested in proper human conduct.

3. *Hsin* as the mind-heart functioning as the locus of the experiential unity of concern-consciousness.
4. *Hsing* as human nature in its role as the active creation of new life-values for civilized human society.
5. *Chu-ching hsiung-li* as the task of residing in reverence in order to exhaust principle; this is the self-reflexive function of critical reason and humane wisdom as a key element in the cultivation of the mind-heart.

According to Mou, each one of these traits is related to a specific philosophic theme as well as being centrally located in one or more classical Confucian texts, including such works as the *I Ching*, the *Analects*, the *Mencius*, the *Ta-hsueh* and the *Chung-yung*.[8] First, the concept of *t'ien-ming* expresses the cosmological aspect of creativity itself as the supreme cosmological trait of the Confucian Way and is best articulated in the *I Ching* and the *Chung-yung*. This cosmic creativity is the foundational basis for Confucian moral metaphysics as the generation of values in the cosmos.[9] Second, humanity or *jen* thematizes creativity as concern or care for others as the response to the Mandate of Heaven by people seeking humane life in community. It will come as no surprise that the patron text of *jen* is the *Analects* of Confucius. In fact, it is with Confucius's sharp articulation of humanity as the key virtue for civilized life that the Confucian tradition finds its point of origin. It is the root metaphor for human virtue as concern-consciousness within human community. However, as Tu Wei-ming has pointed out, Confucians claim that there was a long history to their tradition before Confucius, just as there was a long history of the Jewish people before Moses on Mount Sinai. The story of humanity is the story of the primordial sages' struggle to create civilization.

Third, the Mandate of Heaven *qua* creativity and humanity becomes fused in the experiential unity of human life and conduct in the mind-heart. The fundamental mind-heart (*pen-hsin*) is creative or active reason in terms of unifying cosmic creativity with human life. The *Mencius* is obviously the key early Confucian text for the mind-heart. Fourth is *hsing*, which functions as the general or formal structure of human nature, the proper pattern of all the elements of a humane life in community. Human nature, when fully realized, contributes to the creation of new values for human life. The *Mencius* is again the key text for the early exposition of the concept of human nature.[10] Behind all these concepts is Mou's idea of concern-consciousness as the leitmotif of all Confucian discourse. Mou's summary statement of this moral sensibility is that 'The moral nature of Chinese philosophy is rooted in the concept of concern-consciousness (*yu-huan i-shih*).'[11]

Fifth, Chu Hsi's memorable and controversial formula, *chu-ching hsiung-li*, encapsulates the sense of critical reason and realism that distinguishes the Confucian tradition, at least in terms of its own apologetics, from Taoism and Buddhism. According to Chu's *li-hsueh* school, the notion of critical reason is epitomized in *The Great Learning* and *The Classic of Changes*, because both texts are concerned with the proper role of thinking as a process and method to understand the world and its organization. I should also note that this sense of critical reason never played the same role in the Confucian tradition, even in its most rationalistic aspects, as it has since the eighteenth-century Enlightenment in most forms of Western philosophy.[12] Nonetheless, the proper use of reason and wisdom has always played an important role in the Confucian tradition, as witnessed by the work of thinkers as diverse in orientation as the author of *The Great Commentary* on *The Classic of Changes*, Hsun Tzu,[13] or Chu Hsi and Tai Chen, for example.

Besides the list of key traits, Mou Tsung-san has yet another way of describing the function of concern-consciousness in terms of what he calls the vertical and horizontal aspects of the Confucian tradition. The vertical thrust of concern-consciousness describes the ultimate transformation of the mind-heart from *jen-hsin*, or the undisciplined mind-heart of human passion, to being *tao-hsin* or the mind-heart conformed to the Tao. Mou argues that all the great philosophic traditions pass over into the domain of religion or spirituality, when they manifest a vertical dimension that connects them to the ultimate source of all transforming values of their world-view. However, no great civilizational philosophy is merely a metaphysical way of ultimate self-transformation; it is always concurrently a practical social teaching about how to manifest proper ritual and moral behaviour. The vertical dimension only makes sense as a move from untruth to truth itself, within a community of discourse and conduct that brings civility to mundane human society.

Along with the vertical dimension of transformation from ignorance, finitude and error to true reality, ways of ultimate transformation are also paths of normal social human interaction, of ethical conduct, of artistic sensibility, of economic organization, of political debate, of ritual and moral action. By this Mou observes that ways of ultimate transformation as the defining philosophies or root metaphors of a culture always have well-defined sets of social patterns, rules of ethical conduct, rituals of behaviour and meaning, elaborations of rites of passage, of maturation, of marriage, of birth and death, which help to shape civilized human life. Along with the quest to overcome ignorance, finitude, sin and error, these rituals make up the ultimately transforming nature of the traditions that we call religions or world-views.

In terms of universal religious world-views, Mou points out that Confucianism does not display anything like the organized religious structure or developed theism of Judaism, Christianity or Islam. But this, Mou believes, does not make Confucianism one bit less a religious world-view, because the Confucian Tao does have a path of ultimate vertical self-transformation, along with patterns of ethical conduct and social rites that help guide Confucians through the chaos of everyday life.[14] Indeed, as Fingarette has noted, this is a world-view wherein the secular becomes the sacred when the person fuses the vertical and horizontal dimensions of its world-view.[15]

Furthermore, Mou and his students such as Tu Wei-ming are somewhat controversial in their articulation of the religious dimension of the Confucian Way.[16] We need to remember that Mou and Tu's explanation of religion is a highly nuanced defence of Confucian spirituality that in no way denies the other social, artistic, educational and scholarly aspects of the tradition discussed in detail by other scholars of the tradition. What continues to define all the New Confucians is the perennial engagement with the canonical texts of the tradition, even though the New Confucians tend to take a more irenic view of the tradition than even the most liberal of the Ch'ing evidential scholars such as Tai Chen.[17] The New Confucians view the entire tradition, including Hsun Tzu, as a repository for future philosophical reconstruction.

Actually, according to Mou, there is a descending and ascending movement from the Mandate of Heaven, manifested as humaneness when *jen* becomes the experiential unity of humanity in the mind-heart, the final illumination of human nature. In being illuminated, human nature, as it were, ascends again to unity with the creative forces of the cosmos.[18] While Chu Hsi agrees with the general structure of this process of humanization, he would want to add the element of critical thought to the process. Reason, to borrow a phrase from our Muslim colleagues, is God's finger on the earth. Critical reason is the way humans save themselves from pride and inordinate self-interest through a realistic encounter with the concrete world. Without reason we can never be sure that we escape the worst deformations of individual and communal arrogance and blindness. Reason helps us to understand and to protect the objective nature of the Mandate of Heaven in generating a true inter-subjective autonomous morality. The same point was made clearly centuries before by Hsun Tzu in a number of his essays, but most cogently in 'Dispelling Blindness', and 'On the Correct Use of Names'.

There is always the rhythm of a person's choices, for good or ill, about how one will become an authentic person. Of course, no person does this alone, for we are all part of community. We inherit and then modify the customs, teachings and practices of our community. These include the highest ethical goals of our community, such as the Confucian notion of *jen* as humanity, as well as all the other bits and pieces of our collective culture and personal habits. While it is true that becoming humane is a profoundly personal action, it is an action that only has meaning within community as being understood in the broadest possible way. As Tu has observed, 'We can perhaps restate Neo-Confucian religiosity in terms of a two-fold process: a continuous deepening of one's subjectivity and an uninterrupted broadening of one's sensitivity.'[19] Or, as he states in his interpretive study of the *Chung-yung*, 'the Confucian way of being religious as ultimate self-transformation as a communal act and as a faithful dialogical response to the transcendent.'[20]

Ch'en Ch'un (1159–1223), one of Chu Hsi's most philosophically astute students, notes:

What the sages and worthies have called the Learning of the Way is not a principle that is too obscure and difficult to investigate or any affair that is too lofty and difficult to practise. It is nothing but ordinary human affairs. For while the Way is rooted deeply within the Mandate of Heaven, it actually operates in the midst of daily life.[21]

Here Ch'en clearly joins the notion of Way to that of the Mandate of Heaven. In fact, Ch'en begins his discussion of the most contested parts of Chu Hsi's thought, namely those aspects of *li-hsueh* as a theory of principle, by his extended description of the Tao as the path of human wisdom and perfection. Ch'en argues that the source of the Way must be traced to Heaven, and that it is a creative process. Furthermore, Ch'en rejects the Taoist notion that the Tao is something that transcends daily life, the world as void rather than characterized by solid connection between human beings and the world itself. As Ch'en notes somewhat later, 'In the Learning of the School of the Sage, there is nothing that is not concrete.'[22] One of the functions of critical reason is to help us respond to the concreteness of the objectivity of the reality of nature.

Although Ch'en Ch'un is considered the arch-rationalist of Chu Hsi's students, it is noteworthy that he, like Mou, begins his account of Confucian thought with a discussion of the Mandate of Heaven. If both Ch'en and Mou agree about the centrality of *t'ien-ming*, we can conclude that this is a central characteristic of the entire tradition, and not something germane only to Mou's interpretive stance. The notion of the objective side of the Confucian Tao is heightened by Ch'en's noting that '*Ming* is like an order from a superior or an official order.'[23] Ch'en recognizes the normative, definitive side of the Confucian tradition from its very inception in *t'ien-ming*. According to Ch'en, this objective side of *ming* is essential because the world is not just the flux of dynamic matter-energy without any director or moral foundation. Each object-event must have its principle in order to be distinguished from other things and to have its own integrity, its own unique value in a world of constitutive values. 'There must be something to direct it and that is principle. Principle is in material force and acts as its pivot.'[24]

At the heart of any exposition of the Confucian Way one finds, literally, the mind-heart that we must begin the transmission of the Confucian Tao to the West. But before we begin this exposition, we need to make clear that the Confucian project of the study and cultivation of the mind-heart is only distantly related to the modern Western analytical philosophy of the mind. While most Confucians will want to argue for the unity of humankind as a thinking species, few will find immediate or obvious links to the modern analytic tradition of the philosophy of mind.

However, it is fascinating to speculate that this gap in world philosophy may be closing somewhat, as Confucians become more conversant with the intricacies of the Western philosophic scene, and as Western analytically trained philosophers such as Graham, Fingarette, Rorty, Neville, Cua, Rosemont and Ivanhoe take more interest in non-Western traditions. Who can say what fruitful conversations will emerge? However, it is well to remember that at the beginning there is a great interpretive gap that needs to be filled in carefully and patiently in order that there be more than mutual incomprehension.[25]

It is with the examination of the concept of the mind-heart within Confucian discourse that we return full circle to the question of the possibility of a Confucian-Christian theology. It is a Confucian theme that ought to remind Christians of their own question, how is it with your soul? Further, is there anything in this proposed cross-cultural philosophic experiment that is religiously incommensurable with the broad sweep of the Christian faith?

Conclusion

Having very briefly outlined one Western version of New Confucianism as a basis for philosophic self-cultivation and natural theology, we must return to the question of the possibility of Confucian-Christian identity. From the Confucian point of view, there is really no problem in conceiving of a Christian-Confucian synthesis that preserves the essential contours, sensibilities and traits of their cumulative traditions.[26] After the arrival of the Jesuit missionaries in the later part of the Ming dynasty, many Confucians embraced the Christian faith as something entirely compatible with their Confucian commitment. They argued that the question of theism was simply not the central point of the historical Confucian tradition, and therefore a Confucian was free to adopt a theistic understanding as part of her or his world-view.[27] Personal religious commitment, if it does not violate Confucian ethical and philosophical sensibilities, has always been viewed as essentially a free choice by the individual involved. The point for these early converts to Christianity is that Confucianism continued to function as the philosophic background for Christian faith; in no way did they see themselves abandoning Confucianism. Rather, these early Confucian literati who converted agreed with the Jesuits that the Christian faith made them better Confucians as well as faithful Christians.

I am persuaded that such a viewpoint is possible for a Western Christian, although such an assertion is novel because it is something new when compared to the East Asian case. Nonetheless, I agree with the early Confucian-Christians that there is nothing ultimately incompatible between the notion of concern-consciousness and the five traits as a philosophic world-view that articulates a Christian theistic commitment. If Christianity can have dialogue with Athens, Rome, Berlin, Paris, Moscow and London, it certainly can do the same with Beijing, Seoul and Tokyo. What has happened is that the philosophic and ethical canon for the development of Christian natural theology has been expanded yet again beyond the normal Western, European context. Of course, here again there is nothing novel in such an expansion, because it happens every time the gospel becomes an integral part of any culture. From an ultimate religious point of view, I remain committed to the portrait of Jesus of Nazareth as the Christ – and in Confucian terms this is the place where I cultivate my mind-heart in order to become truly human; from a philosophic perspective I can read the world in a Confucian way.

In fact, the Confucian reading of the world as a reflection on divine matters is extremely valuable at just those points where the modern Western philosophic tradition is searching for ways to expand its vision of the cosmos, as it always has done when confronted with sophisticated alternative world-views. For instance, the notions of moral metaphysics, concern-consciousness and the processive and relational qualities of the Confucian Tao are themes that resonate with modern process and naturalistic and pragmatic philosophic theology. The Confucian tradition, as a form of natural theology committed to a spiritually transforming moral metaphysics based on an organic, relational and processive world-view, demonstrates how one can be religious and also hold a set of philosophic positions in tune with the naturalistic world-view of modernity. At a minimum, such a Confucian-influenced natural theology assists in reducing cognitive dissonance, because it sees nothing wrong with a creative, relational, historical and natural interpretation of the world that still includes a sense of divine things.

Therefore, the question of confused ultimate religious commitments and the fear of MRP turns out not to be the provocative issue that it seemed at first encounter. Real religious commitment is seldom truly confused even if it is complicated. Engagement with the Confucian tradition enriches rather than destroys Christian faith; this is what one would logically expect if it is true that there is one God and if Christ is the creative and redemptive manifestation of divine love transforming any encounter with the cultures of the world.[28] God surely finds new and creative ways for the witness to the nations.

Notes

1. W. C. Smith, the Canadian theologian and historian of religion, argues that there is no such thing as a purely Christian theology, at least if Christians affirm, as they do everywhere and always, that theirs (and mine) is a monotheistic faith in the one Creator, God. Smith points out that theology is the studying of what we can know about the divine reality that Christians confess as the Trinity. Hence theology ought to be a global enterprise. Smith notes that this is certainly what such giants of the Christian movement as Aquinas, Calvin and Wesley thought they were doing.
2. When I worked as the national Interfaith Dialogue Secretary for the Division of World Outreach of the United Church of Canada, I cannot count the times

that worried laypeople confessed to me that they were practising some kind of Hindu yoga or Buddhist meditation, or had been awakened to the ecological crisis by listening to the stories of the Native Elders. Once they sensed that I would not immediately denounce their spiritual searches, they flooded me with their wonderment that no one had ever told them about the richness of the other religions of the world. In one case, a friend who had a Muslim dentist as a neighbour was truly astounded to learn that Christians had held the doctrine that there was no salvation or true revelation outside the Church. Religious pluralism has a way of making old truths uncouth as the hymn by James Russell Lowell (1819–91) teaches:

> New occasions teach new duties;
> Time makes ancient good uncouth;
> They must upward still and onward
> Who would keep abreast of truth.

3. Many Confucian scholars point out that Confucianism is already an international movement. There are Chinese, Korean, Japanese and Vietnamese Confucians. However, for the purposes of this essay I have only focused on the Chinese part of the tradition. For an excellent discussion of the nature of the Confucian tradition, see A. S. Cua, 'The Idea of Confucian Tradition', *Review of Metaphysics*, vol. 45, no. 4 (June 1992), pp. 803–40.

4. Modern examples of other Christian theologians are, for Buddhism: Lynn A. de Silva, *The Problem of Self in Buddhism and Christianity* (London: Macmillan Press: 1979); John B. Keenan, *The Meaning of Christ: A Mahayana Theology* (Maryknoll, NY: Orbis Books, 1989); and for Hinduism: M. Thomas Thangaraj, *The Crucified Guru: An Experiment in Cross-Cultural Christology* (Nashville: Abingdon Press, 1994); Francis X. Clooney, SJ, *Theology after Vedanta: An Experiment in Comparative Theology* (Albany, NY: State University of New York Press, 1993). Each of these authors attempts to frame their Christian theology in terms of a particular form of Buddhist or Hindu thought.

5. Mou himself demonstrates the great internal complexity and intellectual scope of the Northern and Southern Sung Confucian revival in his various studies of the rise of Neo-Confucianism. He tries to show that there were a number of different strains within the schools of thought that find their synthesis in Chu Hsi. In fact, Mou concludes that Chu Hsi is not really the true inheritor of the work begun by Chou Tun-i, Chang Tsai and Ch'eng Hao. The picture is even more complicated when we include scholars other than this particular set of philosophers.

6. One of the reasons that the Western tradition, on its philosophic side, is called Graeco-Roman is to indicate the role of critical, questioning reason along with the religious sensibilities of the Jewish roots of Christianity. Tertullian aside,

Athens has a great deal to do with the actual development of Western thought. Religion may proclaim but critical reason always asks why. As the Islamic tradition teaches, reason is God's finger on earth.

7. The following account is drawn primarily from Mou Tsung-san's little outline of Chinese thought, *The Uniqueness of Chinese Philosophy (Chung-kuo che-hsueh te t'e-chih)* (Taipei: Student Book Company, 1974). His discussion of the four traits is found in chapters 3–10, pp. 14–78. Although later in his career he modifies some of his views, nonetheless, beginning with the monumental *Mind and Nature (Hsin-t'i yu hsing-t'i)*, published in the late 1960s and marking a noteworthy achievement in the reinterpretation and reconstitution of the Confucian Way, the basic outlines of his argument were clearly drawn in this early set of lectures on the Chinese intellectual tradition. It also has the virtue of focusing almost exclusively on Confucianism, which Mou argues is the central thread of the entire Chinese intellectual world.

   In 1983, Mou completed another and more comprehensive set of nineteen lectures on Chinese philosophy, which expanded the range of his reflections to include Taoism and Chinese Buddhism. However, Mou is quick to point out that Confucianism still remains the dominant intellectual tradition throughout Chinese history. These nineteen lectures add considerable detail to the basic outline provided in *The Uniqueness of Chinese Philosophy*. As I also noted above, these works primarily focus on the philosophic reconstruction of the tradition and do not deal directly with the question of ritual or social practice. However, Mou knows as well as any Confucian that social renewal as civilized practice and ritual will need to be part of the New Confucianism as social praxis.

8. Mou's specific bias is clear from this list. For instance, it is not just a recognition of the standard thirteen classica. Also, it does not include the Great Learning. The reason for this is that Mou does not believe that the Great Learning is really part of the mainstream tradition. The mainstream for Mou is centred on Mencius. Mou finds it suggestive that the Great Learning was a key text for both Hsun Tzu and Chu Hsi. Hsun Tzu and Chu Hsi are definitely not the best examples of the mainstream of the Confucian Way for Mou.

9. There has been considerable warranted debate over the last three decades about just which philosophic label best fits the Confucian tradition. Is Confucianism, in its philosophic form as thematized by Mou, an ontology, a metaphysics, a cosmology, a form of humanism, a soteriological narrative, social ethics, or some rich combination of these and more aspects of human thought, action and passion? Mou prefers to call it a moral metaphysics. By this Mou wants to distinguish the Confucian tradition from Kant's metaphysics of morals in order to make the claim that morality is essential to the very core of the Confucian tradition. I have come to believe that the notion of an *ars*

contextualis, as advanced by David Hall and Roger Ames, beginning with *Thinking Through Confucius* (Albany, NY: State University of New York Press, 1987), is a good way to address the question of the philosophic taxonomy of the Chinese tradition. The notion of an *ars contextualis* maintains the close link between ethics and values that everyone agrees is crucial to Confucian self-definition, and yet does not demand immediate consent to the classification of Confucianism under one of the very specific and traditional Western ways of construing reality as metaphysics, ontology or cosmology.

10. I would argue that if Hsun Tzu were included here, we could also add the notion of principle as a part of human nature. However, if we exclude such Wei-Chin thinkers as Wang Pi from the mainstream of the Confucian tradition, it was not till Ch'eng I and Chu Hsi that principle *qua li* again played such an important role in the definition of human nature. Once this lesson was relearned, it always played a crucial role in the articulation of Confucian philosophy.

11. Mou Tsung-san, *The Uniqueness of Chinese Philosophy*, p. 12.

12. For an excellent general discussion of this issue in relation to the modern religious situation in the North Atlantic world, see Peter Berger, *A Far Glory: The Quest for Faith in an Age of Credulity* (New York: The Free Press, 1992). Berger makes the point that all the world's great religions have made a place for critical reason in the sense that they break what he calls the cosmic mythic matrix, the pure connection of the self and world.

13. John Knoblock, *Xunzi: A Translation and Study of the Complete Works*, 3 vols. (Stanford, CA: Stanford University Press, 1989–94), provides us with this short passage that shows Hsun Tzu's concern for critical reason: 'One who is adept at study exhausts principles of rational order. One who is adept at putting things into practice examines problems' (3:225).

14. In fact, Mou has an extended discussion of the religious dimension of the Confucian Way in chapter 12 of *The Uniqueness of Chinese Philosophy*.

15. Herbert Fingarette, *Confucius – The Secular as Sacred* (New York: Harper & Row, 1972).

16. For a summary of the debate about the religious quality of the Confucian Way, see Rodney Taylor's *The Religious Dimensions of Confucianism* (Albany, NY: State University of New York Press, 1990). Mary Evelyn Tucker, *Moral and Spiritual Cultivation in Japanese Neo-Confucianism: The Life and Thought of Kaibara Ekken (1630–1714)* (Albany, NY: State University of New York Press, 1989) and John H. Berthrong, *All under Heaven: Transforming Paradigms in Confucian–Christian Dialogue* (Albany, NY: State University of New York Press, 1994) also have discussions of the topic of the religious nature of the Confucian tradition.

17. Yet I would argue that Tai Chen has as much vertical dimension to his thought as Chu Hsi or Wang Yang-ming. Tai's passionate defence of the way of the

scholar is surely a commitment to move from ignorance to the true, from unreality to true reality.

18. I am indebted for this insight into the structure of Mou's thought to Professor Lin Tongqi's presentation of Mou's thought at the recent Third International Confucian–Christian Dialogue, Boston University, 25–28 August 1994.

19. Tu Wei-ming, *Confucian Thought: Selfhood as Creative Transformation* (Albany, NY: State University of New York Press, 1985), p. 137.

20. Tu Wei-ming, *Centrality and Commonality: An Essay on Confucian Religiousness* (Albany, NY: State University of New York Press, 1989), p. 94.

21. Ch'en Ch'un, *Neo-Confucian Terms Explained (Pei-hsi tzu-i)*, trans. Wing-tsit Chan (New York: Columbia University Press, 1986), p. 176.

22. Ibid., p. 107.

23. Ibid., p. 37.

24. Ibid., p. 38.

25. In the outline presented here one can only hint at some permutations of the notion of concern-consciousness and the five specific Neo-Confucian and New Confucian philosophic traits. The other contrasts and connections must, at some later date, be explicated. In English, the two most accessible alternative models for a New Confucian world-view are to be found in the ongoing work of Tu Wei-ming (see notes 18 and 19) and Cheng Chung-ying, *New Dimensions of Confucian and Neo-Confucian Philosophy* (Albany, NY: State University of New York Press, 1991). For a general discussion of the New Confucian movement and its relation to the modern dialogue movement, see Berthrong, *All under Heaven*.

26. For a brief examination of the issue of joint citizenship as it has emerged in modern Confucian–Christian dialogue, see Berthrong (*All under Heaven*, pp. 1–68; 165–87). This is also primarily a study of the modern dialogue, although it does provide a bibliography concerning the earlier Jesuit mission in the sixteenth and seventeenth centuries.

27. A. S. Cua, in 'The Idea of Confucian Tradition' (see note 3), makes the point that a tradition is a 'cluster' concept that changes over time and with the interpretive choices of individuals and communities of scholars. I should note that such a choice was often seen as somewhat eccentric. For instance, the great Northern Sung Neo-Confucian, Su Shih, has always been recognized as one of the truly great Confucian scholars of the Sung Neo-Confucian revival.

28. A. N. Whitehead, *Religion in the Making* (Cambridge: Cambridge University Press, 1927), pp. 130–1, once noted that, 'A system of dogmas may be the ark within which the Church floats safely down the flood-tide of history. But the Church will perish unless it opens its windows and lets out the dove in search for an olive branch. Sometimes even it will do well to disembark on Mount Ararat and build a new altar to the divine Spirit – an altar neither in Mount Gerizim nor yet in Jerusalem.'

ONE-WORLD FAITH?

Revd Marcus Braybrooke

Revd Marcus Braybrooke is an Anglican clergyman, Chair of the World Congress of Faiths, a Trustee of the International Interfaith Centre at Oxford, and a former Director of the Council of Christians and Jews.

I ENDED MY first book, *Together to the Truth*, with these words:

> One world faith will emerge by a process of reconception. As the great religions respond to the world in which they live and to each other, so their fundamental insights will develop and broaden. This is quite different from an easy and artificial amalgam of diverse creeds. It is the growing together of living, developing organisms. As a Christian, I believe that Christ will stand at the centre of the emerging world faith.[1]

Twenty-five years later, I retain this vision but would want to word it more carefully. Although I disowned a wish to see an artificial amalgam of creeds, it is clear that this is what the term 'one-world faith' suggests to most people, just as the word 'syncretism' is usually used in a pejorative sense.

It would be better to speak of a growing recognition that people of all faiths share a common quest. They seek the one ultimate Reality, who is for ever seeking them. This common quest is shown by the growing together of the life of the world's religious communities, although this is often resisted, sometimes violently, by extremists. It is reflected in the beginnings of global theology, global ethics and global spirituality.

This sense of a common quest, in which differences should be valued, should help to overcome the hostility and rivalry still so evident between many members of different faiths. It should also inspire people of all faiths to work together for a world of peace and justice where all people enjoy the fullness of life and in which the environment is cherished.

I recognize now that the way in which I spoke of Christ twenty-five years ago was too defensive. It is my very faith in Christ, who reveals the unbounded love of God for all people, that has impelled me to a universalist vision.

Reconception

Together to the Truth was based on William Hocking's theory of 'reconception'. It was an attempt to test out his thesis of reconception by comparing developments within Christianity and Hinduism since the early nineteenth century. W. E.

Hocking was an American philosopher who chaired the American Laymen's report *Rethinking Missions, a Laymen's Enquiry after a Hundred Years* (1932). The commission for the report travelled widely and the report's factual observations are still interesting. Controversy surrounded the summary, which was mostly the work of Hocking. The task of the missionary, the report suggested, was to see what was good in other religions and to help their adherents to recover the best elements of their own faiths. The ultimate aim of missionary work, insofar as the report articulated one, seems to have been the emergence of the various religions out of isolation into a world fellowship in which each would find its appropriate place.

Hocking developed these ideas in two longer works: *Living Religions and a World Faith*[2] and *The Coming World Civilization*.[3] He argued that the whole trend of global life was towards unity and community of outlook. There was a need for a single world religion. How, he then asked, might a Christian work for such a world faith? One method was 'radical displacement' – the replacement of other world religions by Christianity so that the whole world becomes Christian. This, it is probably fair to say, was the traditional missionary hope, as shown, for example, in the slogan 'the world for Christ in our generation'. The second method he suggested was 'synthesis'. This would include the adoption of some ceremony and ideas from other traditions into Christianity. This seems to have been, for example, the position of John Henry Barrows, who was the chairman of the 1893 World's Parliament of Religions. He wrote at one point, 'The idea of evolving a cosmic or universal faith out of the Parliament was not present in the minds of its chief promoters. They believed that the elements of such religion are already contained in the Christian ideal and Christian scriptures.'[4] In his Barrows lecture, which he gave in Asia, Barrows further explained why he believed that Christianity was destined to become the universal religion of the entire world. He based his argument on an evolutionary theory of religion, whereby 'lower' forms of religion are absorbed into 'higher' forms. Eventually these 'higher' religions will be assimilated to the religion of Christ. Christianity, he claimed, was 'a celestial seed capable of indefinite expansion and wide variation'.[5]

The third method, which Hocking himself favoured, was 'reconception'. Suppose two religions partly overlap in their teaching or practice. In the way of synthesis the one will reach over and try to include part of the other, but members of the other religion will not agree about what is 'inessential'. In the process of reconception, a religion does not lose its shape, but expands as its growth in understanding increases. Religions are continually growing or rethinking, as they come in contact with new people and ideas. At any one stage a religion is a complete and shapely whole; but it is also in constant need of reconception. In part this is in response to contemporary intellectual developments. For example, the work of Darwin and subsequent thinkers has made it necessary for some religions to reformulate their teaching about the beginning of the world. Advances in genetics studies are causing a similar rethinking about the beginnings of life. Awareness of living in a multi-religious world has caused members of many faiths to re-express their teaching about the attitude of their faith to that of others. The decree of the Second Vatican Council, *Nostra Aetate*, is an example of such rethinking in the Roman Catholic Church, but rethinking that appealed to and based itself on traditional teaching.

Because now more than ever all religions live in the same world, they all have to respond to the same intellectual challenges – not least to secularism and technological advances. There is often a willingness to distinguish that which is inessential, because shaped by particular histories and cultures, from that which is at the heart of a tradition. Their responses to common stimuli mean that to some extent as they change, the common elements become clearer. The argument of my *Together to the Truth* is that the evidence of the last two centuries does indicate that the reconception that has taken place within the world religions has also brought religions closer together.

Reasons to Expect a World Faith

There are other reasons for expecting a coming world faith, in the sense of a growing fellowship of believers. The gradual emergence of a world society seems to require some shared spiritual values. In 1939 Sarvepalli Radhakrishnan asked, 'Should we not give a spiritual basis to the world which is now being mechanically made to feel its oneness by modern scientific inventions?'[6] Quite recently, the Duke of Edinburgh, in his preface to Hans Kung's *Global Responsibility*, comments, 'While it has proved possible to arrive at a broad consensus about the facts of life on earth, so far at least, it has proved impossible to overcome the jealousies, rivalries and the destructive consequences of competing religions and ideologies.'[7] The feeling for a world faith rests also on a belief that the coming together of peoples in a global society is under the guidance of the divine Spirit. This reflects a biblical belief that however ambiguous history may seem, it is the sphere of God's operation.

This emerging world society is bringing together the diverse histories of traditionally separate faith communities. The 'provincialism' of so much of our knowledge was brought home to me when I attended a *son et lumière* at the Red Fort in Delhi. Although my degree was in history, here we listened to the history of emperors of whom I had scarcely heard. No one had noticed that my course ignored the history of whole continents. Religious thinking was carried on in similar isolation. Now gradually members of one faith are becoming aware of the history, teaching and writings of other great religions. This is making possible the emergence of world theology. As Wilfred Cantwell Smith wrote in 1981, 'Henceforth the data for theology must be the data of the history of religion. The material on the basis of which a theological interpretation shall be proffered, of the world, man, the truth and of salvation – of God and His dealings with His world –

is to be the material that the study of the history of religion provides.'[8]

The urgency of the crises that confront humanity is another compelling reason to encourage religious people to work together. Practical co-operation for peace and human welfare has helped many people of faith discover a sense of oneness. Archbishop Fernandes, for example, has described the World Conference of Religion and Peace as 'trying to create a unity of conscience or, if you prefer, a universal conscience around the basic convictions shared by all living faiths'.[9] Again, it was the critical issues facing humankind that was the focus of shared concern at the 1993 Chicago Parliament of the World's Religions. The 'Declaration toward a Global Ethic', in the formulation of which Hans Kung played a major part, was an attempt by the religions of the world to address those issues.[10]

The feeling for an emerging world faith also reflects the view that the mystery of the Ultimate transcends our pictures and doctrines and that therefore, each person's experience of the Ultimate is relevant to us all. Stanley Samartha has written, 'A sense of Mystery provides a point of unity to all plurality. In a pluralistic world, the different responses of different religions to the Mystery of the Infinite of *Theos* or *Sat* need to be acknowledged as valid.'[11] A number of writers speak of convergence. This is why dialogue at its deepest is truth seeking. It is not just a matter of understanding the other, nor certainly of avoiding disagreement, but of entering into a search for deeper truth that draws upon the spiritual heritage of all people. This is why the attempt to enter into the spiritual experience of other traditions, sometimes referred to as 'global spirituality', has a creative contribution to make to our mutual understanding.

A Common Quest

I do not think that at some future point it will be possible to draw up a 'world creed'. This is why it seems better to speak of a common quest or a shared pilgrimage, rather than of an emerging 'one-world religion'. This is partly because there will be new questions and challenges, partly because variety itself is to be valued and partly because there will always be more to learn about the ultimate Reality.

Durwood Foster, writing of what he calls 'ultimology' or a 'universal theology', has this sense of the goal always being on the horizon. 'Ultimology in every tradition, I believe,' he writes, 'in this sense of committed quest, must strive for universality. It will never reach it, as Kipling suggests, short of the great Judgment Seat. Its trajectory is asymptotic, with many dips and squiggles. It is a regulative ideal, in Kant's sense. Like perfection, as John Wesley understood it, it is something to be going on toward, not something a right headed ultimology will ever claim for itself.'[12]

My picture is of the religious history of humankind becoming one history. It is largely true that Christian theology is no longer denominational theology. In considering a theological issue, most students will read those who have made significant contributions to the subject, regardless of their denomination. In the same way, we shall increasingly draw upon insights from the great religious traditions. We need, as Durwood Foster says, 'to be really encountered in mind and heart by the truth of the other, without being able either to dismiss it or subsume it under one's own truth'.[13]

Already, for example, this is beginning to happen in Jewish–Christian dialogue. Christian and Jewish scholars, who have pioneered a new understanding of Judaism and the beginnings of Christianity in the first century of the common era, work together and are in large measure in agreement. Some Christian theologians are grappling with the question of how the Jewish 'no' to Jesus is also within the purposes of God.[14] Another example is the Manor House Jewish–Christian group, which moved beyond explaining different positions to each other, in the attempt to grapple together with some of the deep questions to both faiths.[15] Durwood Foster refers to similar developments in Christian–Buddhist dialogue.[16]

This sense that the goal is always on the horizon may in part meet Raimundo Panikkar's questioning of the assumption of underlying or ultimate unity that seems to be presupposed by those who speak of convergence. He distinguishes pluralism from plurality. 'Pluralism', he says, 'means something more than sheer acknowledgment of plurality and the mere wishful thinking of unity.'[17] He continues, 'Pluralism does not consider unity an indispensable ideal . . . nor is it the eschatological expectation that in the end all shall be one.'[18] Pluralism recognizes that that Being is not fully apprehended by human thought. It rejects 'the monotheistic assumption of a totally intelligible Being' and makes us aware of our own contingency/limitations and nontransparency of reality.[19]

The mystery is not fully grasped by human understanding. We have to beware of searching for a universal system, lest our theological agreement becomes an idol in place of the living Mystery. What we can do is recognize and joyfully affirm that people in every great religious tradition seek and are met by that one Reality. This is why dialogue is not only personally enriching but helps to create a spiritual fellowship in which we recognize the bonds of our common humanity, even whilst acknowledging that our response to the Mystery is expressed in very different pictures, symbols and intellectual systems.

The 'one-world faith' of which I wrote twenty-five years ago was modelled too much on pictures of the universal church. I extrapolated ideas from then current Christian ecumenical thinking and tried to apply them to the 'wider ecumenical movement'. My picture now is that of a pilgrimage. Each year in London a multi-faith pilgrimage is held. This has several starting points, but gradually the pilgrims converge on one shrine. I rather suspect that in this pilgrimage the shrine will always recede into the distance.

Bede Griffiths' Vision

It was whilst I was preparing to write *Together to the Truth* that I first entered into
correspondence with Bede Griffiths. It was also his, *A New Vision of Reality* that
prompted me to look again at what I had written in *Together to the Truth*. Bede
Griffiths, in the final chapter of his last book, *A New Vision of Reality*, speaks of
rediscovering the perennial philosophy, the traditional wisdom, that is found in
all religions and especially in the great religions of the world. Members of the
Semitic religions, he insists, will have to give up their exclusive claims. 'This
would free them to recognize the action of God in all humanity from the
beginnings of history.'[20] Christian theology, he points out, was evolved in Europe,
'We have to look forward to a theology which would evolve in contact with
Hindu, Buddhist, Taoist and Confucian thought and at the same time a liturgy
which would develop from contact with the art, music and dance of Asian and
African peoples.'[21] One characteristic of the new culture, he says, would be its
feminine aspects, 'We have now reached the limit of this masculine culture with
its aggressive, competitive, rational, analytic character.'[22] Bede Griffiths ends his
book like this:

> The only way of recovery is to rediscover the perennial philosophy, the
> traditional wisdom, which is found in all ancient religions and
> especially in the great religions of the world. But those religions have in
> turn become fossilized and have each to be renewed, not only in
> themselves but also in relation to one another, so that a cosmic,
> universal religion can emerge, in which the essential values of Christian
> religion will be preserved in living relationship with the other religious
> traditions of the world. This is a task for the coming centuries as the
> present world order breaks down and a new world order emerges from
> the ashes of the old.[23]

I have three questions about this passage, which in so many ways resonates with
my own thinking. Is it only a rediscovery of the perennial philosophy that we
need? This takes away the sense of newness about the insights we are
discovering, as we relate the inherited wisdom of the great religions to the
amazing advances in so many fields of human intellectual endeavour. Bede
Griffiths partly recognizes this himself when he says that the religions have
become fossilized. Secondly, I have already questioned what the phrase 'a
cosmic universal religion' might mean. My third question relates to the phrase
'in which the essential values of Christian religion can emerge', although this is
not so triumphalistic as my sentence of twenty-five years ago that 'As a
Christian, I believe that Christ will stand at the centre of the emerging world
faith.'

Christ Calls Us to Serve God's Kingdom

A rabbi, who is a good friend, baulked at a sentence in the final section of Paul Knitter's *No Other Name?*, where Knitter writes, 'Perhaps Jesus the Nazarene will stand forth (without being imposed) as the unifying symbol, the universally fulfilling and normative expression, of what God intends for all history.'[24] The rabbi felt that Christian superiority had been smuggled in by the back door to a book that is a plea for pluralism. Knitter, however, continues:

> In carrying on the dialogue among religions, however, Christians must bear in mind that if such a recognition of Jesus does eventually result from the praxis of dialogue, it will be a 'side effect' of the dialogue. Whether the question of Jesus' uniqueness is answered, whether Jesus does or does not prove to be final and normative, is not, really, the central issue or the primary purpose of dialogue. The task at hand, demanded of Christianity and all religions by both the religious and the socio-political world in which they live, is that religions speak and listen to each other, that they grow with and from each other, that they combine efforts for the welfare, the salvation, of all humanity. If this is being done, then the central hopes and goals of all religions will be closer to being realized. Allah will be known and praised; the Lord Krishna will act in the world, enlightenment will be furthered and deepened; God's kingdom will be understood and promoted.[25]

For whose sake does the Christian slip into a universalist vision a plea for the superiority of Jesus? Surely not for the one who did not prize his equality with God, but who humbled himself, assuming the nature of a slave.[26] To picture Jesus and Muhammad and the Buddha and others competing for a prize for their contribution to 'progress in religion' is at once to see the absurdity of the suggestion. Jesus' own message centred on the coming kingdom of God. For those who follow Jesus, the longing and indeed daily prayer is that God's kingdom will come on earth as it is in heaven. Jesus defined that kingdom as good news for the poor, release for the prisoner, recovery of sight for the blind, freedom for the victims of cruelty. The ultimate picture and hope is of a world at peace, a world of justice, where all share God's gift of abundant life. It is not, despite well-known hymns with splendid tunes, a coronation ceremony.

'Jews and Christians,' writes Hans Ucko, 'though in different ways, are both waiting for the Messiah to come.' There is a story about a Jew and a Christian engaged in heated discussion. All of a sudden someone comes in and says, 'We hear that the Messiah is coming.' They run to the place where the Messiah is to appear, and there he is. They both go up to him and ask, 'Is this your first or second visit?' The Messiah responds, 'No comment.' The story doesn't end there. It goes on to say, 'Perhaps now you will understand the true meaning of the Messiah: messianism is the quality of life that we live together along the way.'[27]

God's will is abundant life for all people. Jesus came to proclaim and embody that good news of life in all its fullness. Members of the Church are those who identify with Jesus' vision of abundant life and who seek to promote God's reign of love. All who also seek that goal are to be welcomed as allies. As a student in India, I used to help at a clinic for leprosy patients. One day I walked there with two other students. One was a Muslim from Tamil Nadu and the other a Christian from Sri Lanka. The doctor at the clinic was a Saivite. We were together in service of those in need who ministered to us by their cheerfulness. The urgency of interfaith co-operation in a world of violence and suffering has become ever more pressing.

As we co-operate we discover that we are impelled to do so by the deepest convictions of our particular faith. Twenty-five years ago when I spoke sympathetically of a coming world faith, I was made to feel by fellow Christians that I was betraying Christ. It is, however, my commitment to Christ that has impelled me to work for interfaith understanding and co-operation. The God whom I see revealed in Jesus Christ is a God of boundless love, whose mercy is for all people. God seeks to break down barriers and to reconcile men and women both to himself and to each other. God shares the suffering of the homeless and the hungry, and appeals to the conscience of the world through the cries of the refugees and the victims of torture. 'For Christians,' writes Durwood Foster, 'Jesus Christ is the centre we are coming from, but he is an ec-centric centre, a self-transcending centre, an outward impelling centre.'[28]

My hope for an emerging world faith does not make me feel any less a Christian. For me the various titles of Jesus and the doctrine of the incarnation are primarily ways of saying that in Jesus Christ I, like millions of other people, have been met by God. That others have encountered Divine Reality through other bearers of truth does not lessen the reality of my own experience of the all-accepting, self-giving love of God made known in Jesus Christ. I recognize that they will use very different language to express their convictions. My use of personal and theistic terms indicates that Jesus Christ is the centre from which I am coming. If that to which the Christian is committed is found to be similar to that to which followers of other faiths are committed, this is a matter for rejoicing. My commitment to Christ is a commitment to what I believe to be true.

When Rolf Hochhuth's play *The Representative*, which was critical of Pope Pius XII's acquiescence with the Nazis, was first produced, Pope John XXIII was asked what one should do about the play. He replied, 'Do? What can one do about the truth?'[29] If, as I believe, in Christ I have been encountered by the truth, I do not doubt that he and his message will be of continuing significance. Presumably followers of other great faiths would say the same of their core convictions. My hope is that, whilst continuing to be a disciple of Christ, I might also begin to become a follower of the Buddha, learn from God's word in the Qur'an and the Torah and sense the oneness taught long ago by the rishis of India.

Together in the Presence of the Holy One

The closer we come to the Holy One, the less labels matter. Evelyn Underhill, the English mystic, said that religions meet where religions take their source – in God. As a Sufi poet said long ago, 'On my way to the mosque, O Lord, I passed the Magian in front of his flame, deep in thought, and a little further I heard a rabbi reciting his holy book in the synagogue, and then I came upon the church where the hymns sung gently in my ears and finally I came into the mosque and pondered how many are the different ways to You – the one God.'[30]
John Hick has written:

> The function of a religion is to bring us to a right relationship with the ultimate divine reality, to awareness of our true nature and our place in the Whole, into the presence of God. In the eternal life there is no longer any place for religions; the pilgrim has no need of a way after he has finally arrived. In St John's vision of the heavenly city at the end of our christian scriptures it is said that there is no temple – no christian church or chapel, no jewish synagogue, no hindu or buddhist temple, no muslim mosque, no sikh gurdwara . . . For all these exist in time, as ways through time to eternity.[31]

My ultimate vision now is of a growing awareness amongst people of all faiths that they are embarked upon a common quest. As they share their inherited spiritual treasures and their own experiences, their sense of the beauty and love and wonder of the Divine will grow. At the same time they will be more deeply moved to work for the coming of God's kingdom in which all people enjoy the gift of life in a world without war and poverty, where the life of every being is valued and respected.
A world in agony desperately needs the hope and transforming action that together people of faith can offer. In the words of a children's song:

> There's a dream I feel, so rare so real
> All the world in union, the world as one.
> Gathering together one mind, one heart;
> Ev'ry creed, ev'ry colour once joined, never apart.
> It's the world in union, the world as one;
> As we climb to reach our destiny, a new age has begun.[32]

The dream is of that day when 'nation will not take up sword against nation and every person will sit under his own vine and under his own fig-tree and no-one will make them afraid'.[33]

Notes

1. Marcus Braybrooke, *Together to the Truth* (Delhi: Madras and ISPCK, 1971) p. 156.
2. London: Allen & Unwin, 1940.
3. London: Allen & Unwin, 1958.
4. J. H. Barrows, ed., *The World's Parliament of Religions* (Chicago: The Parliament Publishing Co., 1893), p. 1572.
5. J. H. Barrows, *Christianity: The World Religion* (Chicago: A. C. McClurg, 1897), quoted in Richard Hughes Seager, 'The World's Parliament of Religions, Chicago, Illinois 1893: America's Coming of Age' (Harvard University Doctoral Thesis, 1986), p. 238.
6. Sarvepalli Radhakrishnan, *Eastern Religions and Western Thought* (Oxford: Oxford University Press, 1939), pp. viii–ix.
7. Prince Philip, preface to Hans Kung, *Global Responsibility* (London: SCM Press, 1990).
8. Wilfred Cantwell Smith, *Toward a World Theology* (London: Macmillan, 1981).
9. Marcus Braybrooke, *Pilgrimage of Hope: One Hundred Years of Global Interfaith Dialogue* (London: SCM Press, 1992), p. 149, from *Religion in the Struggle for World Community*, ed. Homer A. Jack (New York: WCRP, 1980), p. 42. Paul Knitter has argued on the basis of liberation theology for religions to work together. See Paul F. Knitter in *The Myth of Christian Uniqueness*, ed. John Hick and Paul F. Knitter (London: SCM Press, 1987) pp. 178–200.
10. Hans Kung and Karl-Josef Kuschel, eds., *A Global Ethic* (London: SCM Press, 1993).
11. S. J. Samartha, *One Christ – Many Religions* (New York: Orbis, 1991), p. 4.
12. Durwood Foster, 'The Quest for a Universal Ultimalogy' in *Visions of an Interfaith Future*, ed. David and Celia Storey (Oxford: International Interfaith Centre, 1994), p. 158.
13. Ibid.
14. See Marcus Braybrooke, *Time to Meet* (London: SCM Press, 1990), p. 59.
15. Tony Bayfield and Marcus Braybrooke, eds., *Dialogue with a Difference* (London: SCM Press, 1992).
16. Foster, 'The Quest for a Universal Ultimalogy', p. 154.
17. Raimundo Panikkar in Hick and Knitter, *The Myth of Christian Uniqueness*, see note 9, p. 109.
18. Ibid.
19. Ibid., p. 110.
20. Bede Griffiths, *A New Vision of Reality* (London: Collins, 1989), p. 287.
21. Ibid., p. 293.
22. Ibid., p. 294.
23. Ibid., p. 296.

24. Paul F. Knitter, *No Other Name?* (London: SCM Press, 1985), p. 231.
25. Ibid.
26. Epistle to the Philippians 2:7–8.
27. Hans Ucko, *Common Roots: New Horizons* (Geneva: WCC, 1994), p. 84.
28. Foster, 'The Quest for a Universal Ultimalogy', p. 160.
29. Hans Kung, *Judaism* (London: SCM Press, 1991), p. 258.
30. Zaki Badawi, *World Faiths Insights*, June 1986, p. 11.
31. John Hick, *God and the Universe of Faiths* (Oxford: Oneworld Publications, 1993), p. 147.
32. 'World in Union' © Charlie Skarbek/Standard Music Ltd, 1991.
33. Micah 4:3–4.

A JEWISH JOURNEY

Dr Dan Cohn-Sherbok

Dr Dan Cohn-Sherbok currently teaches Theology at the University of Kent, is a visiting Professor of Judaism at the University of Wales, Lampeter, and a visiting Professor of Interfaith Dialogue at the University of Middlesex.

I WANTED TO be a congregational rabbi ever since I was a little boy. I pictured myself wearing a rabbinical gown, teaching to a vast congregation in a large synagogue in the Midwest or on the East coast. I hoped my parents would be proud of me. I had it all worked out: first I would go to college, then to rabbinical college, and finally I would end up a distinguished rabbi. But it didn't turn out like that. My spiritual journey took another turn, quite to my surprise. This account is based on my memoir *Not a Job for a Nice Jewish Boy.*[1]

Growing up in the Suburbs

On my spiritual journey, my bar mitzvah was a major turning point. Growing up in the leafy suburbs of Denver, I was exposed to liberal Judaism in a Reform Temple. Although my great-grandparents had lived as Orthodox Jews in Hungary, my family had discarded the traditional trappings of Judaism, yet the Jewish heritage as interpreted in progressive surroundings still held an attraction for me. To my family's surprise, I decided I wanted to be a rabbi.

The Temple in Denver is located in the Jewish section of the city. Surrounded by a gigantic parking lot, it looms over the neighbouring suburban houses. The stained-glass windows of the sanctuary, in abstract designs, dominate the building. On the morning of my bar mitzvah, 1 February 1958, the lot was filled with cars. Proudly my father slid his Jaguar into a reserved space near the entrance. The service would not take place for half an hour, but already friends and relations had arrived. As we walked to the rabbi's office, my parents were waylaid. Seeing so many smiling faces, my father's mood changed. This was an occasion for him as well as for me, an opportunity to show off his only son, to impress guests with his affluent hospitality. My mother glowed. She was secretary of the Temple board; the Temple was her second home. This was her big day too.

The rabbi was a tall, pock-marked man with a hooked nose and straight white hair brushed back over his ears. I knew my parents were important members of the Temple and had considerable influence. It was in the rabbi's interest for my bar mitzvah to go well. Most bar mitzvah boys are terrified, but I was confident if a little apprehensive. I followed the rabbi and my father through a narrow hallway to the sanctuary. We entered through the back and took our seats. I looked at the congregation and saw my grandmother sitting next to my mother. The former, in a matronly black dress, radiated pleasure and pride; the latter looked strained and anxious. Near them was my uncle, and several rows behind sat various cousins. Dotted through the congregation were friends from school.

Behind me the choir began singing. The service started. In a trance I followed the prayers. After an interminable time the Torah scroll was taken out of the Ark. I was called to read my portion. I read it – no mistakes. Then the Haftarah. Again, no mistakes. The Hebrew part was over – so far, so good. But there was still my speech. Out it came as I had memorized it, word for word. It was not my own creation – rather the anguished product of my mother's labours. I thanked my parents; I thanked Rabbi Frankel; I thanked my bar mitzvah teacher; I thanked each and every one of the congregation for coming. I spoke about my grandmother and her late husband. I quoted from my Torah portion. And then it was over. My bar mitzvah had ended as I believed it would. I was a success!

At the reception held in the Temple hall, I was mobbed. My grandmother headed the throng. 'Danny, darling,' she said, 'you were wonderful.' My mother hugged me. She looked profoundly relieved. The burden of my bar mitzvah had been lifted. Her son had triumphed. She could hold her head up among her friends. She simply kissed me. My father shook my hand. He looked almost pleasant. 'Well done, Dan,' he said. Then my friends surrounded me. They patted me on the shoulder. Everyone was happy. And hungry. The crowd moved towards the refreshments. But a hush descended on the room when the rabbi entered. Quickly he recited the Sabbath Kiddush. Guests then surged forwards towards the tables, which were groaning with food. In the centre was a huge swan carved in ice; from its beak, drops of water dripped onto the table. There were piles of chopped liver, mounds of smoked salmon, stacks of knishes and oceans of cocktail dips. And that was just the first course. Eventually, the company broke up into groups, seating themselves at tables festooned with flowers.

I sat with my parents and my grandmother. Guests came up to our table and congratulated me. They complimented my parents.

'You must be proud,' the rabbi's wife said. 'He did a wonderful job. His Hebrew was very good. Even the rabbi was impressed!'

My mother's sister, swathed in mink, came to sit next to me. 'Danny,' she said, 'you were great.'

We were joined by the conductor of the Denver Symphony Orchestra and his wife – my parents' best friends. 'Hello, Aunt Selma and Uncle Saul,' I said. Selma kissed my cheek, being careful not to smudge her lipstick, while Saul gripped my hand.

'Your speech brought tears to your mother's eyes,' Selma said. 'Have you thought of being a rabbi? I think you have just what it takes.'

From the vantage point of our table I surveyed the crowd. Plates piled high, they were having a splendid time. My parents glowed. My grandmother was radiant. I was happy. I was also the most important person in the room. It was my bar mitzvah, and I had triumphed. I began to take Aunt Selma's question seriously. Perhaps I *would* be a good rabbi. At the age of thirteen I was sure I could do a better job than Rabbi Frankel. My parents always said he was mediocre. My performance was *not* mediocre.

As everyone ate and drank, the photographer took pictures, and unbelievable quantities of roast beef, vegetables, gravy, chocolate cake, meringue gateau, passion fruit sorbet and *crème brûlée* disappeared. Eventually guests began to leave. They came over to my parents and thanked them. Again I was congratulated. I'd never been kissed so many times. Finally, only my parents and I remained. On the tables half-empty plates and glasses were left to be cleared away. The reception hall was silent. We made our way back to our car. The parking lot was empty except for my father's Jaguar. We were exhausted. In silence, we drove home.

Over the years, I have often looked at the photographs of my bar mitzvah. Although I can no longer recognize most of the faces, I can clearly remember the atmosphere. For my parents, it was a joyous event. It was a time of hope and promise, a day to remember. For me, it was the turning point of my young life. On my thirteenth birthday I decided what I wanted to do: I wanted to become a rabbi.

And why not? From what others had told me, and from what I knew myself, I was a good speaker. I could stand in front of a congregation without fear. I enjoyed the adulation. Indeed, I relished the praise. Being a rabbi was a respectable job. I could serve the Jewish people. I could gain prominence in the community. Possibly I could even achieve national recognition as a famous preacher. Other rabbis had done it; there was no reason why I shouldn't emulate them.

I wasn't shy about telling my family and friends of my new ambition, but even to myself I did not confess that my desire to be a rabbi was mixed with worldly ambition. I had no desire to follow my father's footsteps and become a surgeon. I had no interest in the law, or in business. What I sought instead was the elation of standing before an awestruck congregation, making them listen to me. I cannot truthfully say I was called to be a rabbi. I was seduced into it.

A Rabbinical Education

After college, I trained for the rabbinate at the Hebrew Union College in Cincinnati, the largest Reform rabbinical seminary in the world. Although my rabbi had recommended me for the course, I never had an interview with the college authorities. Instead I was sent to see a psychiatrist (as were all first-year rabbinical students). The purpose of this productive session was to ascertain whether I was suitable to be the spiritual leader of a modern synagogue. As I was to discover, this interview was in fact a test; but which were the right answers?

Although I did pass the Hebrew exam, this was not the final ordeal of the first year. At the end of the semester, in true Jewish-American style, each of us was required to have an interview with a local psychiatrist. Previously we had each completed an enormous multiple-choice questionnaire. It was not clear, however, what the psychiatrist was looking for. It was like running an obstacle race in the dark.

I drove my car to his office, which was located in the Jewish suburbs. Lavishly decorated with deep carpets, modern furniture and abstract painting, it exuded affluence and culture. In the waiting room I glanced through several magazines. Presently, a receptionist announced, 'Dr Levinson is ready to see you now.' I followed her into the doctor's office. 'Where's Dr Levinson?' I asked. 'He'll be here soon,' she said, smiling, and shut the door. I sat in an overstuffed armchair and waited. On the walls were diplomas from various institutions. In the corner was a skeleton.

When the psychiatrist arrived I stood up and we shook hands. Small in stature, Dr Levinson suffered from a slight nervous twitch. 'Do sit down,' he gestured. Arranging himself across from me, he lit a pipe. The process of stuffing it full of tobacco, striking a match and getting it to smoke took several minutes. At last he looked up. 'So,' he said. 'You want to be a rabbi?'

'Yes . . . I do.'

He puffed on his pipe. 'How long have you wanted to do this?' he asked.

'Ever since my bar mitzvah. I never really wanted to do anything else. My father's a doctor, but I didn't want to follow in his footsteps.'

Dr Levinson looked at me quizzically. 'You don't like your father?'

'That's not what I meant,' I back-pedalled. 'I just don't want to be a doctor.'

'And why not?'

'Because I'm not interested. I don't think I'd be very good at it. I fainted when I saw my first operation.'

'And you like your father?' Dr Levinson persisted.

'Well, yes, I suppose so. He's pretty tough, and very busy. We don't see much of each other. I haven't really thought about it very much.'

'And your father, he's happy you're going to be a rabbi?'

'Well, not exactly. As a matter of fact he's not pleased at all. But my parents want me to do what I want to do.'

Dr Levinson was engulfed in smoke. I could no longer see his tic. I coughed. Continuing his exploration of my family relationships, he asked me about my mother.

'You're fond of her, then?'

'Of course. She is my mother.'

'Not all Jewish boys like their mothers,' he pronounced. 'Tell me about her.'

I explained that my mother was a housewife, a local painter, and that I was her only child.

'You're close to her?' Dr Levinson asked.

'I guess so. Actually, I am very close.'

'And your father, he approves of this?'

'Yeah, I guess he does. I've never given it much thought.'

'It's time you did. Do you ever dream about your mother?'

I couldn't see where this conversation was going, but I suspected the worst. What did my mother have to do with my being a rabbi? What was the interview all about? Did this man really think my relationship with my parents had influenced my decision to become a rabbi?

'Dr Levinson,' I said, 'I thought we were going to talk about my suitability for the rabbinate.'

'But we are.' He smiled coyly. 'We are.'

I was baffled, and then astonished by his next question, 'You've had sex?'

'I beg your pardon?' I said.

'Sex . . . in college, you've had sex?'

'Dr Levinson, this is a bit personal.'

'Personal! Of course it's personal. That's just the point. We are talking about the personal.'

'But I'd rather not discuss this.' I was outraged.

'*You* may not . . . but *I* do. And *we* must. So tell me a bit about your sexual experience.'

I fiddled with my tie. I didn't know where to look. What was I to say? First my father, then my mother, now sex. But there was no choice. If this was an exam, I had to pass it. But what were the right answers?

Reluctantly, I described various sexual encounters. Dr Levinson watched carefully as I stumbled over these exploits. When I stopped, he asked, 'Is that all?'

'More or less,' I said.

Leaning forward, he eyed me suspiciously. 'When you were a little boy, did you play with other boys?'

'Play? Well, yes, I played lots of different games. I played football, if that's what you mean.'

'No . . . that's not what I meant. What I have in mind is something more sexual.'

Peering into his waste basket, Dr Levinson began banging his pipe on the edge. After he had emptied it, he reached into his pocket, took out a leather pouch, stuffed more tobacco into his pipe and then began again the process of lighting it. This gave me time to think. It was now clear what Dr Levinson was looking for: homosexuals. The Progressive Rabbinical Seminary was taking no chances – they were being rooted out before they advanced far in their studies.

After a lengthy pause, I continued, 'No, Dr Levinson, only girls. I've only played with girls.'

'You sound a little defensive about this.'

'Nope. No boys. I've never touched them.'

This seemed to satisfy him. He changed subjects. 'And visions? Have you ever had visions? Or maybe heard voices?'

'No visions, no voices,' I insisted.

'You don't have conversations with God? You don't hear him telling you to do this or that, or to behave in some sort of way?'

'Well, if you are referring to my conscience, I do feel bad or good about some things.'

Dr Levinson's pipe had gone out. His twitch seemed worse. I felt my interview was ending. He picked up a pen and wrote something in a notebook. Then he stood up. 'Well, that's it. Thank you for coming. It's been a pleasure to meet you. Best of luck in your studies.' He opened the door, shook hands and grimaced. The door slammed shut. The receptionist showed me the way out. Dazed, I drove back to the seminary.

Life as a Student Rabbi

During the five years of rabbinical training I secured congregations in various parts of the United States. This was my introduction to the rabbinate. To my surprise, being a rabbi was not what I expected. As time passed my disillusionment increased. Perhaps being a rabbi was not a job for a nice Jewish boy.

Once a month, I visited my congregation in Jonah, Alabama. The president arranged that I had dinner every night with a different family. Invariably the food was the same – matzoh ball soup, fried chicken and vegetables, and home-made pie. But the houses were different – most members lived in modest suburban dwellings, but the richer congregants dwelt in the most exclusive part of the town in sprawling, ranch-style homes. This social division was reflected in the running of the Temple – the president and board members were made up almost entirely of the wealthiest members of the community.

Throughout the year I coached Greg Grossman, the son of the only Jonah millionaire, for his bar mitzvah. On my last visit I officiated at the ceremony. When I arrived at Birmingham airport, I was met by Jack Grossman's chauffeur. Ushering me to a large Cadillac, he told me about the weekend's proceedings. 'It's going to be something,' he said. 'There's about fifty out-of-town guests who've already arrived. Right now most of them are at the house. I'm supposed to take you there right away.'

En route to Jonah he told me about the guests. 'Grandpa Sternberg – that's Jack's wife's father – he's here from New York. He's an old man now, but he was big in New York real estate. The rest of her family are from the East too. Jack's father – old man Grossman – he's from Mobile. That's where the rest of Jack's family's from.'

'And what do the New Yorkers make of Alabama?' I naively asked.

'Your guess is as good as mine. I guess they think of us as small-town folk. But there's nothing wrong with that. No, man. I'd never want to live in a place like New York.'

When I arrived some of the guests were swimming in the pool. Others sat at tables arranged on a large patio, having lunch. 'Come on over, Rabbi,' Jack Grossman shouted. He was dressed in Bermuda shorts and his vast bulk filled out a short-sleeved shirt. 'Have a steak sandwich, Rabbi; they were just flown in from Kansas.' Motioning to a black waiter, he said: 'Johnnie, get the rabbi a drink. What about a beer, Rabbi?'

'That's fine . . . thanks.'

Jack gestured that I should sit next to him. 'The whole family's here, Rabbi. From Alabama and back East. That's Mollie's father,' he said, pointing to a tall, moustached elderly man seated under an umbrella and wearing white trousers and a long-sleeved shirt. He was reading a large paperback novel. Seated next to him was a voluptuous redhead wearing a skimpy bikini. 'The girl's his niece. Hey, Ruth!' he shouted, 'come meet the rabbi.'

As she walked over to our table I tried not to stare. She stretched out a hand with long, red fingernails and smiled. 'I've heard all about you, Rabbi,' she said.

Ruth's bikini hardly kept her suntanned body covered. She fluttered her long eyelashes. I wondered if they were real. Her eyes were intensely green. Were they really that green or possibly helped by coloured contact lenses? There was no doubt, however, that her body was all her own. 'It's nice to meet you,' I said.

'There's the bar mitzvah boy,' Jack announced. I turned around and saw Greg dive into the pool. I hoped his Hebrew would be as good as his diving.

'So, how long are you here for, Rabbi?' Ruth asked.

'Just the weekend. I'm still in rabbinical school and have to go back on Sunday.'

'That's too bad,' Ruth said, twirling her bikini straps. 'I hope you'll have some free time this weekend.'

'Well, I hope so too,' I said.

'Got to go now, Rabbi,' Ruth said, standing up. 'See you later.' I watched as she went back to her uncle.

'That's quite a girl,' Jack whispered. 'Just got divorced a couple of months ago. You ought to get to know her, Rabbi.'

The next day was the bar mitzvah. I arrived at the Temple early. From my office I had a good view of the street. About half an hour before the service, the Grossman family arrived in their Cadillac. Like his father, Greg wore a black suit, and his mother was dressed in a tight-fitting red dress. I shook everyone's hands and reassured Greg. 'You'll do fine,' I said. Greg looked unconvinced. Previously I had made a tape of his Torah portion so he could hear how it should be pronounced – I hoped he had practised. Because I was in Jonah only once a month, I had had little opportunity to hear him read, and he had rehearsed the Torah scroll only a few times. Would my first bar mitzvah be a catastrophe?

Soon the Temple filled up with the rest of the Grossman family as well as the usual congregants. I began the service promptly at eleven, but stragglers continued to arrive. By the time of the Torah reading, everyone had settled into seats. First, Greg recited the blessing and then I guided him through his portion with a silver pointer. When he stumbled, I helped him with the pronunciation. At last he finished. He then recited the blessing over the Haftarah, and read it in Hebrew. Again he stumbled, but he persisted. When it was over, Greg's mother beamed. His father patted him on the back. He hadn't done a very good job, but it appeared that his parents were satisfied.

At the reception Jack Grossman welcomed all the guests, and Greg made a little speech thanking me for all I had done for him. I wished I had done more. After the Kiddush, the entire gathering sat down for lunch. I was seated at the top table next to Ruth. She wore a low-cut dress, and I struggled not to look down her front as we ate.

'You were wonderful,' she said.

'But I didn't really do anything; Greg was the star performer.'

'You're far too modest,' she continued. 'I loved your speech.'

'You did?'

'It was very moving. Didn't you see Greg's mom crying?'

'She cried?'

'It was so sweet. She's awfully choked up about little Greg. By the way, I hope you're coming to the party this evening at the country club.'

'Ah, well . . . I am, as a matter of fact.'

'Good,' she said, stabbing a shrimp. 'I'll see you there.'

For the last time I drove the Mercedes to the country club. When I arrived, a band was playing and the party was in full swing. I greeted congregants, and then went over to the Grossmans' table. Jack stood up and handed me an envelope.

'Rabbi, we sure are grateful for all you've done for Greg. This is just a little present from Mollie and me.'

I didn't know what to say – I had never received a tip before. 'Well, thanks,' I mumbled. 'But it's not necessary . . .'

'Our pleasure,' Jack said.

Later in the evening I saw Ruth. She had squeezed into an even tighter-fitting gown with an even more swooping neckline. 'I hope you'll ask me to dance,' she said.

She held on to me as I tried to waltz to the music. I was not a good dancer at the best of times, and I stepped on Ruth's foot. 'Sorry,' I said.

Ruth giggled and pressed against me. This was all very flattering, but we were dancing closer than I thought prudent. I looked around the room to see if anyone was watching. After we finished dancing, Ruth put an envelope in my pocket and winked as she headed off for the drinks table.

When I arrived at my hotel, I opened both envelopes. In the one from Greg's father was a hundred-dollar bill, and a letter thanking me for teaching Greg his Torah portion. The other was a note from Ruth which read, 'Danny – when you come East I hope you'll look me up. My number in New York is 987654. I think we could have a good time, don't you? Love and kisses, Ruth.'

I wasn't sure which gave me more pleasure.

Being a Rabbi

Alas, life as a congregational rabbi was not very different from what I had experienced as a student. As a boy I envisaged myself preaching eloquently to hushed congregations. But this was not what happened; instead my flock stayed away. The only time the parking lot was full was when my congregation staged a bingo evening. To my horror, I was compelled to call out the numbers.

At eight, the doors opened and masses of people flooded into the Temple. I had never seen such a crowd there before. Members of the Temple dressed in outfits suitable for a casino directed them to the hall where long tables had been assembled. In the middle was a machine with bouncing numbered ping-pong balls. Once everyone was seated, Joe Blumenthal reached into what looked like a suction cup and took out the first ball. As he called out the numbers there was a hushed silence (except for the click-click of plastic tabs on the bingo cards). As more numbers were called, excitement mounted. At last a woman in the corner of the hall called out 'Bingo!'; the monitors rushed into action to check her numbers against those Joe had read out.

As the evening progressed, I wandered around the hall greeting members of the congregation as well as visitors. I also purchased a hamburger and a Coke from a food counter run by the Sisterhood. Eventually it was time for the high point of the evening: bingo for the grand prize. I was summoned by Joe Blumenthal, and he announced that the rabbi would call the numbers. Reluctantly I approached the ping-pong machine and stood next to Joe. We shook hands, and then he told me what to do. As the balls bounced against the glass sides of a large container, I reached into a suction cup and called out the numbers of the balls that emerged. A record number of bingo cards had been sold for the jackpot and I watched as players stared at them and clicked the plastic tabs when I called a number on their card. Tension increased as one number was called after another. Finally a woman wearing trousers jumped up. 'Bingo!' she cried. There was laughter, then applause. The numbers were checked and confirmed.

'Will the winner please come forward,' Joe announced.

I picked up the keys and handed them over when she stood next to me. 'Let's all give the winner a round of applause,' I said. The hall broke into thunderous clapping. The winner kissed me, and more applause ensued.

The evening had been a great success. Over 10,000 dollars had been raised, including money for the food we had provided. Since all the prizes had been donated, this was clear profit; the money would be used to finance the Temple. The members involved were both elated and exhausted. When the last of the bingo players departed, I helped the Sisterhood clean up. The hall was full of litter – paper cups, plates and plastic knives and forks were scattered everywhere. In addition, cigarette butts filled all the glass ashtrays. At last, at midnight, it was clean and everyone departed.

The next day there was a meeting of the Denver Rabbinical Council. This was a body of all the rabbis in Denver – Orthodox as well as Progressive – which met once a month at the largest Orthodox synagogue. As temporary rabbi at Temple Israel, I had been invited to be a member. When I arrived I sensed the other rabbis were uneasy. I sat next to Rabbi Frankel, who handed me an agenda. Pointing at the first item on it, he shook his head. 'Your Temple is in trouble,' he said. Under 'Minutes of the last meeting' was the topic 'Bingo at Temple Israel'. I shuddered; my eczema began to itch horribly. What was this all about?

The chairman of the Denver Rabbinical Council was an elderly Orthodox rabbi who attempted to maintain friendly relations between all the different religious groups in the Denver community. After the minutes were approved, he looked at me. 'Dan,' he began, 'we all know you're here for only a few months. It isn't your fault, what's going on at Temple Israel. We realize you're not in a position to change anything. But we aren't happy about this bingo business.'

Rabbi Frankel spoke next. 'We can't have gambling,' he stressed. 'It sets a bad example for all of us.'

Meekly, I tried to defend the Temple. 'Nobody asked me about bingo,' I explained. 'When I arrived, they put up that big sign in front of the Temple . . .'

'A disgrace!' Rabbi Frankel interrupted.

'Well, I agree, but the Temple wouldn't have bingo if they didn't need the money. And it does seem to work,' I said defensively.

Rabbi Frankel grimaced as I said this. He was becoming increasingly agitated. 'That's no way to raise money!' he exploded. 'Those people would do anything.'

Why was Rabbi Frankel so hostile? He was not making this easy for me. Again, I came to the Temple's defence. 'I'm not sure bingo does much harm,' I said. 'Lots of churches have bingo. And it does bring the members together to do something for the Temple.'

The Rabbis looked down at their agenda papers – it was clear I had convinced no one. After a short silence, the chairman explained that he had drafted a letter to the president of Temple Israel that expressed the Rabbinical Council's condemnation. He passed around copies for all the members. It read:

As members of the Denver Rabbinical Council we wish to express our disapproval of bingo at Temple Israel. Gambling runs counter to the Jewish tradition and is an affront to our community. We insist you stop this activity immediately. If you do not comply with our wishes, we shall be impelled to expel your congregation from the Rabbinical Council.

'I'm sorry, Dan,' Rabbi Levi said, 'but we have no choice about this matter.'

'But I can't sign this,' I explained.

'We realize that. Don't worry about it.' Rabbi Levi then passed around the original letter, which all the rabbis signed, and we turned to other business.

An Academic Rabbi

I failed as a rabbi. Although it had been a lifelong quest to serve my people, they did not want me as their leader. And – to be honest – I did not want the job. I had thirteen years of higher education, yet it was not all in vain – for I became a university academic, teaching Judaism to non-Jews. It was much more pleasant.

Teaching at the university was a delight; in contrast to those of Temple religion schools, the students were actually interested in the subject and wrote down every word I said. What, I wondered, would they do with this written record? To my astonishment some of the students even brought tape recorders to class – it was beyond comprehension that they would want to listen twice to what I had said. How different this all was from my experience in the rabbinate, where I had struggled to attract anyone to adult study groups!

Sprinkled among the undergraduates was a handful of friars who were simultaneously studying at the Franciscan study centre located next to the university campus. Occasionally they came dressed in their habits to my Judaism classes. The cleaning lady, who was a Catholic, was thrilled whenever she saw them with their black rosaries hanging from their belts; before class she chatted to them in the corridor. On one occasion I was explaining about *tefillin*. These, I said, are small leather boxes that contain pages from the Torah; they are worn by Orthodox male Jews on their arms and heads in fulfilment of a biblical commandment. Their purpose, I went on, is to remind the wearer to keep God's law. Listening to my explanation, one of the Franciscans held up his rosary. 'Rabbi Dan,' he said, 'we have something similar, you know; the rosary is supposed to aid concentration in prayer.'

I had never made the connection. I couldn't help but wonder what the rabbis I had worked with or the congregants I had served would make of this scene – my lecturing to Christians about Judaism, and their teaching me about their own faith in relation to mine. This was so utterly different from what I had expected to do in those years I was a congregational rabbi, and infinitely more satisfying.

For me such teaching was bliss – yet I did feel guilty. It had been my aspiration to serve Jews – but there were no Jews in my classes. Was this in some sense a betrayal? When I told Lavinia, my wife, about my self-doubts, she laughed. 'But you don't like synagogues,' she said. 'And quite clearly the members don't like you.'

'That's true,' I admitted. 'But I have a conscience about this. Do you think I'm doing any good?'

'Of course you are. You're countering anti-semitism.'

'I am?' I asked, puzzled.

'Do you think any of your students will end up pushing Jews into gas chambers after they have taken your class?'

'I never thought about that,' I admitted.

'Come on, Dan. As a congregational rabbi you'd just end up making everybody angry. But here you're helping the goyim feel better about Jews. That seems a far more useful activity than driving your board president into suffering apoplexy.'

'Do you think so, really?'

'You're doing a mitzvah, Dan. That's the way to look at it.'

As the university rabbi, it was somewhat incongruous that I should be teaching together with a Christian clergyman, but our course attracted a sizeable number of students; for convenience's sake, we decided to meet at the canonry. Every Wednesday evening, a dozen elderly ladies and William and I sat around the dining table. One week it was William's turn to lead the class, and I took over the next week. Beginning with biblical origins, we traced the development of Jewish and Christian ritual to the present.

As the course was nearing its end, we arranged an outing to a nearby convent of Anglican Benedictine nuns. William had previously been in contact with the Mother Superior, and she readily agreed to have our group. The purpose of the trip was to give our class an insight into the contemplative life. It was to be a day of silence. When we arrived we were ushered into a hall where the Lady Mother addressed us. An impressive figure in her late seventies, she was dressed in black. Silence, she pointed out, is fundamental to the religious life – it is in stillness that the voice of God can be heard. Citing Scripture, she emphasized that the prophet Elijah experienced the divine presence as a still small voice rather than through the tempests, fire and general cacophony that accompanied the revelation on Mount Sinai. For the Christian, she continued, it is in the mysterious depths of silence that Christ can be found.

After her talk, William said a short prayer as we all bowed our heads. This was followed by a long period when no one said anything. I looked at some of our students – most had shut their eyes and folded their hands as they meditated on what we had been told. Finally, the Lady Mother brought us to order and announced that lunch would take place in the dining hall. She instructed us not to say anything during the meal, since one of the nuns would be reading to us from *The Little Flowers of St Francis*.

When we took our places, the Lady Mother said grace. There was a scraping of chairs, and then a clattering of dishes as food was served. The meal consisted of home-made pizza with salad. Unfortunately the jug of water had not been passed down to our end. Was it acceptable to ask that it be handed down? In the background one of the nuns spoke about the adventures of St Francis and his brothers. I looked at one of the nuns near the water jug. I smiled; she smiled back. Could I whisper instructions to pass the water? This was too perplexing, and I decided to keep quiet. As I ate lunch, I looked at those across from me who munched their pizza as the nun continued reading. How different this all was from a Jewish household! It was simply unthinkable for Jews to eat without talking. Unused to the overpowering quiet – except for the incessant reading – I concentrated on the food.

After lunch the students were taken on a tour of the grounds, but the Lady Mother asked that I join her for a brief chat. As we entered her study she urged me to sit across from her in an overstuffed armchair. 'William tells me you're a Progressive rabbi,' she began. 'Do you know that our Lord was a Progressive rabbi, too?'

'I'm not sure "Progressive" is the right word,' I replied.

'Ah . . . but He was, you know. He was critical of the Pharisees, and I dare say you and He would have had more in common than you think.'

'Perhaps,' I mused.

'Now, Rabbi. May I ask you an impertinent question – have you ever thought about accepting Jesus as Saviour?'

I hadn't expected to be faced by such an onslaught on my first visit to a convent – the purpose of our trip had been to give students a taste of the Benedictine experience. Hesitantly, I explained that I couldn't possibly accept the central tenets of the Christian faith.

'Why not?' she said, smiling.

'To begin with,' I stated, 'the doctrine of the Incarnation is unbelievable – at least to me.' I went on to say why I thought it was theologically incoherent.

'Is it more unbelievable than what you Jews believe about God?' she asked.

'Well, yes . . . frankly. We don't think that God could become a man. For us that's impossible.'

'You know,' she continued, 'that's just what one of our most famous fathers of the Church said about the Incarnation. He thought it was impossible too. But that's just why he was so convinced it was true.'

'I don't think I understand,' I said.

Picking up the train of her habit, the Lady Mother stood up.

'Faith is the greatest of all mysteries. You mustn't try to understand with your mind. You should reach out to God with your heart. I will pray for you, Rabbi. Now, let us go and find your students.'

Notes

1. London: Bellew Publishing, 1993.

A Voice Crying in the Wilderness

David Craig

David Craig, an Anglican Christian, has been a member of a religious order and a publisher. He is now Executive Producer of Religious Programmes at the BBC World Service.

THE PROTESTANT WORK ethic endorses the belief that the full utilization of all one's gifts is the only human response to an awareness of God – and I was brought up with lashings of Protestant work ethic. It was the sword of Damocles hanging over my head; whether it was piano practice or prep. If I skipped them – divine retribution was invoked. 'God has given you these gifts. If you don't use them . . .' And that, as far as my limited horizons then permitted, meant practising complicated organ voluntaries for a comfortable and appreciative congregation at church on Sunday, and slaving away at Latin verbs to ensure a place at university, where I would read theology so that I could become an effective clergyman.

So what went wrong? Why, I have to ask myself, do I now find myself shying away from the preaching in most of our churches, cringing at the coverage of religious issues in much of the media and refusing to identify with any professionally associated Christian organization?

Let me come clean from the start; professionally I am involved in the business of communication. As head of religious broadcasting for the World Service of the BBC, I am responsible for programmes which broadcast to people of all religions and none, to people persecuted for their faith, as well as to people persecuting in the name of their god. I am also concerned for the responsible coverage of those news stories that derive from a religious base – and looking at the news agenda day by day, it is difficult to believe that there has ever been a time when religion has been more important, more influential or more inadequately represented.

My work also includes concern for those programmes that reflect the religious imperative of the world's cultures: the Muslim perspective from Bangladesh or Algeria, from Iran or Nigeria; the Buddhist influence on Thai and Sri Lankan politics or on Tibet and Cambodia; the implications of Hindu renewal seen in India and through the enthusiasms of the ubiquitous Hare Krishna movement, the Christian right of the United States and the grass-root communities of South America. A daily dose of disaster does a lot for the Protestant work ethic.

And it's all because of the Christian inheritance!

My first encounter with Islam came when, an idealistic VSO in Tanzania in the 1960s, I went to work at an Anglican boys' secondary school set up on the Makonde Plateau in Tanzania. To the south, the river Rovuma, which marked the boundary between Tanzania and Portuguese East Africa, was clearly visible, winding its way across the plain. To the north the river Rufiji entered the sea at Kilwa, centre of a once famous Muslim empire, source of the Kilwa Chronicle and other *utenzi* literature.

The school was run on English public school lines, with four houses dedicated to appropriate African saints and each housing boys from one of the main tribes of the area – Wayao, Wamakonde and Wamakua. Boys from smaller tribes, or even those from afar whose families didn't come from the remote southern province, messed together in the fourth house, Washahidi wa Africa, appropriately dedicated to all the other saints who weren't Augustine, Cyprian or Thecla.

It was 1962, the year Tanzanian independence had been declared, but the school felt no uncertainty at the change, no crisis in identity. The staff were all dedicated educationalists: the expatriates missionaries from Universities' Mission to Central Africa (United Society for the Propagation of the Gospel), the staff the best graduates from East Africa's Makerere University. It was a proud school, a good school and it changed my life.

Except for the Muslims, chapel was a compulsory feast of high mass, and evensong with benediction on each Sunday and a seemingly endless procession of saints' days, with morning prayer and compline on a daily basis. Its churchmanship was extreme: for a non-conformist like me whose experience of liturgy had been simple hymn sandwiches with thick fillings of Congregational oratory, it was like water in a parched land, or more appropriately, like the richest wine. I absorbed it, I wallowed in it and, regardless of any theological doubt, was totally obsessed by it. Solemn benediction to a seventeen-year-old away from home and with serious responsibilities for the first time can have very dangerous consequences! It was a halcyon year – and in it I made the most significant friendships of my life, discovered that saints were alive and well and still working. I also made innumerable discoveries about religion.

Since my early teenage years, I had single-mindedly pursued what I had interpreted as a vocation to the mission field. I had haunted missionary conferences, hounded missionaries on furlough with intense youthful questions, read endless books and been inspired by speakers such as D. T. Niles with his request for bonelayers – people who would go and live and work and die among their adoptive people. This, for me, was the ideal. My singular inability as a linguist and a personal preference for apple pie rather than curry seemed irrelevant at the time. For me, going on VSO was similar to 'testing one's vocation' – a phrase I learned at Chidya.

It came as no small surprise at the end of year prize-giving to discover that the prize for religious instruction was won by a Muslim student. Abubakr came from the Rufiji, was certainly older than me by a few years and had managed a brilliant eighty-seven per cent in the exam. I looked at him in a new light – I also looked at Islam! During Ramadan the Muslim boys had fasted while a special

Muslim cook was employed to ensure they could eat properly, and the headmaster, a Christian priest, had provided goats for Eid. Abubakr gave me a book about Islam – it was in Swahili and so reading it combined language lessons with religious enlightenments.

The local village mosque he attended was a mud hut, almost indistinguishable from all the others in the village, with the exception that on its walls were terracotta line drawings of grand mosques, complete with impressive minarets and domes. A closer inspection suggested the experience of the hajj – for even in this remote corner of Tanzania the pilgrimage was an achievable reality for some.

Did it seem curious to me that a missionary school run by missionaries, who presumably were committed to bringing the light of the gospel to non-Christians, should tolerate and even encourage Muslims? That it didn't should have warned me that my understanding of the mission field was changing and my concept of vocation, as I thought it, was under attack, but it did not! Muslim boys were integral to a Christian school, and when an epidemic of meningitis broke out and one of our Muslim students contracted it, prayers in chapel were as fervent for his recovery as for anyone else's – through Jesus Christ our Lord.

Back in London, reading theology at university, Islam became book bound, and extracts from Bell's translation of the Qur'an felt more like undiscovered extracts from the Scottish Psalter than the revelations of the divine word. But I was transfixed; those lectures, essays and hours in the library were made live by knowing and being friends with Muslims. During long vacations I travelled and went back to East Africa; it was like homecoming and my former colleagues spoilt the youngest brother horribly!

When postgraduate research was offered, there was no real question – it had to be Islamic studies, but to go any further I knew I had to read the Qur'an in the Arabic. During the year at theological college learning the skills that would have turned me into a congregational minister, I patiently struggled with Arabic verbs in Ahmad and Thatcher, commuted to Redhill where the great linguist Eric F. F. Bishop tailored the perfection of his Arabic to my meagre abilities. Names such as Margoliouth, Massignon, all the French Islamicists, rolled off his tongue, together with stories and anecdotes in an oral history of significance – and I bought a new French dictionary.

When I won a Goldsmith's Company scholarship though, it was to Osmania University, right in the middle of the Deccan Plateau. I travelled via Greece and Lebanon, Syria and Egypt, Iraq and Iran, Afghanistan and Pakistan – my first introduction to 'the Muslim World'. For the first time I saw the places I had read about: al-Azhar, the great Medrasseh at Isfahan, Babylon and Ctesiphon. I went to Friday prayers – so different from and yet so similar to their London equivalent. It had a fantastic influence and the fact that it was done on a shoestring (currency restrictions were still in force) made no difference. Thanks to strong sandals, regular buses, boats and trains, I walked through the streets absorbing a Muslim atmosphere, being woken by the muezzin each morning before dawn, sitting at the back of mosques, and visiting some of the world's most holy places. I even have a photograph of Qum, taken from the bus, the nearest I was then allowed to go to the sacred city.

When eventually I arrived in Hyderabad, I studied what it was like to be a Muslim in a minority community, but after four months, with the civil unrest over the Telengana question, I found myself advised to leave Hyderabad and travel. Six months on Indian trains, in rest houses and on the floors of student friends gave me a good insight into the significance religion has for people and for India! The conversations and exchange of food on the trains were always accompanied by theological discussions. Muslim, Sikh, Jain, Hindu – all motivated by faith, all curious about my faith and as to why I was studying Islam, and in India!

May was hill-station time and I found myself sharing a house-party with a motley collection of missionaries; it was a curious experience, as although I was a Christian, I could not identify with their lifestyle or their behaviour. It felt decidedly odd! They, in turn, found me strange but in a mad season of amateur dramatics, musicals and concerts, the month passed agreeably. But the atmosphere of the hill station puzzled me. It was only when I was on the train from Madras to Bombay that it dawned on me – for the first time I had been in an exclusive Christian ghetto, and it had felt weird and, in India, quite wrong.

When the priest at the parish of the Church of South India in Trivandrum failed to say the prayer of consecration at the Maundy Thursday communion because, when asked, he said he was running late, I decided that Congregationalism and I had come to the parting of the ways. Within days of returning to Africa I was confirmed into the Anglican faith at the Bishop's chapel in Masasi and learned first hand what power of rejoicing there must have been when the prodigal returned to the fold.

After having returned to England I then went back to Africa at the end of the year to work as a diocesan administrator for the first African bishop of the diocese of Masasi. By then the diocese had launched its own missionary activity on the Rufiji. Canon Robin Lamburn, a former vicar-general of the diocese, had motivated a very poor diocese to provide money for him to go and live and witness in a tiny village on the Rufiji river. Robin developed a leprosarium at Kindwitwe and over the years the 'Rufiji project', as it has always been called, developed, with enthusiastic backup from the American school in Dar es Salaam and devoted followers around the world. But Robin's initial object was to do what St Frances had done at the crusades – to go and witness. If by being in the Rufiji he was making his Muslim neighbours better Muslims, then he was doing God's work, he told the diocese, and I agreed.

Uncertain of my own future, I applied to the Islam in Africa Project for a new job, which would be based in Kenya but, probably wisely, they turned me down. I was too young, too green *and* – as one elder on the interviewing panel pointed out – unmarried. Definitely not a good bargain!

Ordination had always been at the back of my mind, and so I returned to England with every intention of training at the College of the Resurrection at Mirfield, but after a brief visit to the community itself, I realized that it was to the monastic life I had been called and so, instead of being a student at the college, I taught Greek and Hebrew for the second part of my novitiate! I adopted the poverty, obedience and chastity of the community. It was both a liberating and painful experience. Good friendships were forged and I discovered, perhaps for the first time, that piety did not produce perfection and that monks were not immune to malice. At times I felt rather as if I were at a prep school where the rules were constantly being changed to my disadvantage by some capricious head. The whole was presided over at the time by a malignant vulture of a man whose personal problems, unbeknown to most, were being worked out on a long-suffering community.

While the Almighty decided I had no vocation for the monastic life I, at the same time, decided that my vocation was not to the ordained ministry – it was obvious the Church had enough problems with recalcitrant and arrogant clergy, it was not for me to add to their number!

Because of various connections, I applied for a job in the Foreign Office and after the usual sort of interview in an elegant terrace office, some written examinations – I managed to fail the maths paper but they seemed not to mind – and more interviews, I was offered the chance to take the first step on the diplomatic ladder. It was a crucial moment. Although ordination was not an option, I still felt the strong attraction of religions and my encounters with diplomats in my travels had not led me to think that there was much sympathy for anything more extreme than matins and Easter Communion. On the morning I had to write my decision to the recruiting officer, a friend telephoned and asked whether I would consider a job in the publicity department of a distinguished religious publishing house where he was a director. I never hesitated, accepted, wrote to the Foreign Office explaining that I was 'going into publishing' and left them flat to learn about publishing.

The next years, first with Darton, Longman and Todd and then with SPCK as a commissioning editor, introduced me to people who would form what would become identified as interfaith action groups. Authors invited me to conferences on Judaism, Christianity and Islam. It was the time of the Masorti schism in Judaism and *A Jewish Theology* had just been published by Louis Jacobs. *To Heaven with Scribes and Pharisees* was on the list and I became more involved with people who, in their writings, speeches and conversations, showed me a religious attitude with which I could identify, but which seemed so at odds with the attitude of my own church where 'Are you going to become a Muslim?' became the stock response to my contributions to church discussion groups, or seminars.

It was through such people that the truth of experience became clear – that the only way to become involved with people of other faiths is to have an honest awareness of and commitment to your own.

An opportunity came for me to work in Nigeria and I grasped it with both hands, partly because the BBC had just turned me down for a job in religious broadcasting – a particularly sour interview during which I fell into every trap set by the chairman, and ended up explaining heatedly, in response to the head of department's theatrical reaction on learning that I didn't even own a television, that if I needed pictures to make an intellectual argument stand on its feet, I wouldn't be a publisher!

Ibadan was a great place to be situated, and apart from the traffic problems of southern Nigeria that guaranteed a fifty per cent attendance rate at any Lagos meetings, it also gave me the chance to go north to spend time in Kaduna, Zaria and above all Kano, to see the Hausa culture with its exemplary form of Islam, to come into contact with university departments where Islam was a very different experience, and to meet great businessmen who regularly made the pilgrimage on planes specially chartered from Kano. It was also a chance to identify manifestations of the great Nigerian tension between Cross and Crescent, as well as seeing the problems that existed between the established Church and the new prophetic movements.

But my abortive interview with the BBC was not without its consequences. After the interview, my inquisitor took me to lunch at the Travellers' Club and told me that he had made a point of being unpleasant because he wanted me to be aware from the outset that I didn't stand a chance of getting that job, but that when the right job came along he, the head of department, would let me know. And, sure enough, a year later he did. A copy of an advertisement that was to appear in *The Listener* was sent to me and I applied for the job, took leave from Nigeria and flew back to London for an interview in Manchester.

I like interviews, they give me a chance to show off, and I had a great job in Nigeria that I enjoyed, and so I started the interview going great guns. Suddenly half-way through, I realized I *wanted* this job, sweat started dripping down my back (it was late October in Manchester) and I began to fight. At the end of the ordeal, I was asked where I would be the next day. 'In Lagos,' I said, 'I'm flying back tonight but you can get hold of me until 8 p.m. at a friend's house near Brighton.' The telephone rang at 6 p.m., would I like the job? Would I *like* the job? I would, and yes I could start as soon as they wanted – how about Monday?

That was fifteen years ago and during that period I learned the techniques of radio production and television direction, the management skills to run departments and I have become increasingly aware of the need to revolutionize the concepts of religious broadcasting: to turn the Reithian vision of broadcasting as a forum for evangelism or of Christian communication into one of public service and religious broadcasting. These are two very different concepts and ideals needing treatment in different ways. I have also found it necessary to fight for the transformation of a religious broadcasting department that had unhesitatingly accepted the Christian calendar at the expense of those of other faiths.

There is no doubt that non-Christian religions regard the coverage of religious issues in the British media as partisan and hostile. Were this perceived hostility to be the result of rigorous journalistic standards it could then become a matrix for creativity, but a perception of it as Christian-based hostility is cause for concern. The recent strategy document published by the BBC now includes statements about religious broadcasting that anyone with awareness of interfaith relations would have assumed to be at the basis of any religious broadcasting policy for Britain.

When I joined the BBC, religious broadcasting was a preserve run by clerics on their way to the purple or influential deaneries. They acted as senior chaplains to the corporation, providing elegant memorial services for the great and the good, ensuring a high standard of worship was maintained each Sunday and Wednesday and that the then Daily Service never moved too far away from the BBC Singers and New Every Morning. If a non-Christian viewpoint was required, some academic would be interviewed about the meaning of the pilgrimage, or the significance of a particular Hindu feast and custom. The phrase 'you never guess what they do with the rice' was coined after a particularly crass account of the celebrations surrounding Diwali had been broadcast on the Sunday programme. The nearest to interfaith awareness the BBC had was the occasional programme such as God without Christ, a series where former Christians explained why they had converted to Islam, Hinduism, Judaism and Buddhism. It was successful and had to be balanced by a second series where a Jew, a Hindu, a Muslim and a Buddhist explained why they had converted to Christianity!

But then history played its card. The 1982 urban riots in Britain electrified the nation. Race relations had never been good but this was the first time such ruthless violence had occurred on such a large scale. It was an apparently national phenomenon and it exploded throughout Britain's major cities.

As a response to it, BBC Radio 4 commissioned me to make a series of programmes – Worlds of Faith – which would explore the societies in Britain that felt such animosity and expressed their alienation in such violent action. It was a bold plan and for almost a year John Bowker, the Professor of Religious Studies in Lancaster, interviewed Buddhists, Jews, Hindus, Christians, Muslims and Sikhs around the country, finding out what personal religion meant to them. We didn't interview priests, imams and bishops, intellectuals, analysts or politicians, we interviewed ordinary practitioners: Muslim shopkeepers and factory workers, Sikh taxi drivers and teachers, Hindu accountants and mechanics, Jewish businessmen and doctors and so forth: for the first time people were speaking for themselves about what mattered to them about religion.

We collected some two hundred hours of material, logged it, and spent anguished weekends in Lancaster deciding what the issues were. After independent consideration it became apparent that there were obvious issues that needed treatment, and so *Worlds of Faith* hit the airwaves in thirteen thirty-minute instalments.

It was a watershed for religious broadcasting, but it was hell to make – the endless editing of people who were not necessarily articulate, for whom English was not a first or even second language and who were not used to putting into words their personal commitment to the religion that inspired their lives.

It was an enormous learning curve for both John and me; he, one of the finest theological brains in the country, certainly the most innovative, moved from the texts and languages to the people and their practice, while I moved from an awareness of relations with people of different faiths around the world to a dawning awareness that one of the causes of the breakdown between ethnic groups was not simple xenophobia, but a failure to understand the role religions played in the lives of non-Christian individuals and communities.

It also convinced me that the BBC's religious broadcasting policy was wrong. Our efforts at producing wonderful liturgy daily and weekly did matter, but we were failing seriously to take into consideration the fact that while Britain was historically and culturally a Christian country, practically it was a place where the religions of the new Britons were stronger, more virile and of greater apparent personal influence than the cultural heritage of the original inhabitants of the country.

I began to realize that we had misunderstood, not the religions themselves, but the significance of those religions to the people who believed in them. It was the empirical expression of English religion versus the rest. The English, unlike the Scots, Irish or Welsh, are, I think, unique in their attitude to religion: it is something that is not discussed, made public or worn on the sleeve. I hardly know which, if any, of my colleagues are Christians, go to church, or play an active role in their religious communities, and this is not atypical English society. This may be because what identifies Christians is not practice but the repetition of credal formulae – not diet but devotion – as a Jewish friend put it! For my Muslim colleagues religion is overt, not least because unselfconscious prayer is part of the daily routine, or that they fast together during Ramadan, but because of their awareness of the significance of religion on the international agenda.

The World Service has provided me with more opportunities to take a practical part in interfaith dialogue around the world by making programmes that have looked at the way religions in South Asia interlink people in human encounters and which, despite such religious excesses as the destruction of the Ayodha mosque or the events in Kashmir, can provide platforms for common action. Other opportunities have been provided by attending the World Parliament of Faiths in Chicago and making a series of programmes about the rich choice of religious experience available in the United States and by spending time in Turkey where the interaction of a secular state and a resurgent Muslim culture is providing a new chapter to the culture that provided not only the Ottoman Empire but also the early Christian Creeds.

As a constituent in the development of interfaith interest and commitment, I would argue that a proper use of religious broadcasting is vital. The significance of stories such as the destruction of the Babri Masjid Ayodha, the attempted assassination of the author Naguib Mafouz in Egypt, the threatened execution of a Pakistani teenager in Islamabad, can only be adequately understood within a religious dimension.

The future of Bakhtivedanta Manor at Letchmore Heath is of sufficient significance not just for the local authorities but to justify direct intervention from the government of India. Fragile relationships between certain South American countries are often maintained only through the direct power and influence of the Church. Who could discuss the role of cities such as Jerusalem, Srinagar or Tehran without an understanding of the religious history of those places?

The realization that the reporting of news and events, often in a negative sense, is common to all religious groups can be a binding and significantly shared experience, as can the realization that the practice so often falls short of the ideal, that twentieth-century Islam is more complex, less clearcut than when the Qur'an was first revealed; and that there is a commonalty in coverage of religious news.

Because the major focus of religious broadcasting should not be dogma or abstract theologies but the critical issues of our time, the personal involvement in interfaith action is essential. It is in the practicalities of life that religion must appeal, inform and inspire if it is to prove relevant to the faithful of a religion.

In some religious traditions, practice has given paramount authority to a priestly caste. Experience, however, has proved that people of faith outside such a caste can influence and act on critical issues – especially peace and environmental protection – and show that service grounded in wisdom and compassion can change the world. This has been interpreted as a threat to authority and so religious people, and by extension, religious broadcasting, have been seen to exercise a radical influence.   There is evidence of a dislocated present and limited future everywhere, from the smallest villages, through cities and nations to continents and seas. In whatever direction we look there are troubling signs: grave and widespread threats to the environment; grotesque extremes of affluence and poverty; such divisions as racism, interreligious hatred, gender discrimination, tribalism and xenophobia. The prevalence of war, and the violence of oppression and injustice destroy any claim to humanity as a family.

Where there is hatred and war, selfishness and injustice, environmental damage and poverty, cause cannot be distinguished from effect, one problem cannot be isolated from another. All are parts of a single problem. How can there be a just and sustainable co-existence, one caring for another and together for the planet that nourishes the community of life?

At the heart of this/these problem/s is a question of values, of creative and collective wisdom.

Because the world has now the means to make mistakes that could threaten the existence of the ecosphere, religious responsibility and therefore religious broadcasting assumes a new imperative. New ways of living together on earth must be explored, discovered, and their progress disseminated. To do that new relationships must be forged sometimes at the expense of old loyalties. The role of religion in the downfall of communism in Eastern Europe should not be underestimated, while the Malawian bishops' letter to the Catholic parishes had the effect of political liberation, providing a captive community with the justification for action against their oppression.

Religions are revolutionary but religions are also prophetic and, while taking on a concern for the revolutionary aspects of religion, religious broadcasting must also provide a vehicle for the prophetic role – failure to embrace such responsibility would jeopardize any integrity claimed by religious broadcasting.

WHY I SAY I AM A BUDDHIST BY CONVICTION

Professor Lily de Silva

Lily de Silva is Professor of Pali and Buddhist Studies at the University of Peradeniya, Sri Lanka.

I WAS BORN to Buddhist parents and I have had a Buddhist upbringing. Apart from abiding by the five precepts, going to the temple on full-moon days, occasionally observing the eight precepts on full-moon days and the monthly offering of alms to the monks at the monastery, in my childhood I hardly knew what it meant to be a Buddhist. As an adult I started studying Pali, which paved the way to my academic career. As a student of Pali Buddhist texts, I now say I am a Buddhist by conviction.

The Relevance of Buddhism for the Modern Age

Buddhism is a fully fledged philosophy of life and it is of timeless value. It addresses itself to the eternal problem of human suffering and shows a systematic way out of it. It assures each individual who follows the path a happy destiny, without their having to surrender to the will of an unknown God. Therefore it is a message of hope, optimism and self-reliance. It does not conflict with modern science, nor does it discourage the freedom of intelligent inquiry. Modern people are far more knowledgeable than their predecessors in history. What they need is wisdom and self-discipline, and this is where the Buddhist way of life becomes relevant.

   The world today has stockpiles of destructive weapons sufficient to blow up the planet many times over. This state of affairs came about because humans discovered many secrets of nature without the emotional maturity to handle them for human happiness. The Buddha and the spiritually advanced saints of the East understood many more secrets of nature, but the difference between them and scientifically knowledgeable people today is that they knew how to exploit this knowledge for human happiness and spiritual advancement. The world today is replete with immense problems, and wisdom contained in the Buddhist texts offers valuable advice about solutions to them.

   In this consumer-oriented world humans are sick in body and mind. They dissipate their energies in sensuality and are like ants that have fallen into a pot of honey. Buddhism shows a way of enjoying sensual pleasures moderately without getting hurt, yet advancing spiritually too. This middle path of moderation is the relevant solution for most of the ills that harass humans today.

   The above is a concise summary of my convictions regarding Buddhism and its relevance for the modern age.

Open-Mindedness

One main reason that makes me appreciate Buddhism in preference to a theistic religion is its frank open-mindedness. The *Kalamasutta* exhorts the disciples not to accept a proposition as true just on the authority of the teacher, scriptures or tradition.[1] Even logic is of limited value. One is advised to exercise one's judgement intelligently to see if a behaviour, when cultivated, is conducive to one's happiness or suffering. Verifiability is an important criterion of truth. Unverifiable propositions regarding the world and humans, such as whether the world is finite or infinite,[2] eternal or not, and whether the world and humans were created by a God or not, for which proofs can never be found, are prudently left aside as useless speculative pursuits. This pragmatic attitude pleases me a great deal.

Triple Gem

Initially one becomes a Buddhist by confessing faith in the Triple Gem: the Buddha, *dharma* and *sangha*. The Buddha is the pioneer teacher, the highest ideal of human perfection for which the potentiality is there in every human being. The lesser ideal is Arahantship[3] and that is the aim of practically every Buddhist. The *dharma* constitutes the path preached by the Buddha for the attainment of that goal. The noble *sangha* consists of Arahants who have attained the goal by following the path, thus furnishing evidence for the efficacy of the *dharma*, and proving the enlightenment of the teacher. Therefore the Triple Gem is worthy of trust.

Scientific Approach

The world-view of Buddhism appeals to common sense and does not go against modern scientific findings. According to the *Aggannasutta*, humankind and society came to be what they are through a long process of evolution.[4] Stimulated by Buddhist notions I am prompted to interpret the famous *Purusasukta* of the *Rgveda* too in terms of evolution.[5] Creation of the *sudras*[6] from the feet of Brahma may allude to the branching off of animate forms from plant life. Feet connote mobility, which fact distinguishes animals from plants, which also live, grow and die, but are rooted in the same place. *Vaisyas*[7] were created from the thighs of Brahma and this must be an allusion to sexual reproduction. Cell division may have been the earlier form of propagation, but sexual reproduction is far superior. Creation of *satriyas*[8] from the arms of Brahma may be a reference to manual dexterity. When the hands were freed from the function of locomotion, the animal (*tiracchana* from *tiras*, 'crosswise' and *carati*, 'to walk'), which walked on all fours with the backbone horizontal to the ground, became *Homo erectus* walking with an upright backbone. At this stage it was very likely that the mammary glands developed too and with the loving suckling of young ones the human family was born.

The *Rgvedic* assertion that the Brahmins were born from the mouth of Brahma must be an allusion to the birth of language, through which culture is transmitted.

Thus, with a knowledge of the ideas contained in the Pali canon, it is possible to interpret more deeply some philosophical hymns of the *Rgveda*, the surface understanding of which has given rise to social ills such as caste discrimination, which sometimes assume inhuman proportions.

World-View

Mind and matter (*namarupa*) are interdependent, and so are humans and nature. Humans are made of the same great elements as the external world (*pathavi*, earth; *apo*, water; *tejo*, fire; *vayo*, air), and have to subsist on food, which they get from the physical environment. From the natural sciences we learn that humans are pulled to the ground by the force of gravity, and are pressed down by the atmosphere above. They are also influenced by the rotation of the planet. The interdependence of humans and nature is expressed in Buddhism through the concept of the five cosmic laws (*panca niyamadhamma*), namely physical, biological, psychological, moral and causal laws.[9] The last mentioned causal laws operate *within* each of the first four spheres, as well as *among* them. This process of interaction is as follows: the physical environment generates plant and animal life suitable to itself, and they determine the psychological attitudes of humans. Moral values of what is right and wrong are developed accordingly by and by.

Conversely, with these developed attitudes, skills, values and goals, humans then act upon plant and animal life and change the physical environment according to their preferences and ability. Nature without human activity grows wild, but humans shape the face of nature for their advantage and comfort. Marching from savagery to civilization, from Stone Age to space age, humans have changed their environment in diverse ways during the course of history, building roads and irrigation schemes, cutting down forests, growing terraced paddy fields and plantations, digging mines, etc., not to speak of the various buildings, secular and religious, erected upon the surface of the earth; so much so that the modern nuclear-cum-space age has brought about an environmental crisis. This world-view is succinctly expressed in Buddhism as *cittena niyyati loko*,[10] 'the world is led by the human mind'. Human intentions, ideas, values and goals shape the world, both physical and human. When the human mind acts with wholesome intentions there is peace; when the intentions are unwholesome and evil there is much strife, unhappiness and suffering. This world-view accords with reason and experience. Therefore it appeals to me more than theological explanations of the will of God.

Moral Responsibility and Survival

The Buddhist theories of karma and rebirth appeal to me as being reasonable and plausible. Each human being is a unique individual as his or her actions – physical, verbal and mental – are unique to him or her. No human being is one hundred per cent good or one hundred per cent bad, and this fact is known through observation and experience. A human being is called *manussa* in Pali because each has an elevated mind (*manassa ussannataya manussa*[11]) as opposed to that of a horizontally walking animal (*tiracchana*). The fact of survival seems fair as it gives a chance to everyone to rise to spiritual heights. Through purposeful cultivation of virtue and wisdom, when one reaches the goal one is not reborn, one attains nirvana. It is a great consolation to learn that there are no permanent hells and the concept of eternal damnation is alien to Buddhism. But nirvana is eternal bliss. It is to be realized through personal effort and not by the grace of an unknown God.

I say rebirth is plausible because it accords with experience. None of us likes to die (suicide is a mental aberration); we try to preserve life throughout life. Even when we miss our footing, we steady ourselves to prevent ourselves falling, because we do not like to be hurt and we fear to die. At the root of all fear, there is the fear of death. When yearning to live is present throughout life, is it possible to imagine that, when we are ultimately faced with death, we would accept death with a sense of resignation? My hunch is that *mentally* we would struggle and yearn to live (*bhavatanha*) until a viable place comes within grasp (*upadana*).[12] Once grasped, growth ensues (*bhava*), and if it is in a mother's womb, birth (*jati*) takes place after the period of gestation. But if one has attained liberation through virtue (*sila*), mental culture (*samadhi*) and wisdom (*panna*) one would have no fear, one would observe the process of death with mindfulness and not grasp another womb (*na gabbhaseyyam puna-r-etiti*).[13] One attains nirvana and the nature of that state cannot be meaningfully explained as it is beyond words, space and time.

The notion of survival brings me to the question of the existence of beings in other spheres of life, such as *devaloka*[14] and *petaloka*.[15] I come to terms with this question logically. As human beings our bodies are formed of the four great elements of earth (*pathavi*, solidity), water (*apo*, cohesion), fire (*tejo*, heat), and air (*vago*, motion).[16] As there is a preponderance of earth and water our bodies are gross and coarse. I imagine that there could be beings who have much less of the earth and water elements, and much more of the heat and air elements. Such beings therefore would be radiant and they could traverse the skies. This agrees with the description of deities in the Pali canon. But they too are subject to the laws of karma and rebirth. I view the *deva* worlds as holiday resorts, but for the cultivation of virtue and wisdom the human world is far superior.

Society

Buddhism advocates a society that recognizes human value on the grounds of merit and not on accidents of birth. Many *suttas* have criticized the Indian caste hierarchy that has gained philosophical support from the *Purusasukta* of the *Rgveda* discussed earlier in this essay.[17] Members for the community of monks are drawn from all walks of life and it is recorded that the Buddha himself invited for ordination a scavenger named Sunita who was working by the roadside, having seen his spiritual potential shining within.[18]

Wealth is not frowned upon, in fact it is regarded as a source of happiness for the layman (*atthisukha*).[19] But it must be righteously earned, avoiding blameworthy occupations such as trading in meat, alcohol, poison, weapons and slavery. (I would add prostitution also to this traditional list). As wealth has only instrumental value, it should be wisely spent and shared. The *Sigalovadasutta* exhorts laypeople to collect wealth like the bee collects pollen,[20] and this simile is pregnant with meaning. As the bee neither pollutes the beauty of the flower nor depletes its fragrance, so should a person be environmentally conscious not to pollute nature nor impede its life-sustaining activity – a very sound economic principle relevant for today.

Kings are admonished to be righteous in conduct, personal life and administration, so as to set an example to their ministers and subjects. They should not fall into error through partiality (*chanda*), hostility (*dosa*), fear (*bhaya*) and ignorance (*moha*).[21] They should consult the clergy in the country from time to time, and install in office wise and competent lay advisers. It is the duty of rulers to maintain law and order in the country, and provide security and employment opportunities for their citizens.[22] The ideal society is characterized by the simple joys of life, where people make their babies dance on their laps and enjoy security of life and property with open doors, as it were.[23] This political philosophy is much more praiseworthy than, for instance, that advocated by Kautilya's *Arthasastra*.

Family Life

The family life advocated by Buddhism is especially appealing. Equality of the status of sexes is recognized and spouses have complementary roles to play. According to the *Aggannasutta*, sexual differences, both male and female, appeared in primordial beings as a result of moral deterioration.[24] Therefore the question of the superiority of the one or the inferiority of the other does not arise. The relationship between husband and wife depends on mutual trust, love and respect, and the reciprocal performance of duties.[25] Both are expected to be faithful to one another, and the husband is advised not to belittle the wife, perhaps because this tendency is there in a male-dominated society, where the husband is economically in a superior position. As a gesture of complete trust and to give the wife a sense of economic security, the husband is expected to hand over to her the wealth he earns. It is she who keeps the money safe and manages the budget. It is her duty to maintain a well-organized household and to look after the domestic servants and detail work according to their individual capacity. Special mention is made of the duty of the husband to provide the wife with clothing and ornaments.

The well-adjusted love relationship between husband and wife is said to survive death, and it is recorded in as many as over thirty *Jataka* stories that the Bodhisattva gained maturity in virtue and wisdom in successive lives in the companionship of his wife Rahulamata.[26] The parents of Nakula, who followed Buddha and became a monk, are portrayed in the canon as ideal spouses who expressed the wish in their old age to be reunited as husband and wife in the next life too.[27] Buddha replied that it was possible to be so reunited if they equally shared the spiritual qualities of mutual confidence (*saddha*), moral virtue, self-denial (*caga*) and wisdom. The possible trans-rebirth continuity of conjugal love deeply satisfies happily married spouses. Just as much as positive emotions continue through *samsaric* life when selflessly cultivated, so there is the danger of bitter negative emotions surviving death, as is for instance shown in the *Kalayakkhinivatthu*.[28] Hence the constant exhortation in Buddhism to give up hatred and cultivate the sublime emotions (*brahmavihara*) of *metta*, *karuna*, *mudita* and *upekkha*: loving kindness, compassion, sympathetic joy and equanimity respectively.[29]

The relationship between parents and children too is warm, loving and duty bound.[30] Parents should set an example to the children in their behaviour by being morally upright. They should educate the children and pave the way to economic independence. They should take an interest in choosing suitable spouses and hand over family inheritance at the proper time. Children in their turn should love, honour and support parents, especially in old age. There is a custom in Sri Lanka for children to worship their parents, at least once on New Year's Day, and this I think is a subtle reminder for the parents too to be worthy of that honour by being duty-conscious and wholesome in behaviour. When the family unit is cohesive and duty bound, it engenders stability and peace in the entire society.

The Mind

The human personality is analysed into five inseparable groups of grasping (*panca upadanakkhandha*), as the physical body (*rupa*), feelings/emotions (*vedana*), ideas (*sanna*), will/volitions (*sankhara*) and consciousness (*vinnana*).[31] They are called groups of grasping because we regard them in terms of I and mine. When one says, I am tall/fat/fair, etc., one identifies oneself with the body, *rupa*, as it is the body that is tall/fat/fair. This identification is universally accepted as each passport carries a photograph of the body with the name label. We identify ourselves with *vedana* when we say, I love/hate, don't hurt my feelings; with *sanna* when we say, I am a democrat/socialist/philosopher, I will not give up my ideas; with *sankhara* when we say, I want to become a doctor/monk, this is my aspiration/ambition; with *vinnana* when we say, I see/hear/smell/taste/think, I keep my thoughts to myself. Thus we identify ourselves with these different aspects of our personality at different times. Moreover, all these aspects keep on changing. The body changes over the years from infancy to old age. Feelings and emotions keep on changing all the time; one moment we are angry, the next we are kind. Ideas change with education and maturity. Ambitions may similarly change from time to time. Sensory consciousness changes with stimuli and food for thought. Thus in our personality there is no place for a permanent unchanging entity that can be called a self/ego. Therefore the famous *anatta* theory in Buddhism seems sensible and factual.[32] That there is an individual stream of consciousness (*vinnanasota*) running through *samsaric* life is maintained in Buddhism.[33] What is denied is changeless identity. If there were an unchanging permanent ego then even the religious life would become meaningless, as a change for the better could not be effected.[34]

What Buddhism says about the nature of the untrained mind can be observed through experience if we only take the trouble to pay attention to the emotional and cognitive changes taking place in our day-to-day life. Sometimes our mind gets caught up in the desire for sensual pleasures (*kamacchanda*). If the desire is so intense and a healthy means of satisfying is not available, we resort to unacceptable means, of which we may later become ashamed. Sometimes our minds are overpowered by anger (*vyapada*) and punishable crimes too are committed as a result. When the mind is gripped by laziness (*thinamiddha*), work gets terribly neglected. The mind that is given to agitation and restlessness (*uddhaccakukkucca*), with constant sense stimuli such as loud music, is unsuitable for concentrated academic studies. Doubt/suspicion (*vicikiccha*) often mars interpersonal relationships. These five emotional and cognitive biases that overpower the mind from time to time are called *nivaranas*, 'coverings' in Pali, as they obscure the clarity of the mind and impair its efficiency.[35] These are observable mental phenomena and one learns to appreciate much of Buddhist psychology as it deals with knowable facts and there is nothing mysterious about it.

The *Samannaphalasutta* states that consciousness is tied up with the body and a highly developed meditator can see it like the thread that runs through a transparent gem.[36] It seems fair to assume that the mind is associated with the breath, as we know through experience that the breathing pattern changes with emotional changes, for we sigh in grief, we yawn in laziness, we snort in anger, we gasp in pain and we hold our breath in fear and wonder. Perhaps because this breath with which the mind is associated gets mixed with blood and is distributed all over the body through the nexus of the heart, the later Buddhist tradition considers the heart as the seat of consciousness.[37] This may be accepted as a probable hypothesis, as experientially too we feel the agitation more in the heart with negative emotional changes. Buddhist psychology satisfies my curiosity regarding the human mind as no other religion does.

Mental Culture

The most important training advocated by Buddhism is mental culture, consisting of the twin branches of meditation, namely tranquility (*samatha*) and introspection (*vipassana*).[38] They help us to understand, calm and free the mind of all impurities and obsessions. The mind, as we saw, is associated with the breath and by being aware of the breath (*anapanasati*),[39] we can understand the nature of the mind. Breathing is normally automatic, but we can also wilfully breathe. Therefore it holds the key to both voluntary and involuntary activities of the body. One can gain access to the comprehension of all physical activities by being aware of the breath to begin with. The mind also has a habit of dwelling on past experiences and future hopes and plans. But it has to be trained to dwell on the present moment, as that is the only time available for us to work in. By dwelling on the past and the future, we only day-dream. Breathing is an activity of the present moment, and it is such an innocuous activity that we do not have the tendency to compare it with past breathing nor plan for future breathing. By being aware of it we train the normally restless fugitive mind to be engaged in the work at hand in the present moment. The mind also has the fallacious tendency to create entities out of processes. In our personalities there are only energies at work, both physical and mental. The body is but a body-building activity as the cells die and get replaced continually; but we regard it as a solid entity that continues through time. The mind changes so fast as to give the impression of an everlasting ego, like the circle of fire that appears when a fire brand is twirled around. The breath is a wonderful object of observation to train the mind to view things as processes of energy, as there is no breath that can be characterized by a noun – there is only an activity of breathing characterized solely by a verb. *Anapanasati*, or the exercise of being aware of the breath in meditation, helps us to confine our activities to the present tense and understand the body and mind as processes of physical and mental energy.

   Vipassana meditation helps us to understand and gain control of our emotions.[40] When one attains a certain degree of mental tranquillity through awareness of breath, one can watch out for moments of emotional weakness. If, for instance, a person recognizes that he is angry when anger has arisen in him, it is a great step forward, as anger normally effaces self-awareness. *Vipassana*, or introspective awareness, consists of observing the physical changes taking place when one is angry, such as restlessness, feeling hot, sweating, faster heartbeat and quick breathing. When attention is paid to these physical changes, anger subsides. There is a physiological explanation for this phenomenon. The emotion of anger stimulates the secretion of adrenalin; when anger is expressed in abusive words and physical assault, more adrenalin is secreted and anger increases. When attention is diverted to the physical manifestations of anger, the adrenalin supply is cut off and anger loses its physical source of stimulation. If this exercise is repeated a few times when anger does arise, its frequency and intensity drastically decreases and an irritable, hot-tempered person is transformed into an even-tempered, lovable character. It becomes easy to generate the positive sublime emotions, such as *metta*, *karuna*, *mudita* and *upekkha*. The meditator experiences and radiates peace and joy.

All religions advocate ethics, but I am not aware of any religion other than Buddhism that elucidates a systematic path for the all-round development of the personality leading to mental discipline and the elimination of negative emotions. It is said that one can go further on the meditative path until one personally realizes the truth about one's previous *samsaric* life, how one has gone from birth to rebirth according to one's own intentional actions (karma).[41] With personal verification of the truth about oneself, all defilements are destroyed and it is said the knowledge dawns that there is no more rebirth.[42]

As the teachings of the Buddha accord with reason, common sense and experience, it is intellectually appealing, and as it has given me satisfactory results so far as I have practised it, I can say I am a Buddhist by conviction.

Notes
(All Pali texts referred to are Pali Text Society editions.)

Abbreviations:

A *Anguttaranikaya*
D *Dighanikaya*
M *Majjhimanikaya*
S *Samyuttanikaya*

1. A I 189.
2. D I 189.
3. Arahant is a saint who realized the goal of nirvana.
4. D III 80–98.
5. *Rgveda* X 90.
6. *Ksudra*: small, small creatures who multiply by cell division.
7. *Vaisya*: agriculturists.
8. *Ksatriya*: warriors, rulers.
9. *Atthasalini*, p. 272.
10. S I 39.
11. *Vimanavatthu Atthakatha* 18.
12. *Tanhapaccaya upadanam, upadanapaccaya bhavo bhavapaccaya jati.*
13. *Suttanipata*, v. 152.
14. *Devaloka*: the world of gods/deities.
15. *Petaloka*: a woeful world of departed beings.
16. S II 94.

17. *Assalayanasutta* M II 147 *Madhurasutta* M II 83; *Suttanipata* p. 115.
18. *Theragatha* 620–31; *Theragatha Atthakatha* I 540f.
19. A II 69.
20. D III 188.
21. D III 182.
22. D III 61.
23. D I 135.
24. D III 88.
25. D III 190.
26. *Jatakas* are birth stories of the Bodhisattva.
27. A II 61, II 295.
28. *Dhammapada Atthakatha* I 37.
29. D I 251.
30. D III 189.
31. S III 28.
32. S III 22.
33. D III 105.
34. S III 147.
35. D I 246.
36. D I 76.
37. *Visuddhimagga*, p. 256.
38. A I 61.
39. M I 56; III 78.
40. M 1 59.
41. D I 81.
42. D I 84.

THE VISIONS OF THE FIRST PEOPLES OF THE AMERICAS AS WE LEAVE THE FIVE-HUNDRED-YEAR CYCLE OF NINE HELLS AND MOVE TOWARDS THE FIRST OF THE THIRTEEN HEAVENS

Voyce Durling-Jones (Walking Bear Woman)

Voyce Durling-Jones is an American Indian of Cherokee/Choctaw/Celt ancestry, a Pipe Carrier, Family Bundle Keeper, Sundancer, and Speaker of the Tenasi Society.

IT APPEARS THAT the foundations of most world religions are based on visionary experience. This knowledge has become an important factor supporting the growing practice of interreligious tolerance during the twentieth century. Thus, in discussions of 'ultimate vision', we may find that we are much closer to the heart of the matter than we would have thought possible a decade ago.

I cannot begin simply with a reflection on why I choose to live by my religion, or what I think my religion has to offer to interfaith dialogue, or how it will contribute to humankind's ultimate vision, without first talking about certain historical events that have happened in the Americas. It has taken five centuries to weave this new spiritual blanket of many colours and songs for today.

The five-hundred-year cycle of the Nine Hells began with the arrival and subsequent invasions of the sacred motherland in the 1490s by the conquistadores, soon followed by other Europeans in North America. As the story unfolds, perhaps the ancient religions of the Americas will quietly appear from the four directions bringing many vision-gifts for the Give-away, for those who see.

Land, Gold and the Cross

The invaders brought weapons and the cross. What they first wanted was land and gold, and then later, 'religious freedom'. The land has always been the reason for Indian, European and American battles, and it continues to be the core of religious–legal issues as well.

It should be noted by the developed Christian nations of Europe and the Americas that the economic foundations of modern Europe and the Euro-nations of the Americas were created primarily from the gold and resources of the so-called 'New World' (followed by other colonized nations) at the expense of the Original Peoples' land, gold, and their religious freedom.

Certain things must be said for the sake of interreligious harmony between Christians and First Peoples of the Americas to honour those ancestors of goodwill and compassion who, through the centuries, lived side by side (Indian and non-Indian) sharing all they had.

The Great Tree of Democracy

Many people still believe the textbook distortions of Indians as portrayed by academia, government and church in the Americas. Thus, a reader with preconceived ideas might not bother to finish this chapter, secure in their conviction that American Indians are godless, without firm footing in this century, much less the next. Film and media have, until very recently, reinforced this image. Because of American 'cowboy and indian' movies and novellas, the Apache, the Comanche, the Lakota (Sioux), and the Cheyenne in particular, will ever be envisioned as the feathered dying warrior, the last noble savage (emphasis on savage), or the drunken Indian, their power and deep spiritual traditions vilified by half-truths and 'Hollywood historians', rewriting past events into the lies of today.

The American public hardly considers the First Nations east of the Mississippi and in the south; yet the League of the Iroquois with its constitution, the Great Law of Peace, based on unity in diversity and representative self-rule, embodies the tap root of the Democracy Tree in the United States. When Benjamin Franklin drafted the Albany Plan of Union in 1754, he patterned it on the Iroquois working model of federalism. It foreshadowed the US Constitution and the Articles of Confederation.

The US Constitution itself, with its separation of powers and system of checks and balances, reflected the Iroquois Grand Council of the time. As a document, it is a combination of the democracy of First Peoples and that of emerging European concepts of democracy influenced by thinkers such as Rousseau and Locke (who in turn had been influenced by the Hurons, Cherokee and Iroquois during their early visits to Europe) and the ancient Greeks and Romans; but nonetheless, it is firmly rooted in the 'red' earth of America. It is interesting to note in retrospect that the First Nations most admired by Franklin, Jefferson and Washington were matri-right people under 'petticoat government' led by Clan Mothers: the League of the Iroquois, the Wampanoag Confederacy and the Cherokee. Perhaps they reasoned that the colonials were not yet ready to have their women elect the leaders and oversee them, with the right to remove any who did not serve for the good of all the people, as did the Six Nations and the Cherokee. Hence, they patterned the Senate after the more patriarchal Greeks and Christianized Romans.

Once the policy of 'Manifest Destiny' (God on Our Side) was entrenched in the halls of power, even the architecture of Washington DC, along the Atlantic seaboard, and in the South, became decorated with Ionic-columned Greek towns, while the southern First Nations east of the Mississippi were being forcibly 'removed' as godless pagans.

Cosmologies and Religious Traditions of the Americas

So let me begin by sharing some of the knowledge that, though known to us, is only now beginning to be understood and accepted by religious scholars – the information that First Peoples of the Americas have practised their rich religious traditions beyond memory. Contemporary archaeologists, assisted by the newest dating techniques, now confirm that First Peoples have been at home in this hemisphere since at least 270,000 BCE.

Our existing traditions and stories of Creation reflect ancient religions that continue to link First Peoples with a ceremonial treasury of spiritual practices, texts, songs, chants, prayers, music and dance that extend throughout the western hemisphere in spite of holocaust and religious persecution.

WE think the IMMANENT flowing from within and around the GREAT MYSTERY is present and mirrored in the universe. WE believe there is a CREATIVE PRINCIPLE that permeates the universe (the Sacred Circle) and all within. Events in the human world mirror their analogues in the celestial sphere of the Star Nations and the Milky Way (Sacred World Tree) that stands in the centre of the Cosmos; AS ABOVE, SO BELOW . . . a reciprocal relationship.

This process of circular time and space is evident in the belief that the Earth is a Living Being and all Life in the Cosmos is related and balanced as it moves within the Sacred Circle or Wheel of the Universe. The circle enclosing and embracing the cross of the Four Directions/the Sacred Tree has been its symbol for more than 10,000 years. In the tribal spiritual traditions there is no transcendent sense of God as distant and removed, existing apart from the material universe; for this would create a process of linear, mechanical time with dominion over space. We exist in ceremonial time/space.

The Great Mystery, Master of Breath, Creator, called by many names and known also as Thought Woman, Corn Woman/Mother, Star/Sky Woman, Great Spirit, All Maker, Spider Woman, All Spirit, Hard Beings Woman, Earth Woman, Heart of Sky/Heart of Earth, Heart of Heaven/Huracan, Grandmother Sun, is joined by other powerful historical or spirit beings such as Sotuknang, the Pale One, Red Lady, White Buffalo (Calf) Woman, Peacekeeper, Quetzalcoatl (Anointed One), the goddess Tinotzin (the Virgin Morena), Kukulcan-Lord of the Dawn, Deganwidah-Master of Things, Sovereign Plumed Serpent, Grandmother Spider, Ancient Red, the Grandfathers and the Grandmothers, Four Winds, the Guardians of the Four Directions and many others.

These prophets, spiritual messengers and guardian beings are comparable to the Christian saints and angels, the Buddhist bodhisattvas and goddesses, and may be referred to by many different names within the diverse tribal languages.

Like most world religions, the spiritual practices of the First Peoples are based upon ancient oral and written traditions, dreams and visions. The tribal, clan and family treasury of teachings and annual renewal ceremonies may include one of the following: the Sacred Pipe and Pipe Fast, the Green Corn Dance, the Sun Dance, the Rain Dance, the Sweat Lodge, the Creation Ceremonies, Sandpainting and Songs, the Horse Ceremony, the Crown Dance, the Great Busk, the

Thanksgiving Ceremony, the Yuwipi Ceremony, the Shaking Tent, the Peyote Ceremony and the Sacred Clowns.

In addition, there are the ancestral shrines, divining with the Maya Tzolkin Calendar and healing with the sacred medicine crystals. Certain southern First Nations have used medicine crystals for millennia, especially the Cherokee, Apache, Hopi, Choctaw and Maya. The ceremonies mentioned above represent only a portion of the spiritual traditions practised in the Americas.

The Zero, Skywalkers and Theology of the Land

The First Peoples of the Americas and all those who embrace the sacred quality of nature are sensitive to the necessity for both silence and sacred sound, seclusion and renewal. The American Indian concepts of land theology and sacred ecology are central to our spiritual traditions.

It seems that whether we were born on the reservation or in the city, we find the source of our personal identity is a spiritual belonging within the cultural matrix, no matter how far removed. This inner solidarity brings 'full-bloods' and 'mixed-bloods' together. Racially, this description denotes the degree of blood (a divisive tactic used by North American governments), but sociologically, regardless of blood quantum, it refers to lived values. For example, an individual of one-eighth or one-quarter may be a sociological full-blood.

Our most important religious practices require sacred sites, and so we continue to return to stomp grounds and secluded holy places for seeking visions, for Pipe Fasting, for Green Corn Dances, for the Sun Dance, for healing, for the Sweat Lodge and other spiritual practices. According to the Daykeepers of the Meso-American calendar, before the five-hundred-year cycle of Nine Hells, we always gathered at our holy places and sacred sites: ancient mounds, shrines, temple pyramids and sacred mountains and rivers, throughout the Americas, to participate in elaborate seasonal religious ceremonials. Where possible, we continue to do so.

The ancestors were Skywatchers and Skywalkers seeking communion with the star nations. They made ancient earth-mound effigies more than fifteen thousand years ago, shaped like snakes, birds, horses, elephants, panthers and men, meant to be seen from above the land, and to mirror the star nations, track the heavenly bodies, identify the earth clan residing in the region and honour the symbols of the Creator. Keep in mind that ancient America was home to the horse, elephant and camel before the last Ice Age.

These skywatching astronomers and temple keepers were excellent mathematicians who kept all the cycles of stars, sun, moon and planets that made up the sacred calendar and arranged the sacred high days of ceremonies accordingly. A paradigm was created, which the Mississippi mound cultures – the Anasazi, the Olmecs, the Toltecs, the Zapotecs, the Maya and the Inca – moulded into scientific and spiritual societies, each in a unique way.

The Mayan civilization discovered the mathematical concept of zero more than five thousand years ago. They produced the world's most accurate and sophisticated calendar and created hieroglyphic writing on bark paper and stone, an early technology they developed. Whether Maya, Inca, Anasazi, or Mississippian society – or among their living descendants today – sacred astronomy was the practice of weaving a celestial tapestry mirrored in the daily lives of the people.

The specially trained priests were required to make precise records of the heavens, which accumulated over countless generations, to discover the patterns of the universe. The alignment of the cities and sacred places provided sight lines to mark significant risings and settings of heavenly bodies. Mother Earth was the warp of this divine weaving. The sacred cosmos was woven and mirrored in a sacred landscape for ceremony and for paths of pilgrimage.

The 'New World' Holocaust

These socio-religious activities continued until the final conquest of the Maya by the Spanish conquistadores, who burned all but four sacred books (an act as senseless as the burning of the great library of Alexandria), killed Mayan priests and gifted people and tried to destroy what the Roman Catholic Church called 'the works of the devil'. The Mississippian societies, the Mother Peoples to the north, met a similar fate under the Spanish, French and English colonials; many were conquered and sold into the slave trade.

Historians using conservative figures estimate that in 1519 in *central* Mexico alone there was an Indian population of at least twenty-five million. By 1600 that number was barely seven hundred and fifty thousand; only three per cent of the First Peoples remained. It is important to remember that the ancient motherland of the Americas was not an empty 'new world' as portrayed by dominant societies; it was an 'old world' with millions of inhabitants (the current estimate is a population of 145–200 million in 1492) who had always lived there until its 'discovery' by Europeans.

It is impossible to separate North and South (Latin) America from each other in relation to the common experiences of the First Peoples with the European Christians; we know the scope of the tragedy that befell them all in the Americas, one by one, and then by the millions, which really began in the West Indies in the early 1500s.

The Spanish vanquished the great civilizations of the Maya, the Incas and the Aztecs, not because they were better soldiers, but because the epidemics of measles, smallpox and chickenpox, which swept before and travelled with the foreigners, struck down the Indian populations. This made it impossible for the weakened warriors to protect the communities from the invading Spaniards outfitted with guns, horses and man-hunting mastiffs. Add to this, in the case of Mexico, the warring factions within the Aztec Empire who sided with the conquistadores, and the picture becomes less blurred.

The conquistadores murdered the royalty, enslaved the surviving people, burned their sacred writings, built churches over their temples, converted their palaces, melted down their art and sacred objects of gold and shipped the ingots and treasures back to Europe. The silver and the seeds soon followed. This was Holocaust!

First Nations of North America: The 'First Americans'

But that was not quite the scenario in North America with the Anglo-Europeans and the First Nations east of the Mississippi River. By the eighteenth and nineteenth centuries the Mississippian societies (by then called the Five Civilized Tribes) in North America were struggling to retain their original homelands in the south. In fact, all the Indian First Nations of the Eastern Woodlands and the Atlantic Confederacies in the United States used every strategy available to stay on their lands – from battles to treaties of alliance.

In Canada and the United States, the First Nations are entitled to powers of sovereignty and self-government because their original occupation of the land has been acknowledged by the Canadian and United States governments through countless treaties. They needed the Indian Confederacies as allies in the wars the Europeans carried across the Atlantic to North America; in the Canadian and Mississippi River fur-trade competition; in the agricultural knowledge of the southern Indian Nations – the mothers of corn, tobacco, indigo, cotton and a vast herbal pharmacopoeia. Eighty per cent of the foods in the world today and sixty per cent of the botanical pharmacopoeia originated in the gardens of the 'New World'.

After the Revolutionary War and the War of 1812, the Americans turned on their former Indian allies and enemies. They made little differentiation as to whether the Indians fought for them or the British: the only good Indian was a dead Indian. To the deep shame of the colonialists and then the United States, the Original Peoples, east of the Mississippi, died primarily from bullets and starvation, with their heads separated from their bodies and hung on stockade posts; not death by measles and smallpox so much as by being outnumbered by a never-ending stream of immigrants with guns.

The Removals: 'Trail of Tears' and Sacred Bundles

The Cherokee formed a republic in Georgia and took their case to the Supreme Court of the land. The Cherokee were a literate nation; they won their case. However, the United States government, under President Andrew Jackson, refused to enforce the law on their behalf. All negotiating efforts failed and the removals began, first with the Choctaw and then the Cherokee. Thousands died on the

'Trail of Tears'. Those who could hid in deep forests and on mountains, and in the cane fields and swamps, refusing to leave their original homelands in the South-East.

The South-West and Plains tribes west of the Mississippi gained an extra half century of freedom before being outnumbered, hunted down and killed or 'confined' in reservation camps by the US Cavalry, following the Civil War and up to as late as the turn of the century.

My mother's family were Cherokee and Choctaw. Only a few relatives had escaped the removal of the 1830s by hiding and then settling in Louisiana before the Civil War. Many Indian families fought for the Confederacy in exchange for a promise that part of the homelands would be returned if the South won the war; slavery was not the issue for them. The South lost and so did their Indian allies. The Cherokee regiment was the last Confederate regiment to surrender in the Civil War. For them it was a double loss and sorrow.

Under the harsh policies of the US occupation of the South, if you were identified as an American Indian you could not own land, testify in court or practise your religion. Those laws are still on the books of some southern states, though rarely enforced in the United States since World War II. There were few safe havens east of the Mississippi, and families known to be Indian were in great peril in certain regions.

Thus, the generation born after the Civil War went into hiding once again during the nineteenth century; this time by marriage to Christians. My Cherokee/Choctaw great-grandmother was to be the first in the family to marry a Euro-American. She married the son of a 'remittance man' (Robert Woodward Sherwood, born in Scotland, who had served as an officer in the Confederate Army but never returned home from the war). Many Indian men and women in the South who had escaped removal and survived the wars of the nineteenth century married Celt-Americans; they shared an interest in music, dance, story-telling, dreams and visions, honoured their ancestors, and were egalitarians who possessed a sense of humour.

Many families, clans and tribes in North America continued to keep Sacred Bundles and Teachings; I am the Bundle Keeper in my family. Only because of the protection given by individual families and clans have certain spiritual teachings survived five hundred years of holocaust in North America alone; years of genocide, disease, missionaries, the war between Britain and France, the American Revolutionary War, The War of 1812, tribal diaspora, the Civil War, the Indian wars, ethnocide and alcohol, federal policies of tribal termination and forbidding the practice of Indian religion. If you are curious about what happened during those same centuries in Central and South America you might like to read the prose-history *Trilogy of Fire*, by Eduardo Galeano.

Observance of the ceremonial cycle is still in use by First Nations in North America today, primarily on the reservations and reserves of the United States and

Canada. In spite of racism in some communities and perhaps because of it, many families maintain a dual religious practice of Christianity and their traditional ceremonies, both on and off reservations. However, during the last decade, more urban Indians, mixed-bloods and tribal members are practising their traditional religions openly.

Tribal Elders are beginning to teach and conduct ceremonies in the urban areas, while more Indians are returning to the reservations and sacred sites for ceremonies such as the Sun Dance, the Green Corn Dance, and the Pipe Fast, which must by necessity be held in secluded places, under the protection of Elder Pipe Carriers (men and women), Stomp Ground Keepers, or traditional priests and medicine societies, who are responsible for the ceremonies.

The drum, the rattle, the flute and the voice represent all of the 'relatives' – the biosphere as a living web of life mirrored by the cosmos and honoured in ceremony. To us, the land is sacred and shaped by spirit and is to be celebrated with humility and reverence. In the heart of the world, now called the Americas, is the knowledge that all life is one and inseparable. In the South, home of the panther and the red hawk, we are the Keepers of the Sacred Fire; Sun is our Grandmother. We are Dreamwalkers and Selu's noble children, who walk in beauty still.

The American Indian Religious Freedom Act (AIRFA)

Without truth there is no justice; and without vision the shape of justice and history can become blurred, for it is the conqueror who writes the history and the law. The conqueror never travels alone. In the Americas he came with the cross and the sword and they are ever at hand.

Until 1978 American Indians could not publicly practise their religion, in spite of the First Amendment that protected all other religions brought to these shores. Both houses of Congress passed a resolution regarding American Indian religious freedom. This public law of the 95th Congress in 1978 recognized the inherent right of American citizens to religious freedom, and finally called upon government agencies to 'protect and preserve for American Indians their inherent right of freedom to believe, express, and exercise the traditional religions'.

Ten years later, in 1988, Sharon O'Brien, Professor of Government at Notre Dame University and scholar of American Indian Law in the United States, noted in her contribution to the *Handbook of American Indian Religious Freedom* published in 1991 that, 'in fact, AIRFA might now be placed in the context of an extended history of U.S. persecution of Indian religions'.

She further indicated that the act constitutes statutory recognition of the federal government's responsibility regarding Indians, while a survey of court cases of the 1980s reveals a judicial disregard for the act. She finds the courts have applied more stringent tests to Indians in their religious cases than to other people's religious claims; Indians have been required to prove that the infringement of certain religious practices will necessarily lead to the demise of their religion, while in other cases the non-Indian claimants must prove only that their religious rights are being infringed upon!

Steven C. Moore, a Native American Rights Fund staff attorney who has represented American Indians seeking to protect sacred sites, argues that 'the U.S. government agencies have resisted the intent of the American Indian Religious Freedom Act (AIRFA) to protect the sacred sites of Native peoples in the United States. The Forest Service and the Bureau of Land Management have regarded AIRFA more as an impediment to their bureaucratic interests and have attempted to subvert it. *It is clear that since land is the crux of historical and contemporary Indian–White conflicts, it also constitutes the central knot of the legal–religious tangle*.'

So ends the Nine Hells. We will enter the first of the Thirteen Heavens in the year 2017 of the European calendar. We have lived to tell the story.

Mythopoeic Vision: Something Sacred Is Moving in the Americas

To undertake ceremonies such as a Pipe Fast, 'to cry for a vision', is to accept a sacred reality of existence and guidance based on visionary experience. In the cultures of American and Canadian Indians in North America these are important religious practices for both men and women. To seek a vision in this manner is not the act of an immature person, for one's life is literally 'on the line'. This is not to be confused with creating an imaginary story while alone in the wilderness; it is understood by all vision-seekers to be a non-ordinary event containing sacred power that could manifest the mythopoeic vision that informs our life. It gives us the experience of the Immanent; a place of our own within the sacred circle.

A Pipe Fast must take place on special land in total seclusion. There is a purification Sweat Lodge ceremony before being put on the hill where one remains alone, without food and water, for four days and nights (offering up the self), emerging on the fifth morning at dawn. Women usually make a small lodge of willows with a canvas covering tied down over the frame; men may use the same type of shelter or just a blanket or buffalo robe. The vision-seeker is briefly visited each day at dawn and before the sun goes down or, among some tribes, remains completely alone for three to four days.

Protection songs, calling songs and prayers are offered to the Creator and the Grandfathers each evening on the vision-seeker's behalf. This ritual varies from tribe to tribe. The vigil is kept through the night with sleeping permitted during the day. Silence is maintained except when questioned by the medicine person directing the Pipe Fast, as to what one 'sees', experiences, dreams, and the directions of emergence. This medicine person is always a Pipe Carrier (whether male or female) and may also be a Sun Dance Priest or Yuwipi man.

On the fifth morning, the medicine people come to help the vision-seeker down the hill or mountain and take them into the Sweat Lodge or another special place for ceremonies. There, in relation to their visionary experience, the vision-seeker may be given a new name, receive a pipe, and be given other special gifts. This is always followed by a feast and Give-away – the visionary, in thanksgiving, gives gifts to those who assisted, prayed and sang at the foot of the hill or mountain during the four days and nights. Pipe Fasts may be undertaken for several reasons: the healing of a family member, fulfilling spiritual obligations by an initiate (such as a Pipe Carrier or Sundancer), or seeking one's life vision.

To experience a vision, to become a visionary, to go through a transformation, is to know one's place in the cosmos. From the vision songs, ceremonies, characters and symbols evolve – animal helpers, clothing, designs and ornaments that can become part of our daily and ceremonial life. Some items may be kept in a Medicine Bundle. The spiritual mythopoeic vision transforms into the physical, and healing renewal thereby becomes mythic.

A vision, though the personal experience of an individual, becomes a vision-story by being shared. While many visions are prophetic of the yet-to-be, the myth or vision-story as experienced by North American Indians is not an imaginary story, or a story about something that either is about to happen, or has already occurred, though it may be a complex metaphysical transmission portraying our relationship to the world. This is how mythopoeic vision and myth are lived in the Indian spiritual tradition, with eyes open.

Sacred Transmissions of Thought: The Weaving of Light

For us the light that Grandmother Spider first carried to the people in the 'long ago time' gave us sight, creativity and power; thus she gave us vision, myth and the possibility of being truly human. By becoming Real Human/Beings, we enter into the heart of the Great Mystery; we integrate the feminine and masculine, the unconscious and conscious, the self and other. With vision-story (myth) we may freely enter all the sacred circles within the galaxies as totally integrated beings. This is the way we create the future and live in the present. It is the way we have always survived as the people.

Perhaps you can understand why I choose to live the religion of my ancestors, even though its weaving is frayed in places and its vibrant colours are now a rich tonal reflection of earth and sky. Yet the ancient pattern created by the Great Mystery is still visible and enlivened by Master of Breath and Star Woman who dreamed us all within this holy place: Mother Earth, the Sacred Tree, Corn Mother, the Sacred Fire, Grandmother Sun, Brother/Sister Moon, the Ancestors, and all our relatives: the winged people, the swimming people, the four-legged people, the crawling people, the standing people, the plant people, the star nations and we, the two-legged people, the youngest of creation.

I have only to wrap its rich folds around my shoulders and feel its weight as it touches the earth where I stand, at home with the Ancient Ones. The Grandmothers and the Grandfathers are with us still; we are all one family, unfolding and enfolding forever.

Declaration of Vision from the United Native Nations

Envision, if you will, how different the world would now be, if the Americas had been discovered by Europeans *after* the Christian inquisitions and reformations; if the 'visitors' had properly thanked and acknowledged the many gifts given to them by the Red Earth Peoples; if they had put into practice the egalitarian system of the Eastern Woodland Nations; had kept their promises and honoured even half the treaties made with the Red Indians; had given moral and political support to the experimental Cherokee Republic in Georgia; had allowed the Apache Geronimo and his band of survivors to remain in their sacred mountains; had not shot down Emiliano Zapata like a dog in Mexico, and on and on, *ad infinitum.*

Even today it is not over. First Peoples of the Americas and their relatives continue to suffer and to be martyred in the final years of a literal 'nine hells' of atrocity and genocide, ethnocide and ecocide, in Central and South America. When will the Turtle Island Dream-Gift of freedom, justice and compassion be returned to the First Americans? Vision on this scale will have to be dreamed again with humility and forgiveness rather than with arrogance and Old Testament justice. Can it be done? There are those who say it can.

References

Allen, Paula Gunn. *The Sacred Hoop* (Boston: Beacon Press, 1986).

Deloria, Vine. *God Is Red* (New York: Grosset, 1973).

Earle, Duncan MacLean. 'Ethnoecology and Maya Adaptations of Time and Space', in *Maya Patterns: Cosmos and Time* (Red Indian Society of the Americas, Earth & Sky Conference, Dallas, 1992).

Galeano, Eduardo. *Faces & Masks, Memory of Fire Trilogy* (New York: Pantheon Books, 1987).

Goodman, Jeffrey. *American Genesis* (New York: Berkley Books, 1982).

Kneberg, M. and T. Lewis. *Tribes That Slumber* (Knoxville, TN: University of Tennessee Press, 1989).

Tedlock, Dennis, trans. *Popol Vuh* (New York: Simon & Schuster, 1985).

Vecsey, Christopher, ed. *Handbook of American Indian Religious Freedom* (New York: Crossroad Publishing Co., 1991).

ISLAM: THE ULTIMATE VISION

Dr Asghar Ali Engineer

Dr Asghar Ali Engineer trained in Islamic theology, Tafsir (commentary on the Holy Qur'an), Islamic jurisprudence and Hadith. He has published widely on Islam, and is the founding chair of the Centre for the Study of Society and Secularism. He is also an ex-member of the Executive Council of Jawaharlal Nehru University, Delhi; and is presently General Secretary of the Central Board of the Dawoodi Bohra Community and Convenor of the Asian Muslims' Action Network (AMAN).

EVERY RELIGION HAS its vision, I should say, visions. Religion is a subjective thing, an inner experience. Thus each follower can have his/her vision realized through a particular religion, whether born into it or through acquiring it, and there are as many visions of a religion as its followers. But this again is an idealistic statement. Not every follower cares to evolve his/her vision in life. More often than not, people follow religion mechanically. No wonder then that every religion, however throbbing with life or deeply committed to certain values, can soon be transformed into a set of fixed rituals. Age-old cultural traditions are absorbed into the religion and the revolutionary potential lost, only to be rediscovered occasionally by one or another radical follower.

Every great religion – Buddhism, Jainism, Judaism, Christianity, Islam, Sikhism – in its origins had a great reformist thrust. Their founders were deeply disturbed by social conditions around them and were inspired by an ultimate vision to reform society. Some – like Buddha and Mahavira Jain – drew their inspiration through the process of deep reflection lasting over several years, becoming enlightened in the process; others got their ultimate vision through revelation – like the Prophet of Islam. But one thing was common among these great religious thinkers – they were dissatisfied with the state of affairs they were born into and had a deep inner urge to set things right.

These thinkers were born into certain historical conditions and their ultimate visions could not escape their societies' deep imprints. Thus each vision, while being transcendent, was also limited by its frame, and this explains the specificity of each religion and its vision. These specificities should not lead to irreconcilable differences – they should be appreciated for their creativity. The human potential for creativity – theological and otherwise – is immense, almost unlimited. Even in the same circumstances the religious visions of two individuals may not be the same, or even similar, each thinking mind imparting its own print.

Every religion has multiple visions, each religion being subdivided into a number of traditions, and each vision claiming to be closest to the original vision of the founder. No major religion has escaped this fate. These subdivisions should not be derided, however, as they have added to the richness of theological thinking.

One must step out of this frame of mind and rejoice in the theological creativity and richness of every sect.

Each religious tradition has laid emphasis on certain values: Hinduism on non-violence, Buddhism on compassion, Jainism on non-possession, Christianity on love and Islam on equality and justice. All these values, a moment's reflection would show, are complementary to each other. It is these values together that can create the ultimate vision. A world without peace, compassion, love, equality and justice would not be worth living in. These values, most fundamental for a humane society, were important tools with which the founders of great religions could create a world worth living in. It is unfortunate that these values have been relegated to the background, if not altogether forgotten, in every major religious tradition. Instead, rituals, shorn of their original significance, were constituted as the core of religion. These rituals became signifiers for every religious tradition. It was the demise of the ultimate vision.

I am not suggesting that rituals have no significance today. Rituals in every religious tradition signify the core values, the ultimate vision. But when vested interests controlling religious establishments severed the links between these rituals and the ultimate vision, they lost their value and were reduced to some mechanical operation. The faithful who only followed (in many cases they were forbidden to think) performed these rituals without understanding their links with a fundamental vision, and these rituals come to life only when linked to the ultimate vision of the founder. Today they are more symbolic of a particular culture and its richness than of ultimate values and visions.

I would like to illustrate the point about rituals from my faith tradition, Islam. *Salah* (prayer) is the most fundamental ritual to the value-system Islam emphasizes and it signifies Islam's ultimate vision. Islam wants to create a society based on equality and justice tempered with compassion. The Islamic prayer has been devised to infuse this spirit among the faithful. The first words of the call to prayer are 'Allahu Akbar' (God is greatest). These words have their own meaning and significance: if Allah is the greatest, the faithful should not bow down before any other power. Bowing before any other power will signify bowing before others' tyranny, exploitation and arrogance. Allah is ultimate in justice, mercy and compassion (Allahu 'adil, al-Rahim and al-Rahman) and hence bowing down before Him one is bowing down before justice, mercy and compassion and raising one's head against oppression, exploitation, cruelty and hard-heartedness. Thus the words 'Allahu Akbar' negate all that is unjust and devoid of mercy and compassion. One who worships Allah worships justice, mercy and compassion.

This justice, mercy and compassion are all-inclusive, not confined to the faithful alone. Imam Raghib, the great Qur'anic lexicographer, maintains that 'Rahman' is all-inclusive and that Allah's *rahmah* (mercy) embraces both believers and unbelievers. Thus it can be seen that the Qur'anic values are inclusive, not exclusive.

Another important act during Islamic prayer is that all worshippers stand in one line, the highest of the high and the lowest of the low. This clearly signifies that Allah recognizes no social hierarchy and that all human beings are equal before Him, whatever their social status, colour, language or territorial origin. No language or colour is superior to another; they are all signs of Allah. 'And of His signs', says the Qur'an, 'is the creation of the heavens and the earth and the diversity of your tongues and colours. Surely there are signs in this for the learned' (30:22). Thus with these words the Qur'an wipes out all distinctions between one human being and another, and any worshipper of Allah who perpetrates them is not worthy of worshipping Him.

Again, according to the Qur'an, it is not the mode of worshipping that is ultimate, but excelling in the above virtues (*khairat*). Thus the Qur'an does not lay emphasis on the mode of worshipping Allah but on cultivating the virtues, whose ultimate representative is Allah. The Qur'an proclaims, 'For every one is a direction in which he turns, so vie with one another in good works' (2:148). A great Sufi saint of fourteenth-century India, Hazrat Nizamuddin Auliya, referring to this verse, used to say that there are as many ways of worshipping Allah as there are grains of sand.

A Muslim also recites certain surahs (Qur'anic verses) in his/her prayers, which give an important message of social significance. The Qur'an's ultimate vision is to usher in a just and egalitarian society, and this is possible only when no one accumulates wealth for his own benefit. Concentration of wealth not only strengthens oppressive and exploitative structures in society but also distorts the entire value-system and deprives life of any transcendental meaning. All efforts are then concentrated on accumulation of wealth and considering that wealth as the ultimate goal in life. The Qur'an thus considers this accumulation a source of great evil. It warns, 'Woe to every slanderer, defamer, who amasses wealth and counts it. He thinks that his wealth will make him abide. Nay, he will certainly be hurled into the crushing disaster. And what will make thee realize what the crushing disaster is? It is the Fire kindled by Allah, which rises over hearts, surely it is closed in on them, in extended columns.'

This surah, 104, is recited every day in prayer by Muslims. Its significance cannot be lost on them if they take prayer in the same spirit in which it was designed by the founder. The just distribution of wealth in society is very central to the Qur'anic teachings. It is not without meaning that *salah* in the Qur'an everywhere has been juxtaposed with *zakah* (an obligatory levy for the poor, the needy, orphans, widows, the indebted, needy travellers and the manumission of slaves). No Muslim prayer can be complete without *zakah*. The Qur'an also requires the faithful to spend surplus ('*afw*) for helping weaker sections of society after meeting their own basic needs (2:219). Thus the Qur'an does not approve of either the accumulation of wealth or luxurious ways of life. Both corrode all the higher values in life. Both rob life of all meaning except instant pleasure, and a meaningful life is much more than instant pleasure.

Islam's ultimate vision, prescribed by the Qur'an and *shari'a* (Muslim law), does not approve of the consumerism of modern capitalist societies, and these capitalist values are alien to Islam, in fact, are alien to all religions that stress one or another set of humanist values. No truly religious person will approve of capitalist values, which are negative: production only for profit and greed, and the encouragement of exploitation because it leads to greater accumulation. In this system one individual gains at the expense of another. It is greed, not need, that is central to the capitalist mode of production. Religion, on the other hand, encourages need-based economies.

Buddhism and Islam both stress the middle path. There is great wisdom in adopting the middle path and thereby avoiding extremity at both ends. Extremity, even if it be in asceticism, is a negative factor in the growth of humanity and human values, as, for example, asceticism only leads to neglecting all corporeal demands. The Prophet is reported to have said, 'There is no asceticism in Islam.' The Qur'an also describes the Islamic community as *ummatan wastan*, i.e. a community following the middle path. Edward William Lane, an Arabic–English lexicographer, describes *ummat wasat* as meaning a just, equitable or good nation.

Thus Islam promotes neither asceticism nor consumerism as both produce negative effects and hence must be avoided. Its ultimate vision is of a just and equitable society, wherein the weaker sections do not suffer and people are not driven by the greed that consumerism promotes. Similarly, Islam accepts the right to private property, but does not make this right absolute, so that if public welfare demands that it be curtailed, it can be done. The noted theologian Imam ibn Taymiyyah (1263–1328) also maintained that public welfare had precedence over private and individual welfare.

The welfare of weaker sections of society is so central to Islamic theology that a revealed chapter of the Qur'an rejects a believer's prayer if that person does not take care of those weaker and does not spare a portion of his/her wealth for them. This chapter says, 'Hast thou seen him who belies religion? That is one who is rough to the orphan, and urges not the feeding of the needy. So woe to the praying ones, who are unmindful of their prayer! Who [pray] to be seen, and refrain from acts of kindness' (107).

Thus the above Qur'anic chapter, which is also recited almost daily by the faithful in their prayers, is emphatic about the welfare of weaker sections being central to Islamic society. Also, in yet another surah that is also generally recited in prayers, deep concern is shown for the poor and needy. It calls those needy who are lying in the dust, i.e. the most wretched of society. And those who disbelieve in these signs of Allah (which include the wretched of the earth), 'On them is fire closed over' (see chapter 91:15–20).

Thus it will be seen that Islamic prayer is no mechanical ritual. Every prayer is a renewal of commitment to the poor, the needy and other weaker sections of

The Qur'anic stand is very lucid and clear: 'Call to the way of the Lord with wisdom and goodly exhortation, and argue with them in the best manner' (16:125). Arguing in this manner retains freedom on both sides, a non-believer being as free to reject a doctrine as a believer is to maintain it.

Real human unity is unity of humankind across the lines of faith, and is not reducible to unity of the faithful only. True unity should not encounter any barrier – ethnic, racial, territorial or religious. This is what the Qur'an also desires, respecting pluralism and pleading unity in diversity. 'And if Allah pleased,' says the Qur'an, 'all those who are in the earth would have believed, all of them. Wilt thou then force men till they are believers?' (10:99). The Qur'anic doctrine is quite clear: it is not difficult for Allah to make all believe, but He does not desire it to be by force; rather, every one should be free to believe. Elsewhere the Qur'an throws a challenge to the believers to live in peace and harmony despite differences of faith: 'For every one of you We appointed a law and a way. And if Allah had pleased He would have made you a single people, but that He might try you in what He gave you. So vie one with another in virtuous deed' (5:48).

The Qur'anic intention is not to create one community of faithful, but to let each one follow their own law and way, and yet vie with each other in good deeds. Again the Qur'an states, 'Mankind is a single nation. So Allah raised prophets as bearers of good news and as warners, and He revealed with them the Book with truth, that it might judge between people concerning that in which they differed. And none but the very people who were given it differed about it after arguments had come to them envying one another' (2:213). Thus, according to the Qur'an, 'Mankind is a single nation.' However, different prophets were raised within this nation, who gave the people a Book so that they could be judged on their conduct. However, the differences between people were not on principles but on account of their vanity or because they rebelled against the law of the Book. Thus just because different prophets arose among them they should not be divided; their basic unity should remain intact. It is a challenge for people to maintain this basic unity as human beings.

The Qur'an wants the believer not to abuse others' religion or gods as this does not serve any higher purpose. The Qur'an declares, 'And abuse not those whom they call upon besides Allah, lest, exceeding the limits, they abuse Allah through ignorance. Thus to every people have We made their deeds fair-seeming' (6:109).

The Qur'an also prescribes how to deal with people of other religions, especially the People of the Book (i.e. the Jews and Christians) (29:46). And it is clear that Allah's intention is for humankind to live in peace and harmony, and to deal with each other in the best manner possible despite religious differences.

Under Islam all religious places, be they temples, mosques, churches or synagogues, must be protected as Allah's name is repeated in all these places of worship (22:40). Also, many verses such as, 'Whosoever submits himself entirely to

Allah and he is the doer of good [to others] he has his reward from his Lord, and there is no fear for such nor shall they grieve' (2:112) could be quoted from the Qur'an, which require competition in good deeds, not in theological dogmas that invariably lead to conflict. These are man-made and reflect our egos and we should not allow these dogmas to rule over us and restrain our freedom, dividing humanity. They should be seen in their historical context. A free human being will always transcend these dogmas. In the pluralist world today this Islamic vision is the best of prescriptions.

Lastly, I would like to submit that the Qur'anic ultimate vision would be incomplete without recognizing and also realizing sexual equality. As far as human beings are concerned, it is woman's humanity, not her sexuality, that is significant. As humans, both man and woman are absolutely equal. The Qur'anic vision includes sexual equality and recognizes women's dignity as human beings. The Qur'an declares that 'women have rights similar to what is against them in a just manner' (2:228). Though the Qur'an also says in the same verse, 'and men are a degree above them', this was nothing but a concession to men in the then prevailing social situation. It is not a statement of intention but rather of the prevailing reality of the time. We find the statement of intention elsewhere in the Qur'an: 'Surely the men who submit and the women who submit, and the believing men and believing women, and the truthful men and truthful women, and the patient men and patient women, and the humble men and humble women, and the charitable men and charitable women, and the fasting men and fasting women, and the men who guard their chastity and women who guard, and the men who remember Allah and the women who remember – Allah has prepared for them forgiveness and a mighty reward' (33:35). Thus the Qur'an has equated the two sexes in all spiritual matters and human qualities, Allah according equality to both as they will be rewarded equally for their spiritual achievements.

However, our society is still far from according this equality, but it is our ultimate vision. If all human beings are equal, this equality certainly includes women too. Our society is changing fast and women too now contribute greatly, economically as well as socially.

It remains to sum up the ultimate vision of Islam. Islam stands for the creation of a just and egalitarian society where there will be no hierarchy or status; where there will be no accumulation of wealth in a few hands; where there will be no master and slaves, physical or intellectual; where there will be complete freedom of conscience and expression; where human dignity will not be trampled upon; where religious, ethnic, racial and territorial differences will not stand in the way of human unity; where dogmas will not divide human beings and restrict their freedom; where gender injustice will not be permitted; and where all human beings will keep their heads high. Such is the ultimate vision of Islam.

missing, though I didn't know what it was.

What was missing, I recognized later, was the visionary experience of God's presence. Not knowing anything but always feeling pulled toward that presence, I was drawn to sit for hours in a great tree. She was a huge magnolia, reaching her arms down to earth so that even a small child could climb up into her lap. Day after day, year after year, I would climb into her arms and then just sit there happily in her peaceful, powerful embrace. When I left her arms and moved about in the world, I could not understand why hatreds and cruelties existed among people. I had a dim memory of a life of perfect harmony and love. It was nowhere evident in the world, but that peace, that love surrounded me when I sat in the tree.

Could it also come forth in the world? When I almost died at the age of thirty, twenty-one years ago, I remembered that this is our mission. This is what we have come here to do. As I lay near death in a hospital room, I chose to become very calm inside so that my body would be free to heal itself. In that quietness, in that surrender to the inner power, I discovered that I was not alone in the room. Rather, the room was filled with an unseen Presence whose nature was absolute, unconditional love. As I basked in the light of that Presence, I prayed to it, 'If You choose to keep this body alive, it is Yours to do with as You will. Please allow it to serve Your mission of love. Please always keep me with You.'

When I recovered, by God's grace, I began searching for ways to stay in communion with and service of that ineffable Presence. I encountered it in many paths. After some years of studying all religions, I was ordained as an interfaith minister by the Sufi Order of the West. With great joy, I conducted worship services and marriages drawing from the wisdom of all the prophets. I published a few inspirational books for people of all ages and faiths, including a little book called *Remember the Light*. At the same time, I was writing introductory college textbooks on many subjects – anthropology, sociology, art, biology, history, education, nutrition, nursing and, at last, a textbook on the religions of the world. I also began producing 'Earthcare', a series of radio programmes broadcast globally from the University of Peace in the mountains of Costa Rica. The programmes focused on solutions to the environmental problems we have created. Around the world, I sought out and interviewed great people from many walks of life – devotees and leaders of all religions, artists, scholars, economists, political figures, scientists, farmers, inventors, businesspeople. I shared their words over the air and in my books so that they might help to uplift others. My great desire in all of this was to bring us closer to the living presence of God, and closer to each other. But I was continually discouraged. I felt that there had to be a more powerfully transformative approach that would really advance us towards that state of perfection I remembered but had never seen in this troubled world.

Because this was my strong desire, and because God always answers prayers in which there is no self-interest but only faith and love and desire to serve, God eventually led me to the great saint Baba Virsa Singh (Babaji). When I went to interview him, I immediately recognized him as a living embodiment of that power, that light, that love that had surrounded me in the great tree and in the hospital room. He seemed very familiar. In his powerful and authentic spirituality and his practical work, he seemed to be the best solution to every problem the world was facing, for he embodied and could connect us to the truth, the power of God. As he continually tells us, it is only God who can transform our lives. It is only closeness to God that can bring peace and harmony to the world.

It is my good fortune that Babaji comes from the Sikh tradition. Before meeting him I knew very little about Sikhism, for Sikhs, having no interest in making converts, have not placed much emphasis on sharing their great treasure with people of other religions. In its pure original form, Sikhism is not even an institutionalized religion. It arose in Guru Nanak and his successors as genuine visionary experience of the presence of God. With that true visionary experience came their clear prophetic criticism of empty ritualism, of manipulation of the people for personal ends, and of divisive hatreds that have been propagated in the name of religions. As Baba Virsa Singh continually asserts:

> All religions are one. All the Prophets and Messiahs have repeatedly said that there is one God. There is one God, and we are to see God in every planet and person, in animals, oceans, mountains. But we will only be able to see God in all of God's Creation when the Love of God emerges within us.
>
> All the Prophets have come from the same Light; they all give the same basic messages. None have come to change the older revealed scriptures; they have come to remind people of the earlier Prophets' messages which the people have forgotten. We have made separate religions as walled forts, each claiming one of the Prophets as its own. But the Light of God cannot be confined within any manmade structures. It radiates throughout all of Creation. How can we possess it?
>
> None of the Prophets belongs to one caste, one creed, or one nation. Jesus is not a Christian; Moses is not a Jew; the Prophet Muhammad is not a Muslim; Guru Nanak is not a Sikh. They have not come to establish institutionalized religions. Those religions are created by humans, reflecting their own policies. By contrast, the Prophets come into the world with a message from God.
>
> Human beings do have spiritual wisdom deep within themselves; the One who creates the world is already sitting in their souls. But it is only when a Prophet of God comes down and starts speaking the divine wisdom that it becomes awakened in people. The Prophet reminds them of the Truth they know but have forgotten.[6]

The Sikh Gurus were prophets, reformers. They came to remind us of the truth revealed by the prophets of all religions and to lead us away from pointless ritualism. They did not claim to have the only way to God. The third Guru prayed, 'Oh Lord, the world is burning. Please protect it with your mercy. At whatever gate people can be saved, protect them there.'[7] The ninth Guru urged, 'Admit that all religions have been created by the God Whom you are praising.'[8]

However, the Sikh Gurus did emphasize that there is a straight and easy path to God: love. As Guru Gobind Singh wrote, 'Only those who have deeply loved God have realized God.'[9] The Gurus came to bring us back to realization of the formless, all-pervading Power who is, as the Gurus say, closer to us than our hands and feet. The distance between us and God is as thin as the wing of an insect.[10] But how do we part the curtain? Through continual remembrance of God, which in Sikh practice takes the form of meditation on a name of God (*Nam*).

Again and again the *Guru Granth Sahib*, the sacred scripture composed of hymns, affirms the transformative power of repetition of *Nam*. Many names are mentioned in the scripture; among them Narain (the One who is present in water), Ram, Sohand, Gobind, Hari and Allah. Some Christians repeat the Hail Mary; some the Jesus Prayer: 'Lord Jesus Christ, have mercy on me, a sinner.' Baba Virsa Singh offers a very powerful *Nam* to people of all religions: *Ik Onkar Sat Nam Siri Wahe Guru*. It can be translated as 'There is one God, whose name is Truth, praise to the One who is wondrous beyond words, who is Master of Light and Darkness.' We are encouraged to repeat it continually in our hearts, to let it clean our minds of all negative tendencies. It makes us fearless but humble; it transforms our lives. As Baba Virsa Singh explains:

> Reciting Nam is a way of thanking and praising the *Nami* – the omnipresent, timeless Creator. It is a path to God for everybody. When you recite Nam and love God without any selfish motives, God will cleanse your mind, there will be great light in your heart, and your whole family will be blessed. Nam will heal your mind, eliminating all negative thoughts; only positive thoughts will remain. The hidden joy and love and fearlessness in you will become manifest.[11]

Nam is 'an ocean of peace',[12] a priceless jewel placed in our hearts by the Guru.[13] It continually draws our awareness from the turmoil of the surface of life to the underlying reality. Remembrance of God's name is the light that sustains us in the darkness, the cooling shade from the terrible heat of the sun,[14] the supremely sweet nectar that quenches our desire.[15] Guru Nanak says:

> Filth is attached to the contaminated soul,
> Rarely does anyone quaff the Nectar of Nam . . .
> When I yoked my mind to the True Name,
> Then did I easily recognize my Lord.

If it please him, I would sing God's praises with the Guru.
How can I meet the Lord by being a stranger to him?[16]

Baba Virsa Singh himself is a stunning example of the power of *Nam*. As a boy, he was drawn to sit hour after hour, day after day, under a *Ber* (jujube) tree on his family's farm in a mud-brick village in the Punjab, Sarawan Bodla. Continually he cried out to God, 'Come! Come!' He had no spiritual teacher, only an inner longing for the Unseen. 'Please forgive me, please bless me!' he would cry, rubbing his nose against the ground until it bled. He did so much *tapasya* there that the very earth is still impregnated with powerful sacred vibrations. The leaves and fruits that fall from the tree and the dirt around its roots are revered for their healing properties.

At last his Guru appeared to him in a vision, as an ascetic youth with matted locks, and began instructing him. His Guru was none other than Baba Siri Chand, the renunciate elder son of Guru Nanak who lived to be 149 years old and taught the path of work, sharing and meditation to people of all faiths. Baba Siri Chand was an extremely powerful spiritual figure in his own right because of his continual meditation on God. The first thing he gave to the young Virsa Singh was *Nam – Ik Onkar Sat Nam Siri Wahe Guru*. As Babaji repeated it he developed the same spiritual powers as his teacher: the power to heal 'incurable' diseases, to bless the childless with offspring, to see throughout time and space with his enlightened inner vision, to transform minds and lives and turn them towards God, to awaken the light and wisdom of God that lie hidden within each of us. He developed the ability to communicate directly with crops and animals and learn from them which nutrients they needed.

As people began to discover Baba Virsa Singh's genuine spiritual power, he urged them not to become his followers but to work for the sake of others, overlooking superficial distinctions of caste and religion. In almost every speech he makes, he insists, 'We all have the same Father; we are all brothers and sisters.' Of himself, he says only:

I am just trying to be a better human being. Give all your love to God, and God will fill you with so much love that you can distribute it to all of humanity. Those who truly love God become full of kindness, love, and forgiveness, and God empowers their work. If you clear your mind and focus your scattered thoughts through meditation, God's power will help you in whatever department you work or whatever subject you study. Those people in whom truth arises become the real priests of God. Those who serve others become God's true ministers. They love God naturally. They put their egos aside and do not stand between the people and God. They tell us to love God.

Religion is the subject of the prophets and saints. They did a lot of research on this subject, and they focused a tremendous amount of energy in this direction. They devoted countless years, countless births, to sitting in God's laboratory. They concentrated for twenty-four hours a day. Then finally God spoke with them.[17]

Baba Virsa Singh is neither a self-proclaimed guru charging money to teach meditation, nor an intellectual speaking on the basis of book knowledge. He is a farmer who never learned to read. Nevertheless, he quotes continually from the scriptures and prophets of all religions to make his points about the truths of *dharam*, of closeness to God and righteous living that transcend all sectarian boundaries. He does not just talk about *dharam*; he practises it daily. In so doing, Babaji demonstrates the reality and the power of God. By reclaiming thousands of acres of barren lands in India and hundreds of thousands of barren souls, he is showing the world what happens when we have great love for and faith in God and are willing to work very hard for higher goals. On his farms, known collectively as Gobind Sadan (The House of God), he has inspired rich and poor to work side by side to transform wastelands into some of the most productive farms in India. The income from the farms is used to uplift the poor of all religions. Gobind Sadan offers them employment, food, free medical care, education, help in receiving government services, and spiritual inspiration according to their own religions. People come to Babaji from all walks of life, and he inspires them to love and live by the teachings of their own prophets, be they Jesus, Moses, Muhammad, Mahavira, Buddha, or the Sikh Gurus.

Babaji's life and work is a contemporary example of the basic teachings of Guru Nanak, who said that the straight path to God is to work hard, share with others, and always remember that it is God who is doing and giving everything. Babaji sees potential value in marshy, flood-prone, or desert-like areas that no one has tried to farm. He also sees the light and power of God hidden within people whom society has rejected.

Rather than seeking professional managers to staff his organization, Babaji empowers the lame, the mad, the weak to do the extraordinary. On his biggest farm, Shiv Sadan, which borders the River Ganges, it is a man with one crippled leg who wades through the mud of irrigated fields broadcasting seed by hand. It is a man with only an eighth-class education and one blind eye who runs the farm's tractor repair workshop so brilliantly that professional engineers with advanced degrees come for his guidance in spotting design flaws in their machines. It is a former madman who offers free, compassionate, and highly effective homeopathic treatment to the volunteers at Babaji's farm near Delhi. It is a woman in her seventies who rises every morning at 1.30 a.m., takes a cold bath, and spends the rest of the night singing the sacred devotions of the Sikh Gurus and vigorously cleaning the room that houses the *Guru Granth Sahib*. It is political figures who have risen quickly from lower positions to posts of great influence, working hard and honestly for the uplift of the people with no self-interest. All of them have been empowered by the *Nam* that Babaji gave them. All of them experience the power of God as a practical reality, not a theory.

Guru Gobind Singh, who has also instructed Baba Virsa Singh in vision, instituted very strong ideals and spiritual practices in his followers in order to make them saints and warriors for religious freedom. His father, Guru Tegh Bahadur, had bravely given his life for the sake of the freedom of Hindus from the forced conversion to Islam. The Mogul Emperor Aurangzeb, with the explanation that he was saving Hindus from 'idol worship', had ordered the destruction of hundreds of Hindu temples, prohibited the sacred riverbank cremations of dead Hindus, and so restricted the social rights of Hindus that thousands were converting daily to Islam in self-defence. This pressure was of course contrary to the clear statement of the Holy Qur'an: 'There can be no compulsion in religion.'[18] Hindu pandits asked the ninth Guru to help them, for he was known as the protector of the weak, helpless and downtrodden. He informed the Mogul Emperor Aurangzeb that the pandits would accept Islam if he did. Imprisoned by the Emperor, he refused to submit to conversion and offered his head without a murmur, for the sake of the religious practices of others, for the sake of freedom of religion. His love for God was so strong that he had no enmity towards anyone.

The ninth Guru's example of courageous devotion to the cause of religious freedom heartened the meek and oppressed people, and his son Guru Gobind Singh further built up their self-confidence through absolute faith in the power of God. He held before them the ideal of Khalsa, the 'pure'. Who is Khalsa? The one who 'does not criticize others, who does battle with and destroys the five enemies within himself (lust, anger, attachment, greed and ego), who incinerates his past karma with the fire of meditation, who renounces conceit and ego, who does not look at others with evil or lustful eye, and who ever contemplates and recites God's Name.'[19]

Sikh tradition, rightly understood, is universal. The *Guru Granth Sahib* is a beautiful compilation of ardent hymns not only from the Sikh Gurus but also from saints of Hindu and Muslim backgrounds, such as Kabir and Shaikh Farid. In it there is no dogma, no exclusive claims on truth. It encourages appreciation of all sacred scriptures. From start to finish, it is adoration of God and exhortations to remembrance of God. 'Sas, sas simro Gobind [Remember God with every breath]', urged Guru Arjun Dev.[20] He himself was tortured to death by the Mogul Emperor Jehangir, but he praised God to his last breath and never challenged the truth as revealed to the Prophet Muhammad in the Holy Qur'an. His writings, like the rest of the *Guru Granth Sahib*, are great devotional treasures that transcend all sectarian divisions. Reminding Sikh audiences of this universality, Babaji has asserted:

I am quite certain that Guru Gobind Singh did not make any one religion. He emphasized that God has no form, no features, no clan, no caste, no dress. From his enlightened vision, he saw that God is all-pervading, that His Light is falling on the whole world, and is also inside us. The mission of Guru Gobind Singh was not just for some few people of one religion. Guru Gobind Singh was the follower of the One All-Pervading God. That which we call dharam, that which we call Sikhism, that which we call the religion of Guru Nanak, that which we call the hukam of Guru Gobind Singh is this: That we should not forget God even for one breath.

Their enlightened vision was for the whole cosmos. Guru Granth Sahib is not for some handful of people; it is for everyone. I think if you study it carefully, you will understand that this scripture gives light to the very atmosphere, to the oceans, to the earth, to all of nature. It gives light to the whole universe because it is the voice of God, not the voice of any man. If it were the voice of humans, the product of meetings and ideas, then it could cause clashes. But it is the direct hukam of God, as revealed in vision.[21]

How then does Baba Virsa Singh feel we can all come together in interfaith harmony? Not by meetings, not by seminars, not by theology. Rather, Babaji urges us to develop our own inner visionary connection to God, through meditation. He also encourages us to return to the original scriptures of each tradition, cherishing them and being enlightened by them as the voice of God speaking directly to us through the prophets in a state of inspiration. We should read and share these original revelations and not change a single word, for with our limited understanding we may misinterpret them. These revealed scriptures are priceless, whereas words and interpretations from the minds of humans have little value and will never enlighten us.

Many of us do not really know or live by the teachings of our own prophets, much less the scriptures revealed to other prophets. But no prophet has ever taught hatred, Babaji assures us. One Christmas, Babaji said:

When great spiritual personalities are born into the world, people who are very faithful recognize them and learn from them. The prophets all bring the same message, the same lesson: love God, love human beings, love all creatures, love even the earth. But where will this love come from? We ourselves have no love. We will become full of love only when we love that Power whom Jesus called his Father.

Our limitation now is that we have turned religion into exclusive circles. In Jesus there was no one religion, for He was created from the Light, and that Light is guiding everything. That Light resides in the trees, in the earth, and in our hearts. So what meaning is there in those fortresses that we call religions? Why is there hatred in us? Why do we turn gurdwaras, temples, mosques and churches into fortresses, refusing to acknowledge other religions within those boundaries? We do this because we are ignorant.[22]

Under the inspiration of Baba Virsa Singh, we celebrate all religions, all prophets at Gobind Sadan. At Christmas we fill our communities with hundreds of oil lamps and candles, and garland images of Jesus. Pictures of Jesus are everywhere in Babaji's simple quarters because he has so much love for Jesus. We also offer our devotions to Mother Ganges, to Lord Shiva, to Lord Krishna, to Durga, and to Hanuman, who are considered Hindu deities. Every Tuesday is devoted to Hanuman. The women start at 2 a.m. to make hundreds of *rot*, thick flat rounds of sweetened bread, for distribution in Hanuman's honour to hundreds of poor villagers who come to Gobind Sadan. As in ancient Indian tradition, we keep sacred fire, or *havan*, continually burning, to bring the light of God into the dark corners of our hearts. We celebrate Diwali, the Hindu festival of light, with special foods, sweets, and multitudes of candles and oil lamps. Babaji has built special structures honouring the tombs of Muslim *pirs* (saints) on his farms, and pilgrims of all faiths keep them clean, offer flowers, and pay their respects to the *pirs* in sincere love for their great compassion and power. As Babaji teaches us, these *pirs'* places have been blessed by the light of God. We have celebrated *Id-ul-Fitr*, the end of Ramadan fasting, with great joy, and hundreds of Muslim peasants from the surrounding villages have come to share in a feast and to enjoy the ecstatic singing of Qawalis who are devoted to Baba Virsa Singh. On one of these occasions, Babaji gave a talk about the greater jihad, control of the raving mind. Mullas from the area compared Babaji's lecture with the Holy Qur'an and concluded that both were saying the same thing. We honour the birthdays of Guru Nanak, Guru Gobind Singh, and our great preceptor, Baba Siri Chand, who has instructed Babaji in the combination of hard work and profound meditation on God.

The prophets and their teachings are not the property of people of any one religion, Babaji instructs us:

> They are all our elders. They all come to love us. They come to remind people of dharam by making it fresh and new again; they come to teach love, to encourage service to humanity, to remove ignorance by enlightening people with the knowledge of God. They come to change our consciousness; they come to show us how to live.[23]

Those of us who are privileged to live near Babaji at Gobind Sadan do not wear the garb of monks or nuns. 'Our real dress is our inner dress,' Babaji emphasizes. Among us are landowners and peasants, writers of books and caretakers of buffaloes, the very old and the very young, of many religious backgrounds. We rise early in the morning for several hours of meditation, each according to their own internal timing and responsibilities, so that we can do battle with our own negativities and welcome the light of God. During the day, we work in the fields, kitchen and devotional areas so that we can not only support ourselves but also support others both materially and spiritually. We are imperfect examples of Babaji's teachings, but even so, we are a microcosm of a more harmonious world in which we are all truly brothers and sisters under the parenthood of God.

Notes

1. Guru Gobind Singh, *Dasam Granth*, p. 19.
2. Guru Nanak, 'Jap Ji Sahib', *Guru Granth Sahib*, p. 4, verse 20.
3. The Qur'an, 2:115.
4. Guru Gobind Singh, *Dasam Granth*, p. 16.
5. Guru Ram Das, *Guru Granth Sahib*, p. 527.
6. Baba Virsa Singh, *Loving God* (New Delhi: Gobind Sadan Publications, 1992), pp. 5, 7–8.
7. Guru Ram Das, *Guru Granth Sahib*, p. 853.
8. Guru Teg Bahadur, *Guru Granth Sahib*, p. 902.
9. Guru Gobind Singh, 'Sawayai', in 'Akal Ustat', *Dasam Granth*, p. 13, verse 9.
10. Guru Arjun Dev, *Guru Granth Sahib*, p. 624.
11. Baba Virsa Singh, *Loving God*, p. 18.
12. Guru Amar Das, *Guru Granth Sahib*, p. 28.
13. Guru Ram Das, *Guru Granth Sahib*, p. 696.
14. Guru Arjun Dev, 'Sukhmani Sahib', *Guru Granth Sahib*, p. 262.
15. Guru Nanak, *Guru Granth Sahib*, p. 688.
16. Ibid., p. 766.
17. Baba Virsa Singh, 'Bringing the Power of God to Your Life's Goal', an address given on 16 August 1994 at Gobind Sadan, New Delhi.
18. The Qur'an, 2:255.
19. Bhai Nand Lal, 'Tankha Nama', *Rahitname* (Amritsar: Bhai Chatar Singh Jiwan Singh, n.d.), p. 59.
20. Guru Arjun Dev, *Guru Granth Sahib*, p. 295.
21. Baba Virsa Singh, *News from Gobind Sadan*, May 1994, p. 4.
22. Baba Virsa Singh, 'The Spirit of Jesus Will Never Die', address given on 25 December 1991 at Gobind Sadan, New Delhi.
23. Baba Virsa Singh, *Loving God*, p. 8.

My Own Vision of the Ultimate: Why Am I an Eastern Orthodox Christian?

Metropolitan Paulos Mar Gregorios

Metropolitan Paulos Mar Gregorios, formerly a President of the World Council of Churches, is Metropolitan of Delhi and the North in the Malankara Orthodox Church.

WHY INDEED AM I an Eastern Orthodox Christian? Clearly, my own choice could only be part of the answer, since I come from a family whose Christian ancestry is traced, rightly or wrongly, to the Apostle St Thomas. I belong to a church that is presumably as old as any other Christian Church in the world, except perhaps the Mother Church of Jerusalem. The Apostle Thomas, one of the Twelve, is believed to have come to India around the middle of the first century, two decades after the crucifixion and resurrection of Jesus. Thomas died in India a martyr, and was buried in Mylapore, near Madras. The Eastern Orthodox community in Kerala has come through many vicissitudes of history, mainly as a result of aggression from Western missionaries, both Catholic and Protestant, but has survived to this day.

The choice was thus made for me, first by whoever was responsible for my being born in India to Christian parents and then by my parents, who decided that I should, like them and my four brothers, be baptized in the Malankara Orthodox Church as our Church is officially known. But subsequently I made that choice my own. I could have joined many other Churches, such as the Mennonite or the Presbyterian. I had the closest relations with the Mennonites when I was a college student (1950–2) at Goshen College, a Mennonite College in Indiana, USA. Or I could have joined the Presbyterian Church when I was a Bachelor of Divinity student (later converted to Master of Divinity) at Princeton Theological Seminary from 1952 to 1954. In fact most of my theological education has been in Protestant institutions (including Yale and Oxford), and my rather comprehensive exposure to Reformation thought has only helped to confirm my commitment to the apostolic tradition as maintained by the Oriental Orthodox Churches.

Later, during my five-year tenure as Associate General Secretary of the World Council of Churches in Geneva, I had occasion to visit and get to know at first hand almost all the main Churches of the Reformation and Eastern Orthodoxy, as well as to lead Bible Studies and conferences and seminars for them. Since most of the Protestant church leaders were also members of the Central Committee of the World Council of Churches, I got to know them personally. Even after leaving the staff of the WCC in 1967, I continued to associate myself with that body, as a member of the Central Committee, a member of the Executive Committee, and as one of its presidents from 1983 to 1991.

During these years I came to see quite clearly that the Eastern Orthodox

Church had been, in many things that matter, more faithful than others to the one apostolic tradition that we all profess. I also saw when that Eastern Orthodox tradition had been unfaithful – in its excessive and sometimes exclusive authority, in its basic failure to love humanity and serve it with everything at its disposal, and in its failure to come to terms with the cultural, spiritual and intellectual struggles and frustrations of the bourgeois capitalist industrial civilization that were sweeping over global humanity. I also saw the most unchristian power struggles going on among the Eastern Orthodox, to a certain degree more deplorably so than in the Churches of the West. Despite all these lapses in practice, my respect and love for the Eastern Orthodox tradition deepened during these years.

I have also exposed myself extensively to the Roman Catholic tradition, both through personal friendships with distinguished Roman Catholics and by fairly voluminous reading. During the sixties and seventies I had close relations with the Vatican, first as a Delegated Observer at the Second Vatican Council (1962–5) and later for twelve years as a founding member of the Joint Working Group of the World Council of Churches and the Roman Catholic Church. I knew personally Popes Paul VI and John Paul I, and likewise know the present incumbent, John Paul II. I have also worked closely with some of the leading theologians of the Roman Catholic Church, in the course of half a dozen unofficial conversations organized by the Pro Oriente Foundation in Vienna in the seventies and eighties between Oriental Orthodox and Roman Catholic theologians.

On Other Religions

I shall presently seek to put down briefly what in my own tradition I find most valuable, but let me add a word about other religions before I get to that point. You can very well ask me the question: being born an Indian, why are you not a Hindu in religion as well?

The answer first is that at no time in history have all Indians been Hindus. That label Hindu is a very late creation (eighteenth century?), and there never was a religion specifically labelled Hinduism until a couple of centuries ago. India has always been a multi-religious pluralistic society. Even before Jaina Mahavira and the Lord Buddha in the sixth century BC, not all Indians followed the same religion. There were the Sramanas, naked mendicant monks, the Ajivikas, the Adivasis with their own comprehensively religious approach to reality; there were also the predecessors of what later turned out to be Tantrics, Shaivites and Vaishnavites, and of the many *bhakti* cults that arose in India from time to time. Most of these did not accept the authority of the Vedas. The Brahmans, who came to dominate the Sanatana Dharma later, were originally newcomers, a distinct minority of immigrants from Central Asia, who later climbed to the top niche of the caste structure they created and reinforced with a thousand-year process of further small group migrations from Central Asia. In this respect Brahmanism is as foreign to the Indian tradition as any other religion. But it too was accepted and domesticated here after many quite violent struggles.

In India today we acknowledge eight great religions, four largely of Indian origin (Buddhism, Jainism, the Sanatana Dharma or the religion of the Vedas and Upanishads, and Sikhism) and four introduced from outside (Judaism, Christianity, Zoroastrianism and Islam), all of West Asian origin. All these eight religions are fully Indian. Even Islam, which came in last, has been here for twelve centuries. Attempts to brand the latter four as non-Indian or 'foreign' have found supporters only among the fanatic followers of a fascist Hindutva of the Sangha Parivar variety.

If there is one thing we can surely say about India's cultural heritage, it is that that heritage has never been uniform or non-religious. I grew up as a Christian in the midst of that heritage; I went to a school where about a third were Christians, the others following Islam or different varieties of Sanatana Dharma. As a child I was not brainwashed by Western missionary thinking forcing me to regard and condemn non-Christians as unsaved.

In fact our community developed its own myths of religious co-existence, not just tolerance for other religions that some advocate, but genuine fraternal friendship with people of other faiths. For example, in my childhood I had my Sunday School lessons in a nearby church, St George's Orthodox Church, Karingachira. During the feast of St George huge church processions (with the cross and white banner of the resurrection) were taken out through the streets of our town. The Vishnu Temple in my town also had similar processions with the image of Vishnu in front. There was always danger of communal clashes as the Hindu procession entered predominantly Christian areas or vice versa, since both communities were equally prone to the evils of triumphalism.

So the myth our community developed, shocking perhaps to Western Christians, held that St George and the Lord Vishnu were blood brothers. I may not have quite believed it as a child, but it helped create the right attitude towards my Hindu brothers and sisters. Muslims were also regarded as brothers and sisters of Christians, sharing together the once honorific title of *Mapillas* or *Mahapillais* – or 'great scribes'. So I grew up as a child with fraternal feelings for people of other religions. I knew something about their practices, but little about their deeper faith and understanding.

That knowledge, such as it is today, had to be developed in the forty years since 1954 when I returned from Princeton, revolting against the cultural arrogance and intellectual parochialism of Western Christianity. I began engaging in dialogues between Christians and Hindus, mostly organized by Christians. I remember particularly one in Stanley Jones's Sat Tal Ashram up in the Himalayas. There were the usual polite papers, in which each religion tried to prove that it was more right than the other, and putting on false poses of universal charity and general benignness. But the best breakthroughs came during the coffee breaks. Two

I remember vividly.

One was a question and comment from a Hindu university professor. He asked me rather bluntly, 'You seem to have some measure of honesty about you. Can I ask you the question: why do you Christians want to have dialogue with Hindus? You have largely failed in your fire and thunder evangelism to convert us Hindus. Is not dialogue your new technique to get our ear, so that you can try to convert us in a devious way?' Unfortunately most of the Protestant and Roman Catholic literature on dialogue seems to give ground for the Hindu friend's suspicion of Christian motives in dialogue.

I decided that day that I would accept two principles for Christian dialogue with people of other faiths. The first was the principle of maximum transparency. Christians should have no hidden motives for dialogue with people of other faiths. They are all people whom Christ loves and for whom He gave His life. I decided that the love of Christ for all humanity must be the propelling motive for dialogue, though other motives such as the affirmation of, and concern for, the unity of humanity, and the need for pluralistic but harmonious local, national and global communities could be a subsidiary motive. But no hidden motive to convert the other. The second principle was that in interreligious dialogue no religion should claim any superiority. In dialogue all are on the same plane, respectfully listening to and learning from each other. You may be convinced that your religion is the only true one. But do not make any claims of superiority over others on that ground. We are all equally contingent and dependent on God's grace and mercy, whether we be Hindus, Christians or Muslims, whether some of us acknowledge that grace and mercy or not.

I spoke above about Christ's love for all humanity. In that connection I must narrate another coffee-break experience in dialogue. Again it was a Hindu friend who engaged me in one-to-one dialogue. 'You seem to be tough enough to take this,' his preamble immediately put me on guard. 'I want to tell you what images go through my Hindu mind, when you Christians talk to us about your "Christian love" for Hindus. I visualize a giant spider, oozing out from the pores of its skin quantities of gooey fluid, called Christian love, and skilfully weaving a glorious web in which it wants to catch me, an unsuspecting Hindu fly.' I was shocked, but kept my cool, for I knew he had justification for the allegation. The Christian love, which came out in the form of charity or of useful social institutions such as hospitals, schools and orphanages, was still governed by the motives of 'witnessing to Christ' and of making Christianity attractive. It may be unfair to regard all Christian social work as an advertisement for the gospel, but non-Christians do see it that way much too frequently.

It was only in about 1967, when I left the staff of the WCC in Geneva and returned to my country and church, that I began taking up the issue of dialogue with people of other faiths more seriously. I saw the damage done to the image and reality of the Christian Church by the unchristian attitude towards other religions fostered by reformed thinkers such as Barth, Brunner and Kraemer. They were speaking out of their cultural parochialism rather than from any genuine Christian insight, it seemed to me.

One of the first achievements was the setting up of a sub-unit on Dialogue with People of Other Faiths in the WCC. We were able to secure the services of a first-rate Indian Christian, Dr Stanley Samartha, to head that unit. He did a masterful job. Despite the strong inhibitions of a culturally narrow-minded European Church, we were able to organize several small significant interfaith consultations, which laid down some of the rules and principles for fair and honest interreligious dialogue. We also ventured into the experience of praying meaningfully with people of other religions in the course of these seminars and consultations. This caused a lot of furore in European Christian circles, and I remember how a friend of mine, a German professor, the late Dr Margull, almost lost his chair in the university, on the charge that he, a Christian, had participated in the prayer services of Muslims. But we kept plugging away quietly, until it all came to a head in the Assembly of the World Council of Churches in 1975, in Nairobi, Kenya.

Some of us presumed, especially in the Dialogue Working Group of the WCC, that the time was ripe to test the claim of Dietrich Bonhoeffer that Christianity, especially European Christianity, had come of age. At the Nairobi Assembly of 1975, we invited a select number of observers from the great religions of the world and devoted a whole section of the Assembly to interreligious dialogue, in the hope that along with the environmental issue being highlighted at Nairobi, the issue of cultural pluralism and interreligious dialogue would move from the margins of the WCC agenda to its centre. I was asked to chair that section on dialogue, with our distinguished non-Christian friends present.

Our hopes were soon to be dashed on the hard rocks of European cultural parochialism. In response to my presidential remarks, a friend of mine, a Norwegian Lutheran bishop, asked me, 'In what sense does the Chairman find the revelation in Jesus Christ so insufficient that he has to go to the non-Christians to learn the truth?'

I was offended, but being in the chair, could not retort in my usual rude manner. So I responded, 'In this sense that the Chairman is not as fortunate as his friend the bishop from Norway, who seems to have so mastered the revelation in Jesus Christ, that he is so totally self-satisfied and does not feel any need to learn from others.' I doubt that the barb got through. But my non-Christian friends saw for themselves the shameful narrow-mindedness of European Christianity. They were hurt, but kept their cool and continued to be polite.

The Assembly decided that the WCC was not to engage in any more multi-religious dialogue, but to stick with bilateral dialogues in which Christians kept the control. The Nairobi Assembly disillusioned me, and I came to the conclusion that neither forms of Western Christianity, Roman Catholic or Protestant, were mature enough to engage in dialogue Christians could not control and manipulate. I am not claiming that Eastern Orthodox Christianity is more mature or more open in this regard. In fact it is only in contrast with the dry scholasticism and exclusivistic dogmaticism of Eastern Orthodoxy that we can see Western Christianity in a better light.

A Crisis of Confidence

Anyway, the process was begun by which I lost confidence in the leadership of the Western Church – Protestant, Roman Catholic or Sectarian. And my own Eastern Orthodoxy was lost on the margins of humanity, quixotically and uncomprehendingly struggling against many hostile forces on all sides – Islam in the Middle East, aggressive Roman Catholic, Protestant and Sectarian proselytizing missions everywhere, atheist communism in Eastern and Central Europe, and liberal secularism reaching out globally with its bloodsucking tentacles. Eastern Orthodoxy developed a barricade psychology of self-defence by sheer negativity, smug in its pettiness, making tall claims about its monopoly on Christian truth, and yet unable to communicate with either the modern world or even with its own youth and laity (including the alienated Orthodox women).

In 1983 the Vancouver Assembly had chosen me to be one of its presidents, a desperate move on the part of the WCC establishment to keep me out of power in its policy making and running. A president of the WCC is always a decorative figure, supposed to represent the WCC on unimportant public occasions, a senior figure who generally keeps out of all controversy. I was the only legitimate candidate to be moderator of the Central Committee, since no one from the Orthodox tradition had been allowed to be general secretary or moderator up till that time, and only the general secretary's post is more powerful than that of the moderator.

I was aware of the antics of power brokering behind the scenes in Vancouver. Philip Potter had been general secretary for some time, and he wanted only a docile and malleable moderator. He chose a Scottish schoolmaster, with neither knowledge of the World Church nor the basic theological competence needed, as his candidate for moderator. He told me, with a measure of defiance shining through his eyes, that that was his choice and that he was going to get him elected, in the teeth of all opposition. He also announced to me that my name was being proposed as one of the presidents. I tried to advise him that he was unlikely to get his candidate for moderator elected. He told me that he would 'show me'. He also wanted his confidant and adviser, Deputy General Secretary Professor Konrad Reiser of Germany, to be his own successor as general secretary when his term ended in a year or so.

It was one of those rare occasions in the WCC when I entered the fray of power brokering. I thought it would be disastrous for the WCC to have the power combination of Potter, Reiser and the Scottish schoolmaster. The Orthodox would feel left out totally. So I acted. And it worked. The Central Committee rejected the general secretary's proposal, and by a muddled process chose the German Praeses Joachim Held as moderator. That dashed to the ground Konrad Reiser's chances for the succession, at least for the time being, since a German moderator and a German general secretary was an unacceptable combination.

With that I became cynical of the WCC as a 'privileged instrument' of the ecumenical movement. There seemed to be more dirty politics in that Christian body than in most nation-states. I served as president until the Canberra Assembly in 1991, but I was systematically kept out of all important decision making, and was seldom allowed to represent the WCC at any important public function. Whenever I announced that I was going to do something on my own, not as president, the establishment grew fearful and tried to stop or circumvent me. When I announced for example that I was going to Managua for the sixth anniversary of Nicaragua's liberation, they decided to send two more presidents and additional persons to hedge me. They were afraid I would say something inappropriate in favour of the Sandinistas.

I did in Managua what I thought was right. In the first place I went to the place where Foreign Minister d'Escotto was fasting in protest against the American threat of aggression and sanctions. I spent a day with him, fasting in sympathy. I saw President Daniel Ortega, and asked him very politely why the Sandinistas had been so racist and mean in their treatment of the Misquito Indians. I still remember Ortega standing up from his presidential chair, and with bowed head saying to me, 'I confess before God and before you that the Sandinistas did wrong. We are doing everything possible to recompense the Misquitos.'

I went to other Central American countries such as El Salvador and the Dominican Republic and visited the people who were being tortured and massacred by powerful pro-US fascist forces. I made a firsthand report on what I saw to the Central Committee meeting in Argentina, and the resolution on Central America was approved without any discussion, partly because of the heavy emotional impact of my report.

I was very grieved that the progressive Latin American Christians, who deplored the oppression in Central America, were not aware of what they themselves had done to the original natives of that continent. Even the so-called liberation theologians are still today unable to establish rapport with the indigenous people whom they have uprooted and decultured.

The net result of my rather extensive ecumenical experience is that I have not been able to spot one Christian Church in the world that is even half faithful to the way of the cross and to the teaching of the Apostles. I have gradually begun to look outside the Christian Church, to see what God is doing.

Where Is History Going?

I see the demand for full manifestation of the freedom and dignity of all human beings – men, women and children – as a major thrust still in the march of history. I see the interreligious movement and the women's movement as significant aspects of the advance of human history. I can conceive of the peace movement with a socialist commitment as bound to come back soon into the centre of things, as the contradictions in the single market global economy begin to reveal themselves more manifestly, quite possibly leading to a world-wide economic crash. Above all I am convinced that until humanity sees that the secular civilization, which denies the centrality of God, has been the greatest mistake in our history, it cannot find the way forward.

I see that I cannot put my trust either in Christian Church activities, or in the work of governments and intergovernmental agencies such as the UN, to begin to lead humanity in the way it has to go. That leadership has to come from groups of committed people of all religions and of no professed religion, in all countries and on all continents, working to enlighten the awareness of people and mobilize their power to act in the best interests of humanity.

My Vision – My Faith

Let me now conclude with a confession of my faith and a brief reference to the vision that impels me, even in my seventy-third year.

I know that the created order is in the hands of God. He brought it into being out of nothingness. It is His will that still maintains it in existence. And that will is good. There is no trace of evil in it. So I shall not be daunted by evil, or be stymied by fear of evil. The good is true; it alone is true and everything else must find dissolution in its own time.

I belong to that created order, but am by no means the centre of it; everything else and everyone else shares in the destiny of creation, which is good. But the separation of good from evil causes not only both joy and peace, but also pain and suffering. That separation happens throughout history, but it will take place in a special way at the 'harvest' – the final consummation and summing up of all history, which happens beyond history.

The created order came into being through the Son; he became the Son of Humanity, part of our human destiny and the destiny of the created order, sharing our kind of peace and joy, and also our kind of pain and suffering. Him I adore; Him I love; He is neither male nor female, though I use the male personal pronoun, since we are yet to create a common personal pronoun in the English language. His I am, and that is my fulfilment. I trust in Him; He is my hope, my compass and my anchor. He is the destiny of the created order.

I need to learn from all, and have indeed learned from many. My major liberation in life has been from thinking that the Western way of thinking, with its specific categories and modalities, is the only way to think and to know. Now that I know a little bit about the Yin–Yang polarity–complementarity way of thinking and knowing in the Chinese Tao, I do not have to be a slave of the Western subject–object mode of thinking, and the logic of the excluded middle. From my own Indian tradition I have learned the principle of *Ekam advitiyam* or One without a Second; I know now that all diversity and difference ultimately find their unity in the One without a Second; that One is more ultimate than the many. My own Eastern Orthodox tradition has confirmed that there is no creation other than God or outside God, because the Infinite Ultimate has neither outside nor other.

I have learned from the Jains the great *Anekanthavada*, which holds that all statements are conditional and qualified truth, which have to be supplemented and completed by other truths; that our *Ahimsa* or non-violence should extend to other ways of thinking, and not just to other beings.

I have learned from Buddhists that all epistemology is finally without basis; that our perceptions of all things, including the world, are but mental events that happen when our kind of mind-sense and whatever is out there come into contact with each other; that this world which the secular mindset takes to be some kind of ultimate reality is neither real nor unreal, and should be taken seriously, but not so absolutely.

And I have learned much from Jews and Arabs, from Sikhs and Zoroastrians, from Adivasis and Aborigines, from Africans and from the indigenous peoples of America. And I hope I am still learning and will continue to do so until the end.

I have also learned a lot from the communists – that most avowedly atheistic wing of the European Enlightenment; I have learned from their weaknesses and failures just as much as from their apparent successes. I cultivated them especially for two reasons: (a) their social goals were more compatible with the Christian idea of a just society than that of liberalism and its capitalist ideology; (b) my Christian brothers and sisters in the West, especially the Roman Catholic Church, but also Protestants, were vilifying everything the communists were doing. I found anti-communism anti-Christian, and therefore decided to associate and work with the communists so long as they were committed to just societies in which oppression and exploitation was reduced to a minimum and in which all human beings could live with freedom and dignity.

Alas, the communists became as dogmatic, corrupt and power hungry as the Roman Catholic Church and dug their own graves. But I still remain committed to socialism as the nearest alternative to the just society I am envisaging as a Christian.

And I have learned much from the Eastern Orthodox heritage: that Eucharistic worship and adoration with thanksgiving are the primary responses to what God has done in Christ – not preaching or witnessing; that the Christian life in the community is more important than Christian talking and doing; that the

Christian's personal life is not an individual matter, but the work of the Holy Spirit in the community of faith; that the Holy Spirit of God has been at work in the whole creation from its very inception, and is still at work, not just in the Church, but in the whole universe, bringing it to fulfilment according to God's plans; that I can trust the Triune God to fulfil the created order according to His plans, despite many apparent failures and regressions. I am privileged to be initiated, by baptism-chrismation, into the great mystery of the universe as God guides it to its destiny.

The vision that beckons defies human word and concept: the mind cannot envision what God has set in store for creation. That destiny is good without mitigation, pure joy in love, peace in community with all, ecstasy without triumph, sweeter than anything our mind and senses can now enjoy. The human mind can neither conceive of nor imagine what God has set in store for us and for all creation. Our fantasy and our imagination cannot soar so high. Even when we finally experience it, it will be beyond all language and concept.

It is the Spirit that assures me of this. And the Spirit leads me there. That Spirit, we have a foretaste of here. Only a feeble foretaste. The reality will surpass all present hope and human expectation.

Glory be to the Father, and to the Son, and to the Holy Spirit, one true God, for ever and ever. Amen.

RELIGIOUS CHOICE IS NOT EXCLUSIVE

Dr Elizabeth Harris

Dr Elizabeth Harris is a Methodist local preacher and is a post-doctoral research scholar and teacher of Buddhism at Westminster College, Oxford.

I WAS BORN into a Christian family and remain a Christian. As a child, Protestant Christianity moulded me, not as enforced dogma but as a gentle and loving force. All my choices in adulthood have inevitably been conditioned by this, both those made in rebellion against the past and those that have grown in harmony with it. No human being, except one who is fully enlightened, can make unconditioned choices about religion. The religious symbols and insights that challenge the core of my being flow from the totality of my life experience. If I had been born within another religion or culture, my pilgrimage would have been different. For no one religion has a monopoly over life-giving spirituality. To claim so is arrogance. It leads to the misrepresentation, distortion, even demonization of religious paths not one's own. I know this from experience, since choice has taken me into the heart of Buddhism. I can now feel equally at home in a Christian church and a Buddhist shrine room. Buddhist vocabulary interleaves and challenges my experience of Christianity. By saying that I remain Christian, therefore, I do not imply that I have rejected or judged inadequate the choices of others. The reverse is true. Any analysis of my own religious vision must include both Buddhist and Christian insights. For I believe that the different religions of the world are allies rather than rivals – rich in their diversity and capable of helping each to reinterpret itself.

The diversity of religious practices can make religion seem like so many stalls in a market place offering numberless answers to the basic question of why we are alive in a world of pain. Choice might seem nothing more than taking the path that works for us. Yet, it is not so simple. At the heart of religious choice is not only the claims of one religion over another, but how we interpret the religion we choose or find ourselves within. There can be equally large differences of opinion within one religion as between religions. No religion is a hegemonic unity. Each responds to historical currents and socio-economic changes. Christianity has been used to justify socialism and capitalism, pacifism and war, accumulation of wealth and voluntary poverty, imperialism and liberation struggles, apartheid and pluralism. My own interpretation of Christianity has not remained static. If there had only been the exclusivist interpretation I accepted as a teenager, I would no longer be a Christian. Choice would have taken me far from church walls. Both life experiences and inner intuition would have led to rejection. Yet, I have not rejected Christianity, although I am critical of some of its expressions. This is because the great world religions hold within them the capacity to provide new riches to explorers within them. To explain how this had happened to me, I shall begin with some key life experiences and the values that have flowed from them. Then I will pass to the elements within Buddhism and Christianity that mould my present religious vision.

As the daughter of a Methodist minister my childhood involved movement. Every four or five years I had a new home, a new school, the challenge of making new friends. In adulthood I've not been able to escape this pattern. A wish to 'know' through experience has seemed to dictate change, travel, a concern to cross boundaries – not to experience for the sake of experience but to widen my awareness of what makes humans function. I've never been tempted to swim the channel, hang-glide, take the controls of a plane, even ski. Rather, what has always excited me has been variety both within human culture and in the physical world. Whether it was crossing America from east to west and from north to south as a student, working in Jamaica for two years as a young teacher or eventually encouraging others to cross cultural boundaries as an executive secretary of Christians Abroad, the pattern of my life has placed great emphasis on exploration within the context of international understanding. Always, I placed this in the context of my Christian faith. Proselytization was not uppermost, far from it. Solidarity with the whole of God's Creation, partnership across race and the need for just relationships between rich and poor nations was what concerned me. All, I felt then, had a spiritual content.

The culmination of this was in 1986 when I gained a World Council of Churches scholarship to study Buddhism in Sri Lanka. My time at Christians Abroad had come to a natural end and my commitment to cross-cultural encounter had developed into a wish to explore religious divides also. A short visit to Sri Lanka in 1984 had sparked sympathy with the country, but my comfortable assumption that I would be away for a year's sabbatical was ripped apart. I stayed seven and a half years, the longest I've worked anywhere. Primarily, my time in Sri Lanka was a 'letting go'. I travelled with the wish not only to study Buddhism but to enter it, to let go of my Christian conditioning as much as possible so that I could see the world through Buddhist eyes. I sought to free myself from the strait-jacket of my previous religious concepts. I didn't want to eradicate them – I simply offered them hibernation. The process wasn't easy. It cannot be romanticized. It took place within a country of tremendous beauty, hospitality and richness, but one that was also racked by war, terrorism, human rights abuse and poverty. There were times of disorientation and anguish, but also an awareness of the richness of the world's religious heritage, a conviction that immersion within Buddhism was necessary for understanding, and a personal awareness that I could only benefit and grow through 'letting go' kept me going. The whole experience pushed my spirituality onto a different plane by opening it to a new vocabulary – a vocabulary still developing.

The experience of Sri Lanka increased my awareness of opposites at the centre of reality: beauty and ugliness; hope and despair; equality and injustice; contentment and anguish; affluence and poverty; acceptance and rejection; relationship and loneliness – in other words, of heaven and hell. At the age of ten, I can remember declaring to my mother after a children's rally at a local church that I would follow Jesus and escape the fires of hell. I shudder now to think of the teaching that rally must have given! For heaven and hell blaze through the present. They are not the sole property of the future, nor is one or the other the sole fate of any one religion.

I now realize that it was this awareness that was informing my spirituality as a child and adult. Whether it was the rejection I sometimes felt as a child because I was a little plump or a minister's kid; or the intense exhilaration that has come to me as mists form and re-form on a mountain top or waves crash on a beach; or the extremes of poverty and wealth I opted to expose myself to in the Caribbean and then in Africa and Asia; or the barbarism of war and terrorism I chose to become vulnerable to in Sri Lanka; or the beauty and pain of love, in all these I have always been aware that happiness is elusive, or rather that life and religion are more than the search for happiness. So, religious paths that stress personal fulfilment only have never appealed to me. Charismatic ecstasy has even repelled me and the search for an intellectually satisfying truth has somehow seemed inadequate. Now, I can say that authentic religion or spirituality must help humans to interpret and face the reality of opposites, of pain and joy. It must help us to enter rather than to escape this reality from a point of security and strength and with the will to work for a better world.

Buddhism eventually spoke to the depths of this spiritual search after I began to study and practise it. The Buddha's invitation four hundred years before the Common Era was 'Come and See' – 'See if the message I give explains reality to you, see if it provides relief to your pain.' His emphasis was empirical and pragmatic and at the centre was the fact of suffering – *dukkha*. The reality of *dukkha*, of an essential unsatisfactoriness within life, was something I never found difficult to appreciate, especially in the context of war in Sri Lanka. Yet, there were some emphases of my Buddhist teachers that I did find hard to cope with. Choice between different interpretations was necessary.

I can remember one meditation session when the leader, a Buddhist monk, said, 'Do you want things to be changed? Are you content with things as they are?' My first reaction was, 'Yes, of course, I want things to change, in myself and in the world.' But my thought did not meet his. He was talking about the need to accept things as they are, in the present, without craving for something new and different to gratify our senses and he was speaking out of the very core of Buddhism. The Four Noble Truths point out the nature of reality and then give the cause – *tanha* or craving. The ordinary, non-religious person is seen as enmeshed in a web of *tanha*, continually placing confidence in what can never bring happiness because of its impermanence. Part of this is the relentless search for new experiences, different sense pleasures, more impressive possessions or totally satisfying relationships. Suffering will end when this craving is torn out by the roots, the Buddha insisted, when the almost obsessive urge of the ego for self-gratification, self-promotion and self-protection is seen as a phantom based on ignorance. My Buddhist meditation teacher was right to insist that becoming mindful of the present and accepting it is an essential part of the process. However, from it has grown what I feel is a distortion – that the practice of Buddhism is essentially individualistic, stressing non-involvement with society. It was when I realized through textual study and Sri Lankan Buddhist friends that this paradigm was a distortion that Buddhism flowered for me as a religious path which could help me both interpret reality and become meaningfully involved in it.

So, let me share how Buddhism has spoken to me, how it has informed, challenged and enriched my spirituality. Firstly, my reading of the Pali texts brought me into contact with a teacher I could respect. Although the sermons of the *Sutta Pitaka* were mediated in a stylized way to facilitate oral transmission, I found a person emerging from them – a down-to-earth, no-nonsense person who cut through the prejudices, confusions and arrogant posturing of others with compassion and directness. The Buddha's approach was empirical and non-dogmatic and it appealed to me. The well-known illustration of a man wounded by an arrow is important here. The Buddha compared those who came to him tortured by abstract metaphysical questions about the nature of the universe to a person critically wounded by an arrow, who, instead of removing the arrow, first demanded such things as where the arrow came from and who shot it. More important than wrangling over belief statements concerning the form of the universe, the Buddha insisted, was tackling the immediate, empirical problems of human pain and social disharmony. His was a non-dogmatism, which pointed out that clinging to views, theories and 'isms' could lead to contention, violence and war.

This empirical approach I found refreshing. It made me realize that religious discourse that concentrates solely on conceptual definition of metaphysical reality is rarely meaningful or practically useful. It concerns questions of ultimate truth about which humans cannot hope to gain consensus. It may pander to our yearning for secure belief systems but it does not do much to improve the world. It may satisfy the mind but it does not address the totality of human need. Religious truth, I suggest, has more to do with a religion's ability to interpret the conditioned reality of human experience and human dis-ease than with its perceived closeness to abstract truth.

Many nineteenth-century British missionaries who worked within countries where the majority was Buddhist condemned Buddhism as pessimistic and fatalistic; pessimistic because of the First Noble Truth, the Truth of *dukkha* or suffering; fatalistic because it seemed to insist that present events were determined by past actions. I believe they were mistaken and have argued elsewhere that the Christian Church in places such as Sri Lanka was built on a distortion of Buddhist doctrine.[1]

For Buddhism impresses me as realistic and even optimistic and it is the reason for this optimism that is important. At the core of Buddhism is *paticcasamuppada* or dependent origination.

The traditional formulation of *paticcasamuppada* is:

> When this is, that is
> This arising, that arises
> When this is not, that is not
> This ceasing, that ceases.

In other words, it insists that everything has a cause and that when the cause is identified and eradicated, the effect will evaporate. Obvious, some might say. Yes, but it is also revolutionary. Neither chance nor coincidence is recognized. The interdependence of all phenomena through cause and effect is stressed. Only nirvana, the Buddhist goal of existence, is unconditioned. Within this is the conviction that through analysis and action, humans can change themselves and the world. It accords with the central Buddhist insight that nothing *samsara*, the round of rebirth, is permanent, neither war nor peace, poverty nor riches. It means that Buddhists can joyfully take refuge in the Buddha, the *dharma* and the *sangha* with faith and hope that liberation is possible, that no situation is beyond change.[2]

Craving, *tanha*, is the cause of pain highlighted in the Four Noble Truths. This is the reality the Buddha continually stressed when pointing to the empirical. It is a generic term with numerous nuances and forms. Christians have been guilty of narrowing it for their own polemical purposes, translating it as 'desire' and then concluding that, if the aim of Buddhism was the eradication of desire, then it logically meant that Buddhists were working towards complete indifference to human feeling, complete detachment. Buddhism certainly speaks of non-attachment (*viraga* or *viveka*). These terms are closely connected with the eradication of *tanha* and the related terms – greed and hatred (*lobha* and *dosa*). Yet the non-attachment of Buddhism is non-attachment to such things as greed, selfishness, jealousy and spite – all the elements of the human personality that contribute to disharmony, strife and communal breakdown. The eradication of craving is the eradication of the selfish greed that tears apart human society. Parallels can be drawn between *tanha* and the Christian concept of sin, but they are not the same. For me, *tanha* has become a very powerful tool in my analysis of reality, and central to this is my awareness that the Buddha did not say that every situation was conditioned by craving in the same way.

One strand of teaching in contemporary Buddhist meditation centres is that the only world we have to be concerned about is the world within us, the workings of our mind. But this does not do justice to the way in which the eradication of *tanha*, craving, is presented in the Pali texts or the way it has been lived over two and a half thousand years within Buddhist societies. To take the texts first, the sermons within the _Sutta Pitaka_ often speak to the individual with the message – purify your mind, penetrate the roots of ego-obsession in your own thinking. Yet, the texts also present paradigmatic illustrations of the way in which the ignorance and craving of one person or group can set off chains of violence in which others become victims through no immediate fault of their own.

I have frequently mentioned the _Cakkavatti Sihanada Sutta_ in my teachings and writing.[3] Through a mythological story, it shows a society sliding into chaos and brutal anarchy. Laws lose their force. Families disintegrate. Eventually, people look at one another as wild beasts and indulge in mutual slaughter. What is significant is that the finger of blame is not laid on the mental processes of the citizens. It is pointed at the king or the state that, in wilful disobedience of advice given, does not give resources to the poor. It is the state machinery, institutionalized craving if you like, that causes breakdown. The message is that societies are interdependent units and that injustice spreading from the top will affect the freedom and objectivity with which others act.

At the end of the myth, the people themselves take their future in their hands. A few citizens suddenly have their eyes opened to the horror of mutual bloodletting and go into meditative retreat for seven days. They then emerge with clear vision, embrace each other in loving kindness and begin to rebuild society in an attitude of complete involvement. This myth lies at the heart of the Buddhism that has spoken to me. It presents impermanence as an optimistic rather than a pessimistic quality. It highlights the dangerous consequences of craving or ignorance present within state structures. It illustrates the interdependence of all elements within society and the need for just relationships, individual mind-culture and community action. What I have glimpsed of traditional Buddhist society tells me that this is the paradigm it has lived by. Harmony flowing from a just state, generosity and ethical living within interactive and interdependent communities, social action to maintain harmony, devotional life and meditation – these are all important. This vision has been an inspiration to me. Its opposite, the barbarism reached in the _Cakkavatti Sihanada Sutta_, is also one of the most powerful pictures I know of the dangerous dynamics of _tanha_, and contemporary parallels are not hard to find.

Before passing to Christianity, there are two other aspects of Buddhism that I must stress further – meditation and compassion. Both have influenced my spirituality. At the core of meditation in the Theravada tradition is mindfulness (_sati_) and bare attention. As we react to the demands and pressures of life, thoughts, feeling and states of mind follow one another in quick succession, conditioned by a lifetime of learnt responses. Usually, we function without reflecting on this, blithely assuming that our thoughts are completely under our wise control. Mindfulness within meditation seeks to break through this assumption by encouraging the focusing of bare, unjudgemental attention on all that is happening within the mind and the body. Absolutely anything is allowed to surface, whether 'demons' repressed for many decades or immediate reactions to sounds or bodily sensations. Nothing is judged bad or good. Nothing is clung to as 'mine'. Everything is watched and allowed to pass. Such practice is hard work. It is the very reverse of making the mind bland – a stereotype sometimes projected onto Buddhist meditation. I have found that it can lead to far greater self-knowledge as we glimpse why anger, for instance, rises or the wish to impress and, more fundamentally, that the thoughts we consider 'ours' are conditioned and impermanent. In Buddhist terms it is a practice that develops insight (*vipassana*). It also spills over into everyday life in a process Buddhism calls 'guarding the doors of the senses'. Christianity does not have a parallel system of mind-culture. It needs it. The *Spiritual Exercises* of St Ignatius may be closest and they have been of help to me in the past, but it is Buddhism that has given me the most valuable path towards understanding the depths of my own mind.

My years in Sri Lanka were some of the most bloody in Sri Lanka's history. I watched the process of increasing militarization and cheapening of life with horror as two wars gripped the country, one in the north and one in the south.[4] Certain friends were killed and others I was close to lived under continual threat. I could not have coped with the pain involved in this if it had not been for an awareness of compassion at the heart of reality – the awareness that my pain and that of my friends was part of cosmic pain, but that there was a positive force that was stronger than it. I found that it wasn't only Christianity that could give me this realization.

Compassion is the sister of wisdom in Buddhism. The enlightened person is both wisdom and compassion embodied. The devotional reverence given to images of the Buddha in Sri Lanka is not worship of a living spirit or godhead. But it does involve reverence for the ultimate symbol of compassion. It involves knowledge that at the heart of *dukkha*, suffering, lies compassion and loving kindness. Theravada Buddhism does not officially recognize the Bodhisattvas of Mahayana Buddhism, epitomes of compassion who stay within *samsara* to aid humans. Yet, compassion is no less important. Out of compassion, the Buddha is seen to have taught humans the way out of their dis-ease. Out of compassion are Theravada Buddhists encouraged to alleviate the suffering of others and it is the *Metta Sutta*, the sermon on living kindness, that is the most popular in meditation practice. At its core is this:

> Just as a mother would protect her only child at the risk of her own life, even so, let the one who seeks *nibbana* cultivate a boundless heart to all beings.
>
> Let his thoughts of boundless love pervade the whole world: above, below and across without any obstruction, without any hatred, without enmity.[5]

The Buddha image in my living room epitomizes compassion for me. In a *Words of*

Faith broadcast for the BBC World Service, I once said this about a massive image of the Buddha in Polonnaruwa in Sri Lanka. As I reread it now, it seems to capture the heart of my appreciation of Buddhism:

> Peace seems to emanate from it and has done so for over 800 years. Yet, it is not the peace of indifference. It is the peace of wisdom and compassion, which arises when the heart-rending nature of human violence and human greed is fully realized. It is not an anguished, twisted scream of torture at the nature of the world's inhumanity but a silent, gentle embodiment in stone of empathy, compassion and strength . . . For me, the Buddha image speaks both of the wisdom that sees into the causes of suffering and injustice and also of the compassion which lies at the very heart of life. And it stirs me to try to do something to demolish some of the pain of our world.[6]

Buddhists have sometimes expressed surprise that I can study Buddhism and yet remain a Christian. The Buddha is believed to be a teacher of humans and gods and it is all too easy for Buddhists to assume that the Christian concept of God can be slotted into a realm of being within *samsara*, below the Buddha. The religious goals and the religious frameworks of Buddhism and Christianity are not the same. They touch at many points, more than the casual observer could dream of. They can enrich and inform one another. They can even complement each other. I can say as a Christian that part of me is Buddhist, that part of my spirituality has become irrevocably linked with Buddhism. I do not believe that religions should be exclusive belief systems, demanding an allegiance that condemns other frameworks as inferior. Scoring ideological points in order to snatch converts from other traditions should be beneath any seriously religious person. Yet, we do make choices about what contains meaning for us and my Christianity will not easily be supplanted. The crux of the issue is the Christian concept of God.

In the early stages of my Buddhist meditation practice, I experienced real tension between what I naturally wanted to do as a Christian and what my Buddhist teachers stressed. My gut-level urge, conditioned by my past, was to seek a closer awareness of the spirit of God flowing through the whole of creation. One meditation centre was high in the mountains and the scenery at first seemed to cry out to me of the presence of God. In contrast, my Buddhist teachers spoke in terms of insight into the impermanence of all phenomena, the non-self of all things. 'Did I want to see this?' was my question. For, in the Buddhist perspective there is no place for a Creator God. The actual experience of meditation for a Christian and a Buddhist may have the same elements of joy, peace, calm and sometimes disturbance. There is no such thing as Christian breathing and Buddhist breathing. Yet, the frameworks within which this is placed will always be different.

There is a point, as I have stressed elsewhere,[7] at which the Christian cannot enter completely the Buddhist experience and vice versa. Faith in a creating and sustaining God as the ground of our being is different from insight into the emptiness and impermanence of all phenomena, although I believe Christians can benefit from practising mindfulness and glimpsing the conditioned and fleeting nature of much that we consider 'ours'. Buddhism can here inform, challenge and complement Christianity. Yet, for me, recognition that there is a divine ground of our being, a divine force of love, compassion and mercy, is central to my spirituality. It touches the Buddhist awareness of compassion but is different in that it links compassion with godhead and a spirit flowing through a created world. It is this that binds me to Christianity together with my biblical understanding of the nature of God and his or her relationship with humanity.

There are certain images of God I reject. I reject them in a truly Buddhist fashion, because they neither accord with empirical observation nor with the totality of biblical teaching. For instance, a God who is believed to have laid down that there is no salvation or liberation outside the Church, or outside an acceptance of Jesus as personal saviour, I reject as contrary to the central points that the Word of God is present within the whole of Creation and that criteria other than belief or even faith are used in the gospels to judge a person's worthiness.[8] Then, the God who gives riches and success to his followers as a sign of love I also reject as contrary to the teaching that those who are righteous will not escape suffering and will be wedded to a non-exploitative lifestyle.

A God who suffers with what has been created – an incarnate God who is crucified again and again in the pain of war, poverty and violence – is the biblical image of God that makes sense to me. Existence is *dukkha* – the term can be as relevant to the Christian as to the Buddhist. Capitalistic consumerism does its best to hide death and imperfection, holding out ever more alluring pictures of material happiness, but any objective analysis of human experience must explode this as a dangerous illusion. Evil exists. Death exists. Buddhism personifies it as *Mara*; Christianity as the devil. Its roots lie within human beings, although its accumulated force can seem outside the bounds of human bidding. The God I worship is one who identifies with human suffering in love and compassion. From the depth of suffering, strength can arise. Out of bereavement, endurance can be born. In the loss of all material things, hope can still be present. I see God as the source of this, the source of the strength that can enable us to look into the heart of darkness with the faith that there can be light within it and beyond it.

The concept of self-sacrifice is important to Buddhism. Gautama Buddha, in the stories of his births before gaining supreme enlightenment, is seen to give his life or different parts of his body numerous times for the good of others. At the heart of Christianity also, there is self-sacrifice. The man, Jesus, was crucified by Roman forces in Jerusalem because he was seen as a threat by the Jewish hierarchy and refused to defend himself when brought before imperial power. A purely materialistic, political reading of this is possible and can indeed serve to challenge

Christians who seem to divorce Christianity from secular realities. Jesus was more than a wandering guru or ascetic. He was a challenge to the religious *status quo* and was killed by secular authority. Yet, the movement that grew from the death of Jesus stressed voluntary self-sacrifice for the purpose of reconciling humanity with God. It stressed that Jesus chose not to escape death but to remain silent when he could have saved himself and continued a mission of teaching and healing. So central to the Christian liturgy of the Eucharist is:

> The body of Christ given for you
> The blood of Christ shed for you.

The Eucharist is very important to me. It touches the core of my need and this has something to do with the power of voluntary self-sacrifice. Wherever it occurs, I believe, self-sacrifice has cosmic significance. In its Christian context, it has given rise to a formula that meets one of the strongest human urgings – for healing and acceptance. The Eucharist begins with a recognition of human failure, of human inability to discover inner peace or create a just world. It encourages a complete offering of self to 'the other' in the awareness that clinging to or protecting our ego is pointless in the presence of God. Buddhism speaks of *anatta* (no soul) or the unreality of the self or ego. Christianity speaks of the need to give up the self in encounter with God. The two touch in meaning. As the Eucharist continues, it has the power to tear our yearning for wholeness from our bodies and transform it by bringing us in touch with the compassion, love and self-sacrifice at the heart of the universe. Part of my faith is that the action of Jesus through the cross has had an effect on history and that our healing is possible through penetrating its full significance.

Buddhism's optimistic stress that we have the ability to purify ourselves through eradicating craving and selfishness is complemented for me by the Eucharist. Although neither my Buddhist nor my Christian friends might agree, I feel each approach needs the other. For, to abdicate human responsibility by assuming that divinity will solve all our problems through faith alone is as unbalanced and perhaps dangerous as putting sole emphasis on human ability. Yet, the paradigm of self-sacrifice embodied in the Eucharist is often too narrowly and individualistically interpreted. It too often ignores the basic challenge that Christianity places before human society – that judgement lies on the other side of love, that bread and wine have different meanings for the rich and for the poor. The God of the Bible passes judgement on all that speaks of greed, hatred and ignorance. There is a judgement on the affluent and on those who exploit or perpetuate poverty by unjust dealings. At core level, the Bible places the affluent and the comfortable in a completely different category from the materially poor, the victims of society's greed. Having lived in the Caribbean and Asia, I have lived with material need on my doorstep. In both areas of the world, affluence, ostentatiously flaunted, and struggle to provide rice enough for the day exist side by side. In both areas, some of the rich seem to assume they have a birthright in their affluence. The stark message of the Bible is that riches come under judgement unless used for the benefit of all and that it is the materially poor, of whatever race or religion, who are favoured in the ultimate scheme of things.

Now is not the time to give a biblical exegesis of this. It has already been done, especially by theologians in the South who see through the lie of so much that passes for Christianity in the West.[9] The important point for my own spirituality is that the God I revere cuts through the received wisdom of contemporary society by passing judgement on what may seem success and by making an alliance with those who possess least. As a comparatively rich Christian, I welcome this challenge. Religion should not only comfort, it should also disturb. For me, a God who identifies with the victims of society is worthy of praise. Empirically and intuitively, it accords with my ultimate vision.

The concept of God that emerges from the struggles of the Jewish community and the writers of the New Testament, therefore, still has a hold over me. The Eucharist continues to define my spirituality. Yet Buddhism, in its awareness of suffering, its analysis of craving being at the root of societal disease and its stress on compassion, has penetrated to the depth of my being. Both religions have helped me to face the reality of heaven and hell and inspire me to embrace the challenge of being alive. Religious choice is not by necessity exclusive.

Notes

1. Elizabeth Harris, 'A Case of Distortion: The Evangelical Missionary Interpretation of Buddhism in Nineteenth-Century Sri Lanka' in *Dialogue*, New Series, vol. XXI, 1994, Sri Lanka.

2. It is possible to describe a Buddhist as a person who is able to say the *Tisarana* or Three Refuges with complete sincerity: I go to the Buddha as my refuge; I go to the *dharma* as my refuge; I go to the *sangha* (order of monks and nuns) as my refuge. This forms a central part of any temple devotion.

3. *Digha Nikaya* iii, vv. 58ff.

4. In the late 1980s in Sri Lanka, an Indian Peacekeeping Force was fighting the LTTE (Liberation Tigers of Tamil Eelam) in the north and the government was fighting the JVP (Janatha Vimukti Peramuna or People's Liberation Front), a terrorist group seeking to capture power in the south.

5. *The Sutta Nipata*, v. 143ff.

6. Broadcast in 1993. Together with other *Words of Faith* by Elizabeth Harris, it will be published by the Buddhist Publication Society, Kandy, Sri Lanka.

7. Elizabeth Harris, 'Buddhist–Christian Encounter with Special Reference to Sri Lanka', presented at Westminster College, Oxford, March 1994, during a seminar on The Contribution of Methodists to the Academic Study of Religions.

8. For instance, the first chapter of the Gospel of John which speaks of the Word of God and Matthew 25:31ff., in which deeds rather than consent to belief statements are the criteria for judgement.

9. I have been greatly influenced in this by Aloysius Pieris sj, a Sri Lankan theologian who has attempted to formulate a liberation theology for Asia, taking into account Asia's poverty and deep religiosity. See *An Asian Theology of Liberation* (Maryknoll, New York: Orbis Books, 1988; and, Edinburgh: T. & T. Clark, 1988); *Love Meets Wisdom – A Christian Experience of Buddhism* (Maryknoll, New York: Orbis Books, 1988), both by Pieris.

A South African Jewish Perspective

Dr Jocelyn Hellig

Dr Jocelyn Hellig is Associate Professor in the Department of Religious Studies at the University of the Witwatersrand, Johannesburg, South Africa.

THERE IS NO single ultimate vision, but many. Individual people, moulded by their religion and historical circumstances, formulate ideals about the way the world should be. Religions project ideas about future fulfilment, visions of perfected reality. The time and place of the believer form the counterbalance to these visions and the ground from which they develop. No ultimate vision derives from a vacuum. On reflecting about my own ultimate vision, I found that the more I thought about it, the more I realized how manifold the factors are that have shaped it. As a white, Jewish, South African woman, living through what is perhaps the most exciting period in South Africa's history, my vision has been shaped by a variety of 'givens' over which I have had little or no control. No less important though are my own personality, my family life, my studies and those numerous little accidents of fate that made me choose one thing rather than another. All these together have determined my vision, my capacity for optimism, and the hopes I can realistically nourish.

Ultimate visions are not that simple. I asked myself, how ultimate is 'ultimate'? Is the ultimate vision something that will happen in the distant future, or is it something that can be realized in the now? Is it something that God will impose on us, or will we play a meaningful part in helping to realize it? Will we have to bring it about completely unaided? Is it something that will be preceded by great cataclysms? Can it come about at all, or are we living in a state of unfulfilled illusion? Is religion, which plays so important a part in the formation of ultimate visions, merely an opiate to help scrabbling humanity to live another day without falling into a state of despair? Religion, whichever way one looks at it, undoubtedly helps us to cope with the frustrations, scarcities, contingencies of human life on an everyday level. It is the matrix in which stability and meaning are given to our lives and in which we are helped to see a little further than ourselves in our limited span on this earth.

Yet religion is also the cause of persistent and serious division in the world. Teaching us to love one another, it frequently causes us to hate and even to justify that hatred. I think about the enmity and violence in the Middle East, so much of which is caused by rigid religious positions: the Jewish religious fanaticism that produced a Baruch Goldstein who slaughtered innocent Muslims at prayer; the Muslim religious fanaticism that led to the bus bomb in Tel Aviv which killed Israeli civilians as they went about their daily lives. Graphic pictures on the covers of *Time* magazine spell out for all to see the indignity of brutal death, the sudden stillness of those whose lives were so unexpectedly snuffed out. And the hate goes on. In far away South Africa, which has its own problems and its own influences, there are echoes of this intolerance, the Jewish and Muslim communities staunchly supporting one side over the other. Each group mourns its own, barely sensitive to the pain of the other. Some are prepared to condemn the acts. Others are so entrenched in rigid religio-political positions that they cannot perceive the tragedy.

So here I am, a product of a religious tradition that developed in a situation of landlessness after CE 70, living in South Africa, a land that my grandparents, fleeing from persecution and poverty in Lithuania, judged as offering a future for Jews. Judaism forms the macro-element of my vision, South Africa the micro-element. The present situation in South Africa provides the challenge, the testing ground for the realization of a vision. And that vision, I believe, is one that will be echoed by several contributors to this book.

My wish is simply for the attainment of peace on earth for all people, no matter who they are or where they live. Peace is not merely the absence of war, but freedom to be authentically human, which means freedom from want, from persecution, from hatred and misunderstanding, as well as freedom to think, believe and worship in the manner one desires. Having been influenced by Jewish ideas, my vision is future-oriented and life affirming. It is not, however, so future-oriented that it cannot be perceived in the present. Human beings are given a decisive role in bringing about the ultimate vision. Without active human co-operation, it will never be realized. Indeed, I believe that even if the ultimate vision is attained, human beings will have to maintain and nourish that blessed state. The need for religion, with both its ritual dimension and its ethical vision, will not disappear. Our religious traditions are so rich, so fulfilling, that we apply them as a meaningful force in our lives, even beyond the end of days.

As I write this, I feel doubt. My vision is clear, but I question whether it can be attained. Human beings are so limited, so circumscribed by the influences around them. How much will it take for us to step outside ourselves and our traditions in order to see the global vista more clearly? We are so timid, so fearful that through ventures such as interfaith dialogue we might 'sell out' our traditions, open them to scrutiny – even ridicule – and thereby destroy the very structures that give us meaning and comfort. We thus hide from mutual encounter and creep ever more deeply into our self-constructed ideological fortresses.

My Jewish Heritage

My vision could never have been formed without my Jewish heritage. Judaism, like any other religion, did not come about in a vacuum. Based on three foci – people, land and Torah – Judaism is both particular and universal. Jews see themselves as the chosen people, a doctrine that arises not out of any sense of superiority, but out of a deep feeling of gratitude to the one and only true God who took them out of the land of Egypt and out of their bondage and suffering. This chosenness is understood in intimate, familial terms such as father to son or husband to wife. It is simply the way Jews understand their relationship to God and should be viewed, like the myths of so many other people, as a myth of origin. It only became a 'scandal' when the idea of chosenness was universalized, first by Christianity and later by Islam.

Judaism is rooted in history and regards the Exodus from Egypt as its pivotal revelatory event. God, in Jewish belief, had chosen a particular people, redeemed them from slavery, and would lead them to the promised land. An important part of this complex of events was the entry into a covenant with the Jewish people. They were to show their indebtedness to God by remaining faithful to the covenant. In the Jewish self-understanding, Israel is a natural community, the 'seed of Abraham', whose existence has a religious significance and purpose. This expresses itself predominantly as an observance of a discipline of life, the purpose of which is not so much to procure salvation as to sanctify the everyday act.[1]

An aspect of Judaism that grew with it was the messianic vision. Promising a perfected world at some time in the future, the nature, details and centrality of Judaism's messianic vision have varied according to historical circumstance. At times, there was belief in a messianic redemption; at others, a more explicit belief in a messianic figure. Judaism's intense focus on a messianic deliverance was probably forced upon it by the claim of its daughter religion, Christianity, that the Messiah promised to the Jews had come in the person of Jesus of Nazareth, and by the denigration and oppression that ensued when the Jews refused to accept this belief.[2]

Rabbinic Judaism, to which all expressions of Judaism today are in some way heir, developed in a situation of defeat and exile after the destruction of the second temple in CE 70. The rabbis of the *Mishnah* and subsequent Talmudic period formulated Judaism's ultimate vision under severely limited conditions. But it was the very limitation that produced the richness of the vision. The rabbis were responding to two major crises: the fall of the temple in CE 70 and the Christianization of the Roman Empire that began in CE 312. While both events shaped Judaism, the former was an especially formative event. Loss of the promised land and the central shrine, and the powerlessness that ensued, necessitated an entirely new religious approach. The latter event, the arrival of Christianity in a position of political power, was to place Jews in an invidious position. With Judaism's refusal to see in Jesus the coming of the Messiah the two religions had gone their own separate ways, each formulating itself in relation to the other and with Christendom developing an ugly stereotype of Jews, one that would negatively influence the world's perception of Jews.

The loss of the land and the temple had been a consummate tragedy that forced Judaism to adapt. So disruptive and of such decisive import was this event that Richard L. Rubenstein has referred to it as the 'holocaust of ancient times'. It instituted a situation of powerlessness that became a primary determinant of Jewish life, he argues. Jewish responses to the outside world became predominantly responses of conciliation. Explanations of the catastrophe and the way of life that the rabbis formulated as a response to the tragedy were to result in particular thought and behaviour patterns that culminated in the Holocaust of the twentieth century. The mechanisms Jews learned in order to survive in an alien world had led them, ironically, to play more easily into Hitler's hands.[3] The destruction of the temple, in which the cosmic and social dimensions of Jewish life had converged, shook the very foundations of Israel's religious life. The temple had been the basis for the many elements of autonomous self-government and political life that the Romans had placed in the hands of the Jews. The rabbis, as the leaders of their people, not only had to explain the crisis and thereby give it meaning, but they had to create a system of Jewish life that would ensure the survival of Judaism. They did this by actively constructing a reality beyond history, one that focused on the meaning of humdrum everyday life and sought eternity in the here and now. Historical events were transcended in order that the people might be able to escape rumours of wars, war itself, politics and public life. The whole history of Israel was interpreted in terms of exile and redemption, and the fall of the temple was attributed to Israel's infidelity to the covenant.

In this fresh reading of the meaning of history it was not the nations of the world that made history, but God. The reality formed in response to God's will was what counted as history.[4] The divinely ordered way of life the rabbis formulated governed every detail of Jewish behaviour from morning to night and from cradle to grave. All God's commandments, whether ritual or ethical, were of equal weight and import.

In the Jewish historical situation of humiliation, persecution and massacre the messianic vision served as a promise and hope that kept Judaism alive. If the situation of the Jews was negative now, there was a promise that it would be rectified in the future. God would redeem his people as he had done in the past. Justice had ultimately to triumph because God as the God of history was also the God of justice. The messianic vision gave succour in the darkest days of Jewish suffering. Few images are more moving for me than the Jews the Nazis had condemned to death walking to the gas chambers with the hymn *Ani maamin* on their lips, 'I believe with complete faith in the coming of the Messiah, and even though he may delay, nevertheless I anticipate every day that he will come.'[5]

No consideration of Judaism – or indeed of its ultimate vision – can today be undertaken in isolation from the Holocaust and the re-establishment of the state of Israel. These are the two *kairoi*, or decisive moments, of Jewish history in the twentieth century, and they are inextricably linked. If the Holocaust was the culmination of Jewish powerlessness, the re-emergence of the historical powerlessness of Jews can be overemphasized – an overemphasis that tends to suggest that the Jews reacted only passively to all events,[6] but there is little doubt that the Jewish people needs Israel for its survival. Jews had lived in the Diaspora as a minority people for almost two thousand years in situations of more or less powerlessness, never feeling entirely at ease or at home. One of the lessons of the Holocaust was that Jews needed to enter, as active participants, into the world of power politics. They needed a state in order to be taken seriously.

In a post-Holocaust, secularizing world, the thread that links the divine and the human has, for me, been broken. The idea of a Messiah seems to be an anodyne that helped to keep my people alive during almost two millennia of pain and humiliation. For this reason, if there is one element of the messianic vision I can still hold onto, it is the prophetic vision of the future. The prophets spoke of a messianic era rather than of a personal Messiah and the essential component of their vision was social justice. The prophets were inspired by the conviction 'that every man simply by virtue of the fact that he is a human being, a child of God, has rights that even kings cannot erase'.[7] No one, no matter how powerful, is immune from censure. Exhortations about human effort directed towards establishing justice in *this* world provide, in my time and circumstance, the most appropriate motivation for action. The prophets argued that if Israel was to be brought back to covenant loyalty, the relationship between human beings dared not be overlooked. Indeed, while ritual was important, it did not and could not take the place of the ethical obligation and would be ignored, nay rejected, without it:

> I hate, I spurn your pilgrim-feasts;
> I will not delight in your sacred ceremonies.
> When you present your offerings I will not accept them,
> Nor look on the buffaloes of your shared offerings.
> Spare me the sound of your songs;
> I cannot endure the music of your lutes.
> Let justice roll on like a river
> And righteousness like an ever-flowing stream
> (Amos 5:21f)

This may sound more like the emphasis of a Reform than an Orthodox Jew, but my approach does not jar within the flexibility of South African Orthodox expression. As difficult as I find it to be wholly optimistic about human behaviour, I find it even harder to believe in supernatural interventions. I cannot believe in the coming of a Messiah. For all the function that the vision may have performed in the history of my people, I believe that if there is to be an improvement in the world, it will have to come about by human effort, not in isolation from God's will, but with the full assumption of human responsibility that God has given us and demands of us.

The South African Matrix to My Ultimate Vision

As a South African Jew I belong to a small but vibrant and well-organized community numbering, according to recent estimates, about one hundred thousand. The community has diminished as a result of the emigration of many of its young people to what are seen as safer and more promising climes, and is, therefore, an ageing one. South African Jews are a highly urbanized community with about fifty per cent living in Johannesburg and twenty-five per cent in Cape Town. They are better educated than the rest of the white population, upwardly mobile and widely represented in the professions. While, on the surface, the community resembles other 'New World' Jewish communities, it has a distinctive character as a result of apartheid. South African Jews have, by an accident of fate, been white and have thus always been part of the privileged white minority in a society in which race has been the primary determinant of people's lives. Although Jews have suffered more indignities than any other white groups in the country – chiefly in the form of restrictive immigration legislation – they have been free to practise their religion, establish institutions, and to flourish in a variety of ways. They have not been educationally or economically hampered in any way. Not having been limited by the apartheid legislation, they have been the only religious minority that was not forced to move its places of worship to enforced areas of habitation under the Group Areas Act.

South African Jews are a product of their Anglo-Litvak legacy. Their institutions are British in organization and Eastern European in ethos. They are religiously conservative with at least eighty per cent of their members affiliated to Orthodox synagogues and less than twenty per cent affiliated to Reform temples.[8] Though there has been a remarkable resurgence of Orthodoxy in the last three decades with the emergence of several *haredi* groupings, the normative form of Orthodoxy may be termed 'unobservant Orthodox'.[9] Arising out of economic necessity, the Lithuanian forebears of the community, though deeply pious and attached to tradition, adopted a pragmatism with regard to the full observance of Jewish law. They were often forced, for example, to work on the sabbath, but continued to observe whatever traditions they could. This grew into unobservant Orthodoxy as a widespread expression of South African Judaism. While Orthodoxy entails the active observance of the variety of *halakhot* (religious laws) that govern everyday life, most South African Jews who belong to Orthodox synagogues feel comfortable driving to synagogue and selecting which laws and traditions to observe and which to neglect. The rabbinate does not encourage the situation, but does not condemn it either. While affiliated to Orthodoxy, they argue there is still a religious ideal to which the community may ultimately aspire. It is the existence of these Jews in large numbers that gives South African Jewry its distinctive flavour.

My vision for ultimate peace takes its ground from the vantage point of my own community within the context of a newly elected democracy in South Africa.

Though political freedom has been achieved, genuine equality has not and there is a great deal of crime and violence. The apartheid years have created a huge economic divide between the privileged and the oppressed. For true peace, there has to be equal opportunity for all. All South Africa's people need access to education, health care, jobs and basic services such as homes, electricity and clean water. It is clear that there has to be a sustained and imaginative programme for some type of redistribution of wealth. As important as material redistribution, if not more so, is the sharing of skills, an area in which South African Jews can make an immense contribution.

From the perspective of my privilege, I feel a great deal of pride that individual members of my community, motivated by the Jewish ethic, were at the forefront of the liberation struggle. It is quite remarkable how many Jewish individuals gave up their freedom to fight apartheid. At the same time, I feel a sense of shame at the failure of my community to make a timely, collective and principled stand against apartheid. It is not easy to excuse such failure and yet the dynamics behind it need to be understood. It is often argued by Jews and others that because Jews, through the Holocaust, have known ultimate degradation and dehumanization, they should be alert to the humiliation and suffering of others. But the issue is not that simple.

Jews have always had extraordinary demands made upon them. Not only is there an elevated moral ethic in Judaism which Jews are commanded to keep, but there is a high level of censure from the outside world if there is even the slightest failure to do so. The doctrine of chosenness had the effect of thrusting the Jews into the centre of world salvation. They are perceived by the world either as the best of saints or the worst of sinners. Through this perception Jews are not permitted to possess and exhibit a full range of human virtues and failings and are thus dehumanized. This dehumanization is a significant feature of anti-semitism, a phenomenon that ranges from vague distrust and dislike of Jews to murder of them. There is a tendency to forget that Jews are people like all others and that communities are not monolithic. Not only are there good and bad among Jews, but each individual has a range of virtues and vices.

Related to this issue, and one that is pertinent to the reactions of South African Jews – particularly to the Middle East conflict – is the fact that healing from the Holocaust has not yet taken place because the full horror of the phenomenon in all its details and complexity is too difficult to confront. The pain and humiliation suffered by Jews have not yet been psychologically fully dealt with. Intense human suffering results in a variety of responses, not all of them positive. Jews themselves need to attribute to Jews of the Holocaust a full range of virtues and vices. They need to come to terms with the fact that the responses of survivors ranged from heroic to cowardly, altruistic to self-seeking. We need 'to recognize that the Nazis got to us in ways that dirtied us, that we were not all innocent survivors but rather complicated and complex human beings facing an extraordinarily distorted and ugly reality, and that we did not all come out so healthy or pure from this encounter'.[10] The entire world Jewish community has been scarred by the Holocaust. In order to avoid the pain of confrontation, there is a tendency to concentrate on Jewish survival rather than on the actual murder of Jews. The return to power, in the wake of the extreme powerlessness of the Holocaust period, tends to be overemphasized and there is an accompanying turning off of moral sensitivity to the pain of others.[11]

Another factor is that Jews in South Africa, as anywhere else, are a product of both their history and circumstances. The context of their responses to the apartheid crisis can best be seen in the events of 1948. Only three years after World War II and the brutal slaughter of two-thirds of European Jewry, the National Party came into power in South Africa and the state of Israel was re-established. Anxiety about the possibility of a Nationalist victory and fear for the well-being of the fledgling state of Israel were the dominant concerns of the South African Jewish press at the time. There was trepidation about a Nationalist victory because the National Party espoused anti-semitic policies and had spearheaded much of the anti-semitic legislation of the 1930s. The concern for Israel arose out of the complete powerlessness that Diaspora Jewry had experienced during the Holocaust, as well as the overwhelming pro-Zionism of the South African Jews, another legacy from their Lithuanian forebears. As it turned out, Jewish fears were unfounded. The Nationalist government abandoned its anti-semitic policy and was receptive to the state of Israel. It was this conscious abandonment of anti-semitic policies by the government that served to intimidate the Jewish community during the apartheid years. A process of Afrikaner–Jewish rapprochement was in progress and Jewish communal leadership was anxious not to do anything that might undermine it.[12] Anxious about the position of the Jewish community and only too aware of the erratic nature and dangers of government-supported anti-semitism, they adopted a policy of collective non-involvement in politics.[13] Jews participated in the political life of the country as individuals, a stance encouraged by the South African Jewish Board of Deputies (SAJBD), the official representative of the South African Jewish community. This was a valid stance in that there has always been a considerable variety in Jewish political opinions and there is, indeed, no collective Jewish viewpoint. The real question concerns the boundaries of a non-involved communal attitude in politics and whether it precluded statements against racial prejudice.[14]

An examination of the statements issued by the Board of Deputies reveals that during the harshest years of the apartheid regime, there was a timidity with regard to denouncing the system. Only in the last decade has a more courageous stance emerged. This, according to Gideon Shimoni, must be understood as a characteristic minority-group phenomenon in self-preservation.[15] It should also be remembered that there were no Jews among the oppressed class, a factor that may have minimized a sense of urgency. Having come into existence to defend Jewish rights, the Board did not consider its terms of reference as necessarily including a collective Jewish response or contribution to the shaping of South African society as a whole. Finding it impossible to separate moral from party political issues, and doubting whether it had a role in wider issues, the Board struggled with statements on controversial public issues not directly affecting Jewish rights. Its resolutions, as Shimoni points out, were so generalized as to be politically innocuous.[16]

The considerations mentioned above are important in relation to the Jewish position in interfaith dialogue in South Africa, particularly with regard to Jewish–Muslim relations, which are at present more bitter than others. Overlying the inherent tension between Judaism and Islam, in South Africa there has been the question of race. Jews have always formed part of the privileged white group while Muslims, who had had far more economic opportunity than blacks, have been part of the oppressed class. I do not believe that the Jewish community has been adequately sensitive to this issue. More serious, however, are the divergent attitudes of the two religious groups to Zionism. South African Jews are intensely Zionist, expressing their national and ethnic identity through Zionism and accepting uncritically the decisions of the various governments of Israel. The Muslim community identifies with the plight of the Palestinians and is openly hostile to Israel, some Muslim leaders opposing the current Middle East peace process. As an expression of this mutual antagonism, there have, over the years, been bitter flare-ups on some of the liberal university campuses. There has been no progress on this issue at any level.

Indeed, Jews and Muslims in South Africa know almost nothing about one another, a condition that was exacerbated by the fact of enforced racial segregation under the apartheid laws. Racial groups live miles away from each other and there has been no way of one religious community observing another in action. We cannot see one another celebrate our yearly festivals or our ties of passage. We are unable to observe one another celebrating our joys or mourning our sorrows. There is little sense of sharing the human predicament. We have not had the opportunity to exchange ideas and argue ideologies. It is only recently that organizations such as the South African Chapter of the World Conference on Religion and Peace (WCRP) have begun to make real inroads into the question of interfaith dialogue. Liberation was, until now, the top priority. Now that a democratic government is in power, there will be new and different urgencies and a new incentive to work together for attainable goals.

There is a great deal of consultative activity in South Africa at the moment at all levels of endeavour. Concerned people are talking to one another and are keen to lay down appropriate blueprints for future action. In interfaith activities, Jewish participation is welcomed. I, however, feel an element of embarrassment when I meet in dialogue with people of other faiths. Jews, as a community, seem to have been shielded, not only from the full horrors of the system but also from the fight. While individual Jews did a great deal in the liberation struggle, it is the members of other religions, collectively, that have done the fighting. But they also *needed* to do the fighting because their members were directly affected. Would they, being human, have done so had they not been affected? At the same time, I sense a certain undercurrent and hostility to Jews. The stereotypical view of Jews as inordinately powerful, rich and influential has, it seems, infected more than just the masses. This perception is exacerbated by the fact that a good deal of anti-semitism in South Africa is expressed in terms of anti-Zionism. The Zionist issue has not been brought into the open, no matter how erudite or sincere the participants in the dialogue.

If we are to succeed in bringing about true peace, we will all have to work together, Jew, Muslim, Christian and Hindu. We have to come to terms with the past and concentrate on the present and future. Jews can contribute a great deal. They have the business experience, the education and the goodwill to do so. The Jewish communal leadership, aware of the privileged position that Jews have had, is anxious to make up for the years of uncomfortable silence. Although in the current period of transformation there is generally a more vocal expression of anti-semitism in South Africa, there is far less Jewish fear with the new government. The government is opposed to any form of racism. In his keynote address at the opening of the 39th Congress of the SAJBD in August 1993, President Mandela assured the Jews that civil liberties would be ensured for all South African citizens. 'The suggestion that an ANC-led government could ever indulge in or connive at anti-semitism is', he said, 'a scandalous slander inspired either by sheer ignorance or malice.' He acknowledged the tremendous contribution of the Jewish community to the development of South Africa as a whole, as well as the disproportionate representation of Jews among those whites who involved themselves in the liberation struggle. Because South African Jews are highly educated and have a variety of skills – professional, commercial and industrial – he appealed for their help in the reconstruction of South African society and promised to address the fears of the Jewish community as a minority within a white minority.

Government assurance is encouraging, but it would be far more creative in terms of genuine co-operation if individual communities could learn to accept and trust one another, an achievement that can only be brought about through genuine interfaith dialogue. Through this process, South African Jews have to become less uncritical of Israeli governments, more sensitive to Palestinian suffering and more aware of the Muslim reality in South Africa. South African Muslims have to become more aware of the Jewish historical reality both generally and in South Africa, more in touch with Jewish fears, particularly in relation to the two *kairoi* of the twentieth century, and to have an insight into their own prejudices. Both groups need, in relation to one another, to make sense of their identification with the Middle East. These issues also need to be raised on the broader interfaith agenda. There needs to be a greater general awareness of Judaism and the Jewish situation in history. The current willingness to communicate is a good sign.

How does my religion help to promote the two areas that are so important for my ultimate vision: interfaith dialogue and a programme for action? The first is a relatively simple issue because Judaism is not a missionizing religion. Although this may cause resentment among some, particularly in the light of the Jewish doctrine of chosenness, it is a plus factor. It stands to reason that a non-proselytizing religion cannot make ultimate claims about the religious position of the rest of the world. God chose the Jews for some mysterious purpose in his ultimate design for the world. Whereas Jews are bound by the covenant, other peoples have other mechanisms whereby they reach God. Judaism's particularism and universalism are evident not only in its religious life in the here and now, but in its messianic vision where two inseparable elements may be observed: a political, national salvation and a religio-spiritual redemption. Jews believe that they will ultimately be restored to their ancient homeland, but this will be followed by the redemption of the entire world. The messianic vision, as Zwi Werblowsky states, is the 'ultimately universalistic sanction of an apparently particularistic religion.'[17]

Among the many prophetic ideals that inform my ultimate vision, the prophecy of Micah speaks most appropriately to our present situation:

> They shall beat their swords into mattocks
> and their spears into pruning knives;
> Nation shall not lift up sword against nation
> nor ever again be trained for war,
> And each man shall dwell under his own vine,
> under his own fig tree undisturbed.
>   (Micah 4:3f.)

Few visions could be more important for South Africa than that of self-sufficient domestic bliss. Each man dwelling under his own vine, and fig tree, in a situation in which there is no outside disturbance of the peace, implies the ability to make one's own living, to live together with one's family in happiness and dignity, forming a vital unit within the wider community. This should, I believe, be an important incentive for South Africans to ameliorate the living conditions of black people whose family life has been rent apart by migrant labour. In fact, it is the family-centred dimension of Judaism that is most appealing to me. With the centrality of marriage and procreation to the entire religion, there is an immense concentration on transmission of religious and ethical values through child-centred rituals. Education itself is hallowed. The Jewish emphasis on education and the consequent high level of education and educational skills among Jews can form a valuable resource in South Africa.

Judaism steps in for me in the promotion of these goals because of its attitude to the material world. Human appetites and urges are not denied by Judaism. They are confronted and then tamed by elevating all acts to holiness. The material world is not to be shunned but hallowed. It is *this* world that forms the ground for the achievement of perfection. Human beings are God's co-workers in helping to mend the world (*tukkun olam*). The prophets, far from suggesting that possession of material things was a bad thing, believed that more people should have more of them. Thus, the prophet Amos condemned the arrogant, wealthy women, the 'Cows of Bashan', who lived on the hill, oppressed the poor and crushed the destitute (Amos 4:1). The rich are called upon to get down from their protected perches, familiarize themselves with what is happening at the lower levels of society, and do something to alleviate the situation. Jews should not see this injunction as applying only to fellow Jews but as extending to all of society. Based on their fundamental revelatory experience as an insignificant slave people whom God had taken pity on and redeemed from their agony, there is a demand for care of the stranger. Jews are asked to imitate their God. 'The stranger who sojourns with you shall be to you as the native among you and you shall love him as yourself; for you were strangers in the land of Egypt' (Leviticus 19:34).

I believe that all religions offer similar injunctions, but that we need to reinterpret them to cover the widest possible area and the greatest number of people. The walls of apartheid are breaking down, and the rights of individuals and minority groups in South Africa will be protected by the constitution. We, in South Africa, can begin to become less defensive of our minority positions and reach out beyond the confines of our own groups. We need to come to know one another as fellow human beings and to recognize the beauty inherent in one another's faiths, respecting the fact that each religion has promoted ennobling values. But we also have to acknowledge that religion, when placed in the hands of people – as it has to be if it is to function – has engendered negative feelings and behaviour patterns such as fear, group-centredness, triumphalism, intolerance and even violence. We have to separate eternal religious values from the historical situations in which religious responses have been moulded. In South Africa, religious claims have become involved with race and privilege under an arrogant Christian hegemony. The start of interfaith dialogue here may have to be modest, but it must ultimately focus on the real areas of contention and division, and not merely paper over the cracks. Small groups need to be set up, for example, between Jews and Muslims, Christians and African traditionalists, Hindus and Christians. These can form the beginning of a sustained focus on gaining understanding of those religious, political and social dynamics that divide us. There is no more appropriate moment than the present, because South Africa is exhibiting an unprecedented openness to the minority religions. They, for the first time, feel accepted.

South Africa forms the ideal ground for the development of my ultimate vision. Much has already been accomplished and the transition has been so basically peaceful that we and the world perceive what has happened here to be a miracle. If the second great battle can be won for true equality and peace – and I believe it ultimately can – South Africa can become a model to the world. We are charged with the task of helping to bring about the transformation in the knowledge that things will not change overnight. My tradition states that he who saves but a single soul, it is as if he saved the entire world. Small beginnings can have enormous consequences. With our human limitations, we, as individuals and as individual communities, can only achieve small things. Lest this drive us into a state of despair in the face of the hugeness of the task, we are enjoined to remember that each act of goodness is worthy. Together, as one united people working for the human good, we can mend the world. We are not expected to do this unaided, but with the divine command that each of our religions has given us.

Notes

1. Z. Werblowsky, 'Judaism', in *Historica Religionum*, ed. C. J. Bleeker and G. Widengren (Leiden: Brill, 1971), p. 4.
2. Z. Werblowsky, 'Messianism', in *Contemporary Jewish Religious Thought*, ed. A. A. Cohen and P. Mendes-Flohr (London: Free Press, 1987), p. 597.
3. See, for example, R. L. Rubenstein, *Power Struggle* (New York: Charles Scribner's Sons, 1974).
4. See J. Neusner, *The Ecology of Religions: From Writing to Religion in the Study of Judaism* (Nashville: Abingdon Press, 1989), ch. 10.
5. The Jewish Prayer Book.
6. See D. Biale, *Power and Powerlessness in Jewish History* (New York: Schocken Books, 1987).
7. H. Smith, *The Religions of Man* (New York: Perennial Library, 1958), p. 277.
8. Within the last three years, two Conservative congregations have been established in Johannesburg.
9. See J. Hellig, 'Religious Expression', in *South African Jewry: A Contemporary Survey*, ed. M. Arkin (Cape Town: Oxford University Press, 1984), pp. 95–116.
10. Editorial, 'Victims and Victimizers', *Tikkun*, vol. 9, no. 2 (March/April 1984), p. 8.
11. In similar manner, the full implications of black suffering under apartheid will have to be confronted.
12. G. Shimoni, 'South African Jews and the Apartheid Crisis', in *American Jewish Year Book 1988*, ed. D. Singer and R. R. Seldin (New York: The American Jewish Committee), p. 28.
13. Ibid., p. 27.
14. Ibid., p. 28.
15. Ibid., p. 27.
16. Ibid., p. 28.
17. Werblowsky, 'Judaism', p. 12.

ROMAN CATHOLIC CHRISTIAN IN A WORLD OF OPTIONS

Dr Monika Hellwig

Dr Monika Hellwig is the Landegger Professor of Theology at Georgetown University, Washington, DC, USA. She has contributed to many interfaith projects and her work has been widely published.

THE FAITH INTO which I was baptized in infancy and fully initiated in stages as I grew up certainly shapes every aspect of my life. But this does not prevent me from asking four searching questions repeatedly in changing circumstances and growing maturity:

1. Why am I still a believer rather than an agnostic or an unbelieving pragmatist?
2. Why am I still a Christian, not a follower of any of the other traditions that I have discovered in my adult years and found immensely attractive?
3. Why am I still a Catholic Christian in spite of seeing so much to admire in the other Christian denominations?
4. Why do I find myself becoming more and more radical within Catholicism on a number of issues: the religious character of social justice and peace issues; the importance of personal experience and individual conscience in the quest for truth; the need to respect that what is ultimate is by definition mystery, beyond comprehension; basic human experience as the contact point for ecumenism; and the conviction that authentic respect and concern for others is more central than beliefs or observances?

In trying to describe my personal approach to striving after an ultimate vision, I find I need to deal with those four questions along the way.

The Journey of the Persistent Believer

As one accumulates experiences and becomes more knowledgeable and sophisticated along life's roads, it seems to become more difficult to distinguish between believers and unbelievers. Certainly it is not a matter of what people say they believe about the source or destiny or meaning of their existence. I have known self-proclaimed atheists, agnostics or radical secularists who shared with me a deep respect for life in any form, for beauty, for the dignity of persons and for an ethical exigence that is not humanly made but somehow transcendent and foundational. I have also known self-proclaimed believers, devotees of a religious tradition, habitual worshippers, punctilious in religious observances, for whom this did not seem to have a personal existential meaning, but rather a superimposed, essentially alien one. Reflecting on this over the years and through the decades of my adult life, I have come to agree more and more with Friedrich Schleiermacher that what is distinctive in the believer is a pervasive sensitivity deeply rooted in personal consciousness and self-consciousness, an awareness of dependence and universal interrelatedness.

In situations where I have been privileged to engage in ecumenical encounters, I have sensed the resonance of this in people of traditions very different from my own, as though separate musical notes were joined in a chord in self-validating harmony that needed no musical theory to justify it. I have also participated in church assemblies that seemed to me to be dealing with something other than religious faith, though they were certainly following patterns of worship, proclaiming religious beliefs, and reaffirming commitment to the ways of life of the tradition.

This sense of what it is to be a believer has, of course, developed in the course of a lifetime. When I look back over my childhood experiences, over what I was taught and what I assimilated, the picture is rather different. It was the experience of a Catholic child in a family of mixed religious traditions – Jewish, Lutheran and Catholic – and among adults of varying degrees of pious immersion or critical distance. Therefore the earliest layers of experience included contrasts tangible to a child, though taken for granted. Elementary schooling underscored the polarities; by courtesy of Hitler's persecution of anyone with Jewish connections, German secular schools were replaced in our lives by intensely devout, not to say passionately partisan, Catholic schools in the Catholic region of Limburg in the Netherlands. This was traditional peasant piety, pervasive, all-embracing, utterly sure of itself, inviting no questions, inspiring a certain innocent pride in knowing the truth so sadly denied to others, and stimulating beyond that a great missionary zeal to share the treasure with those remaining out in the darkness outside the true faith.

Both in these villages of Limburg and later when we fled to Scotland from the invasion of the Netherlands by the Nazi forces of World War II, we lived in a culture where religion was not just one aspect of life but the pervasive character of all life and all experience. Catholic faith shaped the calendar of the year, the shape of the week and of the day, the arrangement of space in a room, a house, a school, a village, the relationships among people, all judgements of value and aesthetics, all sense of society and authority, and indeed the most basic sense of reality. Although my family situation was always religiously pluralistic, the villages of my early years and the convent boarding schools of later years were religiously saturated. To this state of affairs my university years were diametrically opposite. This environment was saturated with a sophisticated atheism, logical positivism, and even a certain supercilious cynicism. It was certainly thought to be more intelligent, mature and courageous to be an unbeliever. Yet in the five years I spent at Liverpool University, collecting two degrees and becoming deeply involved in a variety of student activities almost all concerned with the discussion of ideas, unbelief never appeared to me as a genuine option (though it certainly did so much later in life when I studied theology professionally). Among the unbelievers at the university, the only ones that I found to be satisfactory partners in dialogue were the student Marxists, because their atheism was not an introspective preoccupation but was intertwined with passionate concern to better the human condition of the masses of the world less fortunate than themselves.

    Unbelief seemed to me to be a genuine option later in life. Through the post-graduate study of contemporary Christian theology I became much burdened by the realization that all religious language is very broadly analogical, that all doctrines about the transcendent or ultimate arise out of projection, and that all claims of religious authority (like every other claim of authority) rest on human judgement and consent. It therefore seemed, on first reflection, to be more honest and truthful, more in touch with reality, to acknowledge that our access to truth is within the confines of our ordinary experience. This would also mean a frank acknowledgement that the ultimate source, meaning, purpose and destiny of our existence is a matter for wonder and conjecture without hope of any resolution. At this time, it also seemed to me that the religious imagery commonly employed by my tradition was so crude that it made prayer (a reaching towards the transcendent) difficult for a thinking person.

    While wrestling with these problems, I began to read the work of Paul Tillich, who referred to God as 'the ground of all being', and I found that this made prayer possible for me in a way untouched by the 'demythologizing' of imagery in the tradition. I found that even the Christian perception of the holy ultimate as triune became intelligible in Tillich's interpretation as the ground of being also known as expressive being and as unitive being. Abstract as these terms may sound, they seemed to me then, and do now, to resolve the tension between the need to acknowledge and relate to the transcendent on the one hand and the honest confrontation with the limits of human knowledge on the other hand. This resolution became practical for me with another imaginative formulation of Tillich – the idea of 'taking back the broken symbols'. Religious imagery that is crude, inadequate and of necessity never wholly appropriate may become more serviceable as soon as its frail and deceptive character is fully acknowledged. This may seem to blur the line between the respectful agnostic and the post-critical believer, but it seems to be the appropriately humble acceptance of the relation of human beings to the ultimate.

Drinking from One's Own Well

The very discoveries that validated belief against unbelief for me also opened wider ecumenical vistas. To 'take back the broken symbols' of one's own tradition, having become wiser about the way in which they function, necessarily involves the realization that the symbols of the other traditions function in the same way. Just as

I had learned a religious faith based upon the way Jesus of Nazareth interpreted and embodied the Hebrew tradition, so others had learned a faith based upon the way Siddhartha Gautama, the Buddha, had interpreted the Hindu tradition and given it a new direction. Just so others again had learned a faith and a way that remained in the Hebrew or Hindu tradition, rejecting the new paths that had branched off from older ways. Yet others had learned a faith based upon the events that overtook the prophet Muhammad, or the ancient faith that discerns the Tao inherent in all reality.

The depths of insight, wisdom, harmony and self-transcending dedication to be found in each of the great faith traditions of the world have been an exciting and profoundly moving experience in my life. I have often tried to identify with them and learn from them. I have studied Scripture and prayed in synagogues, studying the Jewish cycle of readings and celebrating (at the gracious invitation of Jewish families) the cycle of festivals. I have prayed in mosques, deeply appreciating the simplicity and quiet of the worship space, the total absorption of the worshippers, the extraordinary unity of the great crowd of worshippers at the end of Ramadan, the potential for world peace of the five pillars of Islam. I have tried to learn meditation from Buddhists whom I greatly admired. I have made some modest efforts in the discipline of *raja yoga* to come to experience unity of body and mind, transcendence of spirit, unity of the self with the all, and I have reflected very fruitfully on the four stages of life according to the Hindu tradition. I have tried to learn something of Confucian wisdom, and though less familiar with the Tao have been beneficiary of an experience of balance and harmony in visiting Taoist shrines and temples and observing something of the *wu wei* in those who were there.

From all these experiences I have been immeasurably enriched, edified, liberated, heartened, reconciled, deepened, enhanced. In all of them I have found truth, wisdom, goodness, beauty enough to sustain a full human life and maintain a harmonious and wholesome human community. By this I do not mean that religious traditions are always understood and appropriated in their full potential by their adherents. Nor can I deny that religions are all too often invoked to stir up hatred, provoke wars, maintain cruelties and oppression, and allow the adherents an appalling screen of hypocrisy for immoral, reckless and destructive behaviour. Unfortunately all these things are possible, and do frequently happen, but they do not express what is really the thrust and intent of any of the traditions.

In every instance of such an encounter, such a learning experience, such a spiritual discovery, one must face the question, 'Why then am I here and not there?' And in every instance, recognizing that truth can be apprehended in many forms and in many traditions, I have realized that I am at home, drinking from my own well, and that the well is never exhausted. Indeed my experience has been that every attempt to learn from another tradition has shown me new aspects of the wisdom and potential of my own tradition. This has been true in a special way in relation to Judaism and Hinduism. Any Christian who studies Judaism is by that fact learning more about Christianity simply because our tradition not only branched out of Judaism in its early phases, but also defined itself in juxtaposition to Judaism in later centuries, and has much to learn that is complementary to itself in the very different paths that post-biblical Judaism followed. This applies in the first place to the reading and interpretation of the Hebrew Scriptures that today's Jews and Christians share as sacred text. But it applies also to certain corrective insights as to what was distinctive and original in the attitudes and teachings of Jesus, and what has developed in the centuries since that is distinctively Christian though not perhaps exclusively so.

My strongest and most surprising experience of deepening knowledge and appreciation of my own tradition from the study of another occurred in a course on Hindu iconography taught by a well-known scholar in that field, Stella Kramrisch. When I entered that course my hope was only to get some better sense of what Hinduism meant to express with its great plurality of gods, and whether there was a decipherable meaning to their esoteric gestures and strange appearances, and what were the legends implicit in particular presentations. I did learn much of this, but the greatest insight I gained was into the sacramental principle so pervasive in Catholic life and practice, the symbolism of the sign of the cross, the point of holy water, genuflections, images of saints, festivals and shrines, and a multitude of devotional customs. All these things on which I had reflected very little gained great depth and coherence as non-verbal means of communion and expression, as symbolic modes that were open-ended and could gain further meaning and coherence with further life experiences. And through this I began to see the symbolic expressions in church tradition in continuity with the parables of Jesus in the gospels – pictures, allusions, stories, events in life all serving as unlimited means of deepening wisdom and understanding. The more I admired and appreciated the wisdom and insight implicit in popular Hinduism's representation of gods and ceremonies expressing communion with the reality behind the representations, the more confirmed I found myself in the official and popular expressions of Catholic Christianity.

What is true of these two instances I have continued to find true in many other encounters with people, teachings and practices of other religious traditions. Buddhist ways of meditation have illumined for me something of the sense of Benedictine and Carmelite traditions of prayer. My tenuous acquaintance with *raja yoga* has alerted me to the potential within my own tradition of the spirituality of Ignatius Loyola. My reflection on the five pillars of Islam has reinforced my understanding of the Catholic Church's renewed attention to radical issues of social justice as inseparable from true personal spirituality. From appreciation of other traditions I have learned deeper appreciation of my own.

The Catholic Exuberance

Though I have constantly had occasion to ask with reference to the other religions why I am here and not there, the question has an even greater urgency with reference to other denominations within Christianity. Given the experience that the wisdom of Jesus becomes more and more convincing the more one lives by it, there still arises the question of whether my particular church lives and teaches that wisdom better than others, and if not then why I remain with it. I must admit very quickly that I have no evidence that the Catholic Church implements the vision and mission of Jesus better than others. My honest attempts to see what is truly happening in the Christian Churches have led to the conclusion that the Society of Friends is consistently more generous, more morally upright, more proof against worldly seductions, and more willing to take on risks and arduous work on behalf of peace and social justice. Most Baptist Churches of my acquaintance have a stronger, friendlier community bond among their members. Most Mormons are more disciplined in their total way of life. Most Protestants of any sort are willing to spend more time in Sunday worship (if they attend) and are far more familiar with the Scriptures than most Catholics (though we are latterly trying to catch up in this respect).

It would be foolhardy to claim that simply being a Catholic makes one a better human being or member of society, or more assured of ultimate salvation, though I realize that all of these claims have been made at some time in a more or less official way. Nor does history justify the claim that ecclesial communion with Rome is exclusively constitutive of the 'one, true church of Jesus Christ' – a claim that has been discreetly modified if not actually rejected by the official proclamation of the Catholic Church at the Second Vatican Council in 1964. Furthermore, it can hardly be said that as a woman I can feel more included and respected in the institutional life of the Catholic Church than I would be in other Christian Churches. The very reverse is true in most cases. Finally, it is clear that aesthetically both the Anglican Church and most of the Orthodox Churches surpass the Roman Catholic by almost any measure, musical, visual or ritual, while also offering greater freedom in theological questions.

In view of all the above, the question remains insistent as to why I am here and not there. It could be a matter of simple inertia, but I have given it much thought, and have made other radical and risky moves in my life. It could be a matter of long conditioning from childhood holding up the fear of infidelity and damnation to the 'fallen away' Catholic, but I believe I have long been liberated from that. It could be simple affection for the familiar, and that certainly plays a role. But I believe when all is said and done, what holds me here and not there is what might be called the 'Catholic exuberance'. What I mean is a kind of expansion into every facet of life, an appeal to both reason and imagination, a concern with both Scripture and tradition, an eagerness to gather up the whole of history, an assembling of a ragtag collection of people, not all fully dedicated, not all entirely truthful or trustworthy, and certainly not all respectable.

What I see as particularly Catholic, and which I value enough to want to stay in spite of what was listed above, and in spite of monumental problems in the contemporary Catholic Church, seems to me to be summed up in five characteristics. I see them as constitutive of the Catholic way of being Christian, certainly not unique, but shared with other Churches here and here, more or less. The first of these is the unquestioned assumption that salvation is a community affair – that one cannot really be a Christian in isolation from others, without support from others, without making common cause with others for the redemption. I believe that this accounts for our obsession with getting every member to Sunday Eucharist every week – an obsession that must look either quaint or dictatorial to other Christians with a more relaxed attitude to church attendance. I think it also accounts for some of the less glorious chapters of our history – crusades, conquests to spread the faith, the Inquisition, and the tendency to Christendom-type of alliances with secular power. But the positive rebound from this is also the newly revived movement to ally with the oppressed and the poor in a critique of the structures of society that oppress, and in efforts to transform those structures. All these factors seem to spring from the conviction that the way of Jesus is concerned with the redemption of the world in all its relationships, values and structures, rather than the redemption of souls out of the world.

A second factor that seems to me to be constitutive of Catholicism is the assumption of a continuity between reason and faith. While some may find it irksome, presumptuous or simply boring to hear believers solemnly and systematically arguing the reasonable foundations of their faith in philosophical terms, it has always seemed to me to be quite important and helpful for three reasons. As an intelligent human being I consider myself responsible for the commitments I make, and want them to be based on the probability that they are more likely to do good than harm, and therefore I find it necessary to use reason before making an act of faith. Secondly, as an intelligent human being I want my faith-based view of reality to be coherent, the parts fitting together to make an authentic and 'liveable' whole, and therefore systematic reflection seems to me to be in order. Thirdly, as a responsible, decision-making human being I want to think through the implications of my religious faith for my participation in the public sphere in a pluralistic society that raises many value questions in relation to public policy. I find that Catholicism has passed on a strong tradition of using reasoning in support of faith, and I appreciate that and would not like to lose it.

A third factor constitutive to Catholic Christianity is a careful treasuring of the cumulative wisdom of the past. It occurs in our rituals of worship, in our theologizing, in our accumulating and celebrating memories of heroes of the tradition (the saints), in our devotional literature and spirituality traditions, shrines and pilgrimages, and much more. I find myself greatly in sympathy with the cry of the Reformers that in a confusion of corruption and conflicting interpretations of Christian life there is one central norm by which to judge, and that norm is Scripture. On the other hand I think it would be a tragic loss to take quite literally the dictum 'by Scripture alone', because our history is not only that of corruption and confusion, but also a history of prayer, discernment, fidelity in discipleship, which has enriched our understanding of the Scriptures and their application in changing circumstances. This treasuring of the cumulative wisdom that comes out of our history seems to me to be a precious complement to the Protestant insistence on the centrality of Scripture, and I would not like to lose either side of this complementarity.

The fourth characteristic that seems to me to be important in Catholicism is one that is in some respects very poorly fulfilled in practice. It is the leaning towards a non-élitist invitation to membership. The baptizing of infants, the concern for religious education of all the children baptized in the Catholic Church, the strong incentives to keep everybody coming to Sunday Eucharistic worship every week though some may be minimally committed in their way of life, the regular availability of a sacrament of repentance – all these seem to indicate that one need not be fully committed or socially respectable or free of sin to belong and be welcome (indeed pressed) to stay. The reason for stating that it is poorly practised is that the Church has not done well in accepting non-European cultures within church life and worship, and the institutional Church has made a habit of excommunicating individuals for certain issues that have become loyalty tests (for example divorce and remarriage). Yet there is a great mingling of races and economic classes and ethnic traditions within the Church as well as a demonstrable democracy of saints and sinners, and that seems to be a good thing.

The final characteristic that I find particularly significant is what is often called the 'sacramental principle', namely the pervasive acknowledgement of the need for many-dimensional concrete mediation of the approach to the invisible, ineffable transcendent. This is expressed in the great elaboration of ritual, in the cultivation of saints as exemplars and intercessors, in the many forms of iconographic representation, in the structure and adornment of places of worship, in the elaboration of devotional practices, bodily gestures of prayer, imaginative legends, shrines and pilgrimages built around reports of visions and personal revelations. It is particularly in the manifestations of the sacramental principle that the Catholic exuberance is demonstrated. It is this pervasive and many-faceted character that exercises such a strong pull on Catholics to remain Catholic even while observing their Protestant neighbours searching for the Church that suits them.

Whenever my thoughts range over the various Christian Churches and denominations, I find myself glad that they are all there, reflecting various emphases and priorities within the Jesus tradition; I find the polarities and contrasts helpful. But again and again I find myself eager to preserve the particular emphases and values of Catholicism, not only because I am at home there, but also because I think the other denominations need this as well.

The Loyal Opposition

An Anglican friend confronted me with a question that puzzled him. All the Roman Catholics he knows are constantly at odds with various rules and decisions made by Church authorities, yet they remain within the Church, where his Protestant friends seem to take the simpler option. If they disagree with Church authorities they find another Church. He wondered why the Catholics remained. My first answer was that I was certainly one of those people who protested but remained because I do not think that the Church 'belongs' to the Pope or any other authority. I think it is bigger than that and belongs to all of us, past, present and future who form this Church community and claim loyalty to its traditions, goals and best interests. I consider it my Church and that of all Catholics, and when I think it is not doing as Jesus would want it to do, I protest in any way that I think can be productive towards change.

I find myself often at odds with the majority of 'First World' Catholics over social justice issues in the world which call for some radical structural changes in economies and national policies of the wealthy and powerful nations. On the whole I find that Church authorities are moving in this direction more surely than the Catholic laity. But there has been some Vatican resistance over 'liberation theology' which looks for structural change to come at least partly by consciousness-raising of the poor and oppressed and the formation of grass-roots church communities among them. I have considered it a matter of loyalty to the Catholic tradition to argue through lecturing and writing for this approach held suspect officially.

Similarly, I find myself at odds with the ecumenical timidity and miserliness of the institutional Catholic Church. The restraints on Eucharistic sharing among fellow Christians based on the failure of Church officials to agree on certain structural compromises or rather esoteric verbal formulations has seemed to me scandalous, and I am willing to argue against it where appropriate. The exclusion of women from decision making on behalf of the Church seems to me simply un-Christian; that is not as Jesus did things. The attempts to silence theologians who raise certain issues, and to deny them due process in the adjudication of their status seems to me to call for protest and efforts to bring about change. In the same vein, efforts to legislate the beliefs of Catholics into detailed and unchangeable formulations belonging to a particular culture, philosophy and time in history, seem so counterproductive in alienating the professions of faith from the experience of life that it seems a matter of loyalty to oppose the process. And to treat moral issues as though they were only a matter of obeying predetermined rules, and required no personal discernment or weighing of circumstances, falls so far short of real life that it requires the raising of protesting voices.

For all these reasons, and many others not mentioned, it may well be necessary, in the wonderful phrase from British parliamentary courtesies, to play the role of the loyal opposition. To disagree with Church leadership in certain issues on grounds of conscience or particular expertise does not seem to be a reason for leaving the Church for another faith or another denomination, but rather a reason to stay and enter the contest over the proper interpretation of what is most in consonance with this tradition.

To sum up, then, the answers to all the questions about why I am here and not there: I have found it more coherent and more true to reality as I experience it to be a believer rather than an unbeliever; I remain a Christian because my growing respect, admiration and gratitude for the other traditions has led me to a deeper appreciation for my own where I am at home; I remain a Catholic Christian while appreciating the complementarity of Christian denominations because I see very important values in my particular Church which I want to preserve; I remain in many ways a protester in my Church because I see the Church as much greater than the authority figures in it, and I think my loyalty must be to the greater, and any tradition continues to be a quest.

A Unification Sense of the Ideal

Dr Frank Kaufmann

Dr Frank Kaufmann, a Unificationist, is Executive Director of the Interreligious Federation for World Peace.

As a RELIGIOUS convert, I am often asked about the faith in which I was raised. 'I am the product of a mixed marriage,' I explain. The person asking often nods to show he or she understands and is with me so far. 'My father was a New York Giants fan', I go on, 'and my mother an avid theatre-goer.' In fact, this is only half a joke, for it comes close to describing the nearest thing to religion I encountered at home. More seriously, however, there was in fact a religiously held commitment in my home, namely belief in the 'value of education'. My parents were secular humanists of the tolerable sort, an a-Jewish New York Jew on my father's side, and an Anglo-Indian raised in Himalayan, British boarding schools on my mother's side. Neither had many thoughts about religion, although my dad had a few complaints about Jews, and my mom a few about Catholics (the religion to which her mother converted).

I, strangely enough, was born religious (latent genes, I guess). I remember at the age of three or four, coming into my parents' room one morning while both were still in bed. I lay stomach down, on top of the covers between them, my head about waist high, their legs stretching down beside me on either side. Resting my head up on my hands, I set out to tell them what I had just carefully figured out on my own: I could prove the existence of God. As I set out to do so they listened carefully, and then calmly refuted each of my arguments point by point. When I realized I could not prove to them that God existed, I finally asked, 'Don't you believe in God?'

'Whether or not you believe in God,' they replied, 'it is still important to think clearly.'

I do not recall another word about God or anything remotely religious spoken in my home again, until I spoke them myself about ten years later. I had returned home from my first semester at a Christian boys' boarding-school a pesky convert to evangelical Christianity. My parents, seeking a good preparatory school, unwittingly chose the pre-eminent evangelical, Christian boys' boarding-school in America, the Stony Brook Boys' School, founded by Frank Gabelein in 1922. My classmates included Franklin Graham, the son of Billy, Harold Lindsell, the son of the inerrancy champion John Lindsell, and sons of other American evangelical leading lights.

I was in heaven, chapel every morning, Bible classes, vespers, the works. For the first time in my life, I met other people who believed in God. My classmates, on the other hand, were in hell still having to hear about God. Just one of those funny things. Towards the end of my first semester I attended the revival preaching of Tom Skinner, a black gang leader turned Christian evangelist, a special event sponsored by the school. Sure enough, I was moved by the spirit, and responded to the altar call at the end of the second evening. Counsellors brought me backstage, where they led me through the steps of confession, repentance, inviting Jesus into my heart and life as my personal Lord and Saviour, and receiving the Holy Spirit.

That moment my life became new, and my world was new. I did not eat or sleep for a week after that, so overwhelming was the experience of re-birth through Jesus and the Holy Spirit. From the first moment I was on fire, anxious to perfect my new-found relationship with Jesus, and grow day by day towards the sanctified state to which He calls His disciples. While raring to go, I had a few simple questions, ones which I knew just needed a little explanation and clarification that I could not figure out on my own. I was sure that any of the lovely Christian teachers and elders around me would be able to provide a simple explanation that I had probably just overlooked. Some that I remember are: 'If Jesus returns on the clouds, how will it be possible for all eyes to see him?' 'At the time of the resurrection of the body, what will become of the complex and massive redistribution of molecules that occurred throughout the centuries?' 'What happens at the time of the resurrection to people who were blown up or died in plane crashes, etc?'

For some reason I really needed answers to those questions, and for some reason the questions seemed to irritate the chaplain, the dean, the Bible teacher and whoever else ventured forth with a little Christian boarding-school-type compassion. By the time I graduated, I felt that either I had not been taken seriously, or that no one to whom I spoke was able to answer my questions. Furthermore, in the intervening years the couple of technical eschatological concerns had blossomed into a more mature 'search for answers'. Thus, upon graduating from high school, I visited every religious centre I could find. I spoke to priests and ministers of every major religion (not a difficult task in New York City). I especially recall having been evicted from a synagogue in Brooklyn because it was Saturday. No one seemed forthcoming with answers, and suddenly college dawned.

After acclimatizing myself to college life, I eventually enthusiastically embraced the Eastern religious option that was seeping through Western youth culture in those years. I gave my all to the practice of Tibetan yoga and constructed my world-view upon the likes of D. T. Suzuki and Hermann Hesse. As I encroached upon and occasionally tripped into cosmic consciousness, I became increasingly disillusioned with the academy and conventional social expectations. Reflexively, I sought to face complete, what I had come to regard as the farce called college, and had plans to travel to northern India in search of my true teacher.

Shortly before graduating, while in a meditative trance, I was shocked to be confronted for the second time in my life by the risen Lord Jesus. The only other time I had encountered Him was on the day I made my covenant with Him nearly seven years previously at the age of fourteen. 'What has become of you?' He demanded, 'Why have you become like this? Where have you been? Didn't we make promises to one another?' He implored. 'I have kept faithful to my end of the promise, but you have strayed and drifted away from me, leaving me alone and broken hearted.' I was shocked and saddened. I had betrayed the one who loved me most.

From that moment on I became somewhat distant from everything, and driven by the need to resolve something deep within myself. I had experienced existentially the absolute truth of the Eastern spiritual reality of transcendental consciousness, *and* I had experienced existentially the absolute, indescribable and overwhelming reality of Grace: the Grace of God, Jesus, and the Holy Spirit. My difficulty was that I knew I could never be fulfilled on any path that allowed only for one and not the other. Thus as college ended I found myself in search of answers once again, just like at the end of high school.

Graduating was meaningless for me. I was already aeons away in another world. In fact, I do not even remember graduating from college. I remember only one thing: the promise to myself that I would investigate any and every spiritual claim, path, community, teacher, etc. that crossed my path, none too staid, none too fringe. This was my one and only firm principle and commitment. But though I would ignore none, my special obsession was with what I dubbed 'the cusp', namely any system, teaching or piety that arose from the spiritual or geographical borderline between East and West. I read Gurdjieff and Ouspensky, Krishnamurti, and all manner of Christian monastics. I was fully absorbed in this quest. All my days were spent reading, visiting teachers, communities and churches. My intuition was becoming acute to such a degree that it felt frightening and painful. I could seize upon the essence of a teaching too quickly. I could see the spiritual quality of communities I would visit too clearly. Mainstream priests and ministers tended to be so fraught with ungodliness that I would spend my nights crying over Jesus' Church.

One night I received a call from my mother; a motherly call, demanding to know what I was doing with my life, what were my plans, was I going to go to graduate school? Was I going to get a serious job? What? At the end of that call, overwhelmed, I slammed the handset down into the hook. CHING the phone rang out (Ching is telephone for ouch!) and I screamed at the top of my lungs into the dark night, 'GOD, WHAT DO YOU WANT ME TO DO?'

The next day there was a knock at my door. I opened the door to find, standing on my step, an odd little fellow, who looked to me as if he had been stuck in a time warp for twenty years. Truly an anachronism, not only with a nauseatingly clean-cut look, but also with an utter lack of the necessary darkness and cynicism that was the trademark of we counter-culture revolutionaries and spiritual types of the sixties. He did not seem to be aware that he was trudging around in sub-zero temperatures, so I figured I'd better save this poor, cheerful little oddity from himself and get him in out of the cold.

Over tea, he explained to me that he represented a 'new spiritual group' in town, and that I should come to hear their teachings. He looked to me about as spiritual as the poster-boy for the navy junior cadets. But how he looked was irrelevant since I had already promised myself that I would study every spiritual teaching I encountered. Strangely, this was the first time I had an aversion. I really did not want to go to this group, no matter what it was. But if I violated my one and only iron-clad principle, I could not live with myself – I would be a phoney.

Upon arriving at the household of this little group, I was perplexed to discover that everyone there was just as straight, just as perky and just as quirky as the fellow who had come to my door. My only thought was 'get me out of here'. Nevertheless I listened as they lectured and found that what they taught was true. I also found the people to be true, in an odd sort of way. As much as I dreaded the possibility of ending my Lone Ranger, spiritual hero adventure of the eternal quest for answers I would never find, I could not in all good conscience deny what was taught, or deny that the truth of the teaching required people of integrity to support the project described. It was unmistakably of God. Why God had to work through such an irksome and anomalous collection of people was beyond me, but I had to allow that that was God's business and not mine. Also I couldn't deny that, as odd as these people were to me, they were more 'good' than any others I had previously met. Without going into the mysteries and wonders involved, I became a Unificationist, heels dragging, and looking back so hard that it is a wonder I did not turn into a pillar of salt.

The moment of personal decision that resulted from the confluence of three or four signs, both natural and supernatural, was 3 February 1974. For me, the decision meant that I accepted to be taught by the Reverend Sun Myung Moon. I write now, at the invitation of the Reverend Forward, as nothing more; a person who has accepted to be taught by the Reverend Moon. To write of ultimate visions is to strain at my own limitations with repentance, and labour to sketch a rough icon of his vision. For lack of a better term, I will herein refer to the Reverend Moon's teachings as Unificationism.

The external appearance of Unificationism is Judaeo-Christian. It may even be substantially Judaeo-Christian. The Reverend Moon's family, dwelling in Pyong An Book Do, now North Korea, converted to Presbyterianism in 1927 when the Reverend Moon was eight years old. In 1935, on Easter Sunday morning, at the age of sixteen, the Reverend Moon was deep in prayer on a Korean mountainside when Jesus Christ appeared to him urging him to take up the original mission of Adam, which remained unfulfilled.[1] After two attempts to refuse the mission, Reverend Moon acquiesced, and has stayed this tortuous course largely due to his promise to Jesus.

The first thing he had to do was uncover just what the mission involved;

what was the mission of Adam that had remained unfulfilled since the beginning of time? The Reverend Moon sought to uncover five basic elements: why did God create? What is the purpose of human existence? What is the origin of evil? By what means does evil perpetuate and expand itself? What is God's relationship with evil?

The search for answers to these questions lasted nine years from 1935 to 1945. He conducted his research in three primary areas, namely the natural world, the 'Old' and 'New' Testaments of the Protestant Bible, and the spiritual world. By 1945, he had secured the essential elements of what today is known in the English-speaking world as *The Divine Principle*.[2] This 536-page volume explains the ultimate vision in its most bare-bones form. Additionally, the Reverend Moon has published approximately 250 volumes of sermons in which he has sought to further clarify this vision for his followers.[3]

Unificationists understand the ultimate vision to be God's original vision. This vision was with God from the beginning, prior to Creation. In fact, this vision is what spawned Creation. It should have already established itself from the beginning of human history. It is long overdue. The only reason our world is anything other than one of boundless delight is due to the fall of the first human ancestors. Despite the fall, the original vision has never changed, and its inevitability remains.

Let us quickly look at a few elements of Unification belief in which to contextualize this vision, and the process whereby it can be achieved. God is real and has personality.[4] He created the universe exactly the way it is on purpose. He created human beings on purpose. He created them male and female for a reason. He created us with physical bodies for a reason. The physical body is meant to die after a natural period of time. The spiritual part of the human being is created to live eternally. This is the original, deliberate, and eternal design for created reality. The ideal world will also be comprised of these elements.

The second coming of Christ will occur in history. He will be the one who is awaited by all religions and His mission will be to fulfil the original purpose for which God created human beings. This original ideal world is completely natural, a reality in which people are born, grow up, marry, have children, grow old, die and go to the spiritual world where they exist for ever. God created things like that. He likes it like that as it is the precise design in which absolutely everybody, including God, can be the happiest, and most fulfilled. Although there is in fact a heaven and a hell, God and good people will eventually devise a means to get everyone into heaven without violating anyone's free will, perhaps like getting a baby who is enjoying crying to stop. Heaven is eternal. Hell is only temporary.[5]

God created because He is a being of love, and He wanted an object to which (and to whom) He could give love. As a being of love, He wanted loving relationships. The one type of creature with whom a completely fulfilling love relationship was to be possible was human beings. They were created specifically for this purpose. What makes the relationship possible is that humans were created with the responsibility to perfect themselves, namely their capacity to love by making free decisions, and fulfil their responsibility to perfect a divine and fully loving character. Therefore, once that is achieved, the person can claim responsibility for the achievement along with God. In a real way, after I perfect myself due to the decisions I make, I can claim, 'I created myself', or more accurately, 'I co-created myself'. This means that with each perfect person, God has a real, true-to-life partner, with whom an honest-to-God loving relationship can ensue.

If this is the explanation of creation (i.e. why did God create?), what might we envision to be the ideal world which would then result? Unificationists believe that this ideal is embedded in its entirety in the extremely thin instruction book that Genesis records as the original blessings God gave to Adam and Eve, 'Be fruitful, multiply and have dominion over the sea and over the birds of the air and over every living thing that moves upon the earth' (Genesis 1:28).

Here's how these blessings are interpreted, and how the ideal world would look if the first human ancestors had actually inherited these blessings based on the fulfilment of their own responsibility. The first blessing to be fruitful is understood to describe the process and achievement of maturing into a person loving enough to be a perfect husband or wife, and loving enough to be a perfect parent. To be fruitful, then, is to mature through the natural process of growing up, until one stands legitimately on the threshold of marriage. A fruitful person is understood to be one who is truly loving, unselfish, and capable of translating their intentions into reality.

The blessing to multiply means to take this mature loving self and plant it in the abundant relations of family, the passions of husband and wife, the wonders of parents and children and grandchildren. To multiply means multiply the loving person you have become. Plant yourself in others, through unconditional self-giving.

To have dominion means to be a person of perfect ecological sensibility and practice; a person whose scientific knowledge, whose artistic creativity, and whose spiritual sensitivity is such that the earth and the natural universe benefit more by their presence than it would if they were not there at all.

The belief is that each and every time any one of the three blessings is fulfilled joy abounds. For all the billions of times it occurs, the joy is just as great time and time again. When God sees a young girl on her wedding night, He experiences joy, He shares the joy and excitement in the girl's heart. When God sees a young man nervously hold his own first baby for the first time in his life, He feels joy. He shares the fathomless wonder in the young man's heart. The billionth time is as great as the first. It never grows old. The cosmos was created as something capable of producing endless joy, endless new joy, first-time joy.

The ideal world, the eternal world is full of wondrous violinists, full of lightning-fast football goalies, ballerinas, Nobel-prize-winning physicists, damned good garbage collectors, yes, and even politicians. But what it is full of above all is men and women experiencing their first moment of love, their first baby, and the 'firstness' of their second and third babies as well. It is full of seven-year-old girls visiting Grandma for the first time. And it's joyful every time. The ideal world probably also has scrapes on the knees, and probably has not getting into the college you hoped for, but those scrapes and those failed tests happen to people who have truly loving brothers and sisters, truly loving parents, truly loving grandparents, and to people who know God personally. Such people easily build a world without inequity, without war, and without ecological rape. People get along with each other, and get along with their world. Quite simple.

To describe this world, the Reverend Moon speaks of the Four Great Realms of Heart and the Three Great States of Royalty.[6] The Four Great Realms of Heart are simply the love of children for their parents, the love of siblings for one another, the love of husband and wife for each other, and the love of parents for their children. The Three Great States of Royalty are grandparents as King and Queen of the Past, representing God and the eternal tradition of True Love, parents as the present rulers, the seated King and Queen, and the children as future Kings and Queens (i.e. princes and princesses). Why Royalty? Because we are the children of God. If God is King (and Queen), then His descendants must also be royalty. In God's original world grandparents, parents and children are all treated with the utmost respect and dignity and preciousness, for we *are* royalty. These foundations of goodness and respect, which are the experience of all people growing up in their families, are those which manifest themselves in all larger social units – clans, societies and nations of a peaceful and unified world.

What went wrong and how is this original ideal ultimately recovered? The proper answer to this should require the reader to invest in the rather sophisticated theological anthropology, angelology, hamartiology and soteriology of *The Divine Principle*. A simple answer is possible, but you must promise you won't succumb to misrepresenting the teachings of the Reverend Moon, and the beliefs of Unificationists (as with all views Unificationism can be rendered silly if misrepresented). The short answer goes like this: the mission, to be fruitful, required the original human ancestors to co-create perfectly loving personalities through the fulfilment of their own responsibility over the period of time it took them to mature into adulthood. Aware that the impulse to love would arise during the course of maturing and before perfect maturity (as we all know it does), God gave a commandment which, if followed, would have protected Adam and Eve through the challenging time period (teens) until they could perfect a truly loving character. The commandment 'do not [thou shalt not] eat of the Fruit of the Tree of Knowledge of Good and Evil' (Genesis 3:3) is interpreted by Unificationists as strong, explicit guidance understood by the first human ancestors. That is the commandment not to indulge one's impulses to love (i.e. engage in sexual activity) until one's love is fully mature, and that each of the partners bear the responsibility for parenthood that can result. Adam and Eve were convinced otherwise, and ended up in the position of parents under conditions that had three serious shortcomings:

1. They never developed a capacity for love and sacrifice that was minimally necessary for decent parenting.
2. They formed their family 'apart' from God. God Himself wanted to give them the blessing of marriage when He knew they were ready. They began having children after their expulsion from God's protective realm.
3. They began life as husband and wife in obedience to a creature who had come to despise God. The foundations of their family were in compact with a being (Satan) who had developed an anti-God agenda.

Instead of starting a God-centred family in which the Four Great Realms of Heart and Three Great States of Royalty could flourish, they began their family under the worst imaginable conditions. As a result of their inability to love one another in a mature fashion and to serve as good parents, their efforts at child-rearing failed dismally. Eventually one of their sons murdered his younger brother. Since the first human parents were not able to demonstrate unconditional love, and reveal their origins in God to their children, human history has inherited this very real and intractable problem. The historical providence of salvation then is nothing other than the effort on God's part, working through the resident, albeit crippled, human capacity for free responsibility, to establish a first set of True Parents, ideal, mature, Godly parents, through whom the ideal of family can begin. Jesus was born to be the husband half of True Parents. What a magnificent husband and father He would have been. When the faithlessness of His followers resulted in His crucifixion, causing Him to carry His perfected Godliness to the spiritual world without multiplying it substantially and physically in this world of God's, Jesus promised to return. The promised return is because the human race still awaits the first *True* Parents, Godly parents.

What is the ultimate vision for Unificationists: my brothers and sisters, my husband or wife, my children and grandchildren, God with us, and an eternal wondrous world around us. This for Unificationists represents the promise of God's kingdom on earth (Revelation 21:3–4).

Heaven

Obviously, Unificationism is strongly 'this-worldly'. Heaven on earth is understood by Unificationists as God's original ideal of creation, furthermore, an eternal ideal. The boundless delights of His earthly kingdom, however, pale in comparison to eternal life in the spiritual world.

Unificationism, like many theistic traditions, upholds the notion of the eternal individual soul. Each person is born only once and lives in three stages: womb life as preparation for earthly life, earthly life as preparation for eternal spiritual life, and life evermore in the hereafter. The twist for Unificationists is that one's fate for life in the hereafter requires no pursuit of 'getting into heaven'. People build the foundations of heaven on earth, and that foundation is the substantial world love that they build through the actions of their lives. Love begins as the infant is held and cared for by his or her parents. That grows through sibling, spousal and parental love. It continues to grow beyond the family to the farthest reaches of social reality. One's place in the spiritual world is nothing other than the measure of how beloved one becomes through living sacrificially for the sake of others while on earth.

Unification people do not focus too much attention on 'heaven' in the spiritual world. We feel a deep responsibility to support God in a co-operative effort to return the cosmos from Satan's regime to God's rightful authority. That heaven awaits is a matter for God, and nature, our business being for the sake of others, not worrying about our own destiny.

Despite this character of Unification piety, the Reverend Moon occasionally does chat about the spiritual world during sermons. To treat this issue properly would require careful theological explanation, grounded in a good grasp of the larger system. Rather than that, however, it may be interesting to eavesdrop on a sermon to close followers, as the Reverend Moon speaks on the spiritual world:

The definition of physical death, in a way, is to transfer oneself from this physical world's train track, to the spiritual world's train track. Let's compare the difference between this world and the spirit world. How superior, how much more exciting is the spiritual world! You can't describe it. You do not have to worry about living situations such as eating, wearing clothes, or housing. Of course you can have a house there, you can have clothing, you can have food or whatever you want. But everybody will be on a level corresponding to their level of achievement of True Love on earth. To the level you achieved, the entire environment of the spirit world will provide for you – but only to that extent, according to the level you reached on earth. How free it is in the spiritual world and what a life you can have! . . . You must mature, you must fulfil your life here. You must form character here as a human being. This is where it must be done, not in the spiritual world . . . The spiritual world is our home, our eternal ideal home country. That's the world we will live in, transcending the concepts of time and space. [If you want to go somewhere] it doesn't matter, even if it is a hundred light years away, you can go there in just a second. Think about it and you are there . . . It won't take even one second to travel from one end of the universe to the other. If your loving spouse is at the other end, it won't take even one tenth of a second for you to get there. It will be as you wish.

When you understand these facts, do you want to live in this limited world with your limited physical body, or do you prefer to go to your unlimited life in the spiritual world? You want to live there, without any limitations of course. You can do anything, everything, there are no boundaries. It takes only one step to reach your destination. In other words, you live in a state of crazy love . . . the original state of nature is living in perfect harmony with love.[7]

It should be added that the 'unlimitedness' that characterizes subjective experience in the spiritual world is accessible proleptically, even during the physical lives of people who attain increasing levels of freedom through the gradual expansion of true love in the self and in their relationships. One is fully spiritual and physical from birth, and while thoroughgoing transcendence from physical limitations is only possible after physical death, the contemporary frequency of utter lack of spiritual quality of life in people who are physically alive, is solely due to the artificial and unnatural severing of the spiritual and physical realms that occurred at the time of the Fall.

The Unification 'ultimate vision' is a unified vision. People grow into oneness and wholeness as each unique expression of true love fulfils and manifests him or herself. The eternal quality of absolute freedom is known in the family. That original information is both within, through lineage, and given by parents, who are also 'other'. This most basic truth of what it means to be human and of divine origins expands eternally to all levels of social and cosmic order, and deepens in ever more profound and overwhelming experience of loving in four endless ways. The wonderment deepens and expands forever, both in the temporal physical realm and in the eternal spiritual realm.

Look forward to meeting you there!

Notes

1. Full biographies of the Reverend Moon are widely available.
2. In order to systematize and teach this knowledge, he spent countless hours in prayer and in study of the Bible. In 1950, he began to teach formally the most important parts of the Principle to his disciples. However, much of the Principle received by the Reverend Moon is still unpublished. More of the Principle revelation will be released according to the progress of the dispensation and the development of the foundation on earth.

   Two texts, entitled *Wol-li Hae-sul* (Explanation of the Principle) (Seoul, Korea: Segye Kidokyo Tongil Shillyong Hopwe, 1957; untranslated) and *Wol-li Kang-ron* (Discourse on the Principle) (Seoul, Korea: Segye Kidokyo Tongil

Shillyong Hopwe, 1966), and published in English as *The Divine Principle* (Washington, DC: HSA UWC, 1973), have been used as the official doctrine of the Unification Church. They were written by Hyo Won Eu, the first President of the Unification Church, who served the Reverend Moon in the early years of his ministry and was taught directly by him.

3. Unfortunately only the first volume has been translated into English so far.

4. Although Unificationists understand God to be a person who perfectly harmonizes the fullness of masculinity and the fullness of femininity into one harmonious, fully integrated being, I will refer to God as He, rather than She, He/She, She/He, S/he or any of a number of possibly legitimate referents. Readers who wish to sue me can get my whereabouts from the editor.

5. *Divine Principle* (New York: HSA UWC, 1973), p. 190.

6. Family Pledge No. 3 (Seoul, Korea, 1 May 1994), and elsewhere.

7. Reverend Sun Myung Moon, *True Parents' 1993 American Speaking Tour Celebration* (East Garden, New York, 1 August 1993).

A Oneness to Behold

Dr Julius Lipner

Dr Julius Lipner is Lecturer in Indian Religions and in the comparative study of religion at the University of Cambridge and Director of the Dharam Hinduja Institute of Indic Research.

I AM SOMETIMES asked what I mean when I say that I am a 'Hindu-Catholic'. I have been saying this with increasing regularity for some years now. Five years ago I would have answered differently if asked to explain myself. However, I do not think that in future years my answer will be substantially different from what I attempt to say in this essay. The editor has invited each of us to reflect on where we stand religiously at present. This is a rare privilege indeed and I am grateful for the opportunity to explore aloud my religious vision and commitment.

However forward-looking we may try to be, we are inevitably children of our conditioning and times. And to many observers (and participants) the world has never appeared more fragmented, incoherent and lacking in direction. Old orders are passing away – traditional structures of normativity in matters of truth, value and authority are being dismantled with unseemly haste; the problem is that nothing enduring seems to be taking their place. Communicational advances are binding the world together more than ever before, not only at the level of a pre-critical technological culture – all sorts of ethnic, cultural and ideological groups are technologically literate in more or less the same technocratic sense – but also consequentially, it seems, with a prevailing sense of instability and foreboding.

Both the technocracy and the sense of bewilderment are pre-critical factors of our experience; they have not been debated or articulated, at least sufficiently, in our societies. The responses to this condition are varied. A well-known response has been an immense consumerism among both haves and have-nots (the difference lying not in the value-system but in the means or lack of means of realizing it) to boost security and self-esteem. On the whole, this strategy has failed to achieve its objectives. A fulfilling sense of security and self-esteem does not notably thrive on so precarious a materialist basis. Another response has been religious, political, social or cultural fundamentalism, whereby the travails and lessons of history are either dismissed or denigrated in favour of the felt need to bring a pristine set of identity-bestowing and renovating fundamentals to rebirth. This kind of attempt to reinvent time and space has bred division and strife, diminishing rather than adding to a sense of global well-being: your set of basics may not square with mine. Then there is the response that invariably interprets life's interactions in conflictual mode, namely, as a dialectic between oppressor and oppressed, or at least between superior and inferior. Rather indiscriminately, for I am not evaluating here, we can include liberalism, sexism, racism, feminism, environmentalism, scientism, etc. in this category. These responsive modes are not exclusive of each other, of course, and usually co-exist in some way in most people's interpretation of the world.

Each of these modes is inherently dyadic, bipolar in structure: self–other; them–us; man–woman; God–the world, and so on. This contemporary *mentalité*, which is pervasive irrespective of ethnicity, gender and culture, has tended towards an absolutizing of the particular. At the level of the person, this gives rise to individualism and a stress, ethically, on rights rather than on duties or obligations; at the level of the collective, it has led to new forms of tribalism rather than to a proper appreciation of the community (though the word 'community' is bandied about a great deal in social and ethical rhetoric).

Philosophically, including the philosophy of religion, a doctrine of incommensurability holds sway. Particulars, we are told, are incommensurable with other particulars (which is interpreted both negatively and positively) even when, apparently, they belong to the same genus or species. Faith is incommensurable with reason' (so religion is 'only belief' whereas science is knowledge proper; or vice versa – faith yields the only knowledge worth having for it bears on eternal verities, whereas science is only provisional knowledge at best); 'God is incommensurable with humans' (so God doesn't exist, or cannot become human); 'some humans are incommensurable with other humans' (hence racism and 'separate development'); 'men are incommensurable with women' (hence oppression, usually of the latter by the former). Indeed, in some contexts, nothing seems able to stop the relentless outreach of the incommensurability-thesis: white middle-class women are incommensurable with women of colour; black women from one culture are incommensurable with black women from another, and so on. So while we are becoming technologically unified, we are at the same time becoming conceptually and culturally atomized.

The solution is not, of course, to seek to reimpose traditional universalisms, whether in politics, morality or religion. For these universalisms have tended to be imperialistic, and hence unegalitarian, in terms of culture and/or gender. Thus 'the original American or Hindu (or other) way of life', or 'traditional family values', or 'the age-old truths' of, for example, Christianity/Catholicism invariably incorporate sets of beliefs and practices that have disempowered significant constituencies of the systems to which they refer, that is, various ethnic or religious groups, non-Western cultures, women and/or children, and so on. The real cost in human terms of seeking to reimpose this past is too great; we must look ahead.

In spite, then, of the undeniable problems generated by our age of fragmentation, I cannot but view this problematic as immensely liberating in important ways. For we have here the opportunity to build afresh, to reconstruct our world in terms of a new and integrative vision, in the process of which our narratives and the lessons of history will hopefully play a most important part. And it would make sense to use our new-found and pervasive technological expertise, as well as those wider or narrower bridge-building conglomerates of human concern –

the United Nations, the Commonwealth, the World Health Organization, the European Union, Greenpeace, the local Mothers' Union, and countless others – as unifying bases for the exploration and fashioning of this new creation.

In this creative programme, each one must play his or her part. In an enterprise such as this, even the humblest effort bears fruit, for the effects, I believe, are organic and cumulative. It is here that religion can play a hugely rewarding role, for it is undeniable, I think, that the vast majority of human beings continue to be religiously sensitive, that is, they continue to be open to the possibility that their lives are not reducible to purely biological or physical or material principles. Put another way, they are open to the possibility that there is a transcendent dimension to their existences, a dimension, for the most part ineffable, that yet ennobles and fulfills them by enabling them to rise above merely material concerns. Some religions call this dimension 'God', the supreme reality. Institutional or organized religion is only one chief way in which this susceptibility seeks concrete articulation. Since it is *de facto* such an important way, the world religions at least can give a crucial lead in helping construct the integrative vision of which I speak. For I interpret each of these religions as susceptible of inspiring a way of life and of conveying a message, which rises above divisiveness, towards an integrative oneness, not only of the human but of all reality. This must be explained further.

But first, have not at least the major organized religions a poor track record when it comes to unifying the human race, providing integrative visions? We answer that they have a mixed record, which reflects the very ambivalence of human nature in its capacity for doing good as well as evil. After all, religion is an eminently human enterprise. On the whole, I think, the major religions have been more benevolent in human history than otherwise. Human nature and our capacity to understand ourselves and one another, and to assess what is good and bad in both enduring and provisional senses, are themselves developing phenomena. Religion has been inextricably interwoven in this process. We cannot expect people at significantly earlier stages of this development to conform naturally to our more considered standards. Nor must we be quick to judge them by our own criteria. Our own gains in insight, in terms of which we are inclined to view the actions of our forebears all the more keenly, have derived from the very experiences of these forebears.

But whilst religion has given humans excuses to do evil (sometimes unconscionable evil), it has consistently provided – not marginally or surreptitiously, but up-front and boldly – ennobling ideals from early times to the present day, and a regular batch of practitioners, both great and small, to implement them. This has had a guiding and elevating effect on our developments. And because it was religion that first set the agenda for our distinctions between what is good and what is bad, and human fulfilment and its opposite, the non-religious (rather than irreligious) ideals of today have inevitably been shaped by their religious predecessors. So religion, I believe, has been overall a force for good, and of good hope, where the aspiring human spirit is concerned.

But have not these ideals themselves, though superficially similar, been exposed by the instrument of contemporary hermeneutics as actually very diverse, embedded each one in its own nexus of separate development, linguistically and conceptually? Are not Hindu notions of good and evil, of person and salvation, and so on, really very different when scrutinized in context, from corresponding Christian or Buddhist notions? As such, are they not incommensurable? And must not the same conclusion apply to our different conceptions of the supreme state/reality, if there is such? Religion, then, does not seem suited to playing a significant part in unifying the human race, or yielding an integrative understanding of the world.

We are faced with one of the crucial questions of our day. It is here that we must take cognizance of the role of faith in our lives. By faith I do not mean specifically a religious faith. I mean, rather, that willingness we all *must* evince in following, intellectually and experientially, certain existential paths on the basis of evidence that is ambiguous or factually under-determined. Thus the scientist who affirms that there is no transcendent reality, that the pursuit of purely empirical sciences is the only hope of the human race for betterment and fulfilment, has put her or his faith in a certain kind of evidence (evidence based on the senses alone), in a certain kind of interpretation of the world, dismissing a priori anything that may count for evidence that there *are* trans-empirical realities as invalid. This is to have faith in scientism. And so on. The reasons for adopting such an approach are inevitably not only 'rational'; they include psychological, social and other factors as well. Such an approach is no less a faith-stance than that of the religious believer. Of course, all kinds of faith-stance must be as critical as possible, weighing up the deliverances of experience as comprehensively as one is able, but they are also required to be as open as possible if they are to be responsible. In this sense, *everyone* has a basic faith-stance, or, more correctly, basic faith-stances, whether pre-reflective or reflective, dogmatic or undogmatic. Most people allow others, or fashion, to do most of their thinking for them. The religious believer then, as believer, must not be singled out as some sort of queer exception.

The approach to the issue of incommensurability also, in the current cult of the primacy of the particular in some influential circles, masks faith-stances. Diversity, the basis of the incommensurability thesis, does not necessarily imply incommensurability, or at least that kind of incommensurability that makes a genuine understanding of the other and an integrative interaction impossible or undesirable. Diversity in itself calls for interpretation, and depending on the faith-stance you choose to follow, you may interpret diversity as betokening a more or less absolute form of incommensurability, or on the other hand, a more or less creatively integrative programme for action. Because women are obviously different from men does not mean that this difference cannot be the basis of a common, interactive fulfilment.

But what about the lessons of history, you may ask, which teach pervasive modes of oppression – sexually, socially, economically, politically – by men of women, say? A word of caution: 'oppression' is a term easy to apply ideologically, and as such is a blunt instrument for interpreting the complex interactions between men and women across cultures and ages. But even if it is agreed that men have indeed tended to discriminate against women *tout court*, this does not mean that gender differences alone are the necessary basis for a continuance of discriminative behaviour. One kind of faith-stance will say that they are; another will affirm that they need not be, that education and legislation can effect change towards a balance of genuine equality-in-difference, that in fact, the possibilities of being truly human are possibilities of integrative fulfilment.

I adopt the latter faith-stance, mindful of how easy it is to be glib about this and of the enormous complexities that lie in the way of achieving the goal. But we must have a vision, and it is here that a specifically religious faith-stance can help implement this vision. Ultimate visions are useless unless one sees ways and means of beginning to realize them.

I am coming increasingly to *see* that the major religions of the world contain traditions, rooted in scripture, that inculcate a way of life or a spirituality that is regulated by a discourse, not of the conventional dyadic 'other', but of an actual underlying *oneness*, mainly between the supreme state/reality and human beings, and between human beings themselves. Sometimes these are called mystical traditions; most are many hundreds if not a couple of thousand years old. In these traditions, the final state is an experience, if not of absolute identity between the ultimate being and our deepest selves, then of a real identity-in-difference. These traditions have invariably produced outstanding individuals who have claimed to experience a foretaste, at least, of this unitive state, and in whose description of this state the conventional, 'orthodox' and 'I–thou' dualistic spirituality is left well behind.

A study of the teachings of the Sufi, of Zen and other Mahayana mystics, of an Eckhart, Teresa of Avila and John of the Cross, of a Shankara and Ramanuja, for example, highlights this *tendency* to 'monism', which more conventional practitioners and theologies sometimes only hint at. There is much scope for genuine debate as to whether the final state is an absolute or a relative identity. There can be no disagreement, however, that there is a tendency to monism among the people I mention. It is this vision – one that teaches us that the undeniably important differences of gender, race, culture and so on are neither fundamental nor ultimately significant – that will give us the impetus to put these differences in perspective in our everyday lives and to pull together integratively.

It is all very well to affirm difference, to proclaim respect for the alterity of the other, but unless you and I begin to realize that in a fundamental sense 'You *are* I' and 'I *am* you', alterity will invariably generate attempts to come to terms with it through egoistic assimilation, domination, or some cult of individualism or tribalism. The world is full of such attempts. The aim must be to shape modes of discourse approximating to the monistic, or rather 'non-dualistic', ideal in which conventional 'I–thou' forms are but provisionally valid, justified only in terms of a higher, unitive mode of discourse and experience.

This is not as utopian as it may at first appear. We have well-established patterns of non-dualistic speech and experience in everyday, secular life. Lovers, friends, families catch more than a glimpse of this condition through such expressions as 'two hearts beating as one', 'two/three minds with a single thought', 'three/four bodies, but one soul' and so on. This entails an actual experience of a non-dualist, non-individualistic oneness. Yet individuals continue to exist in this ennobling state non-assimilatively and in their own right. The higher, more productive unity of non-dualism is evinced in so mundane a thing as an orchestra. The orchestral music of particular instruments, not excepting solos, is lifted up in a higher, more creative oneness, which cannot be simulated by individual instruments or groups of instruments as such. Similarly, we must fashion *contexts* of speech and experience (an orchestra is a context) that function non-dualistically rather than conflictually, dyadically or individualistically. In such contexts, no one will be an island, a discrete particular in a stream of similar particulars.

This integral aim is an inalienable part of the religious vision, or at least of any religious vision worth pursuing. So far as I know, it is embedded in the scriptural bedrock and derived strands of mystical experience of every major religion, and of many minor ones. It is claimed to have been experienced, glimpsed, tasted, by hosts of acknowledgedly upright persons across the ages and cultural barriers. It is not easy to dismiss as pie in the sky; it is something to strive for.

It is here that religious leaders and theologians can play a crucial role in our societies, namely, as 'prophets' of change, *agents provocateurs*, complacency-shakers; as heralds or actual shapers of interreligious bridges and unitive objectives. At present, so many are caught up instead in egoistic verbal or administrative power struggles, in tangled webs of mealy-mouthed diplomacy – men (and women) of poor vision and even poorer spiritual prowess.

In the nature of things, we all have our particular starting points. I can imagine a Hindu beginning (and countless Hindus have thus begun) with the great Upanishadic saying, *Tat tvam asi* – 'That [the all-pervasive Spirit] you *are*'[1] or 'The Spirit [*atman*] was indeed [*all*] *this*, one only in the beginning'.[2] Multiplicity derives from, and is established, now and forever, in the One. Many Buddhists also have non-dualist scriptural starting points, where the radical interconnected oneness of all things is affirmed, and so on for the other faiths.

My own starting point is based in the Christian Scriptures. From one point of view, this may have begun as an accident of birth, but in time it has been consolidated and has developed, through the Catholic Church, as a full-fledged commitment. Basically, I am a Catholic Christian. On one level, this means that I try not to sit lightly to the Church's pronouncements and teachings. If you belong to a club, you must respect the rules. If you want to change features of the club, a good place to try and do this is from within, as a paid-up member. On another level, I acknowledge wholeheartedly the fundamental vision of the Church – that salvation, that is, genuine human healing and fulfilment, comes through Christ – and the distinctive principles that have articulated this vision down the centuries. But this is not as straightforward as it seems. Nor should it be. Religious faith may be a simple thing. Its shaping, growth and meaning are both complex and profound. And this is because faith is a living perspective, a *constructive interpretation* of the world.

The Catholic vision, distinctive though it may be in important ways, is irretrievably plural. It has an open-ended quality, susceptible of accommodating different emphases and points of view. This is not only because of various contingent factors in the history of the Church's interpretation of the so-called deposit of faith, but also, of course, because interpretation *per se* is not a hermetic process; it is inherently pliable and proliferative. The Church's hierarchy, to the present day, has tended not to recognize this. One hopes it will become more realistic.

Yet Church teaching itself appreciates that the term 'Christ' in the statement *'Salus in Christo'* (Salvation in Christ), though signifying normatively through the life, death and upraising of Jesus of Nazareth all those centuries ago, far transcends the historical boundaries of this particular life and death. To put it theologically, the Spirit of Christ has burst through these boundaries in space and time. It betokens a Providence that has drawn in every people and culture of the human race. The Christ of which I speak, for the understanding of whom Jesus of Nazareth remains fundamental, is savingly active, often not recognizably so by Christians themselves, in the lives and cultural patterns of countless non-Christians. I am not speaking of some unknown Christ of Islam, Judaism, Hinduism or some other tradition, as if Christians are advantageously placed, on the basis of their doctrinal histories, to recognize this reality while the non-Christian is not. I am not speaking, in other words, of an *appropriative*, an idolatrous, hold on Christ. I am speaking of a Christ that Christians themselves must learn to recognize by affirming first God's salvific concern for all peoples and for the (cultural) articulation of their humanity, and then engaging respectfully in a dialogue of exploration and discovery. In this process, both partners will grow and learn salvifically in Christ, a Christ ultimately recognizable for the Christian by continued reference to and dialogic reflection upon the life, death and upraising of Jesus of Nazareth. I call this guiding but open-ended reality 'Christ'; the Buddhist may refer to it as the Buddha-nature. Barring conversion of some kind, we must respectfully acknowledge of each other that we cannot leave our starting points entirely behind, for the starting point is consummated in the goal. Some labels are importantly adhesive and must be allowed to remain so.

This means that dialogue is not necessarily, or even usually, some agreement of the lowest common doctrinal denominator. Genuine difference of view and disagreement will continue as part of the unitive process. But difference is of two kinds: difference that complements and is the creative basis for a new synthesis, and difference that opposes. Before we are quick to affirm the latter, we must be slow to abandon the prospects of the former, doing so only when we cannot but (provisionally perhaps) admit that the directions of our mutual differences are really opposed. In that case, there may be residual error in one party's view. But since to err is inherently human (even in the 'true' faith), it will usually be a precipitate act to attribute the error to the other. Though there may be genuine commitment to one faith-stance in this approach, there is very little room for the processes of cultural imperialism or simplistic doctrinal assimilation. The new synthesis in Christ (for the Christian) is a more or less *new* synthesis, producing a new reality of belief or practice, incorporating elements from both sides, depending on circumstance and context. Thus the new Christian synthesis of worship in India, say, will be different from its counterpart in China or Africa. 'Behold, I make all things *new*.'

All this must be worked out, both theoretically and practically. The process is under way, in the Catholic context, not only in India, for instance, but also in institutions of research and learning in the West. The weighting in the dialogue here has been towards the Sanskritic traditions of Hinduism, often unsatisfactorily for various reasons; but a good beginning has been made, one that continues to be subject to critical reflection by Christian theologians (including *dalits* – those belonging to 'oppressed' groups). This pertains to why I describe myself as a 'Hindu-Catholic', for I too, am heir to this tradition of Hindu–Christian engagement. Having been brought up in India as part-Indian myself, and having lived for many years in existential dialogue with a Hindu wife (and her family), I am involved personally and professionally in achieving a Christian commitment that is not only enriched, but also transformed, by Hindu meaning. This meaning particularly pertains to the Vedantic tradition, especially of Shankara and Ramanuja. I find that the monistic, or more correctly, non-dualistic, approach of these theologians (their kind of non-dualism is at odds in important respects) has led me to reappraise my Catholic commitment, to discover more profoundly the non-dualistic heart of my own faith.

Thus the scriptural passages in which I have ended, and re-begun, my spiritual quest are beautifully stated by the Christ in the Gospel of John: 'I am the vine, you are the branches. He who abides in me, and I in him, he it is that bears much fruit, for apart from me you can do nothing . . . As the Father has loved me, so have I loved you; abide in my love . . . This is my commandment, that you love one another as I have loved you . . . Father . . . that they may be one even as we are one, I in them and thou in me, that they may become perfectly one' (15.5, 9, 12; 16, 22–3; RSV). It is this Christ that saves, or rather, God in Jesus the Christ. This, I think, is the highest Christian teaching. There is no ultimate loss of identity here, rather, one discovers one's true divinized identity, an identity one is called to experience and share with every other human being. Buddhist and Hindu scriptures further intimate for me that in the divine being we can experience a oneness with all reality, non-human beings included.

This is a hard teaching to *live* up to (rather than just to believe in). It does not take kindly to a gushing sentimentality, or some ideological excusing of wrongdoing. It does not tolerate evil; evil must be confronted. Criminals must be recognized for what they are and restrained, suffering overcome or alleviated, even, where necessary, wars entered into and fought. There is also a place for retribution in this scheme. But all must be done with a compassion and humanity, supported by instruments of discourse, legislation and other practice, that does not lose sight of the ultimate vision of oneness. Further, even if this vision is implemented, suffering or wrongdoing will by no means evaporate away. People will continue to fall ill, to lose loved ones, to have cherished hopes dashed, to make mistakes, to commit crime, to feel anxious, to die. This is the human condition, though I believe that as we seek to live up to the ideal, suffering and anxiety and wrongdoing will be easier to cope with, and some kinds of affliction will be reduced or absent. But it is as a vehicle of selfless compassion that suffering acts best to accomplish the end I advocate. It is here, I think, that Christian teaching can be very strong.

Does my 'vine theology' eviscerate the theological uniqueness of Jesus of Nazareth, or of the Christ that saves? No. The particulars I celebrate are parts of a larger whole, in which the uniqueness of particularity finds its proper, self-transcending meaning. But it is ill-advised it seems to me, and poor witness to the Jesus who lived and died for all human beings, to glory in some 'scandal of particularity', whereby a particular cultural embeddedness of his life among us and a particular doctrinal formulation of his saving role are absolutized to the detriment, not only of other religious cultures, but also of other cultural expressions of this life and role. This would be a scandal indeed. There is nothing good in it. It is wrong I think, and profoundly unchristian, to insist that different religious languages and the concepts they embed are entirely self-referencing webs of meaning, without actual or potential overlapping, bridges, meeting points, convergences, mutualities, shared horizons, of sense and reference (inclusive of ultimate being).

In fact, history has shown this form of the incommensurability thesis to be false. Christian doctrine itself in the West has evolved synthetically, through the fusion of Hebrew, Greek and Latin elements. New synthetic patterns of religious speech and belief emerged through the fusion of cultures in nineteenth-century Bengal (for example, in the Brahmo movement). To insist on the semantic closure of a religious discourse is to fly in the face not only of history, but of the religious belief and hope that all human beings are called to embark upon the path to the *same* ultimate fulfilling destiny, in this life. This is an article of faith for which I wish to live and in which I hope to die.

Notes

1. See, for example, Chandogya Up. 6.12.1f.
2. Aitareya Up. 1.1.1.

WHEN METHODIST AND HINDU MEET: CONFESSIONS OF A COMPULSIVE RE-VISIONARY

Revd Dr Eric Lott

Revd Dr Eric Lott, *a Methodist minister, has been Professor of Indian Religions at the United Theological College, Bangalore, for many years, edited the* Bangalore Theological Forum, *and is a widely published author.*

HOW RARE THE chance to muse publicly on our ultimacies! Or to probe the paths by which these came to be! Exactly half of my life has been spent in India. And as it is this thirty-year Eastern experience that stands out most prominently in the process shaping the ultimacies of my faith, it is there that I shall begin.

The late 1950s was a fertile, if challenging, time to arrive in India as a missionary. Politically, culturally and ecclesiastically so much in India's life was changing. Yet, even if the colonial period was officially over, a mere decade is a very short time for the fruits of hard-won liberation to show as anything more than a few promising buds. I took to India a passionate concern that Christian faith and worship, that ecclesial lifestyle, be expressed in authentically indigenous ways; I found much that disappointed, but not all.

Much of my first five years in India was lived virtually in the shadow of the Cathedral Church of the Epiphany, on the edge of the small railway-town of Dornakal. Azariah, from the deep south of Tamil Nadu, was the first Indian to become an Anglican bishop. His dream of incorporating Mogul minarets along with Dravidian stone pillars bursting with the fertile buds of plantain trees and embossed with the lotus motif may not meet all aesthetic tastes. It was, however, a genuinely 'epiphanic' place of worship – for the many colourful Lombadi tribal people of that area, for Christians from *dalit* backgrounds (once 'untouchable'), for Hindus too, and certainly for the young missionary I then was. Sitting on mats on the floor, singing the wonderfully evocative Telugu Christian lyrics, which I later realized could well have been in many cases Hindu *bhakti* songs of loving praise to the Lover of Souls – all fused together to create for me a powerful sense of the divine presence.

Unfortunately there was also some rather dreary preaching to be endured in a language ('the Italian of the East') that lends itself to verbosity when not the vehicle for powerful beauty and imaginative evocation that it can and should be. There was, too, the dawning recognition that the much-lauded eucharistic liturgy of the Church of South India, especially when translated from English, as if that were some kind of sacrosanct text, was woefully lacking in indigenous sensitivity. Immaculately 'shaped' though it may be from the point of view of Western liturgical reform, it lacks the slightest allusion to distinctively Indian religious symbolism, or to Indian social realities. It is blandly unacculturated. Later experience was very different. As convener of the Inter-cultural Worship Group at United Theological College, Bangalore, I had the task of drafting many worship-forms that were more indigenously sensitive.[1]

I had been plunged immediately into the struggle to learn the Telugu language, and then Sanskrit and later Kannada and Gujarati, though not all with equal success. Telugu is the only one of them I wrote books in and I still dream in from time to time. Of the numerous struggles called for in order to cross the formidably high cultural boundaries the new missionary faces, becoming at least relatively at ease with a local language was most crucial. And Dravidian languages are extremely sophisticated. Telugu word use is especially extensive and flexible because it has incorporated great tracts of Sanskrit vocabulary as well as its older Dravidian words, as did many other Indian languages to a lesser or greater extent.

I make this point for a number of reasons. One of them is this: a word that frequently popped up in all these languages was *darsana*. 'Vision' is what it means, I was told. It seemed strange, though, that the same word was used in a number of very different situations. Here are some examples. My bishop in Dornakal – Solomon by name, and a man of wise simplicity by nature – placed me early on under the gentle supervision of a long-haired, long-bearded presbyter called Kasala Ratnam. When, years before, in giving birth to their first child, his young wife and the child died, Ratnam had, he told me, been given 'a vision from the Lord' directing him to become a celibate sadhu and set up an ashram in a quiet place by a river. In fact this 'jewel' of a man died near his ashram just a few days after his last letter to my wife and me (and very shortly before I began writing this). He was true to his vision. And many others in India later spoke of similar kinds of divine *darsana*, often experienced at a time of extreme stress when their worlds were in danger of disintegrating. They invariably saw the experience as a breakthrough from a different level of reality. And usually they felt it enabled them to find some new kind of purpose in life, even if this entailed a quite radical redirecting of their lives. Candidates for ecclesial ministry, for example, would very often refer to this sort of *darsana*. My own moments of *darsana* have seemed far less invasive of 'normal' consciousness; they have had more of the character of persuasive *insight*.

Another typical usage of this term occurred when a Hindu friend announced he was going to have *darsana* of Balayogi of Mumadivaram on the River Godavari. Balayogi was a local 'low-born' young swami who himself had received a *darsana* from Lord Siva while out herding cattle in the bush. It was said that he had eventually taken a vow of absolute silence and stillness, and of total abstinence from any food or drink. His silent *darsana* was given each year to a huge crowd of devotees only at the time of *Maha-Siva-Ratri*, or the Great Night of Lord Siva. Those I spoke to who had made this pilgrimage claimed a strange sense of life enhancement. They said they felt in touch with a dimension of being that in normal life had become obscured. Similar accounts are given by many who make pilgrimage (Hindus, Christians, Muslims, Sikhs, Jains) to other persons or places they feel to be endued with strangely numinous power. Indeed, the term *darsana* is used for any visit to a sacred place, and especially for the 'seeing' of and being 'seen' by the sacred Focus of that numinous place. While I would usually claim to be fairly insensitive to the 'feel' of a place, I must confess to a strange sense of enhancement of being when visiting certain sacred places, and when standing before certain sacred figures, or sometimes just being part of an act of corporate worship. And these moments of *darsana* are in no way confined to Christian worship places, however normative the latter may be for the meaning such *darsana*-moments have for me.

There is a third prominent use of 'vision' in the Indian traditions. Each belief-system, each of the diverse metaphysical ways of describing the universe is called a *darsana*, i.e. a distinct way of 'visioning' things. Even within the one great Hindu tradition of philosophical theology called Vedanta, in spite of numerous common features, we should not try to play down (as many Indian religious teachers do today) the emphasis classical Vedantic teachers themselves made on the very distinct kind of system they expound. One kind of Vedantic *darsana* is crucially different from another.

For example (and I labour this point because it is of such great import to the development of more authentic Indian Christian theology) some see ultimate reality in terms of a oneness of being that makes either the difference or the relationship between creaturely beings quite unreal – even if you emphasize this unreality of things as only so from the point of view of the ultimate One. To claim this for the way things really are is crucially different from another Vedantic vision that sees *relationship* itself as providing the clue to ultimacy. This is not just a matter of interpretive or noetic nuance; it is a very different ontic vision. And Vedanta is but one of numerous Indian ontological systems.

We miss the mark if we refer all this to the ancient, and in itself telling, fable of the six blind men who were asked to identify an elephant after each had touched different parts of it. For one thing, Indian visionaries certainly do not see themselves as blindly feeling for a part of all that is. In fact, even if there are religious traditions in which all-inclusive metaphysical matters are treated in a somewhat agnostic way – by the Buddha for instance – whatever the great teachers have spoken of in their religious vision they have spoken of with ontological certitude. That on some points they cannot all be right is another matter. I here merely make the point that religious vision does not have the character of that which we 'feel after, if haply we may find'. And at least in the case of the Vedantic theologians, their intention was to identify the whole elephant. If we come to feel that in reality they are not blessed with such an inclusive vision of things, who is the person we must presume to be fully sighted and thus able to tell us they are blind and that a whole elephant stands there? Here, then, are three further characteristics of religious visions – their diversity, doctrinal shaping, and the sense of visionary certitude they induce.

But this emphasis on the distinctive character of religious vision, each with an undergirding belief-system, or doctrinal framework (however ontologically inclusive) will be attributed by some to a typical missionary stance, with the notorious divide-and-rule policy beloved by imperialists. And the fact is, however ecumenically re-formed I may be, I am at heart still a Methodist preacher, with certain visionary compulsions of my own. And I confess that I find the neo-Vedantic slogan of 'all religions are in essence the same', or merely 'different paths to the same ultimate goal', so wide of the mark in terms of what people see as the goals of their faith as to weaken the sense of visionary reality of those different faiths. I am fairly certain that my stance here is not the result of a Christian preacher's obsession with the 'uniqueness of Christ', which is of course lost if in reality all our gods are the same.

I am fairly sure of my motives here, if only because in my concern that a genuine encounter of visionary stance be allowed to take place (which is only possible if the real diversity of visions and interpretations is acknowledged) I am in fact a convinced, perhaps a compulsive, *re-visionary*. Revisionism is always seen as deeply suspect by hard-edged ideologues. To be willing to modify and restate original doctrines because of the flow of human history is seen as being unfaithful to the purity of true revelation. Just a tinge of fundamentalist spirit is enough to produce a condemnation of the revisionary. And in the case of the Christian tradition, this is in spite of the irrefutable fact that within revelatory Scripture, within the apostolic period, at every stage of Christian history when there has been a compelling breakthrough of the spirit of Christ, there has been new insight into the meaning of the tradition and its revelation. There has been revisioning, and revisioning always as a result of the encounter of compelling features of the tradition with compelling features of some other world of perceived reality. This is not a denial of the need for rootedness in religious tradition; it is in fact an affirmation of the need for rootedness. There is no genuine encounter, no possibility of revision, without that continuing grounding in a tradition.

For me, then, being a Methodist preacher (where I began my ecumenical journey), as much as being a professor of Indian Religions, lies behind this compulsion to continuing revision. For the preacher in me has this need always to try to draw out persuasive meaning for those to whom I found I must relate within the Indian milieu – religious, cultural, social. Preaching the Gospel in terms of trying to impose on people that new world-view that will entirely negate their present world hardly strikes me as 'good' news at all. For whatever diversity of world-view there may be, there are also – inevitable in view of our shared humanness – points of convergence that provide the basis for interchange of vision. In a moment I shall try to show what I mean by such interchange.

First, though, I want to look at why the Methodist preacher part of me also seemed to be pushing me towards a reshaping of what many would regard as traditional Methodism. For various reasons mine was a rather catholic Methodist grounding with some unusual feeder streams making up the mix. My mother, in spite of faithful attendance at the tiny West Country chapel I was brought up in, always remained at heart a good Anglican. My father was a pioneer organic farmer, often eulogizing the 'living soil' by which we lived and on which I worked long hours for seven years when I opted out of school a week after my fifteenth birthday. Most work was done manually; we were literally in touch with the many stages of tilling, growing and harvesting, and the feeding and caring for the animals. The sense that earth is a living body, to be respected rather than seen as an agent for greater production and profit made a deep impression on my adolescent consciousness. Artificial boosting of production and profit-making were utter anathema to my father. The local district council members were totally bemused, I am sure, when lectured from time to time on such matters.

Other influences were shaping me too, as a preaching instinct began to emerge. There was a Quakerish Methodist mystic, a sort of guru to me for a while, for whom every point in life should be seen as an opportunity to commune in a new way with the all-pervading divine Spirit. And there was a high sacramentalist Methodist rural minister who introduced an almost illiterate nineteen-year-old farmhand to such exotic Eastern Orthodox theology as Lampert's *The Divine Realm* (an Oxford doctoral thesis originally!), which has all creation throbbing with hidden divine glory.

The same minister also reinforced in me the vision, embedded deeply if often latently in Methodism, of a transformed human community in which love rules out all violence. It is not surprising that later in London it was the preaching of Donald Soper that I found exciting.

I repeat, mine was an unusually catholic Methodist grounding. Some themes from other religious traditions that later made a powerful appeal to me clearly did so because they resonated with some of these earlier faith-memories. For all my belief in *new* visioning of earlier tradition, resonance and remembering are crucial in the shaping of consciousness, certainly theological consciousness. In our cognizing – our moments when we are sure that 'this is true', 'this has important meaning for me' – there is always some element of re-cognizing.

Before leaving this Methodist section, I can illustrate in a different way the point just made. The cultural attitudes of West Country Methodism can be woefully narrow. Yet deep in this tradition's faith-memory some wonderfully inclusive themes shine out. No more than does establishment status (and for generations chapel-folk were anti-establishment) do proper ecclesiastical structure or correct doctrine carry weight, especially in Bible-influenced West Country Methodism. What does so is the 'heart strangely warmed', melted by the fire of divine love; the need for powerfully purifying love in response to the divine arms opened in grace to all; the urge to sing as though our very being were born in song; the warmly expressed community togetherness resulting from openness to all people of faith – called 'the catholic spirit' by John Wesley.

And these *bhakti*-themes (as Indian God-lovers would call them) have come to have a double significance for me. If this kind of *bhakti*-experience of divine love is at the heart of things, surely only a glad openness to any people of similar life-enhancing religious experience is appropriate. In other words, within our own faith there are resources, indeed strong compulsions, to respond positively to people of other faith-communities.

The opposite of this inclusive spirit that we so often find is to me sinful disloyalty to the heart of Christian faith. That 'fundamentalists' turn this argument on its head is a betrayal of what is truly fundamental to faith.

Secondly, it was the *bhakti*-faiths within the Indian religious life in which I found special resonance as a Methodist preacher. (And is it entirely coincidental that my first reading of ecstatic songs of the Tamil Vaishnava God-lovers was in a pioneering translation by a Methodist preacher, J. S. M. Hooper, whom I met in 1958 when he was around ninety years old?)

It was within one such *bhakti*-tradition that I found resources of imagery and theological concept that were to prove especially significant for the revisioning that took place on my own spiritual journey. I refer to what is often called Ramanuja-*darsana*, that visionary system worked out in the eleventh century within the formal requirements of the metaphysical tradition called Vedanta, but springing from a fusing of God-loving ecstatic poetry and elaborate cultic ritual (both within Vishnu faith-communities). And here I recognize the influence of a youthful Ninian Smart, in the mid-1950s lecturing at King's College, London, and making it clear (to me for the first time) that other religious traditions need not remain inaccessibly alien to our ways of thinking. They are part of the shared experience of the human race, and their conceptual systems are important for our own self-understanding.

As this essay is in part a disentangling of the strands that become woven into a faith-position, it is worth noting that Ramanuja too did not invent *de novo* the Visishta-Advaita system, though his way of integrating and formulating this vision was truly original. He was in fact drawing heavily upon imagery and ideas long embedded deep in prominent strands of the Hindu consciousness. Much of what he writes is very close in fact to the 'vision-of-God-in-the-form-of-the-universe' that the Gita ('the gospel of Hinduism') describes. It was precisely this vision that made such an impact on me, so that some years later, in the great temple at Sri Perumbudur where Ramanuja was born (and where tragically Rajiv Gandhi was so violently assassinated), I was asked to lecture on the contemporary significance of Ramanuja's key image of the world as God's body.[2]

Its corollary, of course, is that God is the great and inmost Self of all. And this is the theme found more prominently in Vedanta generally. Crucial to all theistic experience in India is belief in that Supreme Self as endowed with an unchanging fullness of perfection. And for the Vaishnava *bhakti*-schools, it is the overwhelming love of that Self for all who seek refuge in God that prompts God's special embodiments in the form of avatars 'descending' to restore the proper ordering of things and to be close to those who love God. So there is a correspondence here of cosmological and soteriological themes. The key is God's embodiment in creation, whereby God is 'inseparably related' to all cosmic life.

The credo that I outline in a moment has this body-image at its heart. It assumes that our selfhood, and our embodiedness, has much to tell us about Godhood (in spite of what Barthian-like theology would say in opposition, and however much we allow that in the end it is the compelling vision from within a revelatory tradition that enables such a theology-through-human-experience).

There is, of course, a selectiveness about the kind of interchange that has taken place between my grounding faith-memories and what I encounter in Hindu *bhakti*. Some of the religious life as well as social ideology often accompanying *bhakti* has remained alien, or may even have been repulsive to me. There is, for example, reference above to the 'proper ordering' of things, or the concept of *dharma*, undergirding *bhakti* religion normally. And historically that *dharmic* ordering has meant the caste system – each human community's life and status being determined by birth, which in turn is determined by prior karmic deeds. There is no way I can remain grounded in the teaching of Christ and find room for such a view of the human community, not without a radical critique and reworking of these *dharmic* themes. But I also have to remember that at the climax of the Gita's telling of the *bhakti*-story, at the point where Krishna imparts the 'highest mystery', which is that 'I love you well', there is also the claim that in taking refuge in this love the loved one is to 'give up all dharmas, take me only as refuge; I will set you free from all sin'.[3] Exactly what this means is debated at length. There is then the question of what it can mean for the Christian *bhakta*, or God-lover, given the kind of liberative impulse the Christian tradition, at its best, has been able to find in the Christ-story.

So, then, the imperative to choose, whether in response to other faiths or within one's own faith, remains there all the time. But do we actually choose? Or is it more a matter of being gripped by, being compelled by a certain way of seeing things, a certain way of selecting images and ideas as part of that visioning that will always remain a mystery?

Before my credo there is one more strand in my encountering experience that must be drawn out a little more, in view of the reference to a liberative attitude to human community. The majority of Christians among whom I lived and worked in my early years in India had come from what they themselves now call *dalit* communities. They are the 'Broken Ones'. Previously they had been the 'untouchables'. Gandhi had called them *harijans* – God's people. But they have come to reject fiercely and bitterly Gandhi's softly, softly approach to the transformation of society. Systemic revolution is what is called for, such is the alienation and deprivation to which the Broken Ones have been subjected for centuries by the Hindu caste system, with its inbuilt notions of purity and pollution.

From the moment of arrival in India, therefore, I was compelled to reflect on the meaning of Christian faith for such oppressed people. Basic liberation themes soon peppered my preaching, and have done ever since. Biblical images of the new world we are to struggle for, a world of just peace in which every distinct community is free to be human in the way it is led to be, images of walls broken down, of a new human family built up – such was the stuff of all my sermons. It meant being critical of the way life was in India. But what was I to make of the moving experience of working alongside Hindus in the middle 1960s? It was an ancient Brahmanic town, on the banks of the River Godavari, where our college was. A group of Hindus, deeply sensitive to human suffering (belonging to the Society for Compassion in Life) had set up a leprosy clinic. Anyone who has tended the maggot-filled ulcers in the foot of a leprosy sufferer and seen the cruel disfiguring of facial features and gradual loss of limb extremities will know what nursing in a leprosy clinic means. My primary task was providing appropriate food, clothing and medicines from a Christian agency. I quickly came to marvel at the dedication of the Hindu workers there, many of them voluntary. And these were people supposedly wedded to a lofty indifference to all such human need. But their devotion was not sufficiently radical for the liberation movement that was gradually taking shape, and was even overtaking my own brand of just-sharing talk.

I must confess to a sense of being trapped. For that area was the heartland of the violent revolutionary Naxalite movement committed to creating terror in the hearts of all landowners, moneylenders and suchlike oppressive classes. In the hills and forests of the area numerous young men and a few women, from Christian churches and from other communities, were caught up in the revolutionary fervour and had gone underground. I knew a number of those who were killed by the security police forces. Rejection of this violent solution was a strong part of my religious vision; and yet I felt a sense of identity with their concerns, however naively misplaced. Many of the Naxalites were early *dalit* revolutionaries, though the *dalit* movement today (or Ambedkar's neo-Buddhist movement even then) is not as such committed to violence.

Increasingly I came to the conviction that the *dalit* need for an authentic sense of identity does call for an exclusive stage of self-exploration. There has to be a long period of focusing on that tribal memory – its stories, its distinctive themes, its imagery – that creates that special sense of *dalit*ness. But to do this by deliberately cutting themselves away from all non-*dalit* tribal life, or from any cultural life that has been touched by 'mainstream' Sanskritic cultural life, is merely self-weakening. As I argued fairly recently in my Teape Seminar lectures at Cambridge, what is needed is the recovery of lost strands of primal imagery from within that which has been taken into Sanskritic cultural life, and in many cases has been made effete and enfeebled by the domesticating of middle-class urbanity and privilege. The revolutionary thrust, the self-empowerment the *dalit* people are seeking, *dalit* Christians in particular, must surely be grounded in a stronger sense of cultural identity, rather than sought primarily by political strategies. That there is great empowerment of consciousness through the recovery of primal imagery is an emphasis that, for me, has grown through my reflection of the potently imaginative art of Jyoti Sahi, who draws deeply from the wells of tribal life.

My credo, therefore, is based on and built around one such primal image, an image that was also crucial to the *darsana* of Ramanuja and his faith-community. That vitality has ebbed in this community, that this seminal vision has not inevitably produced all those fruit – theological, cultural, social – that I see latent within it, proves little. When I have spoken in meetings of Vaishnava scholars about the incongruity of believing that all living creatures, *dalit* people too, are part of the body of the Lord, and at the same time practising demeaning caste discrimination, most at least acknowledge the anomaly. And what community, religious or social, does not have its tragic anomalies?

At this point, then, I can say that even though I have been powerfully drawn to certain key features of Hindu theology, especially its body-talk, and even though I have come to admire and love many Hindu people, as far as I am aware, there was never any question of my leaving the faith-community of my upbringing. And this in spite of often being deeply distressed by what seem to me to be dreadful failures within that faith-community. The choice for me, then, has been about what my vision is of the kind of Christian faith that has most potent meaning for the world I live in. What within that faith, as it encounters and interacts with other faiths, provides a compelling new vision for our time?

Finally, then, my credo. Though body-based, it can be expressed quite naturally in fairly traditional trinitarian shape:

I BELIEVE in the great Self of all, source of life in all, inmost being of all beings, yet wonderfully 'beyond' all embodied being.

I BELIEVE in God as personal Being, with purposive power and love embodied in the mystery of creation that flows from God, and with the heart's loving worship as the most appropriate creaturely response to God's being.

I BELIEVE that creaturely life provides key images for our understanding of and relating to a God who can be 'visioned' as Father, Mother, Lover, Ruler, Shepherd, Companion, Dancer; and as Light, Water, Fire, Rock, Tree, Seed, Drum and much more in the imagery of primal vision.

I BELIEVE, in particular, in a vision of creation as the *body* of God, for our own embodiedness provides insight into the 'inseparable relationship' of God to cosmic life.

I BELIEVE that all creation, with its complex and delicately interwoven ecosystems, has sacred worth, and that humans are a 'presence' on earth, sharing in creation's body as bearers of the divine image of self-embodiment in a specially responsible way, with power to destroy and to make peace and thus to share in the creative purpose of the loving Self of all.

I BELIEVE in the mystery of God's embodiedness in human history and in particular human form.

I BELIEVE that Jesus of Nazareth, though conditioned by his particular history, in distinctive and lastingly significant ways embodied God's human presence as creative, normative, healing love: in his obedient role of ministering to others; in setting them free from a wide range of needs relating to their corporality; in opening up doors of forgiveness and acceptance, and to ways of love and care for our neighbour; in creating a body of those who shared, however inadequately, his vision of a new world; in pointing, through his death and the resurrection of his own body – and so in Eucharistic bread-body – to the restored body of God's creation that we long for; and in providing that revelatory point of reference by which we can relate positively to all other epiphanic points of divine presence, in whatever historical or cultural context.

I BELIEVE in that eternal Spirit, focused in Jesus and his body of God-lovers, revealing God's purpose through countless prophets and visionaries in different ages and different cultures.

I BELIEVE especially in the Spirit that has made prophets bold to speak out against all that has embodied evil oppression, to stand by all denied their share in the resources of earth's body, or their right to a place within the full life of the social body.

I BELIEVE, therefore, in the Spirit as the focal point of God's body-restoring action, guiding God's people everywhere and in all ages in all their historical conditionedness, to become God's body of worship and service, imparting those gifts by which the whole human body can yet become the agent of God's loving purpose for the world, the wider body of God.

This, then, is something of the ultimate vision to which I am committed.

Notes

1. Some of these are included in *Worship in an Indian Context* (Bangalore: UTC, 1986), ed. E. J. Lott, and containing my early draft of the Church of South

India's *Alternative Liturgy* that Christopher Duraisingh and I had prepared for the CSI Synod Liturgy Committee.
2. Published along with other papers at the seminar (an annual event for Sri Vaishnavas) in *Studies in Ramanuja* (Madras: Ramanuja Vedanta Centre, 1980). More accessible are my *Vedantic Approaches to God* (London: Macmillan, 1980) and *Vision, Tradition and Interpretation* (Berlin: Mouton de Gruyter, 1988).
3. Bhagavad Gita 18:66.

BECOMING HUMAN

Dr Gerrie Lubbe

Dr Gerrie Lubbe is Secretary of the World Conference on Religion and Peace (South Africa). He lectures on religious studies at UNISA.

HAILING FROM A family of Dutch colonists whose forebears arrived in South Africa in 1692, I grew up as a white, Afrikaans-speaking Christian. With the exception of the local butcher who was Jewish, the other people who were recognized as belonging to a faith other than Christianity were all members of the sizeable Muslim community of Indian extraction. The greater majority, I would say about ninety per cent or more, of the inhabitants of our town and district were black (African). Although most of them obviously adhered to and practised the traditional religion, they were in those days regarded as 'pagans' who had no religion of their own.

What was true of my home town was, and still is, true of the whole of South Africa as far as the presence of faiths other than Christianity was concerned. With the exception of Jews, all adherents of other faiths were and are by and large black, that is, African, Coloured and Indian. In the heyday of apartheid this meant that virtually all people of other faiths found themselves, together with black Christians, being referred to as 'non-whites' and therefore on the receiving end of this notorious and inhuman ideology. It further meant that interfaith dialogue virtually always involved the bridging of the racial divide which, because of institutionalized racism, rarely happened. Besides formal contact such as work, trade and official dealings, very few friendships, let alone dialogue, existed across the racial and religious barrier. Whilst urban life might have been more liberally inclined than that in the countryside, it would nevertheless be fair to say that, until the late eighties, it was totally possible for the average white Afrikaans-speaking Christian to go through life without ever experiencing an encounter on equal footing with someone of a different race or religion. In tracing my own involvement with people of other faiths, I find it of utmost importance first to trace my conscious crossing of the racial barrier.

My father was a schoolteacher and my mother a housewife. Being well-integrated people in their particular context, I do not think that they were necessarily more or less racist than the rest of the white inhabitants of our town. What I do recall very vividly was that both of them were pious, God-fearing people with a very keen interest in Christian mission work. Being children of their time, they probably also regarded all African people as pagans in need of salvation. Because of their missionary interest, we often visited some of the surrounding mission stations in support of the work being done there in the spiritual, medical and educational fields. Their missionary interest was not exceptional, although hardline racists would even have opposed such an enterprise on the basis that blacks had no souls! The Dutch Reformed Church, to which my parents belonged, was very active in the field of missions and became involved in countries as far afield as Nigeria, Malawi, Zambia and Zimbabwe.

In retrospect I often wonder about the real motives behind this almost feverish involvement in bringing the message of eternal salvation to people who were so poor and deprived of basic human rights. Although it would be unfair to say that the Dutch Reformed missionaries had no or little concern for the material needs of people, the greater emphasis was certainly on the need for eternal life. Whilst the latter is certainly a key concept in the biblical understanding of mission, it served as a very important *raison d'être* for white settlers in South Africa. Proclaiming that they had come to bring the light of the gospel to a dark continent, the early missionaries who arrived in South Africa could, besides some typical Western arrogance, not be faulted in Christian terms. What did cast a shadow on their noble motives was the fact that they came in the company of colonial expansionists and opportunity-hungry traders. The firm conviction that God had called them with a very specific task to this sub-continent caused the white settlers to hold on tenaciously to their newly found fatherland. Whilst the pioneering spirit that prevailed certainly made constructive contributions, the feeling of spiritual superiority with regard to the indigenous population paved the way for a self-declared custody over black people and eventually degenerated into the totalitarian control of apartheid.

To return to the question why my folks, like many of their contemporaries, could promote the propagation of the Christian gospel with apparent disregard for the oppression and deprivation the 'missionary objects' suffered, two possible explanations emerge. On the one hand, it could have been argued that, like apartheid, the Christian faith was deemed to be in the interest of the black population. In line with the idea of total custody, the proponents of the ideology saw the preaching of the gospel as a necessary tool in achieving 'civilized' norms and in maintaining white supremacy. On the other hand, it could have been said that whilst blacks had so little in this life, they would at least inherit eternal life hereafter. This would, from the side of ordinary whites, have boiled down to an acknowledgement not only of the material deprivation of blacks, but also of their own powerlessness to change societal structures. I never asked my parents what exactly motivated them, but I would think, and have reason to hope, that it might have been the latter rather than the former line of argument that they followed.

The gain I have made from their interest in mission work was the fact that I was more exposed to contact with blacks other than the stereotyped illiterate domestic servant than most of my schoolfriends.

My pilgrimage across the racial border commenced in my last year at primary school when our class teacher proposed that we should have a class debate on the topic 'Should Kaffirs go to school?' (The derogatory term *Kaffir* for blacks was commonly used in those days.) Strangely enough such a question was a hotly debated issue in society during the apartheid years, since many whites were of the opinion that the more educated black people were, the more susceptible they would be to communist propaganda and influence! Be it as it may, the class debate was arranged and for some or other reason I was asked by the teacher to argue in favour of the motion. What I do recall today about that incident way back in 1954 was that when I was wondering what I should be saying in that debate, I was overcome by an instant, almost naive feeling of justice in the sense of 'Here am I walking home from school, so why shouldn't they be doing the same?' I can no longer remember what was actually said during that debate, but what did stay with me for the rest of my life was what happened when the teacher put the whole issue to the vote: out of the forty children in class thirty-nine voted against the motion, saying blacks should not be educated. I, by the grace of God, was the only one who voted for the motion.

At the time I did not really understand what was happening to me as a thirteen-year-old boy. All I knew was that things would never be the same again. For the very first time I discovered a social awareness within myself. I suddenly became aware of the plight of blacks and their need for education, housing and health care. My discovery of course led to endless arguments with my friends. At this time I also found an urge for more contact with blacks. During my last two years at school I started a small Sunday school in the black community and managed to put together a small group of young people for visiting black patients in the local hospital on Sunday afternoons. Looking back now I realize that two forces were driving me at the time. In the first place I felt the urge to share the gospel and in this sense it was certainly the influence of my parents that came through. In the second place I started discovering that black people were human! In a society where naked racism dominated and where the human dignity of those on the receiving end was trampled underfoot, such a discovery had to be consciously made. However, to develop an ear for the underdog in a society made immune by means of constant and well-designed propaganda is only possible through the grace of God.

I now also recognize that God, through my increased exposure to black people, prepared me for the next stage of my pilgrimage, namely making contact with the local Muslim community. Running at least ten or twelve well-established shops in our town, the local Indian community was active and highly visible. They were in contrast to Africans and were generally regarded as more civilized, and yet they were even less acceptable. Indians were brought to South Africa by the British in 1860 to work as indentured labourers on the sugar fields in Natal. With these labourers came people who were attracted by the commercial prospect of the country. Known as 'passengers' they made their way into the interior and settled in the province of Transvaal. In our local situation it was no secret that Indians were disliked and for three reasons: in the first place their presence was regarded as the result of British initiatives, and with the latter for historical reasons not being liked at all, Indians were regarded as intruders and were therefore unwelcome; in the second place their business skills certainly posed a threat to white enterprises; and in the third place they were different. Belonging to a foreign culture, speaking an unknown language, adhering to a non-Christian religion and, perhaps above all being non-white, prevented them from being accepted. With the so-called Repatriation Act hanging over their heads like the Sword of Damocles, Indians were regarded as foreigners who would be returning to India at any time.

Since I grew up in a proper Afrikaans home I was well acquainted with and observant of the unwritten injunction: 'Do not buy from coolies' (*cooly* being the derogatory term used for Indians). And yet, in spite of the enforced separation and deep-seated suspicion, I, in my last year at school, became extremely interested in the local mosque, three blocks away from our home. I would often visit the mosque on an afternoon and ask questions of the imam. What intrigued me most was the Qur'an, which was displayed in the front of the mosque. Somehow regarding it as forbidden for me to touch, I would open the Qur'an and stare with fascination at the Arabic script whenever the imam turned his back on me. I cannot explain this interest other than connecting it with my discovery of black people in general. Maybe my curiosity was aroused by this unknown group of people in our midst. Perhaps my exposure to the underdog in a most natural way extended my desire for contact.

Several years later, after completion of my university studies and some years in the ministry, God led me to become the pastor of a small congregation in an Indian township near Johannesburg. Here my contact and dialogue with Muslims and Hindus became a living and daily reality. In the eyes of the Dutch Reformed Church, by whose financial assistance I was able to minister to the small Christian congregation, I was a missionary with the obligation to lead Hindus and Muslims to Christ. Although I certainly felt called by God to share the Good News of Jesus Christ with whomever He sent me to, my social awareness was by this time big enough for me to realize instinctively that I would be betraying the essence of the gospel if I were to close myself off from social problems. The fact that Christ had concern for people in a holistic manner started growing on me and I began to realize that I was not a missionary but a pastor whose responsibility it was to minister to the whole person.

Seriously grappling with the context of my people, I became aware of the ugliness of apartheid. Under the notorious Group Areas Act they had been uprooted from their residential area near to the centre of Johannesburg, and resettled against their will in an area about thirty kilometres to the south, with a serious lack of proper infrastructure. With disregard of any personal preferences, they were grouped together in an area exclusively reserved for Indians. I could of course not stay in the area and had to live in a white suburb about twenty-five kilometres away. When I took up my ministry there, the first people who had been moved had already been there for ten years and yet proper roads were still to be built. Before I actually realized it, I found myself campaigning for proper roads in the area. This was followed by campaigns for the establishment of a police station to combat crime in the area, for more housing, for a proper bus service, for hospital services, etc. Whilst my theological training certainly did not in any way prepare me for such social involvement, I had no doubt that that was what the Lord expected of me.

My involvement in these campaigns ushered in my participation in interfaith co-operation. They were not deliberately interfaith in nature. In fact, the interfaith nature of these joint ventures was of secondary importance. The emphasis was on human suffering caused by an unjust system. I recall, in particular, one incident in this regard. One night, during a national mineworkers' strike against inadequate wages, my church was asked by the National Union of Mineworkers to make our hall available for workers who had been expelled from mine hostels. Within an hour after the call, the church was a beehive of activity as Christians, Hindus and Muslims turned up with food and blankets.

My contact with people of other faiths became a dialogue, not so much about faith, but about life. It was a dialogue that was sparked off by oppression, discrimination, separation and dehumanization. And yet, I was aware all the time of the fact that my partners in the struggle were people who were deeply committed to their own faiths. I became exposed, in a very real way, to the value that other faiths attached to human life. I became acquainted with the dreams that people of other faiths, as fellow compatriots, dreamt about the future of our land. I discovered that, albeit from different angles, there was unanimity on the rejection of injustice and oppression. Very vividly I recall how we held an interfaith prayer meeting for peace in the Johannesburg City Hall in 1988, in the midst of tension and violence, caused in particular by the unwanted racial municipal elections. When we arrived at the hall, streets in the area were barricaded and policemen with dogs were posted outside, with plain-clothes members of the Security Branch inside. There we were, members of different faiths praying for peace while the presence of the police suggested the imminent outbreak of violence. In the face of such intimidation, and sharing our common humanity, we were welded together into one body of believers. The conviction of my friends of 'minority' faiths, that they were not free religiously until they were free politically, was crudely emphasized that day.

My journey into the world of faith led me to at least two crucial discoveries. On the one hand I made the discovery that I often had more in common with people of other faiths than with my fellow Christians, especially from the white side. On the other hand, I discovered that there were two Christianities in South Africa – a white one and a black one. Entering the world of the black Church was to me almost like getting acquainted with people of a different religion. I learnt a new way of looking at the Bible and discovered God's liberating power and His concern for the poor and the marginalized.

Instrumental in leading me into this new world was Archbishop Desmond Tutu. I met him when he started his term of office as general secretary of the South African Council of Churches in 1978. Two things about him made an incredible impression on me. First, there was his unconditional acceptance and friendship that has never ceased to inspire me. Second, he displayed the ability of combining a deep spirituality with genuine social concern, and this made of him the role model I had unwittingly been searching for all my life. I also owe my exposure to the international interfaith scene to Tutu. In 1979 he sent me to attend, as the only South African, the third World Assembly of the World Conference on Religion and Peace held in Princeton, USA. In 1984 he asked me to go to London to represent him at the first Interfaith Colloquium on Apartheid organized by Archbishop Trevor Huddlestone. Due to Tutu's initiative and influence both events directly contributed to the establishment of the South African Chapter of WCRP, in which I served as national president from 1984 to 1994.

My increased involvement in interfaith work convinced me of the fact that the pooling of spiritual resources to combat apartheid and to work for social and political liberation was a legitimate and relevant form of interfaith dialogue. In fact, it became abundantly clear that if interfaith dialogue wished to have a future in South Africa, it could not follow an agenda different from the one of the people, namely political liberation and the establishment of a true democracy. In 1987 I was privileged to be part of an interfaith delegation, led by Archbishop Tutu, to hold talks with the ANC in Lusaka, Zambia, on the role of religion in a democratic South Africa. In colourful language we were told, 'Don't, as people of religion, ask us to reserve a room for you in the house we are building. Join us in building that house!'

Looking back on the road I have travelled, I realize that the biblical demand for love and justice became the driving force in my life. The prophetic voices of Isaiah and Amos appealed to me in no unclear terms. It was, however, the sermon that Jesus preached in his home town Nazareth (Luke 4:16–21) that gripped me and moulded my thoughts. On that occasion Jesus first read the moving words of Isaiah 61:1–2:

> The Spirit of the Lord is upon me, because he has chosen me to bring good news to the poor. He has sent me to proclaim liberty to the captives and recovery of sight to the blind; and announce that the time has come when the Lord will save his people.

He then, with authority, stated, 'This passage of Scripture has come true today.' I do not think that I ever lost sight of the spiritual message of this portion or that Jesus became a revolutionary in my eyes. And I felt that to spiritualize away the impact of His words on prevailing social conditions would be not to take Jesus seriously and to minimize His relevance for the world of today. I remember that I once preached on this passage to a white student congregation of the Dutch Reformed Church. To put it mildly, I do not think that there was an awful lot of rapport between the preacher and his audience. Anyway, I was never invited back there again.

It was not only my political outlook but also my interfaith understanding that became influenced by the Bible. I always felt that to co-operate and have dialogue with people of other faiths was an extension of the injunction of the Lord to love my neighbour as I love myself. Without suggesting that the Bible should be looked at as a manual for interfaith work, I need to mention two passages that have been growing on me through the years and which provided me with so much insight.

One is to be found in II Kings 5 and relates how Naaman, commander of the Syrian army, became healed from his leprosy. On centre stage in this drama of life were his wife and her servant, a young Jewish girl who was captured and enslaved and taken to Damascus. Between the lines I here read of a friendship between two women; one an adult, the other a teenager; one in a powerful position and the other totally powerless; one most probably a worshipper of the Syrian god Rimmon and the other believing in the God of the Israelites. That their conversations touched on issues of faith seems certain because it led to the healing of the lord of the house. To me this story speaks of interfaith dialogue and interfaith co-operation *par excellence*!

The other portion of Scripture from which I gained much is the well-known parable of the Good Samaritan (Luke 10:25–37). In explaining the concepts of neighbourliness, concern and care, Jesus depicts an adherent of another faith as the agent of compassion. Conceding that the religious affiliation of the characters in this story is of secondary importance, it nonetheless never ceased to intrigue me. To say the least, it taught me that the virtues of caring for life's victims and of restoring human dignity are not the exclusive property of Christians. The capacity for healing is certainly to be found with all who are fully human, regardless of whether they are people of faith or of no faiths. These two passages immensely strengthened me as I journeyed with like-minded Christians, Hindus, Jews, Muslims and others, towards a new and just dispensation in our beloved country.

Saying that those moral values that South African society was and is so much in need of are human, rather than Christian, values is certainly to state the obvious. And yet it has to be seen against the backdrop of South African history. In keeping with its totalitarian nature, the apartheid regime not only wanted to control the entire spectrum of human life but also wanted to justify it morally. Thus South Africa became known as a Christian country with a Christian government which applied a policy of Christian-National education in state schools. Although the constitution that had been in force for the past ten years stated that freedom of religion was guaranteed, in the same breath it mentioned the implementation of

'Christian values and civilized norms' as one of the national goals! Since there was certainly nothing 'Christian' about the policy of apartheid, I found the way in which the Christian faith was turned into an adjective repulsive to say the least.

To challenge the 'Christian' character of the apartheid state was certainly not a nice thing to do, and for saying that the values we were striving for were human rather than exclusively Christian I was often accused of bringing the unique character of Christianity into question. A second challenge that I had to face was the inner question of what I was doing in an area where people knew religion, where people did have holy books and where people worshipped. A third challenge arose when, after a crisis of conscience, I could no longer accept financial assistance from the white Dutch Reformed Church and decided to take up secular employment while continuing with my ministry. After a short spell at a private concern, I was appointed as a lecturer in religious studies, teaching world religions, of which Christianity was one. Dealing at my working place with Christianity as one of many religious systems and then returning to my parish where there were people to whom Christ was so real that they gave up Islam or Hinduism in order to become Christians became a real, and healthy, tension in which I found myself. In facing all these questions and challenges I kept on finding only one reason for being, and becoming increasingly, committed to the Christian faith, and that was the Incarnation of Christ. I am quite prepared to admit that my being a Christian initially had to do with my genes. In later life, however, God's interest in and concern with humanity, as embodied by the Incarnation of Christ, caused me to make a firm commitment to the Christian faith. The implications of His Incarnation took on great significance in the context within which I found myself. He not only witnessed oppression but also experienced it. He condemned the exploitation of His day and identified fully with the exploited. Christ, as my Lord and Saviour, became the reason why I could never stop fighting and condemning apartheid. Because of His humanity I could discover and appreciate other human beings.

Did I encounter criticism? Oh yes, most certainly! To begin with I found myself amongst the small group of Afrikaners who, for many years, have denounced apartheid as evil and inhumane. The labels that came our way were those of 'renegades', 'communists' and 'revolutionaries'. Much of the criticism was more subtle than that, in the sense that it was the mixing of religion and politics that was pinpointed as the actual unforgivable sin! In the second place I faced critics of my interfaith activities. Here the main objection was the 'inevitable' syncretism and subsequent betrayal of the gospel that such activities would lead to. In more liberal circles I was also accused of politicizing interfaith dialogue. People, mainly whites, who were interested in such dialogue from a purely academic point of view found my particular approach too radical. In reply, I maintained that the model my partners and I were using for interfaith dialogue was only one of several and that people with different objectives were welcome to use different approaches. No other approaches came off the ground and the South African Chapter of WCRP has in the mean time become much more acceptable and kosher and halal!

I am not sure whether what I have said above can qualify being called an alternative paradigm either for conducting interfaith dialogue or for viewing religious pluralism. Maybe it should at best be looked at as a particular approach, and I would like to refer to it as the contextual approach, where the following principles apply to a lesser or greater extent:

1. Religions are practised by people, and the study of religion and religious pluralism should then result in a living dialogue involving people within particular contexts.
2. In a situation of conflict and oppression there seems to be no room for the luxury of safe academic dialogue. If such dialogue does not take cognizance of the wishes and concerns of the people, it is irrelevant and will cause religion as such to be viewed as irrelevant.
3. Contextual interfaith dialogue is meant for people who are deeply committed to their own traditions and who owe honesty and transparency to their partners in dialogue.
4. The ability for self-criticism and concern for the other has to be adopted. In this respect the dominant religion in a particular context has a very important role to play.
5. A distance from political power is essential. This will not only ensure separation between religion and the state but will also prevent favouritism being practised with one particular tradition. It will furthermore enable people to retain their prophetic calling towards the state.

The year 1994 was important in the history of South Africa. It was the year of our final liberation. Room has been created for people to be people. It was also very important to me, and others like me who were working for interfaith understanding. At the inauguration of President Mandela, leaders from four different faiths participated in the ceremony. What is perhaps even more striking, though, was the previous day in Parliament when the president was officially elected and when all members of Parliament were sworn in. At the end of the proceedings the Speaker, a Zoroastrian by faith, asked a Muslim leader to offer a closing prayer. In so doing the latter quoted from the Prayer of St Francis of Assisi! This was a significant demonstration of religious pluralism in our country. South Africa is entering an exciting phase in its history and religious freedom will hopefully be fully guaranteed in the new constitution. I am glad that I am living in this country during this process. I am glad of the opportunities I have had in working and sharing with people of other faiths. I am grateful that I could have made a contribution towards better understanding between people of different faiths.

Why I Am a Bahá'í

Dr Wendi Momen

Dr Wendi Momen has written a number of books, is a Justice of the Peace and is currently Chair of the National Spiritual Assembly of the Bahá'ís of the United Kingdom.

THE GREAT BEING saith: O ye children of men! The fundamental purpose animating the Faith of God and His Religion is to safeguard the interests and promote the unity of the human race, and to foster the spirit of love and fellowship amongst men.[1]

The purpose of religion is the acquisition of praiseworthy virtues, the betterment of morals, the spiritual development of mankind, the real life and divine bestowals.[2]

This vision provided by Bahá'í scripture of the purpose of religion shows its dual dimensions: as a mechanism both for the transformation of the social, collective life of humanity and for the refinement and growth of the individual's personal, inner, spiritual self. The development of one informs the development of the other, according to the Bahá'í teachings. The Bahá'í vision of the world as a God-centred, united, peaceful, globally functioning organism, wherein each individual is enabled to develop his or her own potential – materially, spiritually, intellectually and emotionally – to the highest degree, and in which people are valued individually and collectively for the unique contributions they can make to the greater good of the whole – this vision I find enormously satisfying. Faith, of course, is not entirely dependent on personal satisfaction or a feeling of 'rightness' but in examining one's reasons for committing oneself to a particular religion or way of life, this surely must be an important factor.

    A whole host of questions arises when one reflects on just why one belongs to a particular religion. Why belong to a religion at all? What is the purpose of religion? What does one expect from religion – for oneself, for the world? Should we expect anything? What is my religion's view of the universe? How does it make sense of the physical world, the spiritual world, the afterlife, the fact of other religions? What does it say of the nature of God, if there is one? What does it say about other people and how we are to relate to them? Does it say anything about these things or should it? Is my religion concerned solely with the inner life or does it have a social programme? How does it say the inner transformation informs the outer person? Does it have teachings to effect this? How does it fit in with other religions? Is there a historical connection among them? What are the central issues? Does it go some way towards answering the age-old, persistent questions of life: what is our purpose on earth? How did we get here? Where are we going? How do we get there? And just what is it all about, anyway?

My commitment to the Bahá'í faith arises out of the answers it gives to these questions and others. But perhaps more importantly, I am committed to the religion of Bahá'u'lláh (1817–92) because I see the effect of its teachings working in the world, on me and my family and friends as well as in the wider community. Again, I do not suggest that one's commitment to a religion is determined solely by the effectiveness of its teachings, but if we agree that one purpose of religion is to enable a person to draw nearer to the Creator and to co-exist happily and purposefully with others, then religious teachings that foster this end are, to say the least, compelling.

I believe all religions can do this. Why, then, be a Bahá'í and not something else?

I explain this as a believer. My explanation is coloured by the Bahá'í teachings themselves. I see the world, the universe, the nature of religion in a particular way – this particular way – *because* I believe Bahá'u'lláh's explanation of these things to be 'right'. I find it difficult to divorce myself, my thoughts, from what Bahá'u'lláh teaches. His vision is so compelling that it is my vision. Nevertheless, I will try to analyse just why I am Bahá'í.

One of the prayers revealed by Bahá'u'lláh, one I say every day, begins:

> I bear witness, O my God, that Thou hast created me to know Thee and to worship Thee.[3]

The daily recitation of this statement of the purpose of my life provides me with guidance and direction, grounds me and gives me a sense of where I am in relation to the whole of creation. Perhaps others do not need to have a sense of purpose but I find this vital to my well-being and ability to function in the world.

Of the nature of this God who we are to come to know and to love, Bahá'u'lláh says:

> So perfect and comprehensive is His creation that no mind nor heart, however keen or pure, can ever grasp the nature of the most insignificant of His creatures; much less fathom the mystery of Him Who is the Day Star of Truth, Who is the invisible and unknowable Essence.[4]

The perplexing question of how one can come to know a God who is in His essence unknowable is, for me, answered by the Bahá'í writings. Bahá'u'lláh says:

> Far, far from Thy glory be what mortal man can affirm of Thee, or attribute unto Thee, or the praise with which he can glorify Thee! Whatever duty Thou hast prescribed unto Thy servants of extolling to the utmost Thy majesty and glory is but a token of Thy grace unto them, that they may be

enabled to ascend unto the station conferred upon their own inmost being, the station of the knowledge of their own selves.[5]

Therefore, coming to know myself, to understand who *I* am, gives me some understanding of this God who created us in His image. Further, I believe we come to know God through those He sends to us, those precious individuals chosen by God to impart to us His will, those whom Bahá'ís call Manifestations of God. These Manifestations, whose ranks include Abraham, Moses, Buddha, Jesus Christ, Muhammad and Bahá'u'lláh, as well as others, manifest the qualities of God most perfectly:

> The door of the knowledge of the Ancient Being hath ever been, and will continue for ever to be, closed in the face of men. No man's understanding shall ever gain access unto His holy court. As a token of His mercy, however, and as a proof of His loving-kindness, He hath manifested unto men the Day Stars of His divine guidance, the Symbols of His divine unity, and hath ordained the knowledge of these sanctified Beings to be identical with the knowledge of His own Self. Whoso recognizeth them hath recognized God. Whoso hearkeneth to their call, hath hearkened to the Voice of God, and whoso testifieth to the truth of their Revelation, hath testified to the truth of God Himself. Whoso turneth away from them, hath turned away from God, and whoso disbelieveth in them, hath disbelieved in God. Every one of them is the Way of God that connecteth this world with the realms above, and the Standard of His Truth unto every one in the kingdoms of earth and heaven. They are the Manifestations of God amidst men, the evidences of His Truth, and the signs of His glory.[6]

Therefore, coming to know, love and obey the Manifestation of God in the day in which He appears is, for me, another way of coming to know and to love God.

Beyond this, I look at God's creation, at nature, at the visible universe, and am awed by His handiwork. Bahá'u'lláh says that every created thing has been endowed by God with some of His attributes:

> Upon the inmost reality of each and every created thing He hath shed the light of one of His names, and made it a recipient of the glory of one of His attributes.[7]

By studying nature, then, I can come to know something of God. However, Bahá'u'lláh goes on to add:

> Upon the reality of man, however, He hath focused the radiance of all of His names and attributes, and made it a mirror of His own Self.[8]

So coming to know and understand other people is another way I can come to know and love God.

This explanation of the nature of God and how to come to know Him that is provided by the Bahá'í writings is one of the main pillars propping up my commitment to the Bahá'í faith.

These statements of Bahá'u'lláh, with others, provide insights into the answers to the questions I posed above. Particularly they explain the universe, how it came to be, why it is and how I fit into it. Further, they point to the connectedness of all things: the physical universe to the world of the spirit, people one to the other, ideas to objects, thoughts to events. In short, Bahá'u'lláh's teachings provide me with a cosmology at once comprehensive and comprehensible. Through them I can make sense of the universe.

Another of my questions was also answered by Bahá'u'lláh's teachings: how can one explain the existence of various religions? My father is a Jew, my mother's family Christian, my husband's roots are in Islam. Then there is my cousin's wife, whose background is Buddhist, and my brother-in-law's mother, whose family followed a traditional Amerindian religion.

Some religionists explain the existence of these different paths by seeing in them the work of a devil, leading humankind astray; others, more charitable, see them as the prompting of the human spirit to come to know its God. As a child I found the diversity of religious traditions in my own family a normal aspect of life. Only as a youth did questions arise: which one is right? If only one is right, why does God allow the others to exist? Since they all seem to be saying more or less the same things, why are there so many?

Again, in the Bahá'í faith I found a reasonable and satisfying explanation, one that made more sense than any other explanation I had come across:

> Its teachings revolve around the fundamental principle that religious truth is not absolute but relative, that Divine Revelation is progressive, not final. Unequivocally and without the least reservation it proclaims all established religions to be divine in origin, identical in their aims, complementary in their functions, continuous in their purpose, indispensable in their value to mankind.[9]

> In thine esteemed letter thou hadst inquired which of the Prophets of God should be regarded as superior to others. Know thou assuredly that the essence of all the Prophets of God is one and the same. Their unity is absolute. God, the Creator, saith: There is no distinction whatsoever among the Bearers of My Message. They all have but one purpose; their secret is the same secret. To prefer one in honour to another, to exalt certain ones above the rest, is in no wise to be permitted. Every true Prophet hath regarded His Message as fundamentally the same as the

Revelation of every other Prophet gone before Him . . . The measure of the
revelation of the Prophets of God in this world, however, must differ. Each
and every one of them hath been the Bearer of a distinct Message, and hath
been commissioned to reveal Himself through specific acts. It is for this
reason that they appear to vary in their greatness . . . It is clear and evident,
therefore, that any apparent variation in the intensity of their light is not
inherent in the light itself, but should rather be attributed to the varying
receptivity of an ever-changing world . . . God's purpose in sending His
Prophets unto men is twofold. The first is to liberate the children of men
from the darkness of ignorance, and guide them to the light of true
understanding. The second is to ensure the peace and tranquillity of
mankind, and provide all the means by which they can be established.[10]

Often Bahá'ís describe this process of progressive revelation through the analogy of
the child going to school. The child passes through the different levels of the
education system progressively and systematically. The lessons learned in the first
year are the foundation for all later lessons. That the first-year teacher teaches a
simpler form of mathematics than the second-year teacher says nothing about the
knowledge and ability of the teacher but a lot about the ability and level of
attainment of the student. God sends His divine teachers or Manifestations to
reveal more and more about Himself and His plan for us.

That the forms of religions differ is also explained in the Bahá'í teachings:
while the fundamental teachings of the different Manifestations of God are the
same, the way in which they are applied differs according to the age in which the
teacher appears. This also made sense to me. For example, all the Manifestations
teach that justice is an important personal and social quality to develop. However,
justice today looks very different from its form four thousand years ago. Today we
find alternatives to taking the eye of the criminal who takes the eye of his victim,
alternatives more in keeping with our concepts of what is 'civilized' or 'humane'.
These very concepts have been informed by the development of religious principles
brought by the Manifestations, for instance the tempering of justice with mercy or
the need to re-educate as well as punish the criminal.

Beyond these differences are the varying forms of worship, practices and
rituals. These are similarly explained as different approaches to the same desire – to
worship and remember God. That they differ owes much to cultural expressions of
devotion, as when Bahá'ís look to the scriptures of other religions they find that
there is little in them to uphold the complex forms that have developed.

Bahá'u'lláh's perspective on the panoply of religions was both convincing
and cogent to one who had lived happily for years among good people of different
faith-traditions. His explanations opened my eyes to the common ground that is to
be found among all people of faith and enabled me to make sense of what was
otherwise a jumble of religious beliefs.

Again, it was the circumstances of my own family that convinced me of the soundness of Bahá'u'lláh's teaching of the oneness of the human race. Racial and ethnic differences, like religious ones, abound in my family: blacks, whites, Amerindians, Hispanics, Asians, Europeans, Middle Easterners, going back three generations. My own family is a microcosm of the world; I, my children, my brothers and sisters, my nieces and nephews reflect the diversity of the world's people. It would be impossible for me to give my allegiance to a religion that teaches racial or ethnic superiority or any form of nationalism. To find in the Bahá'í writings this statement of Bahá'u'lláh was a confirmation of something I had personally experienced and knew to be true.

It is not for him to pride himself who loveth his own country, but rather for him who loveth the whole world. The earth is but one country, and mankind its citizens.[11]

The Bahá'í writings, which are replete with references to this basic tenet of the religion, often use images drawn from the natural world:

Ye are all the leaves of one tree and the drops of one ocean.[12]

That the human race is essentially one is a fundamental statement of reality for Bahá'ís. However, it is accepted that at present we do not act as if this were the case. Thus the Bahá'í writings exhort us to behave in ways which demonstrate our oneness and which will enable us to build a united world more suited to the purpose given us by God:

Let your hearts reflect the glories of the Sun of Truth in their many colours to gladden the eye of the divine Cultivator Who has nourished them. Day by day become more closely attracted in order that the love of God may illumine all those with whom you come in contact. Be as one spirit, one soul, leaves of one tree, flowers of one garden, waves of one ocean.

As difference in degree of capacity exists among human souls, as difference in capability is found, therefore, individualities will differ one from another. But in reality this is a reason for unity and not for discord and enmity. If the flowers of a garden were all of one colour, the effect would be monotonous to the eye; but if the colours are variegated, it is most pleasing and wonderful.

The difference in adornment of colour and capacity of reflection among the flowers gives the garden its beauty and charm. Therefore, although we are of different individualities, different in ideas and of various fragrances, let us strive like flowers of the same divine garden to live together in harmony. Even though each soul has its own individual perfume and colour, all are reflecting the same light, all contributing fragrance to the same breeze which blows through the garden, all continuing to grow in complete harmony and accord. Become as waves of one sea, trees of one forest, growing in the utmost love, agreement and unity.[13]

Far from leaving us with an idealized vision of a happy, united, peace-loving world and exhortations on how to achieve it, I find that the Bahá'í writings provide practical guidance on those steps that we as individuals and as communities must take in order to realize this aim. The adoption by the people of the world of a universal auxiliary language, of a uniform standard of weights, measures and currencies and of global institutions of governance are but a few concrete examples of the measures that are to be taken to effect the unification of the planet. For the individual, it is recognized that certain personal attitudes need to be acquired and others discarded. Bahá'u'lláh, for instance, calls for the abandonment of all forms of prejudice and stances of superiority. On the other hand, He calls for the recognition of the equality of women and men, for the realization that the truths of religion and of science are but aspects of one truth, and for an understanding of the fundamental oneness of God's religions.

That a religion should provide such specific advice on issues that might appear to be more political than spiritual is, to me, important. Many creeds inform the inner person, guide the individual on his or her way to God, but are short on advice on how to transform spiritual truths into social actions. For me, one purpose of religion surely must be to make the world a better place in which to live. My observation of people in many parts of the world, holding different religious ideas, is that we generally find it difficult to see the connection between those things that will 'get us to heaven' and our day-to-day lives here on earth. For me, the Bahá'í faith makes this connection. It says that one's personal salvation is bound up with the salvation of the world. Hence Bahá'u'lláh forbids monasticism, requiring His followers to face the challenges of the secular world as well as those of the spirit. Indeed, to the extent that 'our own inner life and private character mirror forth in their manifold aspects the splendour of those eternal principles proclaimed by Bahá'u'lláh',[14] will the world we live in be transformed; that is, God proffers the guidance, we must take it up and apply it.

No doubt some will disagree with the Bahá'í view that one purpose of religion is to effect positive social development. Many believe that as life on earth is ephemeral there is little point in trying to improve it; rather, what we must do is fix our gaze on the next world and try to be accepted there. What I find interesting in the Bahá'í perspective is how one's spiritual development, convictions, thoughts and deeds are seen to be connected and how the application of these on this earthly plane affects one's progress in the next world. Since the Bahá'í faith teaches that we are already in eternity, our progress after the death of our physical bodies is a natural and inevitable event. However, we can make progress more quickly and easily if in this world we have 'packed the spiritual luggage' we need. Thus the acquisition of spiritual characteristics and virtues such as trustworthiness, generosity, kindness and patience are valuable both in the physical world and in the next. The development of these virtues is seen by Bahá'ís to be a fundamental purpose of one's life on earth.

I find the analogy of the baby in the womb to be a helpful way to think about this:

> Consider how a being, in the world of the womb, was deaf of ear and blind of eye, and mute of tongue; how he was bereft of any perceptions at all. But once, out of that world of darkness, he passed into this world of light, then his eye saw, his ear heard, his tongue spoke. In the same way, once he hath hastened away from this mortal place into the Kingdom of God, then he will be born in the spirit; then the eye of his perception will open, the ear of his soul will hearken, and all the truths of which he was ignorant before will be made plain and clear.
>
> An observant traveller passing along a way will certainly recall his discoveries to mind, unless some accident befall him and efface the memory.[15]

Thus, just as the foetus acquires physical characteristics the value of which is only fully realized once the child dies to the womb world and is born into this, so the spiritual characteristics one strives to acquire here are perhaps not fully appreciated until one dies from this world and is 'born' into the next. To take the analogy further, the physical characteristics developed by the foetus appear not only to be useless to it, but even detrimental, in that the functionless arms and legs restrict freedom of movement; so too the spiritual attributes of, for instance, honesty and loyalty can appear to be unnecessary and restrictive. And just as an embryo that does not develop some part of its body has disabilities in this life, so too is the soul that fails to acquire spiritual qualities here hampered in the next life. The analogy is limited, however, in the sense that the foetus cannot decide for itself whether or not to acquire its arms and legs, whereas in this life we must make the decision to acquire spiritual attributes and then act so as to develop them. The Bahá'í explanation of the relationship between this world and the next is, for me, both logical and satisfying as it links positive action here with spiritual progress both in this world and the next.

Many are alarmed by the prospect of their own death. The explanation of Bahá'u'lláh about the nature of the next world and our condition in it has enabled me, for the most part, to overcome this fear. This passage, penned by Bahá'u'lláh in answer to a question about the nature and progress of the soul after death, provides an insight into God's love for us which both gives me joy and draws me closer to Him:

Know thou of a truth that the soul, after its separation from the body, will continue to progress until it attaineth the presence of God, in a state and condition which neither the revolution of ages and centuries, nor the changes and chances of this world, can alter. It will endure as long as the Kingdom of God, His sovereignty, His dominion and power will endure. It will manifest the signs of God and His attributes, and will reveal His loving kindness and bounty. The movement of My Pen is stilled when it attempteth to befittingly describe the loftiness and glory of so exalted a station. The honour with which the Hand of Mercy will invest the soul is such as no tongue can adequately reveal, nor any other earthly agency describe. Blessed is the soul which, at the hour of its separation from the body, is sanctified from the vain imaginings of the peoples of the world. Such a soul liveth and moveth in accordance with the Will of its Creator, and entereth the all-highest Paradise. The Maids of Heaven, inmates of the loftiest mansions, will circle around it, and the Prophets of God and His chosen ones will seek its companionship. With them that soul will freely converse, and will recount unto them that which it hath been made to endure in the path of God, the Lord of all worlds. If any man be told that which hath been ordained for such a soul in the worlds of God, the Lord of the throne on high and of earth below, his whole being will instantly blaze out in his great longing to attain that most exalted, that sanctified and resplendent station . . . The nature of the soul after death can never be described, nor is it meet and permissible to reveal its whole character to the eyes of men. The Prophets and Messengers of God have been sent down for the sole purpose of guiding mankind to the straight Path of Truth. The purpose underlying Their revelation hath been to educate all men, that they may, at the hour of death, ascend, in the utmost purity and sanctity and with absolute detachment, to the throne of the Most High . . . The world beyond is as different from this world as this world is different from that of the child while still in the womb of its mother. When the soul attaineth the Presence of God, it will assume the form that best befitteth its immortality and is worthy of its celestial habitation. Such an existence is a contingent and not an absolute existence, inasmuch as the former is preceded by a cause, whilst the latter is independent thereof. Absolute existence is strictly confined to God, exalted be His glory. Well is it with them that apprehend this truth.[16]

Thus for me the Bahá'í faith provides a vision not only of this world but of the worlds to come. Its answers to those age-old questions are clear and logical yet draw on the profound spiritual truths that, it teaches, have always existed and will always do so.

Notes

1. Bahá'u'lláh, *Gleanings from the Writings of Bahá'u'lláh* (Wilmette, Illinois: Bahá'í Publishing Trust, 1983), p. 215.

2. 'Abdu'l-Bahá, *The Promulgation of Universal Peace* (Wilmette, Illinois: Bahá'í Publishing Trust, 1982), p. 152.

3. Bahá'u'lláh, *Prayers and Meditations* (Wilmette, Illinois: Bahá'í Publishing Trust, 1987), no. CLXXXI, p. 314.

4. Bahá'u'lláh, *Gleanings*, p. 62. In the remainder of this stirring passage Bahá'u'lláh goes on to explain how exalted God is above the comprehension of His creation:

The conceptions of the devoutest of mystics, the attainments of the most accomplished amongst men, the highest praise which human tongue or pen can render are all the product of man's finite mind and are conditioned by its limitations. . . From time immemorial He hath been veiled in the ineffable sanctity of His exalted Self, and will everlastingly continue to be wrapt in the impenetrable mystery of His unknowable Essence. Every attempt to attain to an understanding of His inaccessible Reality hath ended in complete bewilderment, and every effort to approach His exalted Self and envisage His Essence hath resulted in hopelessness and failure.

How bewildering to me, insignificant as I am, is the attempt to fathom the sacred depths of Thy knowledge! How futile my efforts to visualize the magnitude of the power inherent in Thine handiwork – the revelation of Thy creative power! How can mine eye, which hath no faculty to perceive itself, claim to have discerned Thine Essence, and how can mine heart, already powerless to apprehend the significance of its own potentialities, pretend to have comprehended Thy nature? How can I claim to have known Thee, when the entire creation is bewildered by Thy mystery, and how can I confess not to have known Thee, when, lo, the whole universe proclaimeth Thy Presence and testifieth to Thy truth? The portals of Thy grace have throughout eternity been open, and the means of access unto Thy Presence made available, unto all created things, and the revelations of Thy matchless Beauty have at all times been imprinted upon the realities of all beings, visible and invisible. Yet, notwithstanding this most gracious favour, this perfect and consummate bestowal, I am moved to testify that Thy court of holiness and glory is immeasurably exalted above the knowledge of all else besides Thee, and the mystery of Thy Presence is inscrutable to every mind except Thine own. No one except Thyself can unravel the secret of Thy nature, and naught else but Thy transcendental Essence can grasp the reality of Thy unsearchable being. (*Gleanings*, pp. 62–4)

5. Ibid., pp. 4–5.

6. Ibid., pp. 49–50.

7. Ibid., p. 65.

8. Ibid.

9. Shoghi Effendi, *The World Order of Bahá'u'lláh* (Wilmette, Illinois: Bahá'í Publishing Trust, 1980), p. 58.

10. Bahá'u'lláh, *Gleanings*, pp. 78–80.

11. Ibid., p. 250.

12. Bahá'u'lláh, *Tablets of Bahá'u'lláh Revealed after the Kitáb-i-Aqdas* (Wilmette, Illinois: Bahá'í Publishing Trust, 1988), p. 27.

13. 'Abdu'l-Bahá, *Promulgation*, p. 24.

14. Shoghi Effendi, *Bahá'í Administration* (Wilmette, Illinois: Bahá'í Publishing Trust, 1974), p. 66.

15. 'Abdu'l-Bahá, *Selections from the Writings of 'Abdu'l-Bahá* (Haifa: Bahá'í World Centre, 1978), p. 177.

16. Bahá'u'lláh, *Gleanings*, pp. 155–6.

WHY AM I A CHRISTIAN?

Dr Daleep Mukarji

Dr Daleep Mukarji joined the Christian Medical Association (the official health agency of the National Council of Churches in India) as General Secretary in January 1985 and stayed there until March 1994 when he joined the World Council of Churches, Unit II; Churches in Mission: Health, Education and Witness. He is Executive Secretary for Urban Rural Mission.

WHY AM I a Christian? This is not a question I have been asked often nor one that I have asked of myself. I suppose the obvious answer is that I was born into a Christian family, went to Christian schools and colleges and was generally brought up as a Christian. This has not been a narrow mission-compound upbringing. I have been a city-bred, slightly Westernized secular and cosmopolitan person. With this education and background the more difficult question for me has always been, who am I? How do you explain your Bengali name without being one? Others ask how I can be a Christian without having a biblical or Western name. How does one really feel Indian when most are Hindu, identified with a specific caste, language and ethnic or regional community?

Our family is essentially Punjabi or north Indian but we have lived most of our lives in Bengal and south India (Andhra Pradesh or Tamil Nadu). In India people are more easily identified as Bengali, Tamilian, Gujarati, Punjabi, etc. We are really Indian only when we are out of the country, and within it more parochial than one can imagine. To say one is an Indian and not from any specific community is confusing. Yet today, more are willing to be seen as Indians without the regional or religious tag. This has been due to inter-caste or inter-community marriages and the large number of families who for some time have lived outside their own communities. However, recently in India we have seen rising caste- and religion-based politics, where people are being forced to consider their origins and labels. We are now expected to make clear our identity in caste and communal terms. What then does it mean to be Indian or, in my context, an Indian Christian?

Suddenly you realize that you belong to a minority community and that even within this group, your being an educated professional from north India places you in a minority within a minority. Thus, being Indian and Christian implies being part of a very small community. So why be one? My pilgrimage has been trying to understand both my Christian and Indian heritage and to see the implications in my life. As I saw the socio-economic and political realities, the disparity and exploitation, the poverty and marginalization of so many and the essential injustice in all this, I realized that I was part of the community, the urban educated élite, that contributed to so much oppression.

In my impressionable years – college and my early professional time as a doctor in a small rural hospital – I began to realize I had to make serious choices. What do I make of my life, whom do I serve and can I make any impact on the social scene? Many friends in the Student Christian Movement and in college influenced me. They helped me to realize that one could and should get involved in the issues and concerns that troubled me, and that not being involved would in some way deny what I understood to be so important to Christ's life. He came that we may all have life, and have this abundantly. Yet for many there really was no quality and meaning in their lives. Also too many Christians were promising new life in another world after death. Sadly there is too much premature, unnecessary and preventable death. Too many are dehumanized by living conditions and deprivation that are scandalous in our times. For too many, death, darkness and the denial of rights and dignity are everyday realities. Yet Jesus proclaims a new understanding of community, the reign of God, a new creation that can make a difference in this world right now. Christian social activists and many in the non-governmental organization sector helped me to realize that this understanding was important to me.

I spent eight years in a rural health and community development programme in Tamil Nadu. It was my hope to be able to participate in and lead a local education and organization process that would help people to help themselves in the community. This covered a population of a hundred thousand people in about a hundred villages in a backward and traditionally agricultural area. I learnt much from the people as we worked together for social transformation and the building up of a sense of community. It also gave me a different approach to health care services. Thus I chose not to be a traditional hospital doctor but to use my professional training and experience to make health a reality for local communities. I realized that this could only be done in the context of an approach that truly educates, organizes and empowers people to take responsibility for their future and to link health to socio-economic development. This is what I have been trying to do these last fifteen years.

My second major choice was more personal. One sister had married a Hindu and another an American Roman Catholic, and when my turn came I chose a wonderful Muslim girl to be my wife. Ours was a registered wedding and five years later my wife made her private and personal choice to become a Christian. Our children are very fortunate to have relatives and friends who are Muslims, Christians and Hindus. The best man at our wedding was a Hindu Brahman and many very close friends are from different communities. We have valued the richness of this common humanity and the reality of an extended family that has both multicultural and multi-faith dimensions. This has not always been easy and we have felt the tensions and problems in our relationships, dialogue and family life. In some sense this is a reflection of what is happening all over the world as we come to terms with the realities of a pluralistic society. I have enjoyed celebrating some common festivals, understanding each other's traditions and customs, and this has helped me appreciate my own Indian Christian heritage. It has helped me be more open, tolerant and honest about my Christianity.

I never seriously thought of other religions as an option. For me the search was for a more caring, sensitive and open Christianity that challenged me to take sides in the social problems that we faced. This was my third major choice. While I have tried to learn something about other religions I felt it necessary to learn more about my own. The real choices for me were:

1. How seriously would I take Christianity?
2. And if I did, what type of Christianity?

So my real pilgrimage has been within Christianity. This has not been as easy as it appears. On one side there is almost a secular post-Christian reality that looks at religion as a sort of social statement. In this context there is a subconscious declaration about belonging to a certain group with no really shared faith or visible expression of the same. Here one goes through the rituals of religion. In addition to this the Church in India is going through so many difficulties of leadership, personality conflicts, identity crises and petty fights over property, politics and positions of power. Sadly there is much mismanagement and incompetence in key positions. Why stay in the Church? There is also a rising fundamentalism that threatens mainstream Churches often with policies and priorities directed from overseas. This narrow evangelistic and triumphalistic aspect of Christianity offers a simple gospel of personal salvation in another world with little reference to the problems and realities of this world.

The Indian Church is going through difficult days and it is easy to see and emphasize what is wrong. For someone who has spent over twenty years working in the structures I can say I have seen a side that is disgusting and disappointing. Many get put off Christianity; they appear to accept Jesus Christ but find His Church an obstacle. Yet in spite of its problems and politics I have found the Church, as a community, as a support system and as a fellowship very satisfying. I have seen groups who have inspired me and others. At times of national calamities and strife I have seen a response that expresses love, caring and commitment. In the hospitals, health centres, community programmes and leprosy centres, I have seen many who have given of themselves in the service of others.

Within Christianity I have been challenged by a gospel that truly gives hope and is good news for the poor and marginalized. I have been excited by a gospel that appears to take sides and that talks of a new creation – a new community – that is the reign of God. This has given meaning and vision to my own concerns for social transformation in our society. The struggles for justice, identity and a sense of community with dignity now mean more to me. I began then to be influenced by the contextual and liberating theologies that I came across in the ecumenical movement. Mission was something I wanted to be involved in. Not mission if it wanted to make others Christian, or to serve only Christians or to work with only Christians. For me mission was an opportunity to be Christian and to be in solidarity with the oppressed and the marginalized. It meant working with them and supporting the efforts for justice, liberation and community. It meant that we could and must work for a world in which there is no exploitation, disparity or disease. I believed that this was essential in Christ's ministry and it inspired me. So here I was, an Indian Christian doctor who wanted to do something with his life. More importantly, I really wanted to help change things in society.

As I got more socially involved as a Christian in the needs and problems of others, I realized sadly that Christian fundamentalism and intolerance was rising in India. There was little tolerance for people of other faiths and almost contempt for Christians who did not subscribe to this very personal and individual approach to salvation. This form of Christianity appeared to be both arrogant and insensitive. I felt this approach to evangelism and proselytism was harmful to Christianity and our relations with people of other faiths.

I could also see some value in the much-needed spiritual revival of our Churches and community that this movement brought with it. I agree that one should make a personal commitment to one's own religion and beliefs. For me this has meant a personal relationship with God and a daily seeking out of what He would like me to do. I realized that I needed to be spiritually alive, socially relevant and biblically literate to be able to relate to this new dimension of Christianity in India. I could not understand, accept or even be a part of a religious movement that had no social agenda, no concern for poverty or injustice and was so insensitive to the feelings and beliefs of others.

My life has been undergirded by these values and beliefs. All of us are children of God made in His image and it is His desire and hope that nations and peoples will come into a new creation where there is more justice, dignity and peace. We need to believe there is something of God in all people and that on planet earth we have a common humanity, which at its basic level is the survival of humankind. How then can I sum up my vision for humanity? It would certainly have the following components:

JUSTICE: I would dream of a society that is healthy and just. This would require a more equitable distribution of resources and a greater participation of the weak and marginalized in the decisions that affect their future, at the local, national and global level. I would hope for the inclusion in this society of the poor, minorities, women, tribal and indigenous peoples and those who because of race, colour or creed have been pushed out. This appears utopian and it probably is, but it gives me hope and a purpose in my life. Justice must go with healing and reconciliation in a world that is so broken and for whom memories of pain, suffering and death have been everyday realities. This is not easy. How does one forgive and forget the oppression and discrimination that people have experienced through generations?

The building of a new society with justice must not only be a change in the powers that rule, for new rulers will continue to oppress and exploit those they can. We need a change in values, lifestyles and our understanding of power. People of goodwill and social commitment, irrespective of their religious affiliation, need to work locally to enable change to take place. This requires the empowerment of local communities for social transformation.

COMMUNITY: We are moving into a society more plural than anyone had ever imagined, in almost all nations of the South and the North. This creates tensions. The multicultural, multi-ethnic and multi-faith dimension of many societies is becoming a reality. How does one build a sense of community when there is so much diversity? We must avoid false or enforced approaches to homogenization or uniformity. In this context my vision would be for a world where there is harmony, tolerance, respect for others and acceptance of differences. Our ethnic, religious and linguistic diversity could enrich our communities as we learn to live with each other. This requires a common commitment to our being members of one human race who share this one planet. It requires a new understanding of community that recognizes differences and works to build a greater sense of belonging and participation for all. Is this possible? I believe it is and we all need to be working towards this.

HOPE: How does one survive in a context of so much despair, death and injustice? It is here that my faith gives me a sense of hope. I do believe things can and will change. In a world where we have destroyed relationships – between humanity and God, between people, between creation and all of humankind – we realize that restoration of these relationships will bring some kind of order and harmony for all. It is a belief in the somehow present and coming reality of the reign of God that gives me hope. It provides meaning and purpose to my life. It implies we can all be agents of this new reality, builders of the kingdom of God. If we accept that God loves the world and that Christ's Incarnation was intervention in history, we can believe that in Christ and through Him all things will eventually be renewed. It helps to know that He went through this world at a certain time, born into a simple working-class carpenter's family, probably in a slum or outhouse in Bethlehem. His family fled in political exile to Egypt and He lived and grew up under colonial oppression. We see throughout His ministry that Christ moved amongst ordinary people – tax collectors, fishermen, the poor and the marginalized. That Christ was betrayed, denied and finally killed like a common criminal shows something of the pain and suffering He experienced. That He prayed this would not happen and could cry out from the cross, 'My God, why have you forsaken me?' helps me to face some of the painful realities of this world. In the final analysis we believe in a God who does not forsake and who has gone through some of the suffering and hurt we feel.

As a doctor I saw one could not treat the patient only in terms of the body. There was more to each person as we recognized the physical, mental and spiritual dimensions of disease and well-being. We also realized that people could not be healthy in isolation from their environment and community. Thus an integrated approach to health, healing and wholeness required that we be concerned with the totality of the human being. We needed to be concerned with physical, mental, spiritual and social aspects of life and living. In a world of many faiths, ideologies and secular traditions, one needs to examine the essential components of one's world-view. What gives meaning and motivation to life? Sadly for many this is money, materialism, consumerism and the pursuit of profit. This, I believe, contributes to greed, excessive competition, injustice and a craving for power that dominates and controls. The spiritual and social aspects of well-being help us to see that we are not alone in this world and that we are to share what we have. This concern and commitment to the greater good of all humanity can only come when we look beyond ourselves. It calls for tolerance, dialogue and openness that allows us to listen, to learn and to change ourselves. So many of us are afraid of being different in this world, of expressing our religion and our basic spirituality. This then is the challenge for all people to be able to feel comfortable in being openly committed to a faith and to let that faith guide and direct your life. At the same time this encourages you to look at other people, faiths, cultures, languages and beliefs in a more accepting way.

My religious affiliation has been to Christianity. It has had a profound influence in my life in shaping my values and choices. Fortunately it has also encouraged me to be more active and involved in the concerns of others. I would hope that people could take up some religion and look for the best in all. I realize that religion today is becoming a divisive force that is being used in political and ethnic rivalries. We need to guard against this danger and to reach out to all humanity. This basic commitment to a faith has meant much to me. I am also concerned that we bring up children with some understanding of religion and a faith they can value in their lives. At the same time this should not focus on just one's own religious tradition. For many the choice is not which religion should I follow, but should I follow any religion at all? It is here that I would emphasize the belief and practice of a religion that gives meaning and purpose to life. I have found this in Christianity, in the life, teachings and ministry of Jesus. He has challenged me and I believe He can challenge others. Can my being Christian make any difference in the lives of others? I am not too sure, but it has made a difference in my life.

THE LIBERATION TO LOVE

Dr Anantanand Rambachan

Dr Anantanand Rambachan is Associate Professor of the Department of Religion at St Olaf College, Northfield, Minnesota, USA.

I AM A Hindu. What does it mean to you when I describe myself as a Hindu? Most importantly, what does it mean to me?

The name 'Hindu' tells little about me since it is not the personal name of a founder or sage whose teachings I follow. Neither does it describe or identify a central belief to which I subscribe or a discipline that is a regular part of my spiritual life. The ambiguity of the name by which I designate my religious commitment is explicable, in part, by its origin. Hindu is the Iranian variation of the name of a river that the Indo-Europeans referred to as the Sindhu, the Greeks as the Indos and the British as the Indus. Those who occupied the territory drained by the Indus river system were derivatively called Hindus.

In its origin, therefore, my religious label had geographical and not doctrinal or religious connotations. It was not employed to define a common identity through shared beliefs and practices and has always sheltered diverse viewpoints. The relative ambiguity of the name Hindu, as a religious appellation, does not mean that those of us who continue to describe ourselves as Hindus are ambivalent about our commitments. We are Hindus not merely by the fact that we have not repudiated the designation Hindu.[1]

Today, it is common for authors of works on Hinduism to discuss in their prefaces the dangers of generalizing about Hinduism and the difficulties of defining who is and who is not a Hindu. While such introductory remarks may be necessary, it is wrong to give the impression that the Hindu tradition is somehow uniquely afflicted by problems of identity and definition. The complexity and diversity of all the world's religions implies that generalizations are always fraught with risk, and thoughtful adherents of all traditions continuously wrestle with questions of religious meaning and identity. While Hindus, like Christians, Muslims or Buddhists, may not find consensus about the essential beliefs and practices of their tradition, each Hindu will offer an account of the meaning of the tradition for him or her. What is perhaps peculiar to Hinduism is that the tradition has not insisted upon or sought uniformity in matters of belief and practice and has always granted its followers a great deal of freedom in such matters. Problems of definition often belong to outsiders who seek easy generalizations in which to subsume an ancient, complex and dynamic reality.

I write today, therefore, more about the meaning of my identity as a Hindu and less about the abstraction known as Hinduism. Yet, while a religion may reveal itself in a unique and personal way through each adherent, one must also acknowledge the shared beliefs and practices which nourish that individuality and which are contained in it.

Where do I begin? I begin with the Vedas, a collection of writings held by almost every Hindu to be a revelation from God.[2] Following the orthodox Vedanta view, I hold the Vedas to be a source of valid knowledge (*pramana*) in the form of words (*sabda*), which informs me of truths I cannot know through the perception of my senses or the inferences of independent reasoning. If the truths that I gather from the Vedas could be conclusively gained through another source, there would be no need for a scriptural revelation. Even as forms can be uniquely perceived only through the eyes, the Vedas communicate a special knowledge through their sacred words. The Vedas reveal, for me, the absolute (*brahman*) whose existence and nature cannot be determined by sense perception or inferential arguments. My faith (*sraddha*) in the authority of the Vedas as a valid source of knowledge for the absolute does not imply, however, that such knowledge is to be gained only from Vedic words and not from any other scriptural sources.

The acceptance of an authoritative source, especially when such a source is in the form of words, presents unique difficulties and challenges. The meanings of words are not always obvious from the contexts in which they are used, and the terse and poetic quality of the verses of the Upanishads often makes their meaning elusive. These difficulties are compounded by the fact that the Upanishads employ conventional words in very special ways to designate a reality that possesses none of the characteristics of everyday objects. The resources of tradition, therefore, are a necessary aid for grasping the meaning of scripture.

Serious debates among those who have accepted the Vedas as an authoritative source have given rise to a diversity of interpretative traditions. The *Purva Mimamsa* (Prior School of Exegesis) for example, grants priority to the first sections of the Vedas, namely the hymns and their interpretation, and argues that the purport of the Vedas is not to reveal the nature of existent entities but to exhort us to perform desirable actions and refrain from undesirable ones. The *Uttara-Mimamsa* (Later School of Exegesis), on the other hand, ascribes priority to the later portion of the Vedas, namely the Upanishads or Vedanta and sees the purport of the texts in the revelation of *brahman*. Uttara-Mimamsa interpreters such as Sankara, Ramanuja and Madhva differ in their understanding of the character of *brahman*, the status of the world, the nature of the individual and *brahman*'s relationship with both.

My own understanding of the nature and meaning of the Vedas has been shaped most significantly by the Advaita (non-dual) tradition of Hinduism whose principal systematizer and exponent is Sankara (c. 788–820). My faith in the Vedas as a valid source of knowledge and the influence of the Advaita tradition upon my understanding of these texts does not prevent me, however, from struggling with the challenges presented by the claims of other understandings of the meanings of these texts and other views of reality championed on the basis of different authoritative sources. To justify itself as valid knowledge, the revelation of the Vedas must respond to the claims of divergent views.

What is the special knowledge revealed in the words of the Vedas and what is its significance for us? What is the human dilemma and how is it addressed and resolved in these texts? Everyone yearns to be a full being and to attain a condition of self-acceptance in which one ceases to be tormented by multifarious desires generated by feelings of personal insufficiency and lack. It is liberation from *want* that we truly seek. While recognizing the importance and necessity of material things in our lives, the Hindu emphasis is upon the unending stream of desire that springs from a sense of inward emptiness. The satisfaction of our material needs does not appear to eliminate such want.

The basic human yearning for fullness manifests itself in multifarious desires. Common among these are desires for various pleasurable sense-experiences. While these are not wrong in themselves and while our enjoyments ought not to cause pain to others, the enjoyments that are attained through contact between the senses and their respective objects are quite limited. They confer a sense of well-being for a brief moment but leave us in want again. They possess, as the Bhagavadgita teaches, a beginning and an end and cause pain to the one who mistakenly looks to them for lasting satisfaction.[3]

We also seek fullness in the multiplication and increase of our material possessions, in fame and in personal success. While these may grant a satisfaction that is slightly more lasting than that experienced through sense-enjoyment, we are still left with a sense of want and emptiness. Many of these gains derive their value from the fact that they are unequally distributed. Being competitive, they engender fear and insecurity. The gain of another is often a source of anxiety.

We journey through life seeking a fullness that continuously eludes our grasp, leaving us restless and unhappy with ourselves. Our spiritual search begins in earnest when, as the Mundaka Upanishad puts it, we engage in earnest reflection on our experiences and learn that the fullness we pursue is not to be gained through any type of action. All actions are limited and capable, therefore, of producing only limited results.[4] We become awake to the fact that our gains in this world, as necessary and as desirable as these may be, fail to satisfy our most fundamental need. In frustration, we throw up our hands in the air and ask, 'Is there anything more to life than the fleeting pleasures of sense experiences and the insecure gains of wealth and power?' The Hindu answer to this question is resoundingly affirmative and the Vedas reveal the 'more' in life that we need and for which we yearn.

The Mundaka Upanishad verse cited above also instructs the reflective individual who is in search of the uncreated to approach respectfully a competent teacher (guru).[5]

We see here an affirmation of the traditional necessity for a qualified teacher to lead us to the freedom from want that we seek and a specification of the qualifications of such a teacher. The qualified teacher is one who has mastered the *sruti* (i.e. the Vedas) and who is established in the infinite (*brahmanistham*). A knowledge of the scripture equips the teacher with the language and methodology for instruction, but this must be complemented by a life that is existentially enriched by the vision of the texts. William Cenker comments perceptively on the two dimensions of the teacher's identity:

> One who has heard the Veda and more specifically has heard the meaning of the Veda fulfils the intellectual aspect of the teacher, while one who stands in Brahman fulfils the spiritual dimension of teacher. A teacher, according to the Upanisads is a self-realized person whose realization has come through the wisdom of the Vedic tradition. This is the basic perception of the teacher to be found in the Upanisadic literature. The esteem given to the guru in the Indian tradition grows out of this initial conception of the teacher as both a knower of Brahman and a dweller in Brahman.[6]

Ignorance (*avidya*) is the root cause of our failure to find fullness in life, and the knowledge revealed in the Vedas and made accessible by the teacher is meant to remove this fundamental misunderstanding about ourselves and the world in which we live. It must be emphasized that knowledge does not mean a superficial familiarity with the words of the Vedas. This knowledge is addressed specifically to someone who senses the inherent limitations of all finite gains and who yearns for a gain that is not subject to time and change. Such an individual approaches the scripture and teacher with the hope of finding a solution. He attentively listens (*sravana*) to the teaching, reflects and ponders (*manana*) on its meaning in solitude or in dialogue with the teacher and seeks through continuous contemplation (*nididhyasana*) to incorporate its vision and insights into all aspects of his life. It is knowledge acquired by dedicated inquiry and integrated into one's self-understanding that is liberative.

What do the Vedas tell us about ourselves and the world that we cannot know except through revelation? They instruct us that the universe we apprehend through our senses does not comprise the totality of reality and does not have an independent existence. While Hindus may be found under a tremendous variety of names and forms, I think that it will be difficult to find a practising Hindu who advocates that sense data comprehend all of reality or that the universe is without intelligent cause. The Hindu tradition advocates that our diverse universe has its basis in a higher or ultimate reality, referred to as *brahman* (the infinite). That which is seen, finite and changing has its basis in the unseen, infinite and timeless. One of the clearest affirmations of this point of view comes from the Chandogya Upanishad (VII.ii.1–VI.ii.2) during the course of the dialogue between Svetaketu and his father Aruni.

> In the beginning, my dear, this was Being only – one without a second. Some say that, in the beginning, this was Non-being, only one, without a second. From that Non-being sprang Being. 'But how could it be so, my dear?' said he; 'How could Being be born from Non-Being? . . . in fact, this was Being only, in the beginning, one, without a second.'[7]

While other traditions share the Hindu belief in a higher reality in which our universe has its origin and existence, Hinduism posits this reality to be not only the intelligent cause (*nimitta karana*) of this world, but its material cause (*upadana karana*) as well. This important point requires further clarification and this may be achieved by comparing this Hindu doctrine with the Christian teaching of *creatio ex nihilo* (creation out of nothing). The Christian tradition emphatically denies that God created the world out of a pre-existent matter which limits God and upon which God is dependent. Hinduism shares this denial of a pre-existent matter for similar reasons, but has avoided the language of *creatio ex nihilo*. Taittiriya Upanishad (II.vi.1) uses language that is familiar in the Upanishads:

> He [the Self] wished, 'Let me be many, let me be born.' He undertook a deliberation. Having deliberated, he created all this that exists. That [Brahman] having created [that], entered into that very thing. And having entered there, it became the formed and the formless, the defined and the undefined, the sustaining and the non-sustaining, the sentient and the insentient, the true and the untrue.[8]

The Upanishads teach that the universe emerges from *brahman*, while denying that any change occurs in the nature of *brahman*.

Hinduism finds it difficult to think of the universe as existing outside or independent of *brahman*. If we must locate the universe anywhere, it can only be in the all-pervasive *brahman*. If we assert the universe to be as real as *brahman* and to have an existence independent of *brahman*, we seem to end up with a reality that, like pre-existent matter, limits the infinity of *brahman*.

While affirming that the universe comes from *brahman*, the Hindu tradition does not go to the other extreme of claiming that the universe, as it is, is *brahman*. Its relationship to *brahman* is an indefinable mystery. It does not have an existence or reality separate from God, but it is not identical with God. Perhaps the term *advaita* (not-two) best sums up the relationship. Without undergoing any change, *brahman* is both the intelligent and material cause of the universe. The universe has its existence in *brahman*, without in any way limiting *brahman*.

This Hindu insight about the non-separation of the world from *brahman* and *brahman*'s all-pervasive nature has important implications for our relationships with nature and living beings. Sadly, however, these implications have not always been worked out or applied in Hindu communities. *Brahman's* presence in all beings confers value and dignity without exception. Each one is sacred and worthy of service and reverence since that which is of supreme value dwells equally within all. This is the vision of wisdom to which the Bhagavadgita calls us:

> He who sees the Supreme Lord existing alike in all beings, not perishing when they perish, truly sees.
> Seeing indeed the same Lord established everywhere, he does not injure the Self by the self. Thereupon he goes to the supreme goal.[9]

Not only is the universe inseparable from *brahman* and dependent upon *brahman* for its reality, but its emergence from *brahman* is without beginning. We cannot imagine a time when it appeared for the first time or when it will become non-existent. In time cycles of inconceivable spans the universe emerges from a seed-like or unmanifest state, becomes manifest and then reverts back to an unmanifest condition.[10] From this state, it will again appear.

Like the universe itself, living beings also have a beginningless and cyclical existence until liberation (*moksa*). We are born, we exist, we die and we are born again. This is the doctrine of *punarjanma* (repeated births) affirmed by all Hindu traditions. Even as birth is not an absolutely new beginning, death is not the extinction of existence. Birth is our entry on the world's stage with a new and physical dress while death is our exit and dissociation with that garb. This process of birth, death and rebirth, referred to as *samsara*, is likened in the Bhagavadgita to a change of clothing.

> As, after casting away worn out garments, a man later takes new ones, so, after casting away worn out bodies, the embodied Self encounters other, new ones.[11]

The rounds of birth, death and rebirth in which we participate are neither chaotic nor haphazard. They assume moral order and significance from the law of karma which governs all human activity. We believe that every volitional action produces a result that is determined by the nature of the action and for which the performer is responsible. The consequences of any action are not necessarily experienced by us in the same life in which the action is performed. The belief in rebirth allows for the possibility that desirable and undesirable consequences of actions in the present may be reaped in future lives.

While belief in the doctrine of karma may be thought of as denying free will and choice, Hindus, on the other hand, see it as emphasizing responsibility and the seriousness of choice. The present circumstances in which we find ourselves are influenced by our individual and collective decisions in the past. The implication is that proper choices in the present will lead to a new future. Our characters, as the Brhadaranyaka Upanishad instructs, are formed by our choices.

> As it does and acts, so it becomes; by doing good it becomes a good and by doing evil it becomes evil – it becomes virtuous through good acts and vicious through evil acts.[12]

Is there freedom from the cycle of birth, death and rebirth or are we trapped forever? Liberation, asserts Hinduism, is possible and is the highest aim of life. Earlier, I wrote of the aim of life as the attainment of fullness, a condition of self-acceptance and peace in which one ceases to be tormented by multifarious desires originating from a sense of deficiency or personal inadequacy. The attainment of this state is liberation. It brings an end to the cycle of *samsara* and Hinduism teaches that it can be attained here and now.

Driven by the urge to be a full person, we develop desires of various kinds hoping that their satisfaction will bring us the fullness we seek. We discover that the attainment of our desires, while leaving us satisfied for shorter or longer periods, still leaves us wanting. To gain the objects of our desire, however, we engage in actions of various kinds. These actions generate results; some of these we experience immediately while others necessitate future births. Thus the cycle of birth, death and rebirth is perpetuated.

How will we ever attain fullness, if all our gains provide only limited satisfaction leading to new desires, actions and rebirth? The Hindu answer is that the fullness we seek will not be attained through the fulfilment of any number of desires since this fullness is already ours. It will not be created as the result of any finite actions we put forth because it is the inherent nature of our true self (*atman*). It remains undiscovered because of our ignorance. Not knowing the truth of the self, we unquestioningly identify ourselves with the qualities and characteristics of the physical body, limited by time and space and always changing. If in rebirth we assume new bodies, we cannot be identical with any particular body. We identify ourselves also with mental and emotional states but these, like the body, keep on changing. Thoughts and emotions belong to me, but do they constitute my essential nature? Each thought and emotion occupies my attention for a limited time before passing away. If my identity were not different from a specific thought, I would cease to be with the disappearance of that thought.

Unlike the body, which is subject to birth, death and a variety of changes, the self is timeless. It is never born nor will it ever die. The Bhagavadgita defines the essential nature of the human being:

> Neither is this (the embodied Self) born nor does it die at any time, nor, having been, will it again come not to be. Birthless, eternal, perpetual, primeval, it is not slain when the body is slain.[13]

Unlike the mind, which is driven by the desire to be full, the self has no lack or want. It is therefore described as *ananda* (bliss). Unlike the ego or 'I' thought (*ahamkara*), which is individualized, the self is identical in all beings. It is the knowledge of the self and a life lived in harmony with its truth that constitutes liberation.

In what way does this knowledge of myself liberate and free me? It frees me from the anxieties of ageing and dying since I know the self to be timeless and eternal. It frees me from the torment of thinking myself to be an insufficient and inadequate being for I know the self to be full and complete. Through self-understanding, I can live from happiness rather than for it. I am also free from the pain of isolation and separation from the universe and other beings since I am aware of a self that is identically present in all things. By seeing myself in others and others in myself, I can learn to love and to rejoice in the well-being of others as I do in my own. No one is an outcast, no one a stranger.

The attainment of happiness through knowledge of the self liberates me from preoccupation with my own desires for fullness, places me in a position to think of the needs of others and grants the energy to serve them. When I am less obsessed with my own petty needs, I am able better to respond to the needs of others. The liberation to love is the greatest gift of wisdom about the self.

Notes

1. See T. W. Organ, *Hinduism: Its Historical Development* (New York: Barron's Educational Series, 1974), p. 2.
2. The word 'writings' is misleading here. The Vedas were assembled as written texts at a fairly late stage in their history. For centuries the sacred verses were handed down orally from teacher to student and preserved by the power of memory. The effect of the verses (mantras), particularly in their ritual uses, depended largely on their correct pronunciation.
3. 'The pleasures that are born out of contact between the senses and sense-objects are sources of unhappiness, Arjuna, since they have a beginning and an end; a wise person does not indulge in these' (5:22).
4. *pariksya lokan karmacitan brahmano nirvedamayannastyakrtah krtena* (I.ii.12).
5. *tadvijnanartham sa gurumevabhigacchetsamitpanih srotriyam brahmanistham* (I.ii.12).
6. William Cenker, *A Tradition of Teachers: Sankara and the Jagadgurus Today* (Delhi: Motilal Banarsidass, 1983), p. 9.
7. See *The Chandogyopanisad with the Commentary of Sankara*, trans. Ganganatha Jha (Poona: Oriental Book Agency, 1942).
8. *Taittiriya Upanisad*, trans. Swami Gambhirananda in *Eight Upanishads with the Commentary of Sankaracarya*, vol. 1 (Calcutta: Advaita Ashrama, 1965). See also Chandogya Upanishad VI.i.3.

9. *samam sarvesu bhutesu*
   tisthantam paramesvaram
   vinasyatsv avinasyantam
   yah pasyati sa pasyati
   samarm pasyan he sarvatra
   samavasthitam isvaram
   na hinasty atmanatmanam
   tato yati param gatim
                (13:27–8)
   See *Shri Bhagavadgita*, trans. Winthrop Sargeant (Albany: State University of New York Press, 1993).

10. 'Manifest' and 'unmanifest' are appropriate terms to describe these processes. The term 'creation', which suggests something coming into being for the first time, may be misleading. The idea here is one of an already existing entity assuming form.

11. *vasamsi jirnani yatha vihaya*
    navani grhnati naro parani
    tatha sarirani vihaya jirnany
    anyani samyati navani dehi
                (2:22)

12. *yathakari yathacari tatha bhavati – sadhukari sadhurbhavati, papakari papo bhavati;*
    punyah punyena karmana bhavati, papah papena. (IV.iv.5)
    See *The Brhadaranyaka Upanishad*, trans. Swami Madhavananda (Calcutta: Advaita Ashrama, 1975).

13. *na jayate mriyate va kadacin*
    nayam bhutva bhavita va na bhuyah
    ajo nityah sasvato yam purano
    na hanyate hanyamane sarire
                (2:20)

THE HEART OF THE HINDU FAITH

S. N. Rao

*Until his retirement, **S. N. Rao** worked for the Department of Fisheries in the State Government of Kerala. For many years he has been involved in interfaith dialogue, and has taught Hinduism and allied subjects to Roman Catholic seminarians.*

IN THE BRAHMANIC Vedic tradition to which I belong, the vision of *atman* (true-self) is deemed to be the ultimate vision. The purpose of this paper is to present this vision as appropriated by me personally and applied by me in my ordinary day-to-day life. My vision therefore is not original. It is rooted in a tradition. As this vision has been interiorized by me, it is in one sense highly personal. It does not claim to be an objective bias-free presentation of the vision of the Vedic sages as seen and lived by them. I cannot make my own the intimate personal experience of a bygone generation. I can, however, re-enact that experience in my own way because it is part of the total human experience. My experience is just one more example of the assimilation of a rich and complex tradition. I have ventured to speak of this vision, not because it is interesting or ancient but because it is human. This vision belongs to us all. It is our common heritage. Since, by accident, I was born into this tradition, I can be at home in it naturally, unlike in an alien culture. I can speak from the inside, subject to the limitations of my faith, intellect and will.

Simply because I was born a Brahman, I did not come to this ultimate vision as a matter of my birthright. I had to wait for the vision to dawn on me. Belonging to a faith-community implies being properly initiated into the orthodox creed, code and cult of that community. But usually these external or esoteric projections hide from one the vision of ultimate reality. More often, the finger pointing to the moon is mistaken for the moon itself. The esoteric secret is lost in such orthopraxis. One needs a radical breakthrough. One must be the recipient of special grace like Arjuna in the Gita, to share in the simple original insight basic to the tradition. Thus in my case, though the external rite of passage, namely, the investiture of the sacred thread, took place formally quite early in life, it took many more years of suffering, reflection and discipline to know what it is to be a twice-born Brahman. The privileges, responsibilities and obligations of being born again in this ritual sense were revealed to me slowly. Consolidating the insight has taken quite a number of years, and I wonder whether this process of maturation will ever end. Illumination no doubt comes suddenly. But only gradual cultivation over the years gives stability to the transformative vision one has gained. However, there is nothing extraordinary, mechanical or artificial about this cultivation. My ordinary life was transformed in the light of the insight, that is all. This insight led to a simplicity in my behaviour that went beyond conventional religious praxis, be it in the realm of piety, ritual or morality.

This illumination took me out of the confines of ritual-bound high-caste Brahmanism and placed me in the centre of open cosmic space where all boundaries vanished – I could breathe freely and interact joyfully with persons belonging to different nations and cultures without fear or inhibition. It made my outlook ecumenical and I was fortunate enough to live in all parts of the world and enjoy the benefits of this ultimate vision. In the wake of this experience, closed and static religion gave way to an open and dynamic religion, making me more humble, more attentive, more reasonable. It gave me freedom from meaningless taboos. It made me fearless. I could become more authentic and boldly reject what was phoney in institutionalized religion and morality. I could reject the hierophantic and hypostatic entities that are the stock-in-trade of static religion. There was thus a radical paradigm shift in my view of the world.

Father Lonergan says in his book *Insight*:

What we have to grasp is that insight:
1. Comes as a release to the tension of enquiry
2. Comes suddenly and unexpectedly
3. Is a function not of outer circumstances but inner conditions
4. Pivots between the concrete and the abstract and
5. Passes into the habitual texture of One's mind.[1]

These five aspects have proved true in my own case so far as my ultimate vision is concerned – I received the insight when I was in my early thirties, and not at the time of my receiving the Word on the occasion of my sacred-thread investiture ceremony at the age of twelve.

It was a set of axioms contained in the Upanishads that opened my 'third eye', to use a time-honoured idiom. These cryptic axioms are capsule statements though they are traditionally called great sayings (*maha vakyas*). The following four statements are the most famous:

1. *Tat tvam asi* – You are that (Sama-veda-Chandogya Upanishad VI.x.3)
2. *Aham Brahma Asmi* – I am *brahman* (Yajur-veda-Brihad-Aranyaka Upanishad I.iv.10)
3. *Ayam atma Brahma* – This *atman* is *brahman* (Atharva Veda-Mandukya Upanishad II)
4. *Prajnam Brahma* – Pure consciousness is *brahman* (Rig-Veda-Aitreya Upanishad V.iii).

The first statement is in the form of an instruction (*upadesha-vakya*), to be heard with attention and reverence (*sravana*). The second statement is the result of first-order reflection (*manana-vakya*). It is the first-level prima-facie acceptance of the instruction received. The third statement is the result of second-order reflection or a refinement of the first-level thinking (*nidhi-dhyasana vakya*) resulting in an insight (*anu bhava vakya*) relating to ultimate reality. The fourth statement clarifies the content of the above insight in the experiential order by defining the characteristic of the meta-noesis gained after proper reflection (*lakshana-vakya*). This involves a leap from epistemology to ontology or from the mental mode (*citta*) to 'pure' contentless consciousness (*cit*), which is trans-individual and free from the limiting adjuncts of body and mind – the sensory-intellectual contents are inclusively transcended here.

These statements are in the present tense or rather 'tenseless mode' as they indicate to me a timeless fact of nature (*rta*). Syntactically they have a common grammatical form of 'a is b', relating two entities. Semantically they look like tautologies or contradictions. Pragmatically they result in a meta-noetic insight of which nothing can be spoken. Yet this silence (*mauna*) itself has a high transformative value.

This 'unspeakable' mystery was useful to me for solving the problems related to my own life in an ultimate sense. This was not a solution in the usual sense, but rather a meta-solution that changed my whole outlook rather than materially altering the course of my life. These statements became axiomatic, normative, and incorrigible in a persuasive way. I heard the One Word, in the singular, pointed out by these axioms. I accepted the Word in faith and could reap the fruits in actual praxis.

Thus sudden enlightenment became possible in my case through the awakening of faith in the above sense. I could understand that the true self was the ultimate subject, the basic postulate of all knowledge, the transcendental background of the empirical transactional trinity of knowledge, knower and known. *Tri-puti* is the self-luminous and self-proved pure consciousness that manifests itself as the subject and object, as the self and the non-self, and which at once transcends or overreaches that tripartite division. I could understand Sage Yajna-valkya's declaration in the Brihad-aranyaka Upanishad that the self, the ultimate knower, can never be known as an object because it knows all objects, and yet it does not reduce itself to an abstraction because the knowledge of the knower is never destroyed. I could realize that the absolute (*brahman*) manifests itself as the subject as well as the object and transcends them both. The ultimate is as certain as the *atman* and as infinite as *brahman*. This blending of the subject and the object in a transcendental first principle, by the Vedic sages, was accepted by me *in toto*. At one stroke, the absurdity of life that was haunting me all along assumed a transcendental reference. This insight suggested to me day-to-day trust in the hidden ways of the first principle. I could take my life as a bonus, one day at a time with an attitude of trust. I found that this was a good antidote to worry. I felt like a child whose hand is firmly grasped in his father's and I stopped being anxious about my future. I fully realized the meaning of the ancient phrase *ya evam veda* – he who knows thus. And I found to my pleasant surprise that the Christian term 'Amen' carried the same meaning. It puts into two brief syllables the meditative gladness of great assent 'so be it'. In this sense, I could enter into the spirit of the Sermon on the Mount, without bothering too much about the background or setting in which the teaching was given.

When I was a child, I was taught a faith that was different in nature, it was not esoteric but exoteric. It was based on a dualistic subject–object structure, as expressed in the 'faith in' construction. Thus I was taught to have faith in Vishnu, as I belonged to the sectarian Vaishnava faith-community. It took me several years to understand this cultic practice of positioning a hierophantic or hypostatic dummy object for purposes of worship – and when the message of the Upanishad came to me in a non-dual intuition, I could easily transcend this cultic practice as being only optional and not mandatory. The traditional texts I had studied had made this clear to me.

The Upanishads had taught me this fundamental distinction between intentional consciousness (consciousness of objects) and pure consciousness or self-presence. This implicit consciousness is consciousness, not of any object, not even of one's self-image or sense of self, but of one's own interiority. It is the immediate self-presence that is the basis or background of any experience of presence to an object. It can never be grasped by introspection, for any attempt to 'look' at it turns it into an object of intentional consciousness. Yet one can advert to its existence in any moment of consciousness, since it is the horizon within which any particular object or event is experienced, but it is limited by none of them. Thus the Upanishadic insight, at the experiential level (*jnanam, vijnana sahitam*), enabled me to transcend both action (karma) and devotion (*upasana*). When Professor D. T. Suzuki was asked what would happen if a man suddenly had enlightenment while chopping wood, he replied, 'He would go on chopping wood.' I could understand this dark reply in the light of the deliverance given to me by the Upanishads.

Before enlightenment came, I was a bureaucrat in government service, married, and the father of a daughter. After enlightenment I continued to play these roles, as if nothing important had happened. I did not suddenly grow a beard, or shave my head; or wear the ochre robe or retreat to the Himalayas; nor did I practise yoga or enter into samadhi. I lived a normal existence, crying when the occasion arose, and laughing when the time came. These were deemed by me peripheral normal phenomena happening all the time on the screen of *atman* or ultimate consciousness. The classic verse, which Sankara himself quotes in his commentary on Kathopanisad (II.i.1) defines *atman* as that which pervades all, that which is the subject and that which knows, experiences and illuminates the objects, and that which remains immortal and always the same. It is this vision of *atman* that has helped me to avoid so many spurious practices in the name of religion or spirituality. In fact, if the expression the 'vision of *atman*' is not taken in the non-dual sense, this itself will land one onto the subject–object plane leading to unnecessary speculations and practices. The truth is, according to the ultimate vision there is no need for any desperate upstream struggle to reach the so-called other shore, since *atman* is not merely the undivided whole that is the ultimate ground of being, it is also the ultimate subject operative in history and existent beyond history. Academics may write big tomes discussing the transcendent and the immanent and wax eloquent over the priority of contemplation over action or vice versa, but the insight gained by me put an abrupt end to such exercises and I found no use for teleological or eschatological categories. I could take for granted what Gaudapada, the grand preceptor of Sankara, stated long ago in his exposition of the Mandukya Upanishad: 'There is no dissolution, no birth, none in bondage, none aspiring for Wisdom, no seeker of liberation and none liberated. This is the absolute truth.'[2]

This position came to me as a natural corollary of accepting the *atman* as the sole ultimate reality. The paradigm shift here is from the egocentric attitude to the *atman*-centric all-inclusive approach. I found that this position was acceptable to the great south Indian saint, Tayumanavar, who tried to blend Vedanta and Siddhanta viewpoints. He has explicitly stated this in his poem *Chidambara-Rahasyam* or *Akara-Bhuvanam*:

> When egoism in the form of I-sense comes to anyone, primordial *maya* presents multiple facets. Because of this, the manifold suffering to which one becomes subject, who can describe it? All sorts of 'entities' such as flesh, body, internal organs, interior and exterior, all-pervading space, air, fire, water, earth, mountains and forests, rise tier upon tier and cloud the vision. One posits forgetfulness and memory. One posits joys and sorrows caused by countless waves of *maya*. One talks of karma as causing these. One talks of countering this karma by different religious practices. One talks of God. One talks of the religious practitioner [*sadhaka*]. One talks of different *dharmas*. One talks of doctrine and argument. When one sees all these, one thinks they are like the myriad grains of sand on a sea shore.[3]

My behaviour, after gaining this insight, was governed by the advice of Gaudapada himself: 'Therefore knowing the *atman* to be such, fix your attention on non-duality. Having realised non-duality, behave in the world like an insensible object.'[4] This piece of advice was clarified for me by Sankara:

> Having known this non-dual Brahman which is free from hunger, etc., unborn and directly perceptible as the self, and which transcends all codes of human conduct (i.e. by attaining to the consciousness that 'I am the supreme Brahman') behave with others as one not knowing the truth; that is to say let not others know what you are and what you have become.[5]

But my intention to travel incognito did not materialize. My friends found me out and they wanted me to teach. This has led me for the past thirty-five years to interact with all types of groups. I had only One Word to convey. Many have listened but I doubt how many could have really understood. For the field in which I operated was the monopoly of specialists, be they Christian priests, Hindu swamis or Yogic practitioners – and the naivete with which I tried to pass on the Word would have amused them, for their brand of esotericism was of a different kind.

To convey my ultimate vision, based on the 'pure' insights of the Upanishads, was also made difficult by the usual brand of spirituality based on the saccharine devotion of *bhakti*. I found most individuals fixated at the sense-imaginal and emotional levels. Everywhere there was 'charismatic' leadership. The place was full of gurus, swamis, babas, etc. belonging to this exoteric dualistic tradition. They were fanatically revered by their followers. No act of the leader was illegitimate as long as he thought fit to perform it. In the eyes of his followers what this leader did was right because he did it. This held good even in the case of famous leaders such as Gandhi, Vinoba Bhave, Mahesh Yogi, Sai Baba or Rajneesh. So my attempts to draw attention to the seminal insights of the Upanishads, without any frills, did not succeed. Like the child in the story, I said that the emperor had no clothes but people refused to listen. Only a few people, whose number can be counted on my fingers, appear to have benefited from interacting with me. When I started interacting with Christian groups, I found that I could not transmit the insights given to me by Gaudapada or Sankara, without diluting it to suit their monotheistic exoteric religion. These groups, among whom I could count leading theologians and philosophers, appeared to have forgotten the esoteric Christian tradition. They were keen only on external trappings. They were keen only on replacing the candles with brass lamps with a cross on the top. They talked of enculturation; a truncated enculturation that refused to admit the ultimate vision adumbrated above. The usual creed to which they subscribed, both clergy and laity, has been summarized neatly by Jules de Gauliter in *From Kant to Nietzsche*:

> A god outside of the world and creator of the world, a law revealed to the conscience of man either miraculously or naturally and intimating to him a good to practise and an evil to avoid, and provided with a free will which permits him to observe or infringe the laws imposed, hence responsible for his acts, capable of merit and demerit, liable to penalties and rewards conceived now in the spirit of the coarsest realism, now in more refined forms, such is the system of fictions which is embraced by the monotheistic conception in its Christian aspect after the simpler and more entirely dogmatic monotheism of the Moslems has been isolated from it.[6]

Very often therefore I found Christian theology dismissing this ultimate vision of *atman* I have presented above as monism or pantheism. In my ultimate vision, time, space and causality become an apparatus of deformation as a purely human

representative means valid at the empirical level. The conception of a work created
by a force outside itself gives way in this vision to that of a Being (*sat, atman*) that
represents itself to itself. The idea of representation is substituted for that of
creation. All the mental constructions, brought about by the monotheistic
hypothesis, such as dualism, conciliation of finite and infinite, of liberty and
fatality, vanish. Existence is given us as representation and we know it only as such.
Only the scripture, to which we have given assent, 'shows' existence *per se* (*sat*) and
cognate ignorance (*ajnana, avidya*), which conceals this pure existence in an
empirical dress. I have found this position quite unacceptable to most Christians, as
it is to most Hindus belonging to the exoteric tradition. As there can be nothing
external to the infinite, ultimate principle, in the sense of the 'objective' or
'second', any objectivation means not ontological. Knowability in this context can
have only a special sense and clearly not the epistemological one. One can know
the ultimate *atman* or *brahman* only by being it, as the Upanishads hint. The non-
epistemic character of the ultimate is indicated by Yajna-valkya as 'not this, not
this' (*neti neti*) – such apophactism is well known in the esoteric Christian tradition
also. But in my encounter with Christian pundits, who revel in discursive thinking,
vociferous prayers and liturgies, such an approach did not make any appeal. The
ultimate is acosmic, for no cosmic explanation can contain or comprehend it. Only
a negative expression can make a feeble attempt to comprehend the acosmic
principle (*nis-prapancha*) by an oblique reference. Failure of discursive thinking to
characterize the acosmic principle is no indication of its non-existence. No one can
deny it, for at the base of every denial there is the affirmation of the ontological
principle. Even the term 'acosmic' is unacceptable to many, for it is equated with
world-negation and pessimism.

In the ultimate vision, described here, there are three positions:

1. *brahman* is real,
2. the universe is unreal, and,
3. the universe is *brahman*.

In discussions with many Christian scholars, I found that their understanding
stopped at the second position. The bridge between the world of appearance and
the absolute is here, as it were, broken.

Another common fallacy that often emerged during such discussions with
Christian theologians was their opinion that the vision of *atman* put an end to all
moral codes of conduct. According to many Christian scholars, the notion of sin
among Hindus is rather weak or ambivalent and they claim superiority for
Christianity on this score, but this is a gross falsification. A classical formulation of
this position is given by the Catholic professor, R. C. Zaehner:

In other words, the text [Gita] seems to say, once you have truly got rid of

all sense of ego, you will find that you can murder to your heart's content
and feel no remorse at all: You will have passed beyond good and evil.[7]

The professor refers to the case of Charles Manson, the cult leader in America who
brutally killed Sharon Tate and six other people in Los Angeles in 1969. To quote
the professor, 'Charles Manson did *not* blanch and in this he was faithful to a very
ancient and very venerable Indian tradition.'[8] I believe that this is an insult to the
Brahmanic tradition to which I belong. Perhaps the professor's excessive love for
his own tradition has dimmed his vision. If only he had known that the teacher of
the Gita stands on a battlefield of *dharma* (as the opening verse of the Gita itself
proclaims) and teaches Brahmavidya to solve a peculiar problem arising out of
dharma itself, he would not have indulged in such exaggerations. I believe also that
tragic phenomena such as Charles Manson began to appear when the orthodox oral
tradition of teaching scripture to initiates yielded to the public and profane
tradition of written scripture in the form of popular paperback editions of the Gita
and the Upanishads, easily accessible to all and sundry.

No doubt the vision of *atman* as portrayed above calls for radical
transcendence or death of the ego. Ultimately there is no experience of death and
the death experiment is, in the last analysis, unreal because the 'subject' who died
was not real. The ultimate vision leads to an experience of liberation, of freedom
from everything. To be born again does not mean an indefinite and horizontal
repetition of one and the same circle. It means breaking the circularity of time and
reaching the ontological fullness of being, here and now. In the light of this vision,
I could understand the advice of Christ: 'Take therefore no thought for the morrow:
for the morrow shall take thought for the things of itself. Sufficient unto the day is
the evil thereof.'[9] Consolidating this insight demanded great humility from me and
a robust sense of humour.

I would like to conclude this paper on a personal note, since I feel I have
already drifted into academic abstractions. I believe there are ultimately three
solutions to life's problems. I call them, serially:

1. my father's way,
2. my mother's way, and,
3. the way of Yajna-valkya or Jesus Christ.

My father went mad. My mother committed suicide. Yajna-valkya and Jesus Christ,
according to me, committed suicide in principle. They went mad in principle. I
once shocked the Archbishop of Calcutta and the Catholic clergy by bluntly
stating this, without preface or prelude, flouting the rules of normal etiquette
expected at a pleasant post-luncheon meeting. I would like to reiterate this
standpoint as a conclusion to this paper. I am now in my mid-sixties. As I write
this, I have just come back from Calcutta, after teaching Hindu spirituality as part

of a pastoral orientation programme to Catholic seminarians about to leave for
their ministry.

I hope you will agree when I write that I have not committed suicide.
Whether I am mad or not, it is not for me to say. You, dear reader, can cherish your
own opinion about me. But you cannot deny me the privilege of considering myself
sane in my own way and I presume that if the Reverend Martin Forward, the editor
of this book, who has interacted with me personally, had not tuned himself to my
brand of madness, he would not have asked me to contribute this paper!

Notes

1. B. J. F. Lonergan (London: Longman, 1957), p. 4.
2. Swami Nikhilananda, trans. and comp., *The Mandukyopanisad with Gaudapada's
   Karika and S'ankara's Commentary* (Mysore, India: Sri Ramakrishna Ashrama,
   1968), p. 117.
3. *Tayumana Swamigal Patal* (Tiruppananthal, India: Sri Kasi Matam, 1963), p. 70.
   Translation author's own.
4. Swami Nikhilananda, *The Mandukyopanisad*, pp. 128–9.
5. Mandukya Upanishad, Karika 11.36.
6. G. M. Spring, trans. (New York: The Wisdom Library, 1961), p. 10.
7. *The City Within the Heart* (London: Unwin, 1980), p. 10.
8. Ibid., p. 11.
9. Matthew 6:34.

To Become a Muslim: A Dialogue with the Self

Saba Risaluddin

Saba Risaluddin is a founder-trustee of the Calamus Foundation, a registered British charity dedicated to promoting a balanced image of Islam and to fostering understanding between Muslims, Jews and Christians. She is an International President of the World Conference on Religion and Peace, and a member of the executive committee of the World Congress of Faiths. She is also a member of the United Nations Association Religious Affairs Committee and Amnesty International British Section's Religious Bodies Liaison Panel, and belongs to a number of other interfaith groups and committees.

POLITICAL AND MEDIA commentators, asked to account for the resurgence of vicious local wars in so many parts of the world today, are apt to fall back on simplistic and condescending explanations such as 'tribalism'. If by tribalism they mean the same thing as a narrow, exclusivist nationalism, they may be at least partly right; though the word 'tribalism' has the enormous merit for such commentators of suggesting something primitive that 'we', the civilized world, are no longer subject to. It evades, too, the question of the role of colonialism and imperialism (formerly the preserve of Britain and other European states and now almost exclusively confined to the United States) in creating conditions in which exclusivist nationalism could flourish or in failing to support movements that could have defused it.

One of the most striking aspects of the message of Islam, in the shape of the Holy Qur'an and the words and deeds of the Prophet Muhammad, is that it is clearly aimed at redefining the tribal society of seventh-century Arabia, setting in its place the family as the cornerstone of the social structure and, beyond that, the overarching belief-community or *umma*, with the potential to reach every corner of the world and to unite diverse peoples in the process. And it did this, not by denying their diversity (difference is celebrated in the Qur'an) but by emphasizing the direct relationship between every individual and the one, transcendent Creator, whom Muslims call Allah, and in consequence, asserting the unique value of each of us, in complete spiritual equality one with another.

Within this ethos, individual and group identity becomes not a simple monolithic concept of the kind expressed by tribalism or narrowly exclusive nationalism, but a many-layered, infinitely richer possibility. To be a Muslim is not to be constrained within a particular racial or ethnic group, nor to be strait-jacketed (except for purely administrative purposes) as a national of this or that more or less exclusive state, nor to be consigned to an inferior class or caste. It is to take the simple but all-consuming step of declaring oneself in submission to the will of God, and thereby belonging to a community whose adherents, in the course of nearly fourteen hundred years since the revelation to the Prophet Muhammad, have given the world some of its most outstanding intellectual achievements, some of its most compelling and beautiful art and architecture, and some of its finest manifestations of civilization. If it has not always lived up to its highest ideals, this is not to be attributed to the Islamic ethos itself, any more than the slaughter of the Crusades, the tortures of the Inquisition, or the Nazi Holocaust are to be attributed to the Christian or Western ethos, but to the flawed human character which, in pursuit of power or economic self-interest, can at times descend to depths of iniquity that include exploiting religion in the name of evil.

Muslims believe that to submit to the will of God comes naturally to humankind, so that every child is born a Muslim in the broadest sense of one who submits; but that we are all, endowed as we are with free will, more or less apt to indulge our baser impulses in defiance of the divine Will. To *become* a Muslim, in the sense of declaring oneself part of the great faith-community founded by the Prophet Muhammad, involves the simple act of reciting the profession of faith before witnesses: I bear witness that there is no god but God, and that Muhammad is His Prophet. There is no lengthy period of induction, no rigorous study programme to be followed; what matters is the belief in one's heart, and since only God can know our heart, the witnesses to this profession of faith are bound to take on trust the new Muslim's good intentions.

Given the opportunity to choose one's faith – opportunity, because though there are seekers and some find without having consciously sought, most stay comfortable with the faith they were born into or at most drift away from it without embracing another, and it is a privilege to be presented, in a condition of such detachment, with the possibility of choice – given such an opportunity, how does one choose a faith? Is it through an intellectual understanding of its ethos, or a liking for the practice and rhetoric of its adherents, or by the simple accident of knowing individual adherents and finding oneself attracted to them in a way that consciously includes an awareness of the influence of their faith on their nature and self-perception? The very word 'choice' seems problematic in juxtaposition with a concept such as 'belief', which as commonly understood is not likely to be initiated by rational argument, though once attained it may be thus sustained.

How others are aware of their belief, their faith, I cannot say; for myself, it is clearly associated with the intellect rather than the emotions, yet equally clearly lies at least in part beyond the rational intellect. The tension between intellect and emotion, between the rational and the mystic, is present throughout the development of Islamic thought, the pendulum swinging now this way, now that, with ever and again a creative impulse towards synthesis of the two strains. To study these developments is to further one's own understanding of the point at which the rational intellect stands helpless in the face of mystery. Al-Ashari's *bila kayfa*, 'without asking how', has resonance, as does Ibn Rushd's (Averroes) theory of the two aspects of truth: the truth of the philosophers and the truth of religion; both of them, in their different ways, resorting to metaphor, ellipses and even antinomy in order to express the underlying truth itself in terms of reason rather than myth.

The fundamental leap of faith, where rational understanding fails and the intellect is forced to fall back on the awareness of something inexplicable and inexpressible in terms of its chosen tools of argument, does not depend on a particular formal framework, however. That being so, rational understanding seems the only proper basis of choice, and, whatever the original impulse that attracted one, only the intellect can be required to justify adherence to one or another formal religion. The evident danger is that, alongside a firm intellectual conviction, there may lurk in the shadows the arrogant belief that, the chosen faith being 'best' for the chooser, it must by definition be 'best' absolutely, with obvious implications for all other faiths. The suspicion is that, here as so often in matters of faith, the rational intellect is after all not in itself enough, that only the apparent abdication of reason can resolve the contradictions between 'the best' and the equal value of 'the rest'. Perhaps the development of fuzzy logic has something to teach us in the domain of faith as of thought. When fuzzy logic, *la logique floue*, was first conceived, it was, I understand, rejected by those working within a framework of Western science and technology, for whom concepts are still expected to fit into neat Aristotelian boxes. But the Japanese, unencumbered by the legacy of Hellenistic thought, seized upon and developed the idea that something could not only occupy more than one conceptual box, but might also be different things in each box. An intellectual system that has the potential to liberate one from a rigid mindset surely deserves better than to be applied to the controls of automatic washing machines or telephone networks.

Strands of thought that prefigure some of the concerns about belief appear in the Qur'an, where Islam recognizes the distinction between deep-seated faith in the ungraspable higher reality on the one hand and commitment to a particular religion, with all its baggage of ritual and dogma, on the other. The natural religion or *din al fitra* is the former. In that it is natural for humankind to submit to the divine Will, this natural religion could also be called Islam in the broad sense, for the word means the faith of those who submit; and to avoid confusion with Islam as it is understood in the world today, it may be convenient to call it Ur-Islam. Furthermore, though the message to the Prophet Muhammad, in the words of the Qur'an itself, completes the continuum of revelation stretching back to Abraham, it also speaks of the many paths to God and of the diversity of modes of worship, in contexts that by no means suggest that other ways are inferior to that of Islam. The Sufis or mystics of Islam, in particular, have stressed the underlying unity of all religions and have not hesitated to draw upon many traditions, from indigenous desert asceticism to Neoplatonism, Christian Gnosticism, Zoroastrianism, Manichaean dualism and even Buddhism.

The choice, then, of a particular formal religion as a framework into which to fit one's personal Ur-Islam becomes paradoxically more challenging, for if it is to be justified rationally, one must surely take account not only of the underlying ethos, as transmitted in the original message, but also of what its adherents have made of that message and how they have lived up to that ethos. Any understanding of the message and ethos is inevitably coloured by the layers of historical experience, by the theological, philosophical and mystical endeavour, by the politics of power-seekers and power-holders who have occupied the territory of that endeavour in justification of their aims, by the overlay of diverse cultures upon the fabric of Islamic society, and most of all, perhaps, by one's own conditioning.

And the conclusion reached that Muslims, in common with the adherents of other faiths, have not always lived up to their own highest ideals – have, indeed, from the very beginnings of Islam in the seventh century, crudely or subtly, deliberately or inadvertently, departed from or even subverted those ideals – how does the convert engage with the disparity between the ideal and the practice? Is it presumption to challenge what one sees as a distortion of the message? Or would it, conversely, be a personal failure *not* to do so, but to accept unquestioningly, as many would have us do, all the baggage, all the ritual and rhetoric, all the distortions of practice that subvert the Islamic ethos of social justice, as though they were part of the original revelation? Consider the position of all too many (though by no means all) women in Muslim societies, at least as perceived from outside, and compare it with the message of the Qur'an: on the one hand, oppression, restriction of women's freedom of action, control of their sexuality, even sometimes brutal physical punishment, all justified in the name of Islam; on the other, though there are admittedly a few verses that are difficult for women to engage with, which imply that they are less fully autonomous than men, the ethical context is – for women no less than for men – that of equality, rights, justice. And there are today many Muslim women working, at all levels from grassroots to academia, to recover that original ethos. The women's movement in the Middle East antedates Western feminism and has a broader sweep than the secular Western feminist's sometimes narrow agenda of sexual freedom and the right to work outside the home. And we are seeing now, rather as Christianity has for some years been enriched by feminist theology, a resurgence of Muslim women theologians who can, without succumbing to the simplistic appeal of a return to some golden age, draw their inspiration from the very earliest days of Islam when the Prophet's youngest wife, Ayesha, was regarded as 'among all the people, the one who was the most educated and whose judgement was the best'.[1] Muslim women writers, too, are producing some fine work. A European woman who chooses to become a Muslim, as I have, far from being thrust into the repressive environment of the popular stereotype, finds herself in the midst of a tremendously creative and liberating movement.

Nor is this Islamic feminist theology developing in isolation from other encouraging impulses within the Muslim world. One of the more coherent intellectual movements in Islam of recent years is Ismail Faruqi's Islamization of knowledge – a phrase that, unfortunately, lends itself to the simplistic conclusion that all you need do is set a layer of overtly Islamic vocabulary and practice over education and you will thereby, effortlessly, shed all the colonization of the mind that has been the great achievement of the Western cultural paradigm in the twentieth century. Faruqi's argument is more persuasive than that. He believed that the cause of Muslim travails in the modern, post-colonial world was that that very colonization, that intellectual and cultural dominance, had left us attempting to understand and resolve Muslim failures within a framework of inappropriate intellectual and analytical tools; that to engage with the reality of our decline we needed to create or rediscover our own analytical tools. This need not imply rejecting Western concepts, though it does demand that we use and develop them consciously; we have only to look back into our own history to find that our greatest intellectual achievements were attained when Muslim thinkers seized the concepts of Greek philosophy and of Neoplatonism and made them their own, with an entirely new vocabulary to represent the new, Islamic understanding of these alien modes of thought. These Muslim achievements, in turn, fed two great strands of Western thought: mediaeval Christian theology, both directly and through Muslim influence on Jewish philosopher-theologians such as Ibn Gabirol and Maimonides, and among Christian theologians thus influenced one may mention, above all, St Thomas Aquinas; and the Renaissance, which it is no exaggeration to say could not have happened had Muslims not preserved, developed and transmitted the learning of the Greeks. Many lesser strands of influence can be perceived as well; for example, the courtly love tradition of the troubadours drew directly upon the Arabic secular poetry of al-Andalus, or Muslim Spain, and in turn influenced Dante, Petrarch, and the Minnesingers; and the inter-connections between Sufism (Islamic mysticism) and both Christian and Jewish mystics are extensive.

Disentangling all these strands, peeling back all these layers, is an essential part of the task facing the Muslim convert who takes nothing for granted, but seeks to understand in order to challenge the stultifying orthodoxy, the political impotence and the economic decline that afflict much of the Muslim world today, as much as to situate those failings squarely within the context of the global political order. And even before accepting Faruqi's challenge to create new analytical tools, there comes the need to engage with the way in which vocabulary, both familiar and less familiar, can mask understanding. Familiar, because the easy assumption is seldom the most constructive, and less familiar, because there is today no vocabulary so unfamiliar that it does not come ready-loaded with associations that, as often as not, are negative. No discourse is free of such associations, which can be used by the unscrupulous or the unwary to distort our understanding in often quite dramatic ways. Even a perfunctory study of the Palestinian question, or more recently the Bosnian conflict, shows us this.

Misleading associations are not the only means of clouding or skewing our perceptions. One of the most powerful ways in which discourse can affect understanding is in its lacunae, its silences. Two examples shall suffice, one from what may seem to the unwary to be a neutral source, the other from the honourable tradition of the struggle against prejudice, and thus even more influential both in what it says and what it leaves unsaid.

Firstly, the history of French literature on which I was brought up makes no reference to Arab influence on the troubadours; so far as the author of my school book was concerned, the tradition sprang from French soil, and there is no need to look any further than indigenous genius for its roots.

Secondly, in almost all discourse about anti-semitism and racism today, though there is often an acknowledgement that other groups are suffering more direct attacks and are viewed in a more negative light than Jews, these other groups are defined in non-specific terms such as racial or ethnic minorities, foreigners, immigrants or asylum-seekers. This hides the fact that Islamophobia, the anti-Muslim equivalent of anti-semitism, is not only widespread, but forms part of mainstream discourse – is respectable, in short – as, mercifully, anti-semitism no longer is. Muslims, in the view of those who combat anti-semitism in these terms, exist only in so far as they themselves speak or act in what are seen as anti-semitic ways. Yet the interests of both Jews and Muslims would be better served if they both acknowledged the reality of prejudice against the other among themselves and in the world community, and acted together against both manifestations of religio-racial prejudice.

The significance of these factors – the careless use of words, or their absence – is profound for the kind of interfaith dialogue in which, almost from the moment of embracing Islam, I have sought to engage: dialogue that goes beyond the simple though laudable intention to 'get to know one another' or the well-meant but condescending assertion that 'we are all the same, really', and seeks to create genuine bonds of friendship, of shared commitment and of joint action. The internal dialogue, too, must take cognizance of its own lacunae and misperceptions; must ever strive for the most rigorous methods, mistrusting the easy response, the instinctive, unexamined reaction, the carelessly emotive.

Dialogue of this kind stems directly from the Islamic commitment to creating a just society; and with that commitment in view, opportunities for joint action present themselves not only within the interreligious arena, but also in the secular world. Dialogue between the followers of different faiths, though often fraught with tensions and misunderstandings, can go far if all are willing to agree that it is posited on one unshakeable foundation: beyond humankind there is something greater, which many of us call God, and to which we are all ultimately subject. Though we may, and usually do, differ on the particular path we should take towards that ultimate reality, we may encounter our own or others' (sometimes unstated, sometimes unconscious perhaps) conviction that only one path can be the true Way, and we frequently allow political differences to obtrude and further obfuscate our understanding of each other. But dialogue between people of faith and those with none, or to whom faith is irrelevant, finds itself without even this foundation and must seek other bonds.

Sceptics, confronted with the phrase 'the Islamic commitment to a just society', may ask themselves, or their Muslim interlocutors, how it is that Muslim societies today are for the most part so manifestly unjust. It is a legitimate question, and honesty, not apologetics, will answer it. We Muslims are entitled, in return, to expect honesty and self-criticism from those with whom we engage in dialogue, though we do not always find these, any more than we ourselves always attain them.

And here we come to the heart of the most difficult and challenging, and thus also potentially the most interesting and fruitful, dialogue: that between interlocutors with differing and fundamentally opposed narratives, histories and self-understanding; with competing, and often equally legitimate, claims. At this point no amount of comfortable agreement about metaphysics will do, for the debate is urgently actual. I think, of course, of the way in which Arabs and Jews, and indeed Muslims and Jews (so completely has the Middle East become identified, in many minds, with Islam in general and 'Islamic fundamentalism' in particular) must, at some point, confront not just the question of Palestine, but the future of Jerusalem, and the gross disparity in resources in the entire Middle East. I think, too, of the tensions and violence in the Indian sub-continent, between Hindus and Muslims, between Hindus and Sikhs, between the Indian authorities and the people in Kashmir and between India and Pakistan over Kashmir, between the privileged castes and the *dalits*, between secularism and religiosity; and of the appalling violence in the Balkans, whipped up by demagogues who have successfully created in their followers a sense of victimhood quite unsupported by historical fact.

Some say that such dialogue goes nowhere until a common history is agreed; perhaps, though, we need rather to agree on the equal validity of different historical perspectives. I think, too, of the imbalance that is present when Muslims enter into dialogue with Christians of the majority, mainstream Church (in Britain's case, the established, i.e. state, Church) – an imbalance sensed by other minority faiths including non-conformist Christians. To the background of centuries of misrepresentations of Islam, so deeply entrenched now that much of it is probably unconscious, is added the reality of cultural and political dominance. Rather than agreeing a common history, the first need is often to define terms, and to agree to avoid words that explain nothing while seeming to account for everything. Having to find alternatives to such loaded words as 'fundamentalist' or 'terrorist', or even to the language of rights so freely and sometimes so self-righteously used by Western liberals, is no mere semantic exercise, but brings a salutary awareness of just how glibly misleading words can be.

In such encounters, even when against the background of power imbalance or competing claims are set the urgently needed qualities of honesty, self-criticism and openness (being willing to express one's own concerns and to articulate the sticking points, and being open to the concerns and sticking points of the interlocutor), we find all too often one critical commodity lacking: time. It takes enormous patience to work through the superficialities to the core of the encounter, and great determination not to stop at the point where discomfort enters the equation, not to remain in the cosy area of shared values or shared concerns that, however pressing, are in a sense external.

Time is short in more than one sense. Those of us who believe we must go beyond the facile and superficial discourse that sometimes passes for dialogue all have many calls on us, from the mundane demands of daily living to our commitment to our faith or our favourite cause. But even our frenetic days are luxuriously easy compared with those of the victims of oppression or violence on whose behalf, as much as or more than our own, we may be engaged. When women are being raped, families torn apart, children killed or brutalized in so many regions of the world, can we afford the luxury of the struggle with semantics? But if we do not confront the grotesque power imbalances that words, misused, can reinforce or even cause, how shall we ever reach a common understanding that, just possibly, might give us a basis for reinventing the world? There are those to whom the appeal of a suffering child is too potent to ignore; these are the people who, often at great personal risk, go into war zones or disaster areas to bring relief; and there are those of us who, less selfless perhaps, believe that we may be able to do our small part to catalyse change so that war and disaster occur less often and, when they do, are more promptly and creatively responded to. Both these responses are – to use a word that is much abused and misunderstood – a form of jihad, which expresses both the struggle for justice in the world and the personal endeavour of faith. The inner dialogue of discovery and the external, for this writer, meet here.

Notes

1. Ibn Hajar al-'Asqualani, *Al-Isaba fi-taniyiz al-shhabi*, vol. 8 (Cairo: Maktaba al-Dirasa al-Islamiya Dar al-Nahda, n.d.), p. 18.

THE ULTIMATE VISION OF THE LIVING SEED

Jyoti Sahi

Jyoti Sahi *is a Roman Catholic artist who, in his painting and writing, is concerned to further the interaction of culture and faith in the Indian context. He founded the Indian School of Art for Peace, an ashram community near Bangalore in South India, and gave the Teape Lectures at Cambridge University in 1995.*

IN 1963 WHEN I was still studying art at the Camberwell School of Arts and Crafts in London, I first met the Benedictine monk Dom Bede Griffiths. He was visiting his old monastery at Farnborough, having started a Christian ashram in Kerala, South India. He and another Western monk who had come from a Cistercian abbey went to Kerala because they wanted to establish links with the ancient Syrian Christian tradition that has been active in South India possibly since apostolic times. Certainly there is documentary proof dating back to the fourth century of the presence of the Syrian Christians on the south-western coast of India.

The liturgical life of the Syrian Christian Church has been sustained by a rich liturgical tradition that goes back to the monastic schools, one of whose luminaries was the poet-saint Ephraim. St Ephraim drew upon a profound fund of biblical imagery that gave meaning to the liturgical cycle of the year. The contemplative life of the monks was lived through celebrating the continuing round of liturgical seasons, which can be related to the times of birth, growth and death, and which have a cosmic as well as a very simple and natural significance.

After returning to India, I went on a pilgrimage around various temples and holy places, concluding with a visit to the Christian ashram of Dom Bede in the hills that look out over the coast of Kerala. Here, in a very beautiful valley, the ashram had established a farm at the foot of a mountain called Kurisumala, which means 'the mountain of the cross'. I built myself a small cottage overlooking the valley and for three years I attended the monastic hours that follow the seasonal changes of the year, whilst reflecting on how these seasons are also a part of our inner world. I was longing for inner transformation.

It was while I was at this Christian ashram and subsequently at another ashram on the banks of the holy River Kavery in Tamil Nadu, to which Fr Bede shifted in 1968, that I began to realize how important the countryside around one is in giving shape to one's inner spiritual life. I suppose this process of drawing one's inner life from the experience of the natural environment was already a part of my childhood, as I was brought up in the Doon Valley, which lies between the two holy rivers of the Ganges and the Jamuna, at the foot of the Himalayan range, and on the other side of a far more ancient mountainous belt known as the Siwaliks. It was here in this hill country, known in India as the *Terai*, that I spent the first twenty years of my life, very much influenced by the holy places I saw all around me, which had been hallowed by the cultural memory of the Indian epics, the *Mahabharata* and the *Ramayana*, because it was in this wild and forested region that the legendary kings were supposed to have wandered in exile, visiting ashrams on the banks of the holy rivers. I think that my interest in stories, and the connection these stories have with geographical places, also goes back to these childhood roots.

As I recall, there is a passage in the Upanishads that tells of the advice given to a soul concerning the journey beyond the grave.

> He said: Those, in truth, who leave this world all go to the moon . . . The moon, assuredly, is the gate of the heavenly world. Those who answer the moon [properly] are released, but those who do not answer [properly] become rain and rain down [on earth] where they will be born again in different conditions of life . . . When he reaches there, a man is asked: 'Who are you?' He should reply: 'From the radiant one, O seasons, the seed was collected . . . So was I born, brought forth in the twelfth or thirteenth month, sired by a father who is twelve or thirteenfold by nature. Knowing this, I understand; knowing this, I am. By this truth, O seasons, by this Ardor make me deathless! I am season, a son of the seasons.'
>
> 'Who are you?' [asks the man] 'I am you!' [he replies]. Then he releases him. (Kausu 1, 2–6, Vedic Experience, p. 560)

Unfortunately in our modern technological world this sense of being part of the seasons is disappearing. When in 1972, my wife and I first went to live in a village about fifteen miles from the burgeoning South Indian city of Bangalore, we found that most of the villagers were subsistence farmers, who relied for their livelihood on the small agricultural holdings that they had inherited. For them a knowledge of the seasons was vital for their survival. There was a wealth of knowledge about the moon, and its influence on the seasons. There were numerous names for different rains that were related to the cycles of the moon. What to an outsider might appear as just the monsoon period was carefully analysed by local villagers in terms of different *types* of rain, each with its own particular property. The early rains were not good for planting. The earth had to be first prepared through successive rounds of ploughing, after the first showers had softened the surface.

In the little shrines that adjoined the fields offerings were made to the guardians of fertility, and certain omens were consulted concerning which would be good seeds to grow. The custom of sprouting seeds as part of a liturgical offering itself probably went back to ritualistic practices which tested the fertility of seeds that had been collected and kept from the previous crop, ready for replanting. In fact the very term *bija*, which is the Indian word for seed, means 'that which is reborn' or generated (*ja*) again and again (*bi*). In discussing tribal art, Verrier Elwin points out that it is closely interwoven with the whole process of planting and harvesting seeds, and that the seeds themselves are associated with the spirits of the dead.

Now with the advent of technology, the tractor with disc harrows is able to plough deep into the hard crust of the earth, in a way that the primitive bullock-drawn plough could not do. Thus the beneficial process of gently allowing the moisture of the rain gradually to permeate the earth, which has been hardened by many months of hot baking sun, is lost, as top soil is often just submerged or washed away. A neighbour of ours who was able to sell some land to a city developer for a high price, and thus acquired some capital to invest in a bore well, proudly told us, 'Now we will not have to depend on the seasons any more – we can always have water!' The result is that he is pumping up water day and night to irrigate fields he has turned into rice fields, as he calculates that rice brings in the largest yields. He is struggling to harvest three crops of rice from land that was never before used for such cultivation. The result is that he must buy hybrid seeds (which are technically not *bija* in the ritualistic sense, because they cannot be replanted, but have to be purchased again the next year from the seed merchant), and these have to be further supplemented by artificial chemical fertilizers as the life of the earth is drained away. Then the crops need to be protected with various pesticides and fungicides, because they have no natural immunity to local conditions.

Meanwhile, we observe that the water table has dropped about fifteen feet in the last five to ten years, and all the open wells have gone dry, as the local farmers are increasingly forced to go in for deep bore wells. Some of these wells now have to go down more than two hundred feet in order to reach water, and as the water resources are drying up through over-exploitation, there are fewer and fewer ways of replenishing these deep ground resources. Those who cannot afford to have bore wells are planting fast-growing trees such as eucalyptus, whose deep root systems further drain the earth of all moisture and, when planted in big areas, drive away the rain because their leaves sweat a moisture into the air that acts as an effective wall against the rain falling.

And so the cycle continues, as the inevitable process of desertification sets in. Local, indigenous shrubs and trees which do not have deep root systems just wither up and die as they cannot get enough water, and then there is also the constant chopping down of all such undergrowth, as it is being used up as firewood for household burning.

One could go on to describe even more ways in which the need to overcome the season itself leads to the destruction of natural life processes. The great future threat to this planet is environmental and ecological. And perhaps we could trace much of this back to a loss of respect for the rhythms of nature, which is what we mean by the seasons. We notice that this loss of the seasons has entered into the very pattern of our inner prayer life, as the demands of a culture that is no longer part of the rhythm of nature eats away at all those natural periods of rest and prayerfulness that characterized the life of even the busiest farmer. The farmers and the craftspeople who relied on the rhythms of the seasons to provide the resources on which culture depended were naturally able to see the connection between work and prayer. This is because prayer itself is part of this rhythm – it is a way of internalizing the rhythm and creating an inner space that is analogous to our outer space. This is what I would now like to explore as the inner landscape of our prayer life.

Inner Landscape

We often think of prayer as just asking God for something. Perhaps the farmer asked God for rain or a good harvest, or the artisan asked God for skill or the power to control certain negative or destructive processes in nature. But what is often not perceived or recognized is that prayer creates an inner landscape of feelings and symbols. Prayer internalizes our sensations and perceptions, spiritualizing our bodily experience. Prayer helps us to *create* a kind of cosmology whereby our immediate world of physical experience is recreated as a microcosm of a whole universe of inner experience. In this way work, as physical or manual effort, becomes a spiritual discipline that opens the way for an inner vision – it is through work that ritual can lead us inwards to discover the sources of an inner transforming energy.

In Indian symbolic thought there is a whole world of interior landscapes that can be perceived as thresholds of different dimensions of spiritual experience. In ancient Tamil or Sangam literature, five interior landscapes were outlined. These could be categorized in simple modern terms in the following way:

1. The landscape of the mountain;
2. the landscape of the seashore;
3. the landscape of the riverside;
4. the landscape of the forest;
5. the landscape of the wasteland.

Finally, the *bhakti*-schools that drew their inspiration from the poet Ramanuja, who built a whole system of thought around the intuitions of the mystic Alvars, mentioned a sixth interior landscape of the temple, as a sort of promised land.

In the same way that I believe the manner in which we design our holy places – our temples, gardens, stages for dance and drama – arises out of a deep cosmology, and represents a visual theology, so also the way in which we understand the landscape expresses our whole attitude to the environment, and the *oikos* or *oikumene* in the Greek sense of the whole inhabited world. One could study the evolution of Western landscape painting from this perspective, as representing in visual forms our whole approach to the natural world in which we live. As this vision of the earth becomes more and more like a picture postcard that we send back to our friends and relatives when we go off as tourists on holiday, so nature is reduced to just another consumer item, to be devoured by the hungry leisure industry which turns our capacity to play into a very profitable way of making more money. Thus even the beauty of the landscape is exploited by technology.

If we look at the miniature paintings that came out of the *bhakti*-schools of devotion in India, we observe a curious difference of perspective from the way in which landscape art developed in the West. Landscape painting in Europe is essentially a picture that is like a window looking *out* on nature. Initially the subject of art was very human-oriented – very much concerned with figures, often situated in clearly defined rooms, and surrounded by things that somehow belonged to the people represented. Even the objects that saints were depicted as carrying helped in the process of identifying the saint, or other important person, as part of a very individual biography. Landscape began to creep in as a glimpse through a window. Slowly the landscape became more and more important as a thing in itself, but even here it was very soon determined by an underlying concept of the estate of the landowner. Landscape was attractive as showing how cultured human beings could arrange it, and make it part of their world.

If we look carefully at the miniature there seems to be a process of moving inwards from outside. The window is not an important feature. What becomes central is a veranda, or doorway, or open terrace, which is, so to say, the threshold of a private inner world. We move from the depiction of an outer symbolic world into the sanctum sanctorum of an inner chamber. The process is the same as that which in temple ritual is termed *darsana*, that is, a vision inwards to discover the inner image of a god who rules the heart.

The different landscapes are like doorways through which we enter the personalized world of spiritual devotion. Here again we often find an erotic undertone. Each landscape becomes a way of discovering an inner love scene, which is consummated in the enclosed world of the bedchamber. The lover is depicted as coming in from outside, and instead of the convention of a window looking out, we find a whole wall removed so that we can move into the building as though it were only a stage set, the curtain having been lifted.

The Threshold as Experience: *Samdhya Bhasha,* Twilight Language

All art is concerned with borderlands, that is why the horizon has so much dominated the visual representations of Western art. The horizon is the meeting point of sky and earth. But in Indian art there has been another sense of meeting, between what one might call a foreground and a background. Here space is conceived of as a series of veils going successively inwards. But again, this has not been emphasized so much as depth (so important to the Renaissance stress on perspective) as a way of understanding the layers, or surfaces of experience. Perhaps one could almost speak in terms of relief. We have to peel away one layer of

representation after another to discover the ground on which the whole image has
been projected. There is a kind of shallowness in the way in which the picture is
conceived, which relates directly to the Indian concept of *maya* or illusion. What is
deep in the painting is its sense of texture, a sort of intuition concerning the
bedrock or substance that lies beneath the picture, and which is conveyed by a
visual feeling or tone.

This tone in Indian painting is related to something almost musical, or
poetic. It often alludes to a time of day – that of *samdhya*, the meeting of light and
darkness or twilight. How we represent light in the landscape is very significant,
because light becomes the way in which we see. In Western post-Renaissance art,
light itself becomes a thing – it is something that falls *on* objects, thus making them
visible. In the yogic traditions of Indian mysticism, we are told about another form
of light, which is said to circulate, creating a kind of dynamism within nature itself.
This light includes darkness, or shade. Darkness is not just the opposite of light –
rather it is the very condition through which light is revealed. Darkness in Indian
thought becomes *kali*, the primal motherhood of matter. It is something
encompassing like the womb. Light is not conceived of just as dispelling this
darkness, but as circulating within it.

Indian composition has been based on the idea of rhythm rather than a
static structure. It goes back probably to the way in which large panels of images
were created on the walls of caves, where there was no need to worry about 'frames'
or edges – the images just emerged and poured over the surface of the wall. There is
a feeling that the world of the imagination is endless, one form flowing into the
next. The outline cannot define, it can only indicate the way in which energy
flows. The image is just the ripple created by a deeper current of life force. That is
why, at its most elemental, the line with which images are drawn is always intended
to be a vibrant line, not just a dead contour. It is intended as a dancing line, which
is simply descriptive but not prescriptive. It cannot limit anything – there is always
an overflowing life that cannot be contained by an edge.

The Ecology of the Imagination

This brings us back to the interior landscapes. These landscapes cannot easily be
put into distinct categories, or territories. They exist in the very process of
interacting, at their borderlands. The very term *sangam*, which means meeting,
comes from a name applied to a South Indian culture, which arose out of the
meeting of possibly ancient tribal entities that had become identified with
particular landscapes. So the culture is itself the product of a federal approach to
local forms of community self-expression. The tribal confederations were an
integral outcome of pre-Aryan republics, which, whilst maintaining distinct forms
of self-government, were yet able to interact and mutually enrich each other
culturally and economically.

And so when we speak of a hillscape, or the landscape of the shore, we must consider a dynamic relationship between two geographical areas and the way in which the former is, so to speak, the economic hinterland of the latter. All the landscapes are part of a total system of pilgrimage and trade routes that had to be respected. In the same way there is a dynamic relationship between the forest, or *kadu*, and the cultivated lands in the river valleys, or *nadu*. Here we might discern not only the basis for political and economic interaction between geographical areas, but also an underlying symbolic world-view that creates a movement between the need to cultivate the earth with the help of water systems, and the need also to leave the forest systems intact, because it is in the forests that the rivers have their catchment areas. The one landscape depends upon the other. The five landscapes are like five brothers – the Pandavas of the great epic of the *Mahabharata*.

I believe it is from this systems approach to the land that the concept of the land as a body develops. In the symbolic language of Ramanuja, the relationship of the self, or *atman*, to the body or *sharira* is understood as a metaphor for the relationship between *brahman* and creation. But this relationship metaphor has to be carried through into the body as a system in itself. In other words, what we are calling the body is itself a network of relations, and this is where the image of the five landscapes becomes an instrument of interrelated understanding.

It is not possible in this essay to pursue in depth the way in which the image of the body symbol has been used in Indian philosophical systems. In the south of India there was a whole system of thought related to the *siddhas*, who were characterized by intuitions that probably drew on very primal visions developed in pre-Vedic, tribal or *adivasi* societies. The *siddhas* cannot easily be defined, though they used esoteric techniques which may even have been originally shamanistic. There is a link between the *siddhas* and the origins of yoga and the philosophic body of thought known later as the *Samkhya*. In this primal form, the knowledge concerning psychosomatic phenomena may even be termed atheistic, in that these practitioners were not really concerned with a personal deity, any more than Jainism or Buddhism in their most archaic forms addressed problems concerning a divine presence as distinct from the phenomenological world. But of course, later, even in the *Shaiva Siddhanta*, the question of divine intervention became important. That probably is the dimension of reality which takes an increasingly important part in the consideration of theists such as Ramanuja who extends the analogy of the body to even transcend the body, by questioning the relationship of *atman* or soul/spirit to the body organism. Without the *atman* the body could not live, and yet the *atman* is not to be equated with any other bodily function.

In yoga we have the image of the six *chakras* or body-plexuses. The question is whether underlying this concept of the body there is not already a notion of an energy that transcends the body, breaking out through the body to something which lies beyond. Perhaps it would be possible to interrelate the idea of the five interior landscapes with the first five *chakras* of the body, of which the sixth landscape, as the dimension of the body that has been permeated and transformed by the *atman*, is already a threshold to something beyond, an integration that takes place at a higher level than the five senses, or the five elements, of which the physical world as we know it seems to be constructed.

What has fascinated me is how this body–landscape analogy connects up again with the idea of the seasons. Again in India, we speak not so much of *four* seasons, as six seasons, which include two phases in each of the three major times of transition in the year's cycle, from the dry season (which is also spoken of as the lean period) through the rainy season (a time of transformation) to the autumn season (which is characterized by fullness and plenty).

It is working with these images that I have tried to develop an understanding of certain common features which I believe to exist between Indian images of the cosmos and certain early Christian symbols, which seem to spread right across through central Asia to the Celtic spiritual tradition of Europe. Perhaps one of the common themes of creation spirituality that seems to link the East with the West is a relationship between the symbol of the seed, and the energy or spirit within life, and the power of light as a creative principle in the universe.

Spirit, Seed and Sacred Space

In an essay written by Mircea Eliade on the link between light and the seed in the religious language of various gnostic groups, we note the origins of a cosmological understanding of body energy. The centre of the mandala or *chakra* designs associated with meditational techniques that channel the psychic energies lying hidden in matter is called in Indian tantric thought – the *bija* or seed. The seed has a dynamic relationship with the womb of space into which it has been implanted. Here we are to understand this space as a kind of promised land, which is like a dark covering in which the fragile seed can germinate, and be protected. Once the seed has been established, it can grow outwards, releasing its energy like a spark of light. The seed is the inner light, but it is also called forth from the darkness by the outer light of the cosmos. If we imagine a circle, whose centre is the seed, the circumference of the circle is the space in which this seed becomes active, and the radius that connects the outer body to the inner germ is the energy tension we call the spirit, or the power of life. In this rather abstract model of the cosmic system we have the basis for a complete language of creation spirituality.

It is easy to see how this model generates both the symbol of the cycle divided into six segments (in that the radius can be used to measure off six sections along the circumference), but it is also the basis for an image of the circle divided into four quadrants representing what was known in the early Church as the cross of light. The ancient Celtic crosses were cosmological symbols before they became Christian signs, in the same way that the Buddhist *chakras* were images of the universe going back to neolithic times. Both cross and *chakra* represent energy centres that generate creation. It is this image of resurrection within the dying process of the cross, the image of the seed that has to die in order that life might be renewed, that informs both the Buddhist teaching concerning *dukkha* and the cycles of birth and death, and the Christian gospel concerning the promised kingdom that is to be found within every heart. These images can never be properly defined by rational propositional statements – they will remain, always, intuitions of the creative imagination.

It is this link between seed and light that underlies the Indian festival of lights, known as *Diwali*, or the gathering of lights. During this festival a pattern is often drawn in front of the entrance to the home, in which little lamps are placed. This pattern, generally based on a circular design created out of two overlapping triangles, which gives the form of a six-pointed star, is constructed out of a pattern of dots around which are woven a maze-like interlacing design of knotted strands. The dots represent the seeds, which are also points of energy, and it is here that little clay lamps in which vegetable oil is burnt are placed. Connecting these flaming points are the interlocking strands of energy that represent the web of darkness in which the lights are held and nurtured. The strands like the wicks of the lamp are symbolically related to the forms of intertwining serpents, and are connected with the philosophic concept of the *gunas*, from which the whole of creation has been woven. The word *guna* is derived from the Sanskrit term for fibre, but carries the meaning of 'quality'. The dots on the other hand are the essences from which the *gunas* receive life, like the juice or sap that courses through the fibrous body of growing plants. The cotton fibre reminds us of this material quality from which the whole veil of creation has been woven. The oil on the other hand has been pressed out from seeds, and is the *rasa*, or essence, that can be converted into flame for light.

Here in this image of the points of light within the enclosing darkness, reminding us of the seed nourished in the womb of the soil, we find a universal theme from which much liturgical symbolism is derived. The cycle of the seasons is essentially related to the cycles of light and darkness, birth and death, and of the seed that has to be planted in order that life might come forth again. All the elements are brought together in this process: the earth and water in the task of nurturing the seed; fire and air in the process of bringing the seed to life and light.

Towards an Eco-Spirituality

I began this essay by describing how as an art student I met Dom Bede Griffiths and as a result felt drawn to his Christian ashram experiment in South India, where he tried to draw from the spiritual tradition of the Syrian Christian Church. In 1970 I settled down in Bangalore because Fr Amalorpavadas, who became the first director of the National Biblical, Catechetical and Liturgical Centre, had invited me to work in association with the Centre on the question of how Indian symbols and styles of art could be used within the context of the Church. During the years 1973 and 1974 I worked on various designs for the chapel and other buildings of this Centre, which had been established by the Catholic Bishops' Conference of India in 1967 to explore ways in which the insights of the Second Vatican Council could be implemented for the benefit of the local Indian Church. My wife and I settled down in a Christian village outside Bangalore where my wife started a small school for the local village children. In 1983 I was encouraged to establish an 'art ashram' near our home, the purpose of which would be to see how the creative imagination could be a way for spiritual growth within the life of the Church, in the context of the multi-faith cultural environment in which we live in India. Subsequently, a few friends came together to give some form to this vision, and so we started the Indian School of Art for Peace, which we shortened to the name 'Inscape'. The idea of Inscape was also much related to the poetic vision of Gerard Manley Hopkins, giving another dimension to our exploration into the whole area of creating sacred spaces, which could also be common ground for peace between different faiths, rather than causes for contention.

In 1984, soon after we had started the art ashram, Dr Eric Lott, who was then teaching at the United Theological College in Bangalore, and who had been a close friend for a number of years, invited us to work on an exhibition whose theme was to be 'Creation in different religions'. This was an occasion for coming together to discuss how a creation theology, to be found in many faith-systems, could be the way to understanding the spiritual significance of the creative imagination that is present in every human being. The creative imagination can be understood as a *sadhana* or spiritual search, precisely because we are all called to participate in the continuing process of bringing the earth to birth.

The insights of Eric Lott, which he had culled in part from the mystical theology of the Hindu saint Ramanuja, provided a deeply inspiring basis for working on an eco-theology that would be a meeting point between different religious traditions, and also an enrichment of the Christian faith. Here, we felt, was the possibility for finding a way in which an ultimate vision could be realized in both the practical world of faith-commitment and theology.

The winter of 1992, when Hindu extremists destroyed a mosque, was for many of us working in the area of interfaith dialogue and understanding a profoundly traumatic time. I had been working since 1990 on designs for a cathedral that was being constructed in the holy city of Benares. The images that were more and more concerning me were themselves a reflection of an apocalyptic view of history, which in many ways reflected our own times. I was trying to understand how the total thrust of the apocalyptic imagination, to be found in prophetic works in the Old Testament such as the books of Daniel or Ezekiel, and which also contributed profoundly to the gospel message of Jesus, could in fact relate to a mystic world-view to be found in India. And so, I had chosen as my theme for the works I was designing the idea of the holy city on the banks of the holy river.

While I was working on this project, I was also engaged in making designs for a regional theologate in Orissa. Moving between Orissa and Benares, I met again an old friend called Vandana Shiva who had written a very provocative book entitled *Staying Alive*, in which she has analysed, as a professional scientist, the ecological situation in India from the perspective of a woman deeply committed to Hindu cultural values. She told me that she had just set up an organization she had called *Navdanya* or 'Nine Seeds', through which she hoped to research into the whole issue of genetic engineering and the way in which the living resources of India's biodiversity were being increasingly exploited by powerful vested interests. I myself believe that there is a close link between the need for biodiversity and a respect for religious diversity in the world of different faith-systems. Vandana Shiva pointed out that one of the reasons why a state such as Orissa had in the past such rich resources in biodiversity was precisely because of the rich tradition of various ancient tribal communities, who had helped to nurture and sustain different forms of life in their natural habitat.

Vandana felt that the issue of biodiversity should not only be approached from a rational, scientific and technological perspective, but needed also to take into account the deep spiritual significance of life as symbolized by a ritual understanding of the value of seeds. She invited me to focus as an artist on this basic theme of the importance of seeds in our spiritual and cultural traditions. It was in response to this invitation that I began to develop more consciously in my art work the idea of seeds of hope and the spiritual relationship between seeds, sacred space, and the transforming power of the spirit.

Bija Shakti

In Indian thought the seed, or *bija*, is the vessel for *shakti*, or living energy, which is often associated with the feminine principle. Perhaps in this primal vision of *bija shakti* we can glimpse an ultimate vision of life to which all religious traditions are committed. It has been said that there can be no peace on this planet of ours, unless there is peace between different religions. But how can we find this peace? Dogmas have tended to divide, but images do create powerful links. The image of the seed, and its life, has been one such common concern to be found in all faith-systems. Perhaps by discovering for ourselves what this symbol means to us, we can contribute in some small way to the creating of bridges between cultures and faiths.

That, I believe, is the hope that lies within the seed – a hope for a new and better heaven and earth.

The Sikh Vision of the Ultimate

Dr Mohinder Singh

Dr Mohinder Singh, currently Director of the National Institute of Panjab Studies, New Delhi, is the author of several works on Sikh history and religion. He is also the founding Editor of Studies of Sikhism and Comparative Religion *and sits on the editorial committees and advisory boards of several national and international organizations.*

'I BRING FROM the East what is practically an unknown religion.' This is what M. A. Macauliffe wrote in the preface to his *magnum opus, The Sikh Religion*, first published in 1909. While Sikh religion is no longer unknown as a result of the world-wide dispersal of members of the Sikh faith and their encounters with people of other living traditions, not much is known about the Sikh Gurus' world-view and their contribution to the ultimate vision.

Guru Nanak (1469–1539), the founder of the Sikh faith, was born at a time when people of different faiths were fighting over the issue of the supremacy of their respective faiths. Rather than appreciating one and condemning the other, the Guru gave a new message of transcending the narrow meaning of religion and asked them to look for the ultimate vision. '*Na ko Hindu Na Musalman*' (I see no Hindu and no Muslim) were the first prophetic words uttered by the master after his enlightenment. It did not mean that he could not physically see either of the two warring communities, but implied that after realizing the truth the worldly labels of a 'Hindu' or a 'Musalman' had ceased to convey any meaning to him. He described all beings as children of one father. Guru Nanak's definition of the ultimate reality is best given in his composition *Japji*, which Sikhs are enjoined to recite daily in the morning. The *Japji* starts with the *Mul Mantra* or the primal creed of Sikhism. The gist of its translation reads: There is but one God; *Sati* [Truth] by name; the Creator all-pervading, without fear, without enmity, whose existence is unaffected by time, who does not take birth, [is] self-existent; [to be realized] through the grace of the Guru.

The numeral one is the first letter of this *Mul Mantra*. Words may change their meanings in the course of time, but the connotation of a numeral always remains the same. Unity of God is thus emphasized at the very outset to wean away the disciples from the worship of innumerable gods and goddesses of the Hindu pantheon. In several hymns of his, the Guru has portrayed this unity in moving terms:

> All say He is one, but are filled with the pride of I-am-ness. They alone will find His mansion, the eternal abode, who see Him inside [their souls] as well as outside. The Lord is near, do not think He is distant. The One

pervades the whole creation. Nanak! those who know one God and shun duality are merged in Him.[1]

Contrary to the Indian belief that this world was an illusion and therefore to realize the ultimate vision, one had necessarily to denounce the world, Guru Nanak believed that the world was worth living in. 'The World is the Abode of the True One, and the True One lives therein,' said Nanak.[2] He firmly believed that it was possible to live purely among the impurities of life. 'As the lotus lives detached in waters, as the duck floats, carefree, on the stream, so does one cross the Sea of Material Existence, his mind attuned to the Word.'[3]

Worth quoting in this context is Guru Nanak's dialogue with the *siddhas*, the followers of Gorakh, as mentioned in his composition the *Siddha Goshati*. After visiting various centres of pilgrimage on the plains, the Guru went to the hills in the north where he met the *siddhas*. The *siddhas* asked Guru Nanak what the condition of the people was on the plains. The Guru replied:

> The *siddhas* have retired to the hills and found their abode in caves; who is there now to look after and guide the common folk? The kings commit sins and exploit their subjects, whom it is normally their duty to protect. The people are ignorant and freely indulge in misdeeds. The judges being corrupt accept bribes and neglect their duty towards truth and justice. Men and women prostitute their honour.[4]

The Guru had similar dialogues with other saintly figures when he visited various religious centres of the Hindus and Muslims, including Hardwar, Mecca, Medina and Baghdad. After completing his long spiritual journeys the Guru settled down in a new township on the banks of the river Ravi and named it Kartarpur, i.e. City of God. There he worked in the fields and shared his earnings with others. A community of disciples grew up at Kartarpur but it could not be described as any monastic order. It was a fellowship of common men and women engaged in normal occupations of life, earning their livelihood through honest means and sharing the fruits of their labours with others. But what was remarkable about Kartarpur was that this provided a model of living that was to become the basis for the development of Sikh society and the Sikh value system in the days to come. The Guru and his followers got up before dawn and, after ablutions, said their prayers. The spiritual routine being completed, the Guru and his followers ate sacred food from the community kitchen and then attended to the day's work. In the evening they again assembled at a common place and said their evening *Sohila* (songs of acclaim).

The Sikh Gurus laid great emphasis on early rising and remembering God, which is borne out from the following lines of *Bhai Gurdas*:

A true Sikh rises before the night ends
and turns his thoughts to God's name,
to charity and holy bathing.
He speaks humbly and humbly he walks.
He wishes everyone well and he is [joyful in
giving] away gifts from his hand.
He sleeps but little,
And little does he eat and talk.
Thus he receives the Guru's true teaching.
He lives by the labour of his hands and he
does good deeds.
However eminent he might become,
He demonstrates not himself.
He sings God's praises in company of holy men.
Such company he seeks night and day.
Upon the Word is his mind fixed
And he delights in the Guru's will.
Unenticed he lives in this world of enticement.[5]

This new philosophy of life, with emphasis on early rising, working hard and always remembering God, created a new society in which there could be neither exploiters nor exploitation. The emphasis on honest living and sharing one's earnings with others laid the foundations of an egalitarian order. The Sikh Gurus brought about a happy union between spiritual and temporal domains.

Guru Nanak was followed by nine successive Gurus who not only continued his precepts and ideals but also made significant contributions in evolving different institutions for the Sikh community. The second Guru, Angad Dev, evolved a distinct script called *gurmukhi* (coming from the mouth of the Guru) which became the sole medium for sacred writings of the Sikhs. It is in this script that the *Guru Granth Sahib*, the Holy Book of the Sikhs, is written. The third Guru, Amar Das, strengthened the Sikh movement by dividing Sikhs into twenty-two districts called *Manjis*, each with its own head, for missionary purposes, and by appointing a number of women (*Piris*) to work as missionaries to women. For obliterating the caste distinctions, which then plagued Indian society, the Guru made it obligatory for all visitors to eat in the community kitchen before they could see him. There is a Sikh tradition that the Mogul Emperor Akbar who went to see the Guru at Goindwal had to eat *langar* while sitting on the floor with his nobles and servants, all in one line. The Emperor was so much impressed by the Guru's strict practice of equality that he donated a village (which grew into the modern city of Amritsar during the time of the fourth and fifth Sikh Gurus).

The fourth Guru, Ram Das, laid the foundation of the city of Amritsar, which developed as the spiritual capital of the Sikh faith. By encouraging artisans and traders to settle there, the Guru also laid the foundation of a big trading and industrial centre, which developed around the newly founded city. Guru Arjun Dev, son and successor of Guru Ram Das, built the Harimandir, which is popularly known as the Golden Temple, and installed the Holy Book, the *Guru Granth Sahib*, there. The sixth Guru, Hargobind, built Akal Takhat, the Throne of the Immortal, and declared it as the centre of Sikh temporal authority. The seventh Guru, Har Rai, continued the mission of his predecessors and appointed the Bhai families of Bagrian and Kaithal to look after the missionary work. The eighth Guru, Har Kishan, cured the victims of smallpox in Delhi and is remembered in the daily Sikh prayer as 'the one whose very sight dispels all miseries'. The ninth Guru, Tegh Bahadur, set a unique example of religious freedom by sacrificing his life for the protection of *Tilak*, *Janju* – the sacred marks of the Hindu religion. This is described by the tenth Guru as 'a unique event in this age of Kaliyug'.[6] Guru Tegh Bahadur's martyrdom proved to be a turning point in Sikh history.

In order to defend *dharma*, Guru Gobind Singh, tenth and last of the Sikh Gurus, created the order of the Khalsa. On the *baisakhi* day of the year 1699, the Guru called an assembly of the Sikhs at Anandpur, in the Shivalak hills. While addressing a packed audience the Guru demanded the heads of five Sikhs. The five who offered themselves and were subsequently initiated into the Sikh faith are popularly remembered in the Sikh prayer as the *Panj Piare* or the Five Beloved Ones. They came from different directions and belonged to different castes, three of them to the so-called low castes. After each being renamed with the surname of Singh, meaning lion, they were enjoined to support the five symbols of the new order – unshorn hair, a comb, short breeches, a steel bracelet and a sword.

A significant development in the history of the Sikh faith was Guru Gobind Singh's declaring the *Guru Granth Sahib* as the Guru eternal for the Sikhs. Compiled by the fifth Guru, Arjun Dev, the Sikh Holy Book is a unique example of the ecumenical spirit of the Sikh faith. The *Guru Granth Sahib* contains 5,894 hymns, the largest number of them (2,216) having been contributed by the fifth Guru himself. Apart from the hymns of the Sikh Gurus, the *Guru Granth Sahib* also contains the compositions of the Muslim and Hindu saints. Equal respect for all religions is best demonstrated when the devout bow before the Holy Book that contains the hymns of saints from different religious denominations.

Against the prevalent Hindu practice of worshipping idols, the Sikh Gurus advocated worship of the *Akal* (Timeless God). The Sikh temple, called a gurdwara, is not merely a place of worship but also serves as a shelter for the homeless, iron-fort for the destitute and refuge for the helpless, where all visitors, irrespective of their religious affiliations, are served free food and given shelter and protection. In the centre of the gurdwara the *Guru Granth Sahib* is installed on a high pedestal, the idea being that the Holy Book occupies a place higher than the followers who sit on the floor. Since complete equality is preached and practised, there is no special place marked for important persons in the gurdwara. There are gurdwaras in different parts of India, which are historic because of their association

with the Gurus. There are other gurdwaras throughout the world, wherever there
are Sikhs, which are not historic but are built by followers to serve as centres for
their religious worship. The *Nishan Sahib*, a huge yellow triangular flag, with the
Sikh symbol of *khanda*, marks a Sikh religious place. Visitors from all sections of
society can enter the gurdwara after removing their shoes, cleaning their feet and
covering their heads. Doors of the gurdwara are open to all communities. It is
significant that the famous Golden Temple at Amritsar has four doors, indicating
that it is open to all people from all four directions and its foundation-stone was
laid by a Muslim divine named Mian Mir.

Contrary to the Indian belief that *moksa* (salvation or deliverance) could be
achieved only after the liberation of the soul after discarding the bodily and worldly
existence, the Sikh religion believes that a human being can enter the highest state
of bliss and become a *Jiwan-Mukta*, i.e. liberated while living. The Sikh Gurus
believed that since all beings were essentially a creation of the Divine, they had the
potential to realize the divine vision. Through constant meditation, good actions
and living a detached life, a *manmukh* (self-oriented person) can gradually attain
the state of a *gurmukh* (God-oriented person). For this spiritual elevation a human
being has to pass through different stages of spiritual development. Guru Nanak
described these stages at the end of the *Japji*: divided into five, these are *dharam
khand* (realm of duty), *gian khand* (realm of knowledge), *saram khand* (realm of
aesthetics), *karam khand* (realm of action) and *sach khand* (realm of truth) – the
stage of the ultimate vision.

According to Sohan Singh, in our long journey to Him, the first stage is that
of *dharma* – that is, the fulfilment of duties required by our station in life. These
duties are determined by the context in which an individual finds himself or
herself. There is, firstly, the physical context – the days, weeks, months, seasons,
the climate and the soil (the nether regions, that is to say, the regions below the
surface of the earth from which come minerals and in which seeds sprout). All
these determine what we do and how we do it. Secondly, there is the social
context, where are found innumerable temperaments, habits, customs and manners.
In accordance with all these physical and social conditions, society expects its
members to live up to certain standards of conduct. The worthiness or
unworthiness of every one of us depends on this conduct.

Those who live up to the social code and its spirit become respected in their
society. People who uphold social integrity are not many, and further, it is only
from such an elect of the people that a few arise to perceive His vision. That is why
this elect is likened collectively to the court of a king. Those whom the king
favours, he calls near his own seat. Those outside the court have no opportunity to
receive the king's favours. Yet the worthiness of the elect, those who fulfil their
dharma, their social code, has no deeper roots than the sanctions of a limited
society. To one who is not even among the elect, these may appear to be 'ripe'
souls, but in fact this ripeness or mellowness is achieved only when they obtain

within themselves the descent of the universal Spirit, which is entirely a matter of His grace. It is only when the elect have reached that region that they really become what others had thought they already were, namely, ripe souls. And before they reach there, they must pass through the two other regions of knowledge and withdrawal into self.[7]

Without confusing this state with the traditional Hindu concept of *varna-asram-dharma*, it does not specify any special duties except that like other objects of nature, one has to keep on performing one's duties to the best of one's abilities. According to other scholars in the second progressive stage, the person is required to seek tri-dimensional realization. These three *khands* are the *gian khand*, the *saram khand* and the *karam khand*, which are respectively the dimensions of knowledge, aesthetics and action. All three are to be carried to their ideal ends in an integrated manner. It is a simultaneous process of gradual realization in all respects. Action without knowledge and aesthetic feeling would be blind, just as knowledge and feeling not translated into action would be barren sentimentalism – a painted ship on a painted sea. Knowledge and feeling must function in harmony with action. But, insofar as the realization of the ideal of all these three is concerned, they mark a sort of simultaneity.[8]

In the Sikh vision of the ultimate, to love God is to love His Creation. To know Him, we have to know His manifold Creation in all its rich variety. The first condition of obtaining His grace in one's life is to open out one's consciousness so that it may obtain the reflection in it of the myriad created forms and structure in the universe. In knowledge one goes out to seek more and more, to taste of His Creation in all its wondrous variety. In contrast to this, the next stage is that of withdrawing into one's inner life in order to reflect on what knowledge has given us, to put into its proper form and relationship all the material acquired by us in the region of knowledge. As we do this a most beautiful form appears, that of the universe as His mansion of harmonies. In this process our mind and understanding are transformed. From creatures of closed, momentary and rudimentary consciousness, we become persons with widely awakened minds, deep discernment, intuitive cognition and vast understanding. Indeed, we can say that such people possess the consciousness of gods and perfected beings.[9]

The third stage of evolution in the ultimate vision is described as *saram khand*, the stage of aesthetic realization of God. In this stage seekers establish a relationship between their Creator and themselves like that of a beloved and lover. Guru Nanak described this stage of spiritual evolution as the sphere of beatitude. The appointed task in this state is the realization of the ultimate, and seekers enter the stage of perception of the ultimate but are unable to realize the aim due to their inability to fully shed their egos.

The fourth stage of the Sikh vision of the ultimate is named *karam khand*, the dimension of action. According to Guru Nanak, the medium of this dimension is energy, strength and power. God-intoxicated, here seekers acquire spiritual power that makes them brave and mighty. Here the seekers realize, simultaneously with their gradual realization in the dimension of knowledge and aesthetics, the universalism in action that they acquire in the dimension of knowledge. Their actions reflect that there is no distinction of 'mine' and 'others'. Spiritually too, they realize the Absolute, in terms of which all are spiritually related. This realization of universalism is reflected in their actions.

The long and arduous journey of the seekers ends with their final realization of the ultimate vision when they enter *sach khand*, the realm of truth. It is the state where the seekers become one with the Ultimate and find themselves in constant communion with the divine Spirit that is the seekers' ultimate goal.

After realizing the ultimate vision and having been transformed from *manmukh* (self-oriented person) to *gurmukh* (God-oriented person) the seekers become part of the Creator. The zenith of spiritual glory is achieved when it is not the seeker who is seeking God but the other way round. Bhagat Kabir beautifully describes this transformation in the following hymn quoted in the *Guru Granth Sahib* (p. 1367):

> Kabir like the waters of Ganga,
> pure is now my mind.
> And, lo, the Lord now follows me,
> saying 'Thou art mine, Thou art mine.'

Notes

1. Dr Manmohan Singh, trans., *Guru Granth Sahib* (Amritsar: SGPC, 1981), p. 1.
2. Dr Gopal Singh, trans., *Guru Granth Sahib*, vol. 2 (Delhi: Gurdas Kapur & Sons, 1960), p. 457.
3. Ibid., vol. 3 (1964), p. 894.
4. *Varan Bhai Gurdas*, Var 1, Pauri 29 (Amritsar: SGPC, 1952), p. 15.
5. Ibid., Var 28, Pauri 15, p. 312.
6. *Shabadarath Dasam Granth Sahib*, vol. 1 (Patiala: Punjabi University, 1985), p. 70.
7. Sohan Singh, *The Seeker's Path* (Lucknow: Central Gurmat Prachar Board, 1978), pp. 94–5.
8. Avtar Singh, *Ethics of the Sikhs* (Patiala: Punjabi University, 1970), p. 228.
9. Sohan Singh, *The Seeker's Path*, p. 99.

AN ULTIMATE VISION

Professor Ninian Smart

Ninian Smart is Professor of Religious Studies at the University of California in Santa Barbara and Professor Emeritus of Religious Studies at the University of Lancaster in England.

I AM A Scottish Episcopalian – that is how I was raised and that is more or less how I am. I love a certain kind of Christian vision. But I have been deeply influenced by Buddhism, and also in some degree by the Vedantic vision of Ramanuja, in the South Indian Hindu tradition. I first encountered Buddhism in Sri Lanka, at the age of twenty, when I was in the army. I came to love it and learn from it. That did not stop me being a Christian, though I had a period as a Marxist when I first went up to Oxford. But during my first long vacation I converted to social democracy and an intense liberalism, largely through reading Popper's *The Open Society and Its Enemies*. To put my vision briefly:

I see the heart of the Christian faith as lying in the Trinity: with the Father suffering through the Son, and vivifying the living world through the Spirit. Above all, the Creator knows that freedom involves suffering and She suffers with the cosmos.

I see the heart of Buddhism as diagnosing our troubles in the world as arising through greed, hatred and delusion (so much more realistic than the mythology of the Fall).

I see the heart of Hinduism as seeing the cosmos as God's body.

I see the heart of liberalism as knowing that we may be mistaken, and so being tolerant.

I see the heart of life as creative love.

Above all our ultimate vision has to focus on our planet as a whole: our ultimate concern must focus on humanity (and beyond that living beings) as a whole.

There are some obvious fallacies in popular religion, and I deplore them, though I can understand why weak humans can sincerely hold to them.

One fallacy is to suppose that our vision – our faith – has the whole truth. This is ridiculous; to suppose perhaps that we have more of truth and ethical insight than others might be excusable, but to suppose that we alone have the truth is crazy. How can we know this in advance of knowledge of other world-views? Unfortunately Christianity, like other religions, often supposes that its scriptures are wholly true. This is enough to alienate sensitive people. A major problem with all religions is the claim to authority, whether this be held to reside in the Church or in a Bible. The trouble is that people confuse certitude with objective certainty. I can have certitude that my faith is right, but that in no way warrants my claim that it has objective truth, to be forced in effect upon others. Let me spell this out with an example.

Suppose a Muslim says that the Qur'an is the mind and the revelation of God. Well, that is a common article of Islamic faith. He backs up his claim by appealing to the undoubted poetic genius of the text. How could a relatively uneducated trader such as the Prophet have composed it on his own? The genius indicates its revealed status. This is a reasonable argument. But is it a proof? Of course it is not a *proof*. One can suppose that genius can arise in unexpected places. There are questions raised by the existence of other and incompatible works of spiritual depth, such as parts of the Buddhist canon, or the Gospels . . . and so forth. So though it is a good argument it does not bring certainty.

Moreover, there are obvious places where the Bible is – taken literally at least – wrong. There are questionable historical claims made about Jesus. Did he really turn water into wine in Cana in Galilee? It is a lovely and instructive story. But true? Why should one have to sacrifice common sense to be a Christian? Now these points that I have been making, about lack of certainty and the fallibility of scripture, may sound negative, but they have a positive side to them. They should allow us to be open-minded about other faiths. They make way for liberal knowledge. It is one of the glories, in my view, about modern Protestantism that it has pioneered liberal Christian faith. It has shown how faith can be self-critical. It has shown too how faith can be in harmony with modern advances in scientific and humanistic understanding. Such modernism is an important ingredient in daily living. It paves the way for toleration. Maybe some people think that too tolerant a faith is wishy-washy. But to me it is part of the open vision that we need in our global civilization. We have lots of intolerance, and we have had burnings, condemnations, narrowness enough in the past.

If we take up a liberal faith, drawing on the rich resources of our tradition or traditions, we must also allow a *nostra culpa*. Our present vision surely differs from our past. I am an Anglican, as I have said, but I do not believe the 39 Articles, and imposing them as a test of faith now seems absurd. It is true that Anglicanism managed within itself to breed a certain degree of toleration, more than most denominations. It manages to embrace both Catholic and Protestant principles, and keep good relations with the Orthodox. It is thus strangely universalistic. For these reasons I like the tradition and admire it. But it had aspects of intolerance as exhibited in its Establishmentarianism, and I believe in separation of church (and mosque and sangha) and state. Catholicism has its culpabilities too, of course: its long resistance to modernism, its invention of cardinals, its absurd infallibilities, its mindless anti-contraceptive stance, and so on. Well, to be true to my own principles I have to admit that the Church might be right on such issues after all, though I vigorously doubt it. Orthodoxy is culpable of a great deal of mindlessness, in harking back to the Fathers and paying little attention to modern intellectual issues. Yet all branches of Christianity have their glories, and more generally all faiths too have their riches. I am sure the Spirit works creatively throughout human achievements.

It is interesting that my life has so much been bound up with religion, and I want to say a bit about it here because it shows something of my real commitments. First of all I was brought up as an Episcopalian in Scotland, though I had a paternal uncle who was a Church of Scotland minister. I think this pluralistic environment was healthy. But at the end of the war I went into the army and was fairly soon projected into quite a different environment. For a year and half I participated in a course in intelligence in Chinese at the School of Oriental and African Studies in London. This was a far cry from the ideological milieu of my school in Scotland. I began to see something of the riches of Confucius. Later, in going to Sri Lanka as a young officer, I saw some of the riches of Buddhism (and to a lesser degree Hinduism). When later, after my undergraduate classics and philosophy at Oxford, I went on to do graduate work, I was determined to do something about the dreadful colonialist mentality of Western learning in those days. It happened that in due course I came to study Sanskrit and Pali, reinforcing both my interest in and engagement with religions and my pluralistic mentality.

So it came to be that my major achievement in academic life from an organizational point of view was founding the Department of Religious Studies in Lancaster, which helped to revolutionize religious education at university and school levels. I was attacked in my Church for this, alas. But I am sure that the Church too has benefited from religious studies. There is for me no conflict between faith and openness. I also have spent nearly two decades in America, dividing my time with Lancaster for the most part. America has a lot of dynamism in religious studies. And as people get a deeper understanding of other cultures, so more real exchanges occur. I have long thought that dialogue is a vital ingredient of studies, and complements the exercise of imaginative and informed empathy in entering into other people's experiences.

One of my major books is called *The Religious Experience*. In it I made the numinous and mystical experiences important poles of faith. It seems to me that religion is warm in people's hearts, as they listen to the prompting of the Lord without and the Spirit within. It is obvious that such a polarity is to be found in varying forms in the major traditions of humankind. This is perhaps the ultimate basis of dialogue.

Maybe we are coming to a new period of human history. Interestingly, academic life has been suffused over the last fifty years with ideology, notably Marxism. There are post-Marxist hangovers too, such as deconstructionism. Most of these philosophies are nonsense, and I am sure future generations will be ashamed of our stupid lip-service to dead men's thought. Not only was Marxism a dangerous form of reductionism, eschewing the importance of imagination and empathy in human beliefs and feeling, but it also helped to fuel the most bizarre, cruel and self-destructive period of totalitarianism. It is for me a wonderful satisfaction to have lived through both the Nazi and the Marxist periods. It still amazes me that there are creative, yet wrong-headed historians and others who remain Marxists. It also is striking that we still have Freudians. Yet Freud's theories have virtually no empirical basis. But perhaps as I have said, we are entering a new age in which a warmer view of religious experience will take over.

Let me now go back to my vision of the Trinity. In proposing this I wish to present it in a way that does not force it on anyone as dogma, but rather indicates it as a picture that is open to those who love the Christian tradition. It is meant as a picture in the gallery of faiths. What the human race will eventually conclude about the truth is of course open to question. Perhaps we shall always be somewhat divided, and able to hold differing portraits of the ultimate side by side. For me, the numinous experience of reality seems to echo a Spirit, so to speak, behind the world. This is the divine Being shining through what we see around us. Yet in trying to understand the Divine, perhaps the chief obstacle lies in the terrors and sufferings of living creatures in this world. If God is all round us, shaping our world, how can She be so cruel? Can the Father and Mother of us all be so carefree that He does not worry about the very act of creation? Does it not inevitably forebode pain and despair as well as joy and hope? The very fabric of the cosmos contains both life and suffering. Well, for me, the Christian faith contains a vitally important message. It is this: God, in creating, foresees His own suffering. This is because She willingly enters Her own world, according to the Christian message. The cross is written, so to speak, at the very heart of the willing creative act. This is what makes the Christian story distinctive.

There is something else too, which links up with the Vedanta of Ramanuja. His picture is of the cosmos as being the very body of God. For him a body is that which is instrumental to the soul. If I wish to lift my hand I just do it. The hand and arm are under my control, or if you like, under the control of the soul. It is true that human bodies are only imperfectly under the soul's command. I can hardly influence the operation of my gall bladder or my kidneys. So human and more generally animal bodies are but partly under psychic control. But according to Ramanuja, God is different. She has complete control over Her body. Thus, the cosmos, as the divine body, is completely controlled by its Lord, or Lady. God is omnipotent over the universe. Now this can give us the picture too of the Divine Being as most intimately feeling the cosmos, as we feel the operations of our bodies. Further, Ramanuja held too that God stands to our souls as the soul does to the body. In other words, God is the soul of souls. She is within me as the Spirit that is the inner controller (in Sanskrit, the *antaryamin*). Now this image depicts God as the soul of souls and as the Spirit within. This means that God in some way shares our joys and sorrows from within. So Christ is not just there on the cross but within the very fabric of suffering life (and joyful life – in the kitten's purr as well as the rat's death). And so if we can imagine God on the brink of His fiat, about to create from nothing this whole vast cosmos, we imagine Him too foreseeing His suffering, both within the body of the cosmos and on the cross.

It seems to me that the weakest part of the Christian myth is the story of Adam and Eve. In any case the modern theory of evolution relegates it to a fanciful story. The fact is that evolution involves a rise rather than a fall; and suffering is intrinsic to independence and is thus part of the fabric of freedom, even amid the relative freedoms of the snake and the grasshopper. The fact is that the Church, in noting its deep faith in the Incarnation, wished to provide a cosmic explanation for the need for the atonement. It overloaded the story of the Garden with sin. Yet there was always an explanation for the Incarnation in the need for the Creator to take on the suffering that inevitably would follow the benefits of the freedom She confers upon Her creatures. In any case, I think the Buddhist account of suffering is more realistic, for in a way the very incidence of greed, envy and delusion is the negative side of freedom. As creatures we are inevitably self-centred. We have the impulse to gather to ourselves the fuels and protections we need – hence greed. We also have the tendency to hate other individuals, since we can see ourselves in a competitive situation. And we suffer from a kind of ignorance as we begin on our way to acquire knowledge (and so control). The Buddhist trio that diagnoses our troubles is realistic in part because it goes beyond the idea of defective will. It is misguided action – action controlled by ignorance – that causes half our problems.

This also helps to make sense of the liberal ethos of modern religion. Although academic knowledge often suffers from delusion, as the example of Marxism shows, nevertheless the quest for learning is correct. It is not that learning is everything – far from it. In fact you have to purify your consciousness and feeling in order to achieve genuine self-criticism, which is a vital ingredient in the learning process. This is one area where the tasks of mysticism and self-awareness are in a state of solidarity with self-critical liberalism.

One lesson we can learn from Theravada Buddhism is this – that you can have mysticism without God. You can have the purification of consciousness without the experience of union. If there is nothing out there such as a divine Being, how can there be any union? This thought helps to make sense of some of the varieties of religion; you can have God without mysticism, and mysticism without God: mysticism without the numinous and the numinous without mysticism.

Now this polarity helps to explain something vital about our world. The numinous experience gives a feeling of depth to the cosmos. It gives us the sense of mystery that illuminates what we know and perceive; it lends a sense of depth to the cosmos, hinting at the Divine that lies beyond the universe. It tells us that the cosmos depends upon the Creator. It 'explains' our world out there. On the other hand, the mystical purification of consciousness reveals the nature of ourselves and thereby shows us something else about our cosmos. We generally have a tendency to grasp for the basic nature of the universe; yet its highest flower is also indicative of its true nature. It is as if we should judge the world by its flowers, not just its quarks; by the orchid and the lion, not just by the molecules that make them up; and above all, by the highest consciousness, which we exhibit in ourselves. The mystical quest leads us to the pure and high apprehension of this. The numinous lies at the base of the cosmos; the mystical at the height of its evolution. Religious experience embraces both poles.

Although I embrace the Christian faith, well suffused with Buddhist values, the view that I have just put forward about types of religious experience is bound to give positive meaning to a whole spectrum of religiosity – to Islam's prophetism and Sufism, to Judaism in both its heroic and prophetic moments and to its Hasidism, to Sikh truth and devotionalism, to the Tao and the quest for heaven, to vibrant kinds of African experience, to the ancient accents of Neoplatonism, and so on. And this width of hospitality to religious experiences in turn suggests that we should take seriously the leaders of all religions. This should be part of a wider acceptance of the human race as a whole, with its many ancestors. For in our modern world we tell our stories through history, and while we may be especially fond of British or German or whatever history, depending on our nation, or of Christian or Jewish or Buddhist history, depending on our religion, ultimately our race is the human race and so our ultimate history is human history (and beyond that evolutionary history). In turn that means that we have to celebrate all our worthy ancestors – not just Shakespeare or Cromwell or Brunel or Nelson (if we are British), but all the great people of the past. Let me list a few: Confucius, Mencius, Hsun-tzu, Bodhidharma, Chuang-tzu, Honen, Shinran, Nichiren, Hokusai, Meiji, Chu Hsi, Yi T'oegye, Yi Yulgok, Sankara, Ramanuja, Asoka, Buddhaghosa, the Buddha, Nagarjuna, Vivekananda, Gandhi, Nehru, Timur, Akbar, Guru Nanak, Guru Gobind Singh, Rumi, Zarathustra, Muhammad, Cyrus, al-Hallaj, al-Ghazali, Saladin, Mehmet II, Dostoevsky, Pushkin, Catherine the Great, Plotinus, Augustine, Shaka, Nelson Mandela . . . and so forth.

We should honour the great of all nations and cultures. It is a kind of universal ancestor worship, not just a communion of saints, but a communion of great achievers.

In the last two centuries or more we as humans have gravitated into nations. There is little doubt that nationalism has become the greatest focus of loyalty. Thousands and hundreds of thousands of human beings have sacrificed their lives and their health fighting terrible wars on behalf of national causes. And to reinforce our patriotisms we have invented histories and legends and even religious commitments to sustain our heroisms and hatreds. In many cases we in effect turn ourselves into separate ethnic species. It is as if we are justified in shootings and ethnic cleansings and purges and massacres, when we are dealing with others. We have perpetrated racisms, and often scarcely treat one another as human beings. These appalling crimes seem, alas, sometimes quite natural to us. But the message of the great religions is quite different. We should treat each other with brotherliness and sisterliness, with love and compassion, with universal humanheartedness. It is of course above all the Christian message that we should love one another, and love our enemies as well as our friends.

Now although I present the differing segments of my vision as above, there is a sense in which my vision is not ultimate. On the one hand, my eyes do not reach for ever – the picture they delineate is necessarily imperfect. On the other hand I note that different eyes see differing things. The love that our vision expresses varies. After all, it is part of the liberal message that the differing faiths are not necessarily compatible. Yet that liberalism has in the long run to be in harmony with our belief in the divine reality. We have to see the openness and creativity of our intuitions *sub specie aeternitatis*. This involves us in a certain view of history. It involves more particularly a vision of the Spirit. Creativity in the spiritual life, whether in Chinese belief, or South Asian or African or European, means that the Divine allows of a freedom which creates a degree of complementarity between different traditions. It is as if God allows of the possibilities of divergences because that is the nature of knowledge. Our idea of divine knowledge must correspond to our conception of natural knowledge. If criticism and the variation of ideas are part of the warp and woof of knowledge it must also be part of the nature of revelation itself. Or we could put it in a different way. God allows of differences in order that different traditions keep one another honest. This is of course a somewhat anthropomorphic way of putting it. But it contains within it a truth. It is also a view that reminds us of the fallibility of revelations, which is part of my vision. It is a far cry from the pretensions of omniscience which have plagued so many traditions. If we eschew omniscience in science, how much more should we give it up in the name of faith? All this implies, however, that the truth of religion is much nearer to aesthetics than it is even to science, with all this critical stance and fallibilities.

As we weave between the types of religious experiences and thread our way among the kinds of spiritual adventures, and as we sum up our ethical intuitions, we surely will recognize that in the future we shall arrive at a global agreement (with luck) which will assemble the diverse spiritual aims together. Why should it not work out in the end that global insights may after all converge?

There is a vital feature of the Christian picture that helps us perhaps to understand this creative convergence. The notion I have tried to spell out suggests a collective activity. Knowledge and insight are not so much individual events as the precipitates of a social activity. This is one way we do not want to postulate some divine and finished omniscience. Rather we see the Divine as advancing the universe in an unheralded way. It is a vision which is like that of the artist, built up from paints and lines. It is a creative construction. So we have two sides to the conception. On the one hand it is collective; on the other hand it is constructed. Both sides suggest a kind of working together. Now these aspects of the picture chime in with the vision of the Trinity. It is itself a social collective (at least according to the delineation found in the book by Steven Konstantine and myself, *A Christian Systematic Theology in a World Context*). Not everyone accepts the model of a social trinity; but we do, somewhat passionately. This is in part because from our perspective it makes much more sense of the ideal of love, which lies both at the heart of the Divine and at the heart therefore of the Christian gospel. It helps to weld together also the structures of both love and knowledge – both lie in collectivities. In turn, this makes sense of the obverse of those Buddhist cankers that infect conscious life. Greed, hatred and delusion are matched by self-control, love and insight, which work together in the divine triad.

There are other features of our worldly vision. In order to see the earth, as controlled by the divine Being, in a realistic way, we need to pick up some of the elements of Teilhard de Chardin's vision. He, of course, saw the working out of the divine plan in evolutionary terms. We need no doubt also to see the human race in its evolutionary history, and beyond that into the future. We have already seen something of the inadequacy of the story of Adam and Eve. More entrancing is the adventure of human beings as they fashioned civilizations. This account of great cultures and the variegated experiments in living which men and women have undertaken chimes in with the exploratory themes of the great faiths, which have both shaped and been shaped by historical cultures. All this suggests a future continuation of the human race's quest. Our vision suggests that spiritual experience is to be taken centrally in our historical quest. The perception of the mystery and the purification of consciousness are clues to the ways in which we might as human beings reform ourselves. At the moment, I suspect that the ethical values of humanity are shallow, when not driven by spiritual progress. We are perhaps too obsessed with technical and scientific education, important as these are, and insufficiently motivated by desire to improve human impulses and dispositions. The importance of gentleness, love and insight are paramount in a world whose violent dangers have become terribly mutilated by technological expertise. See how attractive are the hatreds of nations; see how little we prize ways of love among peoples; see how we prize cleverness; see how little education values goodness. So we need for the human race a reappraisal of a kind of spiritual ethics which can draw upon the virtues and not the violences that religions and ideologies have in the past helped to foster.

One aspect of de Chardin's vision is rapidly coming true – his idea of the noosphere. As the communications revolution develops speed, so we find human minds more closely entangled in one another. We have yet to see some of the spiritual fruits of this half-disembodied closeness.

Let us go back to recapitulate and consolidate some of the aspects of language we may use in articulating our vision. The notion that the Divine is 'beyond' the world is important, but it has to wed with the notion of the cosmos as God's body; in other words, the otherness of God mates with the idea of Her closeness and presence. The faithful person must be very aware of the nearness of the divine mystery, suffusing the world all about us. Also, the inwardness of God is important, as part of the very fabric of humanity in and through the pure consciousness that lies at the heart of each one of us. We need to notice that God is neither male nor female, or colloquially is both. Anyone who thinks God is either male or female has very primitive views about gender. That is one of the troubles about taking scriptures too seriously. They tend to be very misleading. We may also note that the Divine is not literally in some heaven, but occupies a kind of transcendent hyperspace which lies all around us. And because She lies within us, as the soul of souls, God can enjoy our life and suffer too with it. Because too the Christian vision includes the cross of Christ, we must stress that God does not create us independent creatures without being willing to pay the price of Her creative act. At the same time, because our nature as creatures is free (and animals have their own freedoms too), ultimately our life must involve a kind of creativity. So our moral and intellectual life has to be open, and is thus ultimately driven by liberal principles. So it is that there are no fixed dogmas and no unrevisable affirmations of faith. Our faith has to be open, outward-looking, and so bound up with free seeking of the Spirit. Moreover, our knowledge is always open, ranging from the flourishing of spiritual experiences to the new discoveries of science. In this vision it is possible to fuse together the insights of science, faith, the numinous, the mystical, the incarnational, morality, open politics, artistic creativity . . . We look forward to a great collective human quest, which takes up the themes of differing civilizations. Let them complement one another.

That is my vision such as it is. I hope that my own spiritual life has in some degree been enriched with the insights I have come to see along the way.

The Vision of the Bahá'í Faith

Dr Robert Stockman

Dr Robert Stockman obtained a master's degree in world religions and a doctorate in the history of religion from Harvard Divinity School. He is currently Co-ordinator of the Research Office of the National Spiritual Assembly of the Bahá'ís of the United States, and serves on the editorial boards of World Order *magazine and the* Journal of Bahá'í Studies.

ALL RELIGIONS OFFER some sort of ultimate vision for the future. Usually these visions are conveyed in symbol or myth; for example, the four beasts of the Apocalypse of St John are mythological images that have been interpreted and reinterpreted by Christians for thousands of years. Eschewing myth, the Qur'an offers images of mountains crushed to dust and heavens cleft in two when the Day of Judgement comes.[1] It has long been the task of theologians, religious leaders, or even the rank-and-file believers themselves to offer scenarios explaining how the myths or symbols will be played out in history.

The Bahá'í faith is no different in that its scriptures[2] contain symbols and images of uncertain meaning and that the Bahá'í community has often constructed scenarios of future events to explain them. The Bahá'í scriptures, however, are different from the Bible and Qur'an in that their vision of the future is more concrete and this-worldly; they envision a peaceful, united human society, built on this earth primarily by human hands. And they claim to provide the blueprint that guides the construction.

A comparison of the Bahá'í concept of the future with Christian visions of the kingdom of God on earth reveals both similarities and differences. In the nineteenth century Protestants found it convenient to divide their scenarios of the end of times into two major types. Many views were *postmillennialist:* they believed the millennium, or age of human happiness and perfection, would result from the process of building human civilization and culture, and Christ would return only after that process was complete. These scenarios tended to be very optimistic about humanity's perfectibility – for humanity would largely perfect itself – and thus were usually associated with liberal Protestants. Other views were *premillennialist:* they argued that humanity, burdened by sin, was not perfectible and only Christ's return and direct intervention would make the millennium possible. In the nineteenth century premillennial views were the minority and often were linked to extreme ideas, such as setting exact dates of Christ's return. But two world wars and the repeated failure of social programmes inspired by liberal Protestant ideals destroyed the optimism behind the postmillennial views. Simultaneously the premillennial scenarios have become more sophisticated. Consequently the latter dominate popular Christianity in the late twentieth century.

The Bahá'í vision contains elements from both approaches; or, to be more exact, it has a premillennial framework but draws many postmillennial conclusions. Bahá'u'lláh made the remarkable claim that He was the promised one of all the world's religions and was the return of Jesus Christ.[3] He claimed that all the world's religions have promised a time when the swords will be beaten into ploughshares and peace will reign on earth, and that these prophecies refer to His dispensation. The promises will find concrete fulfilment when humanity accepts Bahá'u'lláh's revelation, internalizes it and implements it, thereby reforming society and culture.

The Bahá'í vision, thus, is 'premillennial' in that Christ must return – in the form of Bahá'u'lláh – before the millennium can be established. But the millennium will not be actualized through divine fiat, voiced by Christ and enacted by angels; it is heavily dependent on human effort. Thus there is an element of 'postmillennial' optimism in the Bahá'í vision as well. The Bahá'í concept of humanity certainly does not deny the evil human beings are capable of inflicting; no theology in the nuclear age can deny it. But the Bahá'í scriptures argue that a new divine revelation has set forces in motion that transcend human society, and that human beings are capable of enough transformation to play a significant role in bringing about the millennium.

The name the Bahá'í scriptures give the millennium itself constitutes a description of it: the Most Great Peace or, in Arabic, *solh-i-akbar*. It will be a time when humanity will not be divided by barriers of race, nationality or religion. The Bahá'í scriptures do not define precisely how much of the effort to create the Most Great Peace will come from Bahá'ís, though the scriptures state the revelation of Bahá'u'lláh will be foundational to its creation. The Most Great Peace is preceded by the Lesser Peace (Arabic, *solh-i-asghar*), a time when nations will have implemented tentative mechanisms for ending war and fostering a world economy. The establishment of the Lesser Peace is a task not of the Bahá'í community, but of the governments of the world. The Bahá'í writings clearly suggest that the process whereby the Lesser Peace is instituted may be extremely tumultuous.

Principles Defining the Most Great Peace

The Most Great Peace may be further characterized by describing the Bahá'í principles on which it is to be based. Centrally important to understanding the Most Great Peace is the Bahá'í concept of the oneness of humankind. It has been described as 'the pivot round which all the teachings of Bahá'u'lláh revolve'.[4] The oneness of humankind is not simply a call to recognize the biological fact of our common origin as a single species, nor is it a mere plea that we all must love and assist each other. Both are aspects of the oneness of humankind, and are as yet inadequately understood and practised. Rather, the oneness of humankind goes beyond both. It necessitates the inculcating of new attitudes of tolerance and the appreciation of diversity in the consciousness of the body politic and all of humanity. It requires the creation of an almost mystical understanding of our common humanity, an innate sense of responsibility towards all and, above all, a faculty of the conscience that evaluates every idea and action, of one's own or of others, based on its impact on all. Inculcating a consciousness of the oneness of humankind is a specific goal of the Bahá'í faith, implemented through its literature and educational programmes; it is an element of faith inculcated in every believer. In the Bahá'í faith it is concretely demonstrated through support for interracial marriages and through the creating of ethnically and racially diverse local Bahá'í communities.[5] Many passages in the Bahá'í scriptures offer symbolic descriptions of the oneness of humankind, such as this one:

> The tabernacle of unity hath been raised; regard ye not one another as strangers. Ye are the fruits of one tree, and the leaves of one branch.[6]

In addition to implying the oneness of the races, the oneness of humankind implies equality of the sexes. Bahá'u'lláh Himself, though living in the late nineteenth-century Middle East, emphasized that women should have equal access to education and should receive training for a vocation. 'Abdu'l-Bahá added that should a family be forced to choose between educating a son and a daughter they should choose the latter. In 1912 He stated that in the future women would become equals to men at all levels of service to humankind, even as heads of state.[7] Bahá'í communities have a long history of striving to foster equality of men and women, and women have served on Bahá'í governing bodies since these were first created at the beginning of the twentieth century.

The oneness of humankind also implies a single future for all of humanity. The Bahá'í scriptures describe the human species as steadily ascending a ladder of social evolution that has led to larger and larger social units. Today, with instantaneous communication and efficient global transport, the logical social unit is no longer the nation or the empire, but the entire world. A global society is a key element in the Bahá'í scriptures' vision of the future:

> The unity of the human race, as envisaged by Bahá'u'lláh, implies the establishment of a world commonwealth in which all nations, races, creeds and classes are closely and permanently united, and in which the autonomy of its state members and the personal freedom and initiative of the individuals that compose them are definitely and completely safeguarded. This commonwealth must, as far as we can visualize it, consist of a world legislature . . . a world executive . . . [and] a world tribunal . . . A world metropolis will act as the nerve center of a world civilization, the focus

towards which the unifying forces of life will converge and from which its energizing influences will radiate. A world language . . . a world script, a world literature, a uniform and universal system of currency, of weights and measures, will simplify and facilitate intercourse and understanding among the nations and races of mankind. In such a world society, science and religion, the two most potent forces in human life, will be reconciled, will cooperate, and will harmoniously develop . . . The economic resources of the world will be organized, its sources of raw materials will be tapped and fully utilized, its markets will be coordinated and developed, and the distribution of its products will be equitably regulated.[8]

A key mechanism for converting the ideal of the oneness of humankind into a social reality is the Bahá'í concept of consultation. Consultation is not a single Bahá'í principle, but a collection of Bahá'í principles and concepts about the nature and purpose of communication and decision making. Consultation includes principles concerning people: that all are capable of finding truth and that all must be empowered to contribute to the decision-making process. In order to encourage all to contribute, an environment of sharing, of tolerance yet frankness, of detachment from one's own opinions, and of prayer must be created. All must feel respected and free to contribute. Consultation involves principles about truth itself: that all ideas contain elements of truth and thus must be affirmed even if their eventual contribution is limited. It includes principles regarding the group process: that after one has contributed an idea to the group it is the group's property, and therefore one need not feel an obligation to advocate the idea or defend it if someone proposes a modification to it. Bahá'ís have been struggling to internalize and express these principles in their Bahá'í community life and in their contributions to society for over a century. A world based on such principles would be one where race, sex, and ethnicity would not be barriers to equal contribution to the betterment of humanity; a world where tyranny would be forever banished and where freedom of thought and conscience could reign.

No sketch of the Bahá'í vision of the future would be complete without some mention of the Bahá'í concept of justice. Bahá'u'lláh links justice to the future when He says that 'the purpose of justice is the appearance of unity among men'.[9] A unified world is impossible unless it is a just world. Bahá'ís see the Lesser Peace as a time when social mechanisms for creating justice will steadily improve. However, Bahá'u'lláh created a special institution, the house of justice, to be established by Bahá'ís in every locality, every nation, and at the world-wide level. The latter body, the Universal House of Justice, Bahá'u'lláh and 'Abdu'l-Bahá envisioned as playing a key role in the eventual establishment of justice in the world, especially during the Most Great Peace. Already governments have occasionally turned to the Universal House of Justice for advice, a practice Bahá'ís expect will increase greatly in the future.[10]

Future Stages in the Development of Humankind

The division of the human future into two stages – the Lesser Peace and the Most Great Peace – is further nuanced by 'Abdu'l-Bahá in a famous work of His called the 'Seven Candles of Unity':

> The first candle is unity in the political realm, the early glimmerings of which can now be discerned. The second candle is unity of thought in world undertakings, the consummation of which will ere long be witnessed. The third candle is unity in freedom which will surely come to pass. The fourth candle is unity in religion which is the corner-stone of the foundation itself, and which, by the power of God, will be revealed in all its splendour. The fifth candle is the unity of nations – a unity which in this century will be securely established, causing all the peoples of the world to regard themselves as citizens of one common fatherland. The sixth candle is unity of races, making of all that dwell on earth peoples and kindreds of one race. The seventh candle is unity of language, i.e., the choice of a universal tongue in which all peoples will be instructed and converse. Each and every one of these will inevitably come to pass, inasmuch as the power of the Kingdom of God will aid and assist in their realization.[11]

'Abdu'l-Bahá does not claim to be giving developments in chronological order. Only one of the seven candles – unity of the nations – does He ascribe to the twentieth century. Political unity – glimmerings of which, He said, already could be seen in 1906, when He wrote the 'Seven Candles' – perhaps refers to the myriad international organizations that have been created to carry out tasks as diverse as co-ordinating postal regulations, sharing weather information and counting whales.

One cannot help but wonder whether the political events of the last decade have not represented the achievement of some of the other 'candles'. Unity of thought in world undertakings was impossible when the world was divided into communist and capitalist spheres of influence. The end of the Cold War, the creation of a new treaty on world trade, the holding of a summit in Rio de Janeiro about the environment and one in Copenhagen about development, and the convening of conferences in Vienna, Cairo and Beijing about human rights, population and the advancement of women respectively – all have laid foundations for a unity of thought in world undertakings inconceivable a decade ago. The collapse of totalitarianism in most countries of the world, the rising emphasis on human rights, and the remarkable spread of democracy in Latin America in the 1980s – and now to some extent in Africa in the 1990s – suggests that 'unity in freedom' will soon be achievable.

Unity of language may also have taken a major step forward in the last decade with the advent of satellite television, which has further strengthened the position of English. The Bahá'í principle of a universal language does not call for the elimination of other languages, but for supplementing them with an auxiliary tongue. The role of that tongue may easily change from decade to decade; its fortunes may wax and wane, and it may even be replaced, eventually, by another auxiliary language. Regardless of the language that ultimately serves as the international auxiliary tongue, its role will be to facilitate communication among humanity, for everyone would need to learn only two languages – their own and the auxiliary – in order to be able to speak to any other human being.

'Abdu'l-Bahá promises that the unity of nations will be 'securely established' in this century; its consequence He describes as 'all the peoples of the world [will] regard themselves as citizens of one common fatherland'.[12] It will be easier in retrospect – say, fifty years from now – to know what event represented the establishment of the 'unity of the nations' than it is to imagine that event before its occurrence. The event or chain of events will apparently be such that it will promote a consciousness of world unity or citizenship. This consciousness inevitably will have consequences – at some point further in the future – in fostering world peace and eliminating barriers between the nations.

The other candles describe unities that are more difficult to envision. How can 'unity of the races' be achieved in a world torn by racism and ethnic cleansing? If establishment of a consciousness of the oneness of humankind is an essential foundation for the unity of the races – for racial unity is an aspect of human unity – then the oneness of the races will require more than the creation of political and social mechanisms. Rather, it will require a spiritual transformation of human culture. It thus appears to be a part of the distant future, perhaps of the Most Great Peace.

Finally, 'Abdu'l-Bahá lists 'unity of religion' as 'the corner-stone of the foundation itself', thus stressing that its importance is the greatest of all. But what is unity of religion? The Bahá'í scriptures include this challenging and puzzling discussion of the concept:

> The Faith standing identified with the name of Bahá'u'lláh disclaims any intention to belittle any of the Prophets[13] gone before Him, to whittle down any of their teachings, to obscure, however slightly, the radiance of their Revelations, to oust them from the hearts of their followers, to abrogate the fundamentals of their doctrines, to discard any of their revealed Books, or to suppress the legitimate aspirations of their adherents. Repudiating the claim of any religion to be the final revelation of God to man, disclaiming finality for His own Revelation, Bahá'u'lláh inculcates the basic principle of the relativity of religious truth, the continuity of Divine Revelation, the progressiveness of religious experience. His aim is to widen the basis of all revealed religions and to unravel the mysteries of their scriptures. He insists on the unqualified recognition of the unity of their

purpose, restates the eternal verities they enshrine, coordinates their functions, distinguishes the essential and the authentic from the nonessential and spurious in their teachings, separates the God-given truths from the priest-prompted superstitions, and on this as a basis proclaims the possibility, and even prophesies the inevitability, of their unification, and the consummation of their highest hopes.[14]

The latter half of this passage – describing the unity of nature and purpose of the religions in the revelation of Bahá'u'lláh – may be seen as a clarification of the first part, which stresses their uniquenesses. In this passage one encounters the major claim of the Bahá'í faith to represent and continue the essential teachings of the previous religions, yet also to represent their unification. A 'fulfilment theology' is definitely implied. Clearly, Bahá'í scholars of religion have their work cut out for them by this passage. How are Bahá'ís to justify their belief that the Buddha was sent by God? How are they to explain to Christians that the Trinity is not an essential part of Christianity? How are they to explain to Hindus their rejection of reincarnation? How are they to explain to Muslims their rejection of common Muslim understandings of Qur'anic passages?

A major instrument for essentially redefining other religions is history. Scholarship has shown how difficult it is to reconstruct the life and teachings of the historical Jesus, and to date efforts to reconstruct the historical Abraham, Moses, Zoroaster and Buddha have yielded even less certainty. History shows that reincarnation was not a teaching in the Vedas – Hinduism's oldest and most venerated scriptures – and that only hints of the Trinity may be found in the Gospels. Much of religion is the cumulative tradition created by its adherents; it is here where much of its diversity and contradiction may be found.

Further complicating Bahá'í participation in interfaith dialogue is its apparent claim that the world civilization to be created will be 'sustained by its universal recognition of one God and by its allegiance to one common Revelation'.[15] Of course, the language of 'Abdu'l-Bahá and Shoghi Effendi may be symbolic or hyperbolic rather than literal. In any case, it may be five hundred years before the Bahá'ís can definitively decide how to interpret these passages.

All religions have truth claims that serve as barriers to interfaith understanding. One of the challenges facing Christian theologians has been to define Christianity in such a way as to maintain its distinctive teachings, yet eliminate or minimize any claims that it is better than other faiths. Bahá'í scholars face a similar challenge as they seek to understand the many statements in the Bahá'í scriptures about other religions in the light of those traditions' self-understandings. The fact that the Bahá'í faith itself claims not to be final, but that it will be superseded by another religion eventually, helps to eliminate claims that the Bahá'í faith ultimately is any different from or better than the other religions.

More important to Bahá'í involvement in interfaith dialogue is Bahá'u'lláh's exhortation to 'consort with the followers of all religions in a spirit of friendliness and fellowship'.[16] This passage not only makes dialogue an imperative, but sets the tone of Bahá'í involvement in it. Bahá'í efforts in dialogue must be based on love, consultation, and a search for mutual understanding, not on a sense of superiority. Bahá'u'lláh urges Bahá'ís to be 'anxiously concerned with the needs of the age ye live in'[17] and presumably such concern should be a major focus of interfaith efforts, for religions usually find the performing of acts of service together more useful than the debating of doctrines.

Conclusion

The ultimate vision of the Bahá'í faith is decidedly this-worldly. The kingdom of God (to use a Christian phrase) is ushered in not through a purely divine intervention, but through the forces of history. The forces of history, of course, include God's periodic intervention in human affairs through prophetic figures, the latest one of whom lived a mere century ago. They also include divine forces working behind the scenes in a way difficult for mortals to discern.

The kingdom of God will not be heaven on earth; humans will still experience pain, struggles and suffering. However, they will struggle and suffer in a social climate that is far more equal and just, and far less violent and prejudiced, than the contemporary world. Bahá'u'lláh identifies two purposes for humanity; His short obligatory prayer gives one as knowing and worshipping God and in another work Bahá'u'lláh states that 'all men have been created to carry forward an ever-advancing civilization'.[18] Presumably neither of these purposes will ever find an ultimate end as long as humanity exists, for humans will always have to struggle to know their God, and civilization will always be perfectible. In that sense no vision of humankind's future can ever be ultimate, because there will always be a road to travel until the human species, in the course of time, ceases to exist. If, as the Bahá'í scriptures assert, there is an afterlife, perhaps it will only be in collective retrospect from beyond the veil that humanity will know its true and ultimate purpose.

Notes

1. The Qur'an 69:14, 16.
2. The Bahá'í scriptures consist of the writings of Bahá'u'lláh (1817–92), founder of the faith; 'Abdu'l-Bahá (1844–1921), Bahá'u'lláh's son and successor, whom Bahá'u'lláh authorized to offer official interpretation of the Bahá'í teachings; and Shoghi Effendi (1897–1957), 'Abdu'l-Bahá's successor and Guardian of the Bahá'í Faith, whose writings are also regarded as official interpretation. Bahá'u'lláh wrote in Persian and Arabic; 'Abdu'l-Bahá in Persian, Arabic and

a little in Turkish; Shoghi Effendi in Arabic, Persian and English. Bahá'ís regard Bahá'u'lláh as a messenger of God and His writings as the Word of God.

3. Bahá'u'lláh's claim to be the return of Christ is explicitly stated in His Tablet to Pope Pius IX; see *The Proclamation of Bahá'u'lláh to the Kings and Leaders of the World* (Haifa: Bahá'í World Centre, 1967), p. 83. The Bahá'í claim that Bahá'u'lláh fulfils the promises of all the world's religions is summarized by Shoghi Effendi in *God Passes By* (Wilmette, Illinois: Bahá'í Publishing Trust, 1944), pp. 93–100.

4. Shoghi Effendi, *The World Order of Bahá'u'lláh* (Wilmette, Illinois: Bahá'í Publishing Trust, 1938), p. 42.

5. Unlike many religions, Bahá'ís are not divided locally into separate groups by ethnicity or race, nor are separate groups based on such criteria allowed. Because of their stress on the oneness of humankind, local Bahá'í communities, to a large extent, are racially and ethnically diverse.

6. Bahá'u'lláh, *Gleanings from the Writings of Bahá'u'lláh*, trans. Shoghi Effendi (London: Bahá'í Publishing Trust, 1935), p. 218.

7. See, for example, Bahá'u'lláh, *The Kitáb-i-Aqdas* (Haifa: Bahá'í World Centre, 1992), paras. 33, 48, note 76; 'Abdu'l-Bahá, *The Promulgation of Universal Peace* (Wilmette, Illinois: Bahá'í Publishing Trust, 2nd edn., 1982), p. 375.

8. Shoghi Effendi, *World Order*, pp. 203–4.

9. Bahá'u'lláh, *Tablets of Bahá'u'lláh Revealed after the Kitáb-i-Aqdas* (Haifa: Bahá'í World Centre, 1978), p. 67.

10. The Universal House of Justice is the supreme governing body of the Bahá'í faith today. It was first formed in 1963 and is re-elected every five years at an international convention, where the members of the various national Bahá'í governing bodies (currently called national spiritual assemblies) serve as the voters.

11. *Selections from the Writings of 'Abdu'l-Bahá* (Haifa: Bahá'í World Centre, 1978), p. 32.

12. Ibid.

13. By 'Prophets' is meant the major prophetic figures of the world religions: Abraham, Moses, Zoroaster, Krishna, Buddha, Jesus, Muhammad, the Báb (the forerunner of Bahá'u'lláh), and Bahá'u'lláh. Bahá'u'lláh asserts that God has always sent truth to humanity through such figures, the names of most of whom having been lost to history.

14. Shoghi Effendi, *The Promised Day Is Come* (Wilmette, Illinois: Bahá'í Publishing Trust, 1941), p. 108.

15. Shoghi Effendi, *World Order*, p. 204.

16. Third Glad Tidings, in Bahá'u'lláh, *Tablets*, p. 22.

17. *Gleanings*, p. 213.

18. Ibid., p. 215.

CREATING CROSS-CULTURAL SPIRITUAL IDENTITY

Karma Lekshe Tsomo

Karma Lekshe Tsomo is Secretary of Sakyadhita: International Association of Buddhist Women, and founder of Jamyang Choling Institute, an education project for women in India. An American Buddhist nun and doctoral student in philosophy at the University of Hawaii, she is author of Sakyadhita: Daughters of the Buddha *and* Buddhism Through American Women's Eyes.

MY EXPERIENCE OF Buddhism began in the fifties, as an American teenager growing up in Malibu, California. My Prussian surname 'Zenn' led to readings in Zen and then to Buddhist philosophy in general. I can still recall the bronze-coloured cover of *The Way of Zen* by Alan Watts and the resonance I felt when I read it. My Baptist mother was quite astounded when, at the age of eleven, I announced that I was a Buddhist. From the very beginning, Buddhism struck me as a convincing view of life. Through successive incarnations as Malibu surfer, high-school cheerleader, beatnik, world traveller, folk musician, Berkeley radical, to Buddhist nun, these teachings have been my guide and impressed me as being a sensible explanation of the human condition.

As a child I felt intensely drawn to spiritual life, but could not accept the idea of a creator God or the concept of salvation by faith alone. To say I believed these things when I did not would have been dishonest, contrary to one of the Ten Commandments. Thus, ironically, as intense as my spiritual aspirations were, I found myself shut out of the religious faith of those around me.

In those early years, while singing in the Presbyterian choir and accumulating a long string of attendance awards on my lapel, I accommodated by adopting those Christian teachings that I could relate to. I gained inspiration especially from Christ's teaching on compassion, service, humility and purity of spirit. Silent prayer helped me access feelings of inner peace and light, a valuable counterpoint to the disturbing events around me. The moral precepts of the Old Testament seemed quite reasonable, though the thought of eternal damnation was frightening and seemed to arouse guilt more than genuine transformation. I rejected the virgin birth, the resurrection and the notion of original sin, as well as the hell-and-brimstone approach of my grandmother. Most disturbing was not being able to get answers to questions about life and life after death. These questions led me to search further afield.

At nineteen, I travelled by ship to Japan on a surfing expedition and did Zen meditation during the lulls. The peace and beauty of the temples were inspiring, as I searched for some explanation of human existence and tried to sort out the confusion in my mind. I thought about the theory of cause and effect, which stresses personal responsibility and the significance of every action, and found it a plausible way to explain the disparities of fortune that human beings encounter. I learned the value of meditation practice in developing mindfulness and self-awareness. Each moment became precious – rich with spiritual possibilities.

After some time, I wandered further, to Vietnam, Cambodia, India, Nepal and beyond, seeking a teacher and the meaning of life. The smiling faces and kind-hearted people in the Buddhist countries impressed me deeply. It was refreshing to find in Buddhism a spiritual tradition that affirmed the potential of all living beings to achieve perfection – women and animals included – but did not require me to accept any doctrine on the basis of faith alone. The Buddhist tolerance and respect for other spiritual paths was also refreshing. In this perspective, the various dispositions, needs and karmic affinities of human beings resonate with different spiritual teachings. Rather than expecting everyone to accept just one religious tradition, religious diversity gives humanity spiritual depth, cultural richness, greater openness and understanding, and more range to explore the mysteries of the universe.

Over the years I met many great Buddhist masters – women and men, Asian and Western – who embodied positive human qualities. They explained how the mind works and taught methods for overcoming habitual negative patterns of thought and behaviour. Their own personal qualities lent credence to their words. As I experimented with the methods they taught, I found them very useful for coping with conflicting emotions. They were meditations on patience to help overcome anger, on impermanence to overcome attachment, on rejoicing to overcome jealousy, and on emptiness to overcome self-centredness. The law of cause and effect made sense because I could verify it through first-hand experience – wholesome actions led to enjoyable results and unwholesome actions led to problems. In place of dogma, there were many practical techniques for enriching my life and improving the quality of my relationships with others.

The Buddha's path to freedom means letting go of hatred, greed, jealousy, arrogance and other negative attitudes. It means generating compassion and loving kindness for all living creatures. To me, it seemed like just what the world needed. The ensuing years have been a time of learning more about these teachings and trying to put them into practice. The teachings have helped me through many difficult situations.

Little by little, however, I found that it was not so easy to create the causes for enlightenment in the present day. There are so many complications in our modern world, so many fads, attractions and distractions. Whenever I returned from Asia to the West, I noticed the intensely sensual orientation. Everything seemed designed to arouse desires – for people, possessions and sense experience. We are tempted to taste it all, sampling here and there, yet sense-pleasures leave us hungrier than before. Indulgence in sensual pleasures only leads to more desires and more disappointments. In seeking happiness, we often create a lot of misery for ourselves and others.

As I observed this cycle of craving and dissatisfaction, I grew more and more strongly attracted to monastic life. I watched with boredom the monotonous syndrome of intimate relationships and experienced how time-consuming and frustrating they can be. Monasticism was an unfamiliar concept, but since dreaming aboard a ship to Singapore of myself in robes, I had wanted to be a nun. Still, not finding a monastic community for women in my travels, I drifted aimlessly from one adventure to another, involving myself in fruitless relationships and pursuits.

After years of searching, at long last I found teachers in India who revealed worlds of spiritual insight. Finally, longing for solitude and a chance to devote myself wholeheartedly to spiritual practice, I packed up robes and sleeping bag, and set off to become a Buddhist nun. After receiving novice precepts from the Tibetan master Gyalwa Karmapa in southern France in 1977, I studied Buddhist texts and meditation for years at the Tibetan library in Dharamsala, India, under the guidance of a strict, traditional, but extremely compassionate master who spoke only Tibetan, Geshe Ngawang Dhargyey. Despite problems of health, visa and subsistence, receiving authentic Buddhist teachings from this kind master who obviously embodied them was the treasured experience of a lifetime. Jewels of wisdom seemed to flow directly from his heart to mine, a joyful balance of the mundane and profound.

Discipline did not come easily and sometimes it was hard to set aside my rebellious attitudes. Having always reacted against authority figures, particularly men, I found this period of training in monastic discipline a valuable exercise in reversing habit patterns and developing some inner restraint. Learning to adapt to monastic discipline proved very useful in subsequent years, while staying in various Asian cultures and monastic settings. Living the simple life of a Buddhist monastic in Asia has been a window on the diverse streams of the human heritage and taught me some universal human values.

Living for many years in India brought me into contact with diverse religious traditions and gave me a deep appreciation for each. Interestingly, it has been the monastic aspect of the spiritual life that has brought me full circle, into contact once again with my Christian roots. One day in Dharamsala, I was invited to meet some Benedictine contemplatives engaged in intermonastic dialogue with Tibetan Buddhist monks and nuns. The open-minded attitude of these contemplatives made communication on a very deep level possible. Representing a spectrum of philosophical standpoints within their own tradition, their comprehensive understanding of Buddhism was impressive. They had clearly done their homework for these encounters, which made the discussions very worthwhile, as we exchanged views on topics ranging from the nature of God to women's status in religious hierarchies today. These friendships have continued throughout the years, enriching our mutual understanding and our individual commitment to spiritual life.

It has become apparent that the purpose of interfaith dialogue is not to erase the distinctions between the world's religious traditions. To gloss over their uniqueness not only misrepresents these valued traditions but is an injustice to world culture. In the beginning stages of dialogue, efforts are made to identify commonalities in an attempt to establish friendly communications between scholars and followers of various faiths.

Some discussants forge hopefully ahead, confident that their disparate paths lead ultimately to the same goal. Yet as the ice melts and terms are defined and ever-deeper levels of understanding are reached, it often becomes clear that the goals are many and that is just fine. The fruit of interreligious dialogue is the realization that human beings can have different ideas, not merely different ways of saying the same thing, and still be good friends and neighbours. Similarity of beliefs is not necessary for creating a peaceful world. In fact, a world of people with identical beliefs would be very boring. More importantly, attachment to the ideal of similar beliefs can lead to intolerance of different opinions. Attempts at universalism, without tolerance, may result in either stifling conformity or disputation. Therefore it is necessary to reject religious hegemony and work in a spirit of acceptance and respect for religious pluralism. Since every religious tradition gives priceless guidelines for living a happy life, we can benefit immeasurably by learning from each. We enrich our own world-view by sharing others' spiritual treasures. If our particular world-view shatters upon analysis, so much the better – we are brought to a new level of understanding which would be impossible without such an open attitude.

In the Buddhist tradition, there are many meaningful treasures of wisdom, including teachings on death and impermanence, and on compassion and loving kindness. In the harsh climatic conditions of Tibet, where temperatures dip far below freezing and nature's fury is a constant threat, the Tibetan people have always emphasized the importance of meditation on death. Change and the inevitability of death are a regular part of their daily meditations. The masters say, 'If you don't meditate on death in the morning, you will waste the day. If you don't meditate on death in the evening, you will waste the night.' Only by reflecting on the meaning of death and impermanence can we gain a deeper understanding of life. Without understanding impermanence, we waste our lives in petty pursuits, empty words, and the accumulation of possessions that will only cause us grief at the time of death.

Ordinarily in Western culture, people are somewhat removed from the reality of death. When animals get old, people do not kill them, they 'put them to sleep'. The residents of the old people's home where I worked did not die, they 'expired', more like an old driving licence than a human being. When the residents were 'expiring', we had no time to help them with the transition or to say goodbye. They were immediately whisked off to die in the hospital, away from human contact, then jettisoned in the cold morgue.

Being protected from close encounters with death in this way, we learn to see death as threatening and naturally shy away from it. Our attitude becomes one of fear and denial: 'Me? I still have quite a few good years left in me. Don't be morbid.' Yet death is something we must all deal with sooner or later and if we do not face this eventuality, it will come as a terrible shock and we will be totally unprepared for this important moment.

The Buddha did not try to hide the reality of death from his followers. Instead, he listed it as one of the four miserable experiences that all human beings encounter. Of the Four Noble Truths that he taught, the first was that living beings necessarily experience the sufferings of birth, sickness, old age and death. He taught that we must face these problems and their causes honestly, and seek solutions for them. He recommended contemplation on death, not to make us depressed, but to help us live more fully and meaningfully. Teachings and meditations on death are very valuable for dealing with grief and loss.

If we do not contemplate death and understand its inevitability, we will be taken completely unaware and suffer greatly when death comes to us, our friends, or family members. I learned this intimately when I nearly died from a poisonous snake bite in India. Whether we believe that an afterlife exists, does not exist, is eternal life with God, or a bridge to rebirth, it is wise to prepare well for that significant moment of transition. Only by reflecting on the meaning of death can we gain a deeper understanding of life. After three perilous months in the hospital, every flower, leaf and pebble seemed so extraordinarily beautiful to me. By gaining an awareness of impermanence, I learned to live more fully and mindfully in the present moment.

Living mindfully in each present moment, we become aware of the fiction of an independent 'self'. Deluded by this fiction, we mistakenly see our self as distinct and more important than others, setting up barriers in our relationships and creating innumerable unwholesome actions of body, speech and mind. The Buddhist teachings on the wisdom of selflessness help us see through this fiction, while the teachings on compassion teach us to value others more than ourselves.

Most human beings have compassionate moments, but great compassion means generating the thought of compassion continuously and with ever greater intensity. Many religions teach compassion, but great compassion is distinctive in aiming to liberate all beings from suffering for once and for all. Although relieving the specific sufferings of living beings is important, ultimate benefit comes from extricating all beings from the cycle of birth and death altogether. This is the task of a fully enlightened one. With this enlightened attitude, every action becomes a cause for the awakening of oneself and others.

Awakening is thus the goal of the Buddhist path and every living creature has the potential to achieve it. A person does not need to assume the label 'Buddhist' to practise wisdom and compassion. Purifying the mind of all negative emotions and engendering all positive qualities, each moment becomes transformative and ultimately meaningful. It is really a very simple matter.

ULTIMATE VISION AND ULTIMATE TRUTH

Professor W. Montgomery Watt

Professor W. Montgomery Watt was Head of the Department of Arabic and Islamic Studies at the University of Edinburgh from 1947 until his retirement in 1979, and is now Professor Emeritus. He is the author of many books on Islamic subjects and on Muslim–Christian relations.

MY ULTIMATE VISION is of the human race as a whole accepting the ultimate truth about the world and its own place in it and about what controls human life. Before I explain this more fully, however, it will be helpful to say something about my own religious development.

I had a Christian upbringing. My father was a minister of the Church of Scotland. Before his theological studies, however, he had changed his allegiance to the Church of Scotland from the United Presbyterian Church. I think he did so because of 'High Church' beliefs about such matters as the observance of Easter and other Christian festivals. He died in 1910 when I was a year old, and I was an only child; and from then until 1925 my mother and I lived with relatives, her parents and then her married sister. I was taken to church every Sunday and later attended Sunday school and Bible class. All this, however, was in the United Free Church of the relatives (an amalgamation of the United Presbyterian Church and the Free Church). Latterly, when I was at school in Edinburgh, my mother often took me to 'our' church in the evenings. From 1925 we had our own small flat in Edinburgh. When my mother died in 1937, I myself changed allegiance from the Church of Scotland to the Scottish Episcopal Church. I was in need of much spiritual support at the time, and felt I could get it best from a Church where the main Sunday service was the Eucharist. A service that culminated in a sermon often gave little support, since the sermon tended to rouse intellectual questions in my mind. I thus became a 'High Church' Anglican, though not an extreme Anglo-Catholic. I sometimes wonder whether my change of allegiance was a kind of continuation of the change my father made.

When I was about fifteen my ambition was to become a research scientist in atomic physics. Perhaps I was vaguely aware that exciting discoveries were about to be made in this field, for this was 1924. None of my relations or advisers, however, knew how one became a research scientist. One knowledgeable friend insisted that the safest course was to concentrate on my classics (Latin and Greek) and that this would lead to study at Oxford and an academic career. Reluctantly I accepted this advice and dropped my school science. After obtaining an Honours degree in Classics at Edinburgh University, I went to Oxford with a scholarship in 1930 and read for 'Greats' (*literae humaniores*), which was a combination of ancient history (Greek and Roman) and philosophy, mainly Greek. I had gradually been coming to see philosophy as the subject through which I could achieve something of my desire to be a scientist. I had become deeply interested in the relations between science and religion, and this came within the field of philosophy. I spent a third year in Oxford writing a thesis on a philosophical subject for the degree of B. Litt.

In 1933 I returned to Edinburgh University to work for a Ph.D. on another philosophical subject. From 1934 to 1938 I was an assistant lecturer in the Department of Moral Philosophy. When I submitted my thesis, however, it was rejected. In this I think I was badly treated, and should have been asked to resubmit, which I was not; and I say this as one who was later chairman for a time of the committee that supervises the award of Ph.D. theses. At the same time I realize that I had not consulted my supervisor to the extent to which most Ph.D. students do. The post I had at the university was of limited duration, and there was no automatic promotion. I was thinking of applying for a vacancy in philosophy in Scots Church College, Calcutta, when a new factor came into my life.

From September 1937, in order to help to pay for the housekeeper I now required, I invited a friend to come as a paying guest. He was an argumentative Ahmadi Muslim from what is now Pakistan, and we had long religious discussions over breakfast and supper. Then I heard that the Anglican bishop in Jerusalem was wanting someone to work at the intellectual approach to Islam, and this seemed to me much more interesting than teaching philosophy in Calcutta, and I offered myself and was accepted. While most of my time was to be given to Islamic affairs, I had also to be able to conduct services. For this purpose I had a crash course in theology at Cuddesdon College, Oxford, and was ordained deacon at Michaelmas 1939 and priest a year later. I served curacies in London (to February 1941) and at my old church in Edinburgh. Because of the war I was not able to reach Jerusalem until January 1944. Later that year my wife was able to join me, and our first child was born in Jerusalem. At the end of my first tour of duty in August 1946 I decided not to return to Jerusalem. Apart from the difficulties arising from the end of the British mandate and the transition to the state of Israel, I felt that Jerusalem was not a suitable place for the work envisaged by the bishop who appointed me, because it contained no institution of Islamic higher education.

I was fortunate in gaining a job at once. When I asked the Edinburgh philosophy professors about possibilities, they more or less thrust me into the lectureship in ancient philosophy, whose holder had died a week or so earlier. This enabled me to apply for the lectureship in Arabic, which became vacant in summer 1947 on the retirement of my former teacher, Richard Bell. I had begun the study of Arabic while a curate in London, and continued it under Dr Bell after returning to Edinburgh. I also wrote a successful Ph.D. thesis under his supervision on 'Free Will and Predestination in Early Islam'. Thus from 1947 until my retirement in 1979 I was in charge of Arabic and Islamic studies at Edinburgh, at first on my own, but soon with an increasing number of colleagues, because Edinburgh had been selected as the main centre in Scotland for the development of oriental studies. In

1964 I was given a personal chair. My position in Edinburgh proved an excellent one for pursuing the intellectual approach to Islam for which I had gone to Jerusalem. I had to supervise a large number of Muslim Ph.D. students, of whom many subsequently rose to important positions in their own countries. One even became Shaykh al-Azhar, head of the leading Islamic university. At conferences, too, and in other ways, I came to know many distinguished Muslims as friends. My career was marked by a trail of books. The most scholarly were those on the biography of Muhammad and the early history of the Islamic sects; the rest were largely what Sir Hamilton Gibb called 'haute vulgarisation'.

As I look back on my involvement with Islam, I cannot but see the hand of God behind it all. Although it began in a personal way, it was not because of any attraction to Islam, but because I became aware of it as a challenge to some Christian doctrines. I think I may claim to have attained to a positive appreciation and understanding of Islam and of Islamic truth, and I have tried to correct the false and negative images of it current in the West; but it has never occurred to me that I might become a Muslim. There is a further curious point, however. In the course of my father's theological studies, he gained a prize for ecclesiastical history (in 1897), and the book he chose (I presume he had a choice) was Sir William Muir's *Life of Mahomet*. This makes me wonder if there is something in the Arabian idea of predestination.

During my years in the Arabic and Islamic department at Edinburgh I continued to think about the challenges to Christian belief not only from science but more generally from the contemporary Western intellectual outlook. I had a book dealing with 'the reality of God' in terms of modern thought published in 1957, and one on 'truth in the religions', published in 1963. Since my retirement in 1979 much of my thinking has been along these lines, and I have recently published a book called *Religious Truth for Our Time*.[1]

After this autobiographical introduction let me try to present the position I now hold. The first thing that has to be realized is that the age in which we live is in many ways completely different from all previous ages in world history. This is because there has been a process of unification which has turned the world into a global village. Travel has become faster and easier, and likewise the movement of goods. The communication of ideas and news has also been speeded up, and the media, especially radio and television, have come to dominate the thinking of masses of people in virtually every country in the world. All are exposed to the secular Western intellectual outlook propagated by the media. This outlook is for the most part not anti-religious, but it gives a minor place to the matters with which religions are concerned, and fosters secular, materialistic and consumerist values.

The present age raises important new problems for all the religions. More than ever before their adherents are mixing with those of other religions, and also with people who have no religion; and this means that all have to face difficult questions. Many doctrinal statements are challenged by the Western intellectual outlook. For a century and a half Christians have been trying to deal with the problems about creation raised first by the geologists and then by Darwinian evolution; and, though many have found answers that satisfy them, there has not yet been any official credal statement. More recently the other religions have found themselves up against these and similar problems. Some Muslims have tried to shut themselves off from the Western intellectual outlook, but this is really impossible. Most of the adherents of all the religions want to belong to the modern world and to share its cars and aeroplanes and television sets, and the politicians also want its armaments; but it is impossible to have these without being exposed to the whole Western outlook.

I regard all the main world religions and most of the minor ones as being based on revelations from God, even if they do not think of these as such. God has in some form or other been working through special individuals in all of them. This does not mean, however, that they are all wholly and finally true. It may seem strange to assert that a revelation from God is not altogether true; but a little reflection shows that this is something to be expected, and the point may be illustrated from the Old Testament. Joshua believed that God wanted him to kill the whole population of captured towns – men, women and children – and in one case Samuel told Saul to do the same; Moses believed that God wanted a man stoned to death for picking up a little firewood on the sabbath. Christians may think that the God and Father of the Lord Jesus could not possibly have given such orders; but the Bible asserts the opposite. The point is that what comes to people from God must be appropriate to their stage of civilization and to the nature of the wider community in which the group finds itself; and it must also be in terms of their conception of the world. It is stupid to suppose that God could give to a primitive people a final religion suitable to the humanity of the global village. What God gives is something appropriate to the situation in which people are and which will serve to improve their lot. To later generations God will then give what will enable them to build on and develop what they have received in the past.

At this point I may add a word about the activity of God in Islam as I now understand it. I always took the view – contrary to most previous scholars of Islam – that the Qur'an was not something Muhammad had consciously produced. For long, however, I hesitated to speak of him as a prophet, because Muslims would have taken this to mean that everything in the Qur'an was finally and absolutely true, which was something I did not believe. More recently, however, I have said that Muhammad is a prophet comparable to the Old Testament prophets, though with a different task, namely, to bring the knowledge of God to people without such knowledge, whereas their task was mainly to criticize the conduct of those who already believed in God. Early Christian scholars thought that the Qur'an showed a wide familiarity with the Bible, and that Muhammad had worked up biblical material. In the last few years, however, I have become more aware of the

ignorance of the Qur'an and of Muhammad about Judaism and Christianity. The
Qur'an has some biblical stories, mainly from Genesis and Exodus, but shows no
knowledge of the central beliefs of Judaism; and it has absolutely no knowledge of
Christianity apart from a variant account of the Virgin Birth, while it denies that
Jesus is divine and that he was put to death by the Jews. The fact that there is in
the Qur'an much profound knowledge of the God of Abraham would seem to show
that Muhammad was genuinely being inspired by God. It would seem, too, that
God was behind the later expansion of the Islamic religion.

In considering the relations between the religions, it is important to realize
how language is used in most of their doctrinal statements. The basic or root words
of a language refer to what was familiar to the first users of the language, such as
material objects and simple actions and relationships. This is the primary sense.
The words could also be used in a secondary sense, however, for something that
resembled the primary object, for example, when a river is said to run (like a man
or animal). For the matters about which the religions are concerned it is usually
necessary to use words in a secondary sense. It is sometimes said that the words are
being used metaphorically or symbolically, but these terms are best avoided, since
they are often taken to imply unreality. Science also uses words in a secondary
sense, as when it speaks of waves of light; these are only 'something like' waves in
the primary sense of waves in the sea, but they are entirely real. For this use of
language I have suggested the term 'iconic', because an icon is a two-dimensional
representation of a three-dimensional object, that is, something known to be
inadequate but accepted as a true representation. In English the secondary use of
words is often concealed by their being Greek and Latin derivatives. An atom is
what is 'uncut', and the current of a river is only something like a human or animal
running.

The iconic use of language in religious matters is linked up with the inability
of the human mind to have a full comprehensive knowledge of the being of God.
The word 'god' and its equivalent in other languages may be a primary word for
something sacred or with some control over human life, but that is still vague.
When people try to say more about the being of God, they can only say that it is
something like various things. The biblical writers were well aware that it is
impossible for human beings to have a full and perfect knowledge of God.

When language is used in an iconic fashion, what would be a contradiction
with words in a primary sense is then not necessarily a contradiction. God's being
something like a father is compatible with his being also something like a mother;
and his being transcendent (climbing across or above) is compatible with his also
being immanent (flowing in). This point is of special importance when beliefs in
different religions are being compared, for it implies that the intellectual
comparison of doctrines will not necessarily take us very far. Most Buddhist thought
has no belief in God, yet when that great Christian thinker, Thomas Merton,
talked about spiritual matters with friends who were Buddhist monks, they found

themselves very much in agreement with one another. More important than an assessment of religions by their doctrines is an assessment of them by their fruits in the lives of their adherents. This is in accordance with the principle laid down by Jesus in the Sermon on the Mount, that the value of religious teaching is to be known by its fruits.

In the past when two religions were in contact, they tended to regard one another as rivals or enemies, and each formed a false and negative image of the other. In our present unified world I hold that the main religions should regard one another as partners, since they are all opposed to and struggling against the secularism, materialism and false values that have become so widespread. There are already a few spheres in which they might be able to co-operate – perhaps in working out principles for the reform of the United Nations to strengthen it; and further opportunities of co-operation should be looked for.

Beginnings have also been made in dialogue between the religions, and this is something that should be encouraged. Those involved in the more formal types of dialogue should be people well rooted in their own faith, and there should be no attempt at conversion. Each should, of course, present the truth as it sees it and help the others to appreciate its strengths and to correct any negative images that they have of it. From such a presentation members of the other religions will almost certainly gain deeper insights into their own religions.

The nineteenth-century Christian missionary movement aimed at converting people to Christianity, and it had successes and also did good work in education and medicine. The missionaries, however, had little appreciation of the positive value of the world religions, and still less of the African traditional religions. Moreover, the missionary movement was mixed up with the spread of European culture and with European colonialism. Some of their successes were among people who were marginalized and spiritually starved, but others were rather among people whose chief desire was to share in European life. There may still be a place for this traditional type of missionary work where whole communities are lacking in proper spiritual nourishment, but otherwise I think its day is past. It looks as if none of the great religions would make a significant number of conversions in the foreseeable future. I would allow, however, that there may be a few cases where a change of allegiance is needed for an individual's spiritual health (as it was in my own case), and here conversion should certainly be allowed.

While the traditional type of missionary work has largely become inappropriate, it is still necessary and important that there should be a presentation of the Christian faith to non-Christians and of the other faiths to Christians. The points to be emphasized by Christians will vary with the audience. There are similarities between the Christian conception of God and those of the Jews and Muslims. An important element in Christian teaching is what may be called the unique achievement of Jesus. Through his passion, death and resurrection he achieved something of great value for all humanity, though it is difficult to put this precisely into words. In the New Testament it is variously described as the redemption of the world from sin, the salvation of souls, the reconciling of God with the human race and the mediation of a new covenant between God and humanity. This last I understand as the inauguration of a new and deeper relationship between God and human beings. Part of Jewish belief was that God forgives the sins of those who are penitent; but the mere statement of this belief, even by Jesus, does not seem to have been sufficient in some cases to remove a person's sense of guilt, and the first Christians thought that this had somehow been done by the death of Jesus. The modern Westerner is not familiar, as these people were, with animal sacrifice, that is, the killing of animals for sacred purposes; and this may make it difficult for him or her to appreciate their thinking. It is best to regard the different descriptions of the achievement as complementary but not exhaustive.

It was because of what they saw Jesus having achieved that the first Christians came to believe that he was divine. This belief did not come out of the blue, but was prepared for by various strands of Old Testament thinking. Men and women were held to have been made in the image of God, and this would seem to imply that in God there is a human-like element. It was also held that God's creative activity is directed towards a consummation in a human society (later described as the new Jerusalem). Human beings are occasionally spoken of in the Old Testament as the sons and daughters of God, and in particular the expected Messiah, a king descended from David, is spoken of as God's son. Thus before the time of Jesus the phrase 'son of God' usually meant a human agent for God. It was after the resurrection of Jesus that the meaning of this phrase began to change. The first disciples had known Jesus as fully and completely human, and this point was asserted in later formulations of the Christian faith. At the same time, however, activities such as redemption and salvation had previously been ascribed to God, and so the first Christians came to think of Jesus as a human being wholly identified with God, or as having God present in him in a special way: 'God was in Christ reconciling the world to himself.' Earlier prophets and later saints may have been closely identified with God, but the tasks assigned to them were less important. Through Jesus God was leading the human race into a fuller and deeper relationship with himself, a relationship capable of developing into the final consummation. In Jesus we see the profundity of God's love for humanity in going out to seek and to save the lost.

In the presentation of the Christian faith to non-Christians I hold that the emphasis should be on what Jesus achieved through his humanity, and that the later theological interpretations should be omitted. The non-Christian would then be allowed to understand the achievement in his or her own traditional terms. Christians believe that no similar achievement has been claimed by any other religion; but if another religion claims that it has something similar, Christians should certainly look carefully at the claim.

Closely linked with the achievement of Jesus is the most distinctive element in Christian belief, the doctrine of the Trinity or the threefoldness of God. With the present intermixing of religions this is something to which much more attention ought to be given by Christians, so that it becomes possible for ordinary Christians to explain to their non-Christian friends how they believe that God is one and yet can speak of Father, Son and Holy Spirit. The first point I would make is that the word 'person' needs to be abandoned; perhaps it should even be removed from official statements about 'three persons and one substance'. This is not to indicate any change of doctrine, but because the word 'person' has changed its meaning since it was first used in the sixteenth century to translate the Latin *persona*. The predominant meaning now is 'an individual human being', and Father, Son and Holy Spirit are not even something like three individual beings. 'Person' is by no means the only word to have changed its meaning. The Holy Ghost is not what we now mean by a ghost; and when the Church of England Prayer Book asked God to 'prevent us in all our doings', it meant almost exactly the opposite of what 'prevent' now means.

In Latin *persona* is an actor's mask and then a role in a play. There is something to be said for thinking of God as having three roles, for there are three main ways in which the divine activity affects human beings. There is the activity of creating or giving being to people, the activity of redeeming or bringing salvation, and the activity of sanctifying and strengthening. These three activities, however, are not wholly distinct from one another. The Fourth Gospel speaks of the Word of God (the Son) directing the creative process; and Paul says in one passage, 'I live, yet not I; Christ lives in me', although one would have expected the indwelling divine to be called the Holy Spirit. If ordinary Christians can be encouraged to think about the threefoldness of God along such lines, then there is also hope that they will be able to explain to others their belief in God's oneness. This may not be a full and perfect statement about the being and nature of God, but because of the limitations of the human mind, no account of God is full and perfect.

As I look back on my religious pilgrimage I see in it a central concern to reaffirm the truth of Christian belief, in the face of the challenges posed by science, by elements in the contemporary Western outlook, and by Islam and the other religions. In the course of time my ideas have changed on some secondary matters, such as seeing the Old Testament as the record of a changing and developing religion, and reaching a more subtle understanding of the relations between language and truth. I foresee a world in which there is a degree of mutual recognition between all the great religions, so that they consider one another as partners sharing, to a large extent, in the same basic truth about ultimate reality, and this truth would have to contain something about the human achievement of Jesus. Thus my ultimate vision is of a world in which nearly all the human race has accepted the final truth to which all the religions bear witness, even if that truth has not been expressed in a monolithic form, and the religions are not fully united. There might be progress towards something more monolithic, but I doubt if a completely monolithic religion is ultimately desirable.

Notes

1. Oxford: Oneworld Publications, 1995.